BLOOMSBURY
GOOD READING GUIDE

BLOOMSBURY
GOOD
READING GUIDE

Kenneth McLeish

BLOOMSBURY

First published 1988

Copyright © 1988 by Kenneth McLeish

Bloomsbury Publishing Ltd, 2 Soho Square, London W1V 5DE

British Library Cataloguing in Publication Data

McLeish, Kenneth, *1940-*
  The Bloomsbury good reading guide.
1. Fiction. Encyclopaedias
I. Title
  809.3'003'21

ISBN 0 7475 0079 7

Printed in Great Britain by Butler & Tanner Ltd
Frome, Somerset

CONTENTS

Introduction   ix

Author entries A-Z   1

INCLUDING SPECIAL READING 'SKEINS':

Jane Austen, *Pride and Prejudice*   14
Agatha Christie, *Ten Little Niggers/Ten Little Indians*   44
Charles Dickens, *David Copperfield*   60
E.M. Forster, *A Passage to India*   82
William Golding, *Lord of the Flies*   92
Robert Graves, *I, Claudius*   98
Joseph Heller, *Catch-22*   110
Georgette Heyer, *Regency Buck*   116
James Joyce, *Ulysses*   136
Thomas Keneally, *The Playmaker*   140
John Le Carré, *The Perfect Spy*   147
Alison Lurie, *The War Between the Tates*   156
Iris Murdoch, *An Unofficial Rose*   175
George Orwell, *1984*   185
Mervyn Peake, *Gormenghast*   189
Salman Rushdie, *Shame*   211
Lev Tolstoy, *War and Peace*   238
Lew Wallace, *Ben-Hur*   252
Edith Wharton, *The House of Mirth*   261

AND 'MENUS' OF SUGGESTED READING:

Action Thrillers   2
Adolescence   3
Against the Stream   3
Agents and Double Agents   3
All the World's a Stage   6
Ancient Greece   9
Ancient Rome   9
The Animal Kingdom   10
Art for Whose Sake?   11
Autobiographies and Memoirs (Ghosted!)   15
Bible: New Testament   22
Bible: Old Testament   23

The Booker Prize   25
Children   41
Cities: New World   43
Cities: Old World   43
Classic Detection   46
Comedy Thrillers   47
Country Houses   51
The Countryside   51
Culture-clash   52
Deep South, USA   55
Depression and Psychiatry   57
Dreaming Spires   66
Families: All-engulfing   72
Families: Eccentric   72
Families: Many Generations   72
Fantasy Adventure   73
Fantasy Societies   73
The Film Business   76
Friends (?) and Neighbours   86
Future Societies   86
Good and Evil   93
Great Detectives   100
Growing Up: Teenagers   101
Growing Up: Young Adults   101
High Adventure   115
Higher (?) Education   118
Historical Adventure   120
The Human Comedy   124
India   126
Into the Wilderness   127
Larger than Life   145
Madness   159
The Middle Ages   170
Money   171
Murder Most Mind-boggling   174
Music   176
Newspapers   181
Nineteenth-century England   181
Old Age   183
Old Dark Houses   183
'Only Connect'   183
On the Edge of Sanity   183
Other Peoples, Other Times   186
Parents and Children   187
Perplexed by Life   190
Places   190
Police Procedural   192

Politics (1)   192
Politics (2)   192
Private Eyes   196
Publish and be Damned   197
Renaissance Europe   201
Revisiting One's Past   203
The Rhythm of Nature   204
Roman Catholicism (1)   207
Roman Catholicism (2)   207
Schools   215
Ships and the Sea   218
Shipwreck   218
Something Nasty . . .   224
South Africa   225
Terrorists/Freedom Fighters   234
Trains   240
Unlooked-for Friendships   245
US Small Town Life   246
War: Behind the Lines   253
War: Front Line   254
Weddings   255
Weepies   255

Index   273

INTRODUCTION

Reading is one of the most satisfying of all human skills. We can survive – people do survive – perfectly well without it, and yet many would list it high among the things which make life worth living. Even such eager readers, however, can be daunted by the sheer number of books on offer. Libraries and bookshops are stuffed with treasures; like explorers in some vast, landmarkless new continent, we hardly know where to turn.

The *Bloomsbury Good Reading Guide* seeks to answer two main questions: 'Where shall I start?' and 'Where shall I go next?' The bulk of the text is articles on some 300 authors, describing the kind of books they wrote, listing titles and suggesting books, by the same authors and by others, which might make interesting follow-ups.

There are also, scattered throughout the *Guide*, 19 'skeins' and over 70 'menus' of suggested reading. The menus, listed alphabetically alongside the author-articles, are straightforward lists of about seven or eight books of a similar kind, ranging from **Action Thrillers** (see page 2) to **Weepies** (see page 255). The skeins, on the other hand, range wider; each one starts with a specific book and suggests follow-ups both predictable and unexpected, a haul of reading as varied as fish in a net—E.M. Forster's *A Passage to India*, for example, leads to both Paul Theroux's *Fang and the Indians* and John Le Carré's *The Perfect Spy*. Also included as a menu is a list of all Booker Prize short-listed authors and titles as well as each year's winner (see page 25). These are generally considered to be the best books of their year and so act as reliable pointers to good reading.

The *Guide* deals with prose fiction only. There is no literary criticism: I wanted to describe books, not to be clever at their expense. In particular, I tried to avoid ranking authors by 'literary merit', on assessments of whether their work is 'great' or 'light'. The length of each entry depends solely on how much needed to be said. If this had been a travel guide, New York (say) might have had more space than the commuter village up the line – but that would have had no bearing on where one might choose to live.

Throughout the text, ▷ before someone's name means that that person has a main entry of his or her own. All books mentioned in the *Guide* were written in English or are widely available in translation. We have tried to cover as wide a range of writers of English as possible and have included authors from Australia, Canada, New Zealand, the Republic of Ireland, South Africa and the USA as well as the UK. Some books may be published under different titles in the USA. If this is the case the UK title is given first, followed by the US title:

Daphne Du Maurier: *The Apple Tree/Kiss Me Again Stranger*

Books originally written in a foreign language are listed by their English titles. Original titles follow in brackets where they may be familiar to readers or where they may be used for some English editions.

Emile Zola: *The Boozer* (L'assommoir)
Andre Gide: *The Pastoral Symphony* (La symphonie pastorale)

Main author entries are listed alphabetically by surname. Each author-article contains some or all of four different strands of information:

1 a paragraph about the author's work and style in general
2 description of a particular book, a good example of the author's work
3 list of main books by the author
4 suggestions of follow-ups
   by the same author   ●
   by other authors   ▶

The cut-off date for inclusion in this edition was October 1987. We hope to update the *Guide* regularly, and to include good new books as they come along. We welcome ideas, comments and suggestions, especially for follow-ups and skeins.

Throughout the *Guide*, the final choice of books and authors, the comments and the text were my responsibility: I take the blame. But many people helped, and the *Guide* has benefited from suggestions and comments from Lucy Banister, Sian Facer, Sheila Hardy, Pamela Henderson, Simon McLeish, Kathy Rooney and Stella Yates. I warmly thank them all. As always, my greatest debt is to my wife, Valerie McLeish: her inspiration and encouragement were essential to every page.

Kenneth McLeish,
October 1987

A

ACHEBE, Chinua • *(born 1930)*
Nigerian novelist.

Things Fall Apart (1958), Achebe's best-known novel, is a story of the people of Umuofia on the river Niger, and especially of Okonkwo, a rich and headstrong elder. To British readers the period seems early Victorian; to the men and women of Umuofia it would have no date, it would be part of the gentle continuum of existence. Their lives depend on the harmony between human beings and spirits, and that is preserved by a precise set of rituals and beliefs, established by precedent, explained by folk-tale and so familiar that instead of constricting the soul they liberate it. White people are as mythical as the tortoise in the story who learned to fly: they live far away, snatch slaves, laugh at the gods; no one believes in them. Okonkwo wins respect among his people by a magnificent wrestling-throw when he is 18, and keeps it by his hard work as a farmer, his love for the land. Then, by accident, he kills a relative, and is forced by custom to live out of the village for seven years. While he is away Christian missionaries come; they speak through interpreters, understand nothing of the people's beliefs and are followed by white commissioners whose laws destroy the society they were devised to 'civilise'. Achebe's points are blunt, and (for ex-colonialists) shamingly unanswerable. But his novel's main fascination is not political but social. External observers, however sophisticated their cameras or meticulous their anthropological methods, can only describe the surface of timeless, tribal societies: they report and explain events. Achebe, by contrast, uses a series of direct, uncomplicated scenes, reverberant as poetry, to reveal his people's souls.

Achebe's other novels are No Longer at Ease, Arrow of

READ ON ▷

▶ Amos Tutuola, *My Life in the Bush of Ghosts* (making a denser, more Homeric use of Nigerian folk-styles). ▷I.B. Singer, *Satan in Goray*. Janet Lewis, *The Trial of Sören Kvist*.

God, A Man of the People *(a satirical farce about what happens when the white imperialists leave and black politicians set up a 'western' state) and* Anthills of the Savannah. Chike and the River *is a children's book, sweet as a folk-tale.*

ACTION THRILLERS

▷Richard Condon, *The Manchurian Candidate*
  Clive Cussler, *Cyclops*
▷Ken Follett, *Lie Down With Lions*
▷Frederick Forsyth, *The Day of the Jackal*
  Martin Cruz Smith, *Stallion Gate*
  Scott Turow, *Presumed Innocent*
  Walter Wager, *Telefon*

Agents and Double Agents (p 3); High Adventure (p 117); Historical Adventure (p 120); Terrorists/Freedom Fighters (p 234)

ADAMS, Douglas • *(born 1952)*
British novelist.

In *The Hitchhiker's Guide to the Galaxy* (1979), the first of Adams' genial SF spoofs, Earthman Arthur Dent is informed that his planet is about to be vaporised to make room for a hyper-space bypass, and escapes by stowing away on an alien space-craft. This is the beginning of a wild journey through time and space, in the course of which he meets the super-cool President of the Galaxy, Zaphod Beeblebrox, discusses the coastline of Norway with Slartibartfast (who won prizes for designing it), watches the apocalyptic floor-show in the Restaurant at the End of the Universe, and discovers the answer to the 'ultimate question about life, the universe and everything'. Adams himself is on a spree, spray-painting the stuffiest corners of the genre. There are three Hitchhiker sequels (*The Restaurant at the End of the Universe*; *Life, the Universe and Everything*; *So Long, and Thanks for All the Fish*); *Dirk Gently's Holistic Detective Agency* (1987), whose title suggests the plot, is a cascade of equally loony fantasy, ▷Chandler and ▷Vonnegut swapping one-liners on an intergalactic roller-coaster ride.

> **READ ON**

▶ **SF spoofs in similarly lunatic vein:** Terry Pratchett, *The Colour of Magic*; ▷Harry Harrison, *The Stainless Steel Rat*; ▷Kurt Vonnegut, *The Sirens of Titan*.
▶ **Non-SF books featuring bewildered heroes at the centre of chaos:** Patrick Dennis, *Auntie Mame*; Charles Webb, *The Graduate*; William Boyd, *Stars and Bars*; ▷Evelyn Waugh, *Decline and Fall*.

ADOLESCENCE

▷Maeve Binchy, *Echoes*
▷Colette, *The Ripening Seed*
▷Miles Franklin, *My Brilliant Career*
  Jane Gardam, *Bilgewater*
  Rumer Godden, *The Greengage Summer*
  Harper Lee, *To Kill a Mocking Bird*
  Sue Townsend, *The Secret Diary of Adrian Mole, aged 13¾*
▷Antonia White, *Frost in May*

Children (p 42); Families: Eccentric (p 72); Growing Up: Teenagers (p 101); Parents and Children (p 187); Schools (p 215)

AGAINST THE STREAM
(people at odds with the society around them)

▷James Baldwin, *Go Tell it on the Mountain*
▷Charles Dickens, *Oliver Twist*
▷Maxim Gorky, *Foma Gordeev*
▷Nathaniel Hawthorne, *The Scarlet Letter*
▷Somerset Maugham, *Liza of Lambeth*
▷John Steinbeck, *The Grapes of Wrath*
▷Émile Zola, *Nana*

'Only Connect' (p 183); Perplexed by Life (p 190); Revisiting One's Past (p 203)

AGENTS AND DOUBLE AGENTS

▷Ted Allbeury, *The Secret Whispers*
▷Joseph Conrad, *The Secret Agent*
▷Frederick Forsyth, *The Fourth Protocol*
  John Kruse, *The Hour of the Lily*
▷John Le Carré, *The Perfect Spy*
▷Ruth Rendell, *Talking to Strange Men*
  Hardiman Scott and Becky Allan, *Bait of Lies*

Action Thrillers (p 2); High Adventure (p 117)

ALDISS, Brian • *(born 1925)*
British novelist.

For the last 30 years Aldiss has been a major propagandist for British SF, editing anthologies, speaking at conventions and writing several non-fiction books including *Billion Year Spree* (revised version: *Trillion Year Spree*), a critical history of the genre. His own SF covers the whole range from space opera (eg *Non-stop*) to future-catastrophe (eg *Hot-house*, about the 'greenhouse effect' when the Earth's air-temperature rises uncontrollably), from philosophical fantasy (eg *Frankenstein Unbound* and *Moreau's Other Island*, extensions of themes from earlier SF masterpieces) to stories of alternative worlds (eg the Helliconia trilogy: see below). He is also known for non-SF novels. These range from a comic trilogy about the oversexed 1950s adolescent Horatio Stubbs (*A Hand-reared Boy*; *A Soldier Erect*; *A Rude Awakening*) to *Life in the West*, a ▷Bellow-like book about the plight of a man who has made his reputation preaching science and technology as the salvation of humanity, and is now forced, by the disintegration of his own emotional life, to give his views more intimate analysis.

THE HELLICONIA TRILOGY • *(1982–5)*
Helliconia is one of four planets which revolve round Batalix, itself a satellite of the giant star Freyr. Helliconia seasons last not for months but for hundreds of Earth years, and the planet is inhabited by two separate and incompatible races, one adapted to winter life, the other to summer. The three novels (*Helliconia Spring*, *Helliconia Summer*, *Helliconia Winter*) explore the effects of Helliconia's enormous seasons, each long enough for whole civilisations to rise, flourish and die. Colonial wars, racism, ecology, the clash between religion, science and the arts, are underlying themes – and all the time, Helliconia is observed: watching it provides entertainment, a blend of travel-documentary and soap-opera, for the bored inhabitants of Earth.

Aldiss' other SF books include Earthworks, The Saliva Tree, Barefoot in the Head, Enemies of the System, *and a dozen short-story collections including* Starswarm, Cosmic Inferno *and* New Arrivals, Old Encounters. *His non-SF novels include* The Brightfount Diaries, The Primal Urge, The Male Response *and* The Malacia Tapestry.

READ ON ⟩

- ● *The Dark Light Years.*
- ▶ **To the Helliconia books:** ▷Ursula Le Guin, *The Left Hand of Darkness.*
- ▶ **To Aldiss' SF in general:** Ray Bradbury, *The Golden Apples of the Sun*; ▷Isaac Asimov, *The Foundation Trilogy.*
- ▶ **To the Horatio Stubbs books:** Leslie Thomas, *The Virgin Soldiers.*
- ▶ **To *Life in the West*:** ▷John Fowles, *Daniel Martin*; David Lodge, *Small World.*

ALLBEURY, Ted • *(born 1917)*
British novelist.

Allbeury writes packed, fast spy thrillers, usually with cold-war settings. His titles include *A Choice of Enemies*, *Moscow Quadrille*, *The Man With the President's Mind*, *The Lantern Network*, *The Alpha List*, *The Crossing*, *Children of Tender Years* and *The Secret Whispers* (about a double agent attempting to escape from East Germany). He also uses the pseudonym Richard Butler (*Where All the Girls Are Sweeter*; *Italian Assets*).

READ ON ▷

▶ Duff Hart-Davis, *The Heights of Rimring*. Ted Willis, *The Churchill Commando*. ▷Richard Condon, *The Manchurian Candidate*. ▷John Le Carré, *The Spy Who Came in from the Cold*.

ALLENDE, Isabel • *(born 1942)*
Peruvian novelist.

The House of the Spirits, Allende's first novel, was a glowing family tapestry in the manner of ▷Márquez' *One Hundred Years of Solitude*, spanning five generations and thronged with larger-than-life characters and supernatural events. Her second book, *Of Love and Shadows*, takes a narrower, more political focus, to devastating effect. Irene Beltrán, a journalist, and her photographer-lover Francisco Leal are investigating the disappearance of a disturbed, possibly saintly adolescent. In the jackbooted dictatorship in which they live, however, the child is not simply missing but 'disappeared', one of thousands snatched by the authorities who will never be seen again. Allende surrounds the four main characters – the fourth is Lieutenant Ramirez, the child's abductor – with a web of fantastic personal history in true magic-realist style. But the further the investigators thread their way through the sadism and ruthlessness of a labyrinthine fascist state, the more fact begins to swallow fairy tale. The investigators themselves begin to lose reality – their love-affair becomes a swooning parody of romantic fiction – but what they discover grows more and more uncomfortably like real South American life, like nightmare fleshed.

READ ON ▷

▶ Carlos Fuentes, *A Change of Skin*. ▷Günter Grass, *The Tin Drum*. ▷Richard Condon, *Winter Kills*. ▷Mario Vargas Llosa, *Captain Pantoja and the Special Service* gives a more farcical view of Allende's terrifying haunted world.

ALLINGHAM, Margery • *(1905–66)*
British novelist.

Allingham wrote 'crime fiction' only in the senses that each of her books contains the step-by-step solution of a crime, and that their hero, Albert Campion, is an amateur detective whose amiable manner conceals laser intelligence and iron moral integrity. But instead of confining Campion by the boundaries of the detective-story genre,

READ ON ▷

● *Death of a Ghost* (set in London's eccentric art-community and involving – what else? – forged paintings); *Hide My Eyes*.

Allingham put him in whatever kind of novel she felt like writing. Some of her books (*More Work for the Undertaker*; *The Beckoning Lady*) are wild, ▷Wodehousian farce, others (*Sweet Danger*; *Traitor's Purse*) are ▷Buchanish, ▷Amblerish thrillers. Her best books are those of the 1940s and 1950s, and especially two set in an atmospheric, cobble-stones-and-alleyways London filled with low-life characters as vivid as any in ▷Dickens, *The Tiger in the Smoke* and *Hide My Eyes*.

FLOWERS FOR THE JUDGE • *(1936)*
Strange things are happening at the old-established publishing firm of Barnabas and Company. First the junior partner turns a street-corner in Streatham and vanishes into thin air, then there is skullduggery over a priceless but obscene manuscript, and soon afterwards the firm's stuffy senior partner is murdered and Mr Campion has three intertwined mysteries on his hands.

Allingham's other Campion books include Coroner's Pidgin, Police at the Funeral, Look to the Lady *and the short-story collections* Mr Campion and Others *and* Take Two at Bedtime. *After Allingham's death, her husband* P. Youngman Carter *wrote two further Campion novels, one of which,* Mr Campion's Farthing, *is up to his wife's most sparkling standard.*

▶ ▷Michael Innes, *The Daffodil Affair*. Edmund Crispin, *The Case of the Gilded Fly*. H.R.F. Keating, *A Rush on the Ultimate*. ▷P.D. James, *An Unsuitable Job for a Woman*. Joan Smith, *Masculine Ending* is a tongue-in-cheek whodunnit starring a feminist sleuth.

ALL THE WORLD'S A STAGE
(books about theatre)

Richard Bissell, *Say, Darling*
Caryl Brahms and S.J. Simon, *A Bullet in the Ballet*
Bamber Gascoigne, *The Heyday*
H.R.F. Keating, *Death of a Fat God*
▷Thomas Keneally, *The Playmaker*
▷J.B. Priestley, *The Good Companions*
▷Mary Renault, *The Mask of Apollo*

ALTHER, Lisa • *(born 1944)*
US novelist.

Kinflicks (1976) is the 'autobiography' of Ginny Babcock, a 'typical' US adolescent in the late 1960s and early 1970s. The book sends up every cliché of the genre and of the period: Ginny spends her high school years jerking off a muscle-brained football star, discovers lesbian love at

READ ON ⟩

▶ **To *Kinflicks*:** ▷John Irving, *The World According to Garp*; ▷Philip Roth, *Portnoy's Complaint*;

university, joins protest marches, takes up macrobiotic diets, zen and LSD, marries, has a child and divorces – and treats each experience as if she were the first person in the world ever to discover it, as if she were hypnotized by her own adventurousness. Alther intersperses Ginny's first-person narrative with chapters set ten years further on, when Ginny visits her dying mother in hospital, trying to come to terms with her feelings about herself, her family and her future. These sections give the book a harsher, more elegiac tone: the young Ginny symbolises a whole adolescent generation, as rebellious and zestful as any other but engulfed by the age they live in. Alther's second novel, *Original Sins* (1980), similarly blends satire, slapstick and irony. A 1980s equivalent to ▷Mary McCarthy's *The Group*, it traces the experience of five childhood friends as they grow to adulthood, discovering in the process civil rights, the women's movement and the pleasures and preposterousnesses of the sexual revolution. *Other Women* (1985), a less larky exploration of women's experience in the last generation, counterpoints the lives of two utterly different people, a 'flower-child' depressed at the first wiltings of middle age and the prickings of lesbianism, and her English psychiatrist.

AMBLER, Eric • *(born 1909)*
British novelist and screenwriter.

The deadpan style of Ambler's thrillers lets him move easily from violence to farce, and he either sets his books in exotic places (the Levant, the Far East, tropical Africa), or else makes familiar European locations seem exotic as the scene of sinister and unlikely goings-on. His central characters are minor crooks, conmen, or innocent bystanders trapped by circumstances or curiosity into a chain of bizarre and dangerous events. His supporting casts are crammed with improbable, unsavoury specimens, very few of whom are quite what they seem to be. Films and TV series have made this kind of thriller endlessly familiar. But Ambler was one of the first to write it, and he is still among the best.

THE LIGHT OF DAY • *(1962)*
Arthur Simpson, a middle-aged, scruffy conman (played in the film version, *Topkapi*, by Peter Ustinov), is blackmailed into driving a car across the border from Greece into Turkey – and is promptly arrested and forced by the police to spy on the car's owners. They are a dangerous gang of – what? Terrorists? Drug-smugglers? Criminals? Simpson spends the whole book trying to find

Letting Go; Marge Piercy, *The High Cost of Living*.
▶ **To *Original Sins*:**
▷Mary McCarthy, *The Group*; Rona Jaffé, *Class Reunion*.
▶ **To *Other Women*:**
▷Alison Lurie, *Foreign Affairs*.

READ ON ▷

● Ambler continued Simpson's sleazy career in the appropriately-named *Dirty Story*. His more serious thrillers include *The Mask of Dimitrios/ Coffin for Dimitrios*, in which a bored writer sets out to track down an elusive Levantine criminal, and *The Levanter*, a story of terrorists in Palestine.
▶ **To *The Light of Day*:** David Dodge, *Bullets for the Bridegroom*; ▷Graham Greene, *Our Man in Havana*; Donald Westlake, *The Busy Body*.
▶ **To Ambler's less larky thrillers:** ▷Len

out, and at the same time to save his own sweaty dignity and to make as much profit as he can.

Ambler's other thrillers include Cause for Alarm, Dr Frigo, Epitaph for a Spy, Passage of Arms, The Schirmer Inheritance *and* To Catch a Spy. *He also wrote thrillers (eg* The Maras Affair; Charter to Danger) *in collaboration with* Charles Rodda, *published under the name* Eliot Reed. *They are more straightforward, but no less gripping, than his solo books.*

AMIS, Kingsley • *(born 1922)*
British writer of novels, poems and non-fiction.

In the 1950s, when Amis' writing career began, the end of post-second-world-war austerity had led to an upsurge of optimistic egalitarianism in Britain. Since this mood was not reflected by actual British society, which remained class-ridden, snobbish and élitist, writers of all kinds – the 'angry young men' – began shouting in plays, films and novels about the inequity of life. Whingeing became an artistic form – and Amis' novels showed its funny side. The working-class hero of *Lucky Jim*, a yuppie 30 years before the word was invented, tries to conform with his madrigal-singing, right-newspaper-reading, wine-savouring university colleagues, and in the process shows them up for the pretentious fools they are. The central character of *That Uncertain Feeling*, a small-town librarian, thinks that devastating sexual charm will carry him to the pinnacle of local society; the results are farcical. The hero of *Take a Girl Like You* finds it hard to persuade anyone else in his circle that 'free love' and 'the swinging sixties' are the good things glossy magazines crack them up to be. In the 1960s and 1970s Amis' farcical fires burned low. He began to affect a ponderous, self-consciously right-wing fuddy-duddiness, and abandoned satire for books of other kinds (a ghost story, a James Bond spy thriller and several science fiction books). In the 1980s, however, he returned to the satirical muttering which he always did better than any of his imitators – and his most recent books (eg *Jake's Thing*, about a middle-aged man trying to recapture the sexual energy of youth, and *The Old Devils*: see below) are among his funniest.

THE OLD DEVILS • *(1986)*
A group of old men, acquaintances for over 40 years, meet daily in a Welsh bar to grumble. They are obsessed by failure, their own and the world's. Nothing has ever gone right, and nothing now is as good even as it used to be (which wasn't much). They are especially vitriolic

Deighton, *Horse Under Water*; ▷Richard Condon, *The Manchurian Candidate.*

READ ON ⟩

● *Jake's Thing*; *Stanley and the Women.*
▶ ▷Malcolm Bradbury, *Eating People is Wrong.* A.N. Wilson, *Love Unknown.* ▷Tom Sharpe, *Porterhouse Blue.* William Boyd, *A Good Man in Africa.* Howard Jacobson, *Peeping Tom.* William Cooper, *Scenes from Provincial Life.*

about other people's success – and their discomfort with the world is brought to a peak when one of their 'friends', a famous TV Welshman and an expert on a Dylan-Thomasish poet, comes to settle in the town.

Amis has published several books of light verse, and numerous works on literary matters (eg New Maps of Hell, *a history of SF). The best of his comic novels not mentioned above are* One Fat Englishman *and* Ending Up; *the best of his serious novels are* The Anti-Death League, *about a top-secret army unit whose aim is to abolish death, and which is therefore in direct conflict with God, and* The Alteration, *set in a fantasy contemporary Britain in which modern science and modern religion have never happened, so that we are still organising our lives in medieval ways.*

ANCIENT GREECE

▷Robert Graves, *The Golden Fleece/Hercules My Shipmate*
Peter Green, *Achilles His Armour*
▷Homer, *Odyssey*
Naomi Mitchison, *The Corn King and the Spring Queen*
▷Mary Renault, *The King Must Die*
Rosemary Sutcliffe, *Flowers for Adonis*
Henry Treece, *Electra*

Ancient Rome (p 9); Bible: New Testament (p 22); Bible: Old Testament (p 23); Other Peoples, Other Times (p 186)

ANCIENT ROME

Edward Bulwer-Lytton, *The Last Days of Pompeii*
▷Robert Graves, *I Claudius; Count Belisarius*
Peter Vansittart, *Three Six Seven*
▷Gore Vidal, *Julian*
▷Thornton Wilder, *The Ides of March*
Marguerite Yourcenar, *Memoirs of Hadrian*

Ancient Greece (p 9); Bible: New Testament (p 22); The Middle Ages (p 170); Renaissance Europe (p 201)

ANDREWS, Virginia • *(born 1933)*
US novelist.

Andrews writes domestic chillers: claustrophobic stories of tense relationships in 'ordinary' US families. Her books include a quartet about the unhappy Dollenganger family: it begins with *Flowers in the Attic* (about a brother and sister kept prisoners in an attic until an inheritance is claimed), and continues with *Petal on the Wind*, *If There be Thorns* and *Seeds of Yesterday*.

READ ON ▷

▶ ▷Patricia Highsmith, *The People Who Knock on the Door*. Elizabeth Peters, *The Love Talker*. Celia Fremlin, *The Trouble Makers*. Josephine Tey, *The Franchise Affair*.

THE ANIMAL KINGDOM

Richard Adams, *Watership Down*
Rowena Farre, *Seal Morning*
Paul Gallico, *The Snow Goose*
▷Ernest Hemingway, *Fiesta/The Sun Also Rises*
▷Jack London, *White Fang*
Tony Weeks-Pearson, *Dodo*
Henry Williamson, *Tarka the Otter*

ANTHONY, Evelyn • *(born 1928)*
British novelist.

Anthony's early books were historical romances: they include *Imperial Highness/Rebel Princess*, *Curse Not the King/Royal Intrigue*, *The Heiress/The French Bride* and *Anne of Austria/The Cardinal and the Queen*. In the 1970s she made a second name as writer of romantic thrillers and 20th-century espionage stories. These include *The Tamarind Seed*, *Stranger at the Gates/The Occupying Power*, *The Persian Ransom/The Persian Prince* and *Voices on the Wind* (in which an ex-resistance worker relives her second-world-war fight against the nazis, her love-affairs and a betrayal).

READ ON ▷

▶ **To the historical romances:** ▷Jean Plaidy, *Perdita's Prince*; ▷Dorothy Dunnett, *Queen's Play*.

▶ **To the thrillers:** Helen MacInnes, *The Snare of the Hunted*; ▷Mary Stewart, *Airs Above the Ground*.

ANTHONY, Piers • *(born 1934)*
US novelist.

With R. Fuentes, Anthony has written half a dozen martial arts thrillers, including *Bamboo Bloodbath* and *Ninja's Revenge*. On his own he is a prolific SF writer whose novels range from the 6-volume 'autobiography' of a fu-

READ ON ▷

● *On a Pale Horse.*
▶ Alan Dean Foster, *Spellsinger*. Terry Brookes, *The Sword of*

ture tyrant of Jupiter to the adventures of Death. In his best-known books, instead of winning through by sword and sorcery, his heroes and heroines have to use their wits: in *A Spell for Chameleon* (1977), for example (the first of a series set in the country of Xanth), everyone except Bink (the hero) has a magic talent, and Bink's quest is to find some quality in himself which will prevent him being exiled for ordinariness.

ARCHER, Jeffrey • *(born 1940)*
British novelist.

Archer writes incident-packed stories of intrigue in high and low places. His books include *Not a Penny More Not a Penny Less*, *A Matter of Honour* and the 1970s trilogy *Kane and Abel*, *The Prodigal Daughter* and *Shall We Tell the President?* (which begins with the separate but interlocking careers of two rivals in the worlds of business and politics, and continues with the daughter of one of them, who becomes the first woman president of the USA).

ART FOR WHOSE SAKE?
(painters; fakers; patrons; art-enthusiasts)

▷Marjorie Allingham, *Death of a Ghost*
  Michael Ayrton, *The Mazemaker*
  Joyce Cary, *The Horse's Mouth*
  Mary Flanagan, *Trust*
▷Wyndham Lewis, *Tarr*
▷Somerset Maugham, *The Moon and Sixpence*
  Irwin Shaw, *The Agony and the Ecstasy*

ASIMOV, Isaac • *(born 1920)*
US writer of novels, short stories and non-fiction.

Since the age of 19, when Asimov published his first story, he has written over 300 books, ranging from Bible guides and history text-books to the SF novels and stories for which he is best-known. Unlike many SF writers, he never puts ingenious ideas above character, plot or literary quality. His books are carefully, even tortuously plotted and his characters have depth; he adds scientific detail as the final flourish and the more extraordinary his ideas, the more deadpan their presentation. All this gives his fiction intellectual as well as literary appeal. Flattered that we

Shannara. ▷Anne McCaffrey, *Dragonsong*.

READ ON ⟩

▶ ▷Frederick Forsyth, *The Fourth Protocol*.
Jon Cleary, *Spearfield's Daughter*.
▷Dick Francis, *Risk*.

READ ON ⟩

● **The best Asimov follow-ups are his robot books:** the short stories in *The Complete Robot* and the novels *The Caves of Steel* and *The Naked Sun*.
▶ **To Asimov's short stories:** ▷Italo

know more science than we thought we did, we feel that we are sharing in the wonders Asimov reveals rather than (as with most SF writers) merely gaping in astonishment.

THE FOUNDATION SAGA • *(1951 to present day)*

The first three books, a self-contained trilogy, appeared in the 1950s; Asimov began adding new novels 30 years later, and two have so far appeared. The Saga is 'space opera' (SF soap opera) on a huge scale, an account of political manoeuvrings among nations and civilisations of the far future. Hari Seldon, a professor of psychohistory (statistical and psychological prediction of the future) foresees a disastrous era of war in the galactic empire, and establishes two Foundations on the galaxy's edge, dedicated to safeguarding civilised knowledge until it is again required. The saga describes the nature and work of each Foundation, their uniting to defeat external threat (from an alien intelligence, 'the Mule') and their subsequent internecine struggles. For, like all human constructs, they are themselves prey to emotion and irrationality, to a bias which can lead towards dark as well as light.

Asimov's SF novels include Pebble in the Sky, The Stars Like Dust *and* The Currents of Space *(all on themes related to the Foundation Saga). His short SF stories are gathered in* The Early Asimov *Volumes 1-3.* Opus *is a useful anthology, an excellent sampler from his dazzling list of works.*

Calvino, *Cosmicomics.*
▶ **To the Foundation saga:** ▷Frank Herbert, *Dune*; Gordon Dickinson, *Tactics of Mistake.* ▷Tom De Haan, *A Mirror for Princes* uses SF techniques to describe a mesmeric society not of the future but of the past. For anyone who finds Asimov's ideas too poker-faced, they are magnificently sent up in ▷Douglas Adams, *The Hitchhiker's Guide to the Galaxy.*

ATWOOD, Margaret • *(born 1939)*
Canadian writer of novels, short stories and poems.

Atwood is a poet as well as a novelist, and her gifts of precise observation and exact description illuminate all her work. She is fascinated by the balance of power between person and person, and by the way our apparently coherent actions and words actually float on a sea of turbulent unseen emotion. Her books often follow the progress of relationships, or of one person's self-discovery. The heroine of *Life Before Man*, for example, is caught up in a sexual quadrilateral (one of whose members, her lover, has just committed suicide), and our interest is as much in seeing how she copes with her own chaotic feelings as in the progress of the affair itself. Many writers have tackled similar themes, but Atwood's books give a unique impression that each moment, each feeling, is being looked at through a microscope, as if the swirling, nagging 'real' world has been momentarily put aside for something more urgent which may just – her characters consistently put

▷ **READ ON**

● *Surfacing* (about a woman trying to discover the truth about her relationship with her father, by re-examining her childhood in the Canadian wilderness).
▶ **To *The Handmaid's Tale:*** ▷George Orwell, *1984.*
▶ **To *Surfacing:*** Lynne Reid Banks, *Children at the Gate;* ▷Alison Lurie, *Imaginary Friends.*
▶ **To Atwood's work in general:** ▷Doris

hope above experience – make sense of it.

THE HANDMAID'S TALE • *(1985)*

In the 21st-century Republic of Gilead, fundamentalist Christianity rules and the laws are those of Genesis. Women are chattels: they have no identity, no privacy and no happiness except what men permit them. Offred, for example, is a Handmaid, and her life is devoted to one duty only: breeding. Public prayers and hangings are the norm; individuality – even looking openly into a man's face or reading a woman's magazine – is punished by mutilation, banishment or death. The book shows Offred's struggle to keep her sanity and her identity in such a situation, and her equivocal relationship with the feminist Underground which may be Gilead's only hope.

Atwood's other novels include The Edible Woman *and* Bodily Harm. Dancing Girls *and* Bluebeard's Egg *contain short stories.* The Journals of Susannah Moodie *and* True Stories *are poetry collections, and her* Selected Poems *are also available.*

AUSTEN, Jane • *(1775–1817)*
British novelist.

Austen loved the theatre, and the nearest equivalents to her novels, for pace and verve, are the social comedies of such writers as Sheridan or Goldsmith. The kind of novels popular at the time were epic panoramas (like those of ▷Sir Walter Scott), showing the human race strutting and swaggering amid stormy weather in vast, romantic landscapes. Austen preferred a narrower focus, concentrating on a handful of people busy about their own domestic concerns. Her books are about the bonds which draw families together and the ambitions and feelings (usually caused by grown-up children seeking marriage-partners) which divide them. Her plots fall into 'acts', like plays, and her dialogue is as precise and witty as in any comedy of the time. But she offers a delight available to no playwright: that of the author's own voice, setting the scene, commenting on and shaping events. She is like a bright-eyed, sharp-tongued relative sitting in a corner of the room watching the rest of the family bustle.

PRIDE AND PREJUDICE • *(1813)*

Genteel Mr and Mrs Bennet and their five grown-up daughters are thrown into confusion when two rich, marriageable young men come to live in the neighbourhood. The comedy of the story comes from Mrs Bennet's mother-hen-like attempts at matchmaking, and the way

Lessing, *Martha Quest*; ▷Nadine Gordimer, *A Sport of Nature*.

> READ ON

● *Emma* (about a young woman so eager to manage other people's lives that she fails, for a long time, to realise where her own true happiness lies); *Mansfield Park* (a darker comedy about a girl brought up by a rich, charming family who is at first dazzled by their easy brilliance, then comes to see that they are selfish and foolish, and finally, by unassuming persistence, wins through to the happiness we have always hoped for her).
▶ The 'taming' aspect of Austen's plots has inspired a library-ful of lighter fiction by others, of which the best by

Jane AUSTEN

PRIDE AND PREJUDICE (*social comedy in Regency England: choosing marriage-partners*)

William **THACKERAY, VANITY FAIR**
(*social comedy; girls conforming with or rebelling against society*)

Edith **WHARTON, THE CUSTOM OF THE COUNTRY**
(*social comedy, New York 1910s: young people prey on foolish elders*)

Miles **FRANKLIN, MY BRILLIANT CAREER**
(*young Australian, 1910s, preys on follies of European bourgeoisie*)

'TAMING' OR 'BEING TAMED'

ROMANCE

Georgette **HEYER, REGENCY BUCK**
(*England, 1810s: will he tame her or will she tame him?*)

Baroness **ORCZY, THE SCARLET PIMPERNEL**
(*languid English milord is really romantic hero of French revolution*)

Catherine **COOKSON, THE PARSON'S DAUGHTER**
(*spirited girl 'tames' philandering husband in 19th-century English town*)

Colleen **MCCULLOUGH, THE THORN BIRDS**
(*Australian outback: will hero put priestly vocation before earthly love?*)

Anthony **TROLLOPE, BARCHESTER TOWERS**
(*marriage and career-machinations in 19th-century English cathedral city*)

H.G. **WELLS, KIPPS**
(*personable young man makes his way in 1910s London society*)

P.G. **WODEHOUSE, THE CODE OF THE WOOSTERS**
(*problems in idyllic 1920s English country house? Ring for Jeeves . . .*)

Mary **MCCARTHY, BIRDS OF AMERICA**
(*likeable 1960s young American dismayed by Europe*)

COMEDY OF MANNERS

STYLISH, BEADY-EYED SATIRE

Mrs **GASKELL, CRANFORD**
(*gossip and intrigue in small 1830s English town*)

Barbara **PYM, A GLASS OF BLESSINGS**
(*gossip and foolishness in 1950s London high Anglican parish*)

Robertson **DAVIES, A MIXTURE OF FRAILTIES**
(*intrigue and the arts in small 1950s Canadian town*)

Alison **LURIE, FOREIGN AFFAIRS**
(*Americans in 1970s England cling to each other for comfort and affection*)

fate and the young people's own inclinations make things turn out entirely differently from her plans. The more serious sections of the novel show the developing relationship between Elizabeth Bennet, the second daughter, and cold, proud Mr Darcy. She tries to 'tame' him, to show him the effects of his character on others – and in the process she both falls in love with him and is 'tamed' herself. Although secondary characters (henpecked Mr Bennet, snobbish Lady Catherine de Bourgh, Elizabeth's romantic younger sister Lydia, the dashing army officer Wickham and the conceited bore Mr Collins) steal the limelight whenever they appear, the book hinges on half a dozen magnificent set-piece scenes between Elizabeth and Darcy, the two headstrong young people we yearn to see realising their love for one another and falling into one another's arms.

Apart from a number of unfinished works (eg The Watsons; Sanditon), Austen's output consists of six novels: Northanger Abbey *(a spoof of romantic melodrama, unlike any of her other books),* Sense and Sensibility, Pride and Prejudice, Mansfield Park, Emma *and* Persuasion.

far are the Regency novels of ▷Georgette Heyer.

► Of more serious writings, the ones which most nearly share Austen's ironical, satirical insight into human character and behaviour are ▷Mrs Gaskell, *Wives and Daughters,* ▷William Thackeray, *Vanity Fair,* ▷E.M. Forster, *A Room With a View,* ▷Alison Lurie, *Only Children,* and the short stories of ▷Anton Chekhov and ▷Katherine Mansfield.

► Joan Aiken, *Mansfield Revisited* is a lively sequel to *Mansfield Park,* the best of many authors' attempts to follow in Austen's steps.

AUTOBIOGRAPHIES AND MEMOIRS

(GHOSTED!)

Alan Brien, *Lenin: the Novel*
Margaret George, *The Autobiography of Henry VIII*
▷Robert Graves, *I Claudius*
▷Joseph Heller, *God Knows (King David of Israel)*
Stephen Marlowe, *The Memoirs of Christopher Columbus*
▷Robert Nye, *Falstaff*
Augusto Roa Bastos, *I, The Supreme* (Francia, dictator of Paraguay)

B

BAGLEY, Desmond • *(1923–83)*
British novelist.

Many of Bagley's tense thrillers are set in Africa, and involve groups of people forced together by circumstance and battling not just outsiders and the environment but each other. In *Juggernaut* (1985), for example, an English adventurer leads a convoy through the war-torn state of Nyala. At the convoy's heart is a huge truck carrying the transformer for an oil-rig, and as it trundles across the countryside it becomes a mobile hospital, a battle-wagon and a symbol of hope for streams of refugees who flock round it like pilgrims, making their way to a new home somewhere beyond the war.

Bagley's other thrillers include The Golden Keel, High Citadel, Landslide, The Spoilers, The Freedom Trap, Flyaway, Windfall *and* Night of Error.

BALDWIN, James • *(1924–87)*
US writer of novels, plays and non-fiction.

In a series of non-fiction books (*Notes of a Native Son*; *The Fire Next Time*; *No Name in the Street*), Baldwin described the fury and despair of alienated US blacks, urging revolution as the only way to maintain racial identity in a hostile environment. His plays and novels tackle the same theme, but add two more, equally passionate: the way fundamentalist Christianity is a destructive force, and the quest for sexual identity in an amoral world. *Go Tell it on the Mountain* (1953) is a novel about a poor Harlem family torn apart by the pressures of born-again Christianity. *Another Country* (1962) shows people living lives of increasing desperation in a corrupt, all-engulfing and

READ ON

- *Running Blind.*
- James Graham, *The Khufra Run.* Lionel Davidson, *The Rose of Tibet.* ▷C.S. Forester, *The Gun.*

READ ON

- In Ralph Ellison, *Invisible Man* a rootless black American travels the USA in search of identity, and finally – as the book becomes increasingly surreal – continues his quest in hell.
- A surrealist Harlem, a fantasy-land of crime, jazz, drugs and

terrifying New York. *Giovanni's Room* (1956) is about an American in Paris, having to choose between his mistress and his (male) lover.

Baldwin's other novels are Tell Me How Long the Train's Been Gone, If Beale Street Could Talk *and* Evidence of Things Not Seen; *his short stories are in* Going to Meet the Man. *His plays include* The Amen Corner *and* Blues for Mr Charlie, *and his other non-fiction books are* Nobody Knows My Name, Nothing Personal *(with photos by Richard Avedon) and* A Rap on Race *(written with Margaret Mead).*

graveyard humour, is the location for Chester Himes' detective novels (eg *Cotton Comes to Harlem*): crime plots apart, they are as unsparing and compulsive as Baldwin's books. Maya Angelou's autobiographical sequence, beginning with *I Know Why the Caged Bird Sings*, give sunnier reactions to equally abrasive Southern US black experience. Books as bleak as Baldwin's about the conjunction of sex, violence and despair are Jean Genet, *Querelle of Brest*, John Rechy, *The City of Night* and John Edgar Wideman, *A Glance Away.*

BALLARD, J.G. (James Graham) •
(born 1930)
British novelist.

Ballard's SF is pessimistic and satirical about the human race: each of his novels takes an aspect of the way we treat the planet and each other and extends it towards catastrophe. In some books (eg *The Drowned World*, about the melting of the polar ice-caps, or *The Burning World*, about the coming of permanent drought) our actions trigger natural disaster. In others (eg *Concrete Island*, which imagines the Earth engulfed by motorways, and *High Rise*, about the effects on human nature of living in ever-higher tower-blocks) we laboriously reconstruct the world as a single, megalopolitan prison-cell. His most savage, most dazzling SF novel is *The Unlimited Dream Company* (1979), a fable about human credulity. A youth who has never flown before steals a plane and crashes in the London suburbs. The people take him for a wonder-worker, even a messiah – and their credulity spirals into a religious cult involving orgiastic sex, telepathy and levitation. The story is told by the bewildered boy himself. At

READ ON >

● *The Day of Creation.*
► ▷George Turner, *The Sea and Summer.*
▷Robert Silverberg, *Master of Life and Death.* ▷Gore Vidal, *Kalki.*

first disgusted and appalled, he gradually comes to believe in his own magic powers, and slowly but surely metamorphoses into the ultimate being, the god-figure everyone takes him for. Apart from SF, Ballard is best-known for *Empire of the Sun* (1984), a powerful autobiographical novel about a young teenager in a second-world-war Japanese internment camp.

Ballard's other books include The Atrocity Exhibition/ Love and Napalm: Export USA, The Four-Dimensional Nightmare *and* The Vermilion Sands. The Voices of Time *and* Low-flying Aircraft *are collections of short stories.*

BALZAC, Honoré de • *(1799–1850)*
French novelist.

Photography was invented during Balzac's lifetime, and there was talk of using it to produce an encyclopedia of human types, catching each trade, profession and character in a suitable setting and at a particularly revealing moment. Balzac determined to do much the same thing in prose: to write a set of novels which would include people of every possible kind, described so minutely that the reader could envisage them as clearly as if they had been photographed. He called the project *The Human Comedy*, and although he died before completing it, it still runs to some 90 pieces of fiction – which can be read separately – and includes over 2000 different characters.

OLD GORIOT (Père Goriot) • *(1834)*
Goriot is a lonely old man obsessed by love for his two married daughters. He lives in a seedy Parisian boarding-house (whose contents and inhabitants Balzac meticulously describes), and gradually sells all his possessions, and even cuts down on food, to try to buy his daughters' love with presents. They treat him with a contempt he never notices – in fact everyone despises him except Rastignac, a student living in the same house. Goriot's death-bed scene, when he clutches Rastignac's hands thinking that his daughters have come to visit him at last, is one of Balzac's most moving passages, a deliberate reminiscence of King Lear's death-scene in Shakespeare's play.

The best-known novels from The Human Comedy *are* César Birotteau *(about a shopkeeper destroyed by ambition),* Eugénie Grandet *(a love story, one of Balzac's few books with a happy ending), and* Cousin Bette *(about a man whose obsessive philandering tears his family apart).* Droll Tales *is a set of farcical short stories, similar to*

READ ON ▷

● *The Curé of Tours* (a similarly detailed, and almost equally moving, study of desolate old age).
▶ **To Balzac's power and emotional bleakness:** ▷Émile Zola, *Nana*; ▷François Mauriac, *The Woman of the Pharisees*; Theodore Dreiser, *An American Tragedy*; ▷Carson McCullers, *The Ballad of the Sad Café*; Hugh Walpole, *The Old Ladies*.
▶ **To his evocation of city life:** ▷Somerset Maugham, *Liza of Lambeth*; ▷Saul Bellow, *Mr Sammler's Planet*.
▶ **To his vision of the 'ant-hill of human aspiration', the senseless, self-destructive bustle of affairs:** ▷Charles Dickens, *Dombey and Son*; George Gissing, *New Grub Street*.

those in Giovanni Boccaccio's Decameron *or* The Arabian
Nights.

BARBER, Noel • *(born 1911)*
British novelist.

Barber writes romantic thrillers, usually set in the Middle
East. His books include *The Other Side of Paradise*,
Farewell to France and *A Woman of Cairo* (1984), in
which two lovers are drawn together and pushed apart by
the pressure of events in war-torn Egypt.

READ ON

● *Tanamera.*
▶ Valerie Fitzgerald,
  Zemindar. M.M. Kaye,
  Shadow Moon. ▷J.G.
  Farrell, *The Singapore
  Grip.* ▷Olivia Manning,
  Fortunes of War.

BARNES, Djuna • *(1892–1982)*
US novelist and short-story writer.

Nightwood (1936), Barnes' best-known novel, is a dark
tale of lesbianism, adultery and madness among US exiles
in Paris in the 1930s. T.S. Eliot compared it, for 'horror
and doom', to Elizabethan tragedy; it is also like
▷Sartre's play *Huis Clos*, a glimpse of damned souls in
an ultra-modern hell. The characters – a transvestite doctor, a womanising German baron, a frail young girl and
the bisexual publicist for a travelling circus – spend their
time alternately betraying one another emotionally or
spending maudlin, boozy nights discussing their own and
each other's erotic preferences. Barnes' style is a poetic
version of the stream-of-consciousness monologues of
Freud's patients, halfway between ▷Proust and Molly
Bloom's soliloquy in ▷Joyce's *Ulysses*. *Nightwood* is no
easy read, but it is compulsive and unforgettable.

Barnes' other fiction consists of the novel Ryder *and the
story-collections* The Book of Repulsive Women, Spill-
way *(originally published with poems and plays, as* A
Book *and* A Night Among the Horses*) and* Vagaries
Malicieux. *She is also known for her plays, especially* The
Antiphon.

READ ON

▶ ▷Jean Rhys, *Good
  Morning, Midnight.*
  ▷Angela Carter, *The
  Infernal Desire
  Machines of Doctor
  Hoffman.* Desmond
  Hogan, *A New Shirt.*

BEERBOHM, Max • *(1876–1956)*
British artist and writer.

A caricaturist and satirist, Beerbohm published cartoons,
parodies, essays and articles ridiculing literary and social
figures of the day. His only novel, *Zuleika Dobson* (1911)
is a send-up of the university-set romantic novels of Ouida

READ ON

● *Seven Men* (short
  stories).
▶ Nancy Mitford, *Don't
  Tell Alfred.* Angela

(in which gels' hearts thud as they watch their heroes' rippling muscles in the rowing or boxing teams). Beerbohm turns Ouida's conventions on their heads. His Oxford undergraduates, whether gentlemen (world-weary and overbred) or scholars (weedy and obsessive) think of nothing but themselves, until Zuleika, the beautiful grand-daughter of the Warden of Judas College, sweeps into the university and every male in the place (even the statues on their pedestals) starts swooning for love of her. There are arguments, duels and suicide-pacts, and Zuleika is blind to them all. Her quarry is the Duke of Dorset, the handsomest, best-connected man in England, and her head will not rest easy, blessing the pillow it lies on, until she makes him her slave. But what, dear reader, if she should fall for *him* ...?

Thirkell, *August Folly*. ▷Jerome K. Jerome, *Three Men in a Boat*. Noel Langley, *Cage Me a Peacock*. Oscar Wilde, *The Portrait of Dorian Gray* takes a darker view of similarly self-obsessed characters.

BELLOW, Saul • *(born 1915)*
US novelist and playwright.

In Bellow's view, one of the most unexpected aspects of life in the modern world, and particularly in the post-Christian west, is that many people have lost all sense of psychological and philosophical identity. All Bellow's leading characters feel alienated from society. Some are content to suffer; others try to assert themselves, to invent an identity and live up to it – an attempt which is usually both bizarre and doomed. The hero of *The Adventures of Augie March* (1953), trying to model himself on one of ▷Hemingway's laconic men of action, takes his sophisticated girl-friend lizard-hunting in Mexico with a tame eagle, and is amazed when she leaves him. The hero of *Henderson the Rain King* (1959) goes on safari to darkest Africa, only to be taken prisoner by a remote people who think him a god-king and mark him for sacrifice. Devices like these warm Bellow's books, adding life and energy to what is already philosophically intriguing. His novels are compelling intellectual entertainments, thrillers of the mind.

HUMBOLDT'S GIFT • *(1975)*
The book's hero, Charlie Citrine, is a wise-cracking, street-wise failure. He is a writer whose inspiration has run out, a husband whose wife is divorcing him and whose mistress despises him, an educated man terrified of brainwork. Unexpectedly, a legacy from a dead friend, a drunken, bawdy poet, turns out not to be the worthless pile of paper everyone imagines but a scenario which forms the basis for a hugely successful film. Wealth is now added to Citrine's problems, and he is battened on by

READ ON ▷

● *Herzog* (about a panic-stricken intellectual who revisits the scenes of his past life trying to find clues to his psychological identity: cue for a magnificent travelogue through the city of Chicago, Bellow's consistent inspiration and this book's other central 'character').
▶ **To Bellow's theme of people searching for identity:** ▷Albert Camus, *The Fall*; ▷William Golding, *The Paper Men*; Max Frisch, *I'm Not Stiller*; ▷Jean Rhys, *Good Morning, Midnight*; Bernard Malamud, *A New Life*; ▷Margaret Atwood, *Surfacing*.
▶ **To his vision of the city (in his case, Chicago) as a metaphor for the turbulence of the soul:** James Plunkett,

tax officials, accountants, salesmen and an unsuccessful crook who tries to extort from him first money and then friendship. As the novel proceeds, Citrine keeps nerving himself to make the decision – any decision – that will focus his life, and is hampered each time by ludicrous circumstances and by the contrast between his own inadequacy and the memory of his larger-than-life, dead friend.

Bellow's other full-length novels are Mr Sammler's Planet, Herzog, The Dean's December *and* More Die of Heartbreak. Dangling Man, The Victim *and* Seize the Day *are mid-length novellas, and his short stories are collected in* Mosby's Memoirs *and* Him With the Foot in his Mouth. *He has also written plays and a fascinating political memoir about a visit to Israel,* To Jerusalem and Back.

BENNETT, Arnold • *(1867–1931)*
British novelist and non-fiction writer.

Bennett wrote hundreds of thousands of words each year, and much of his output was pot-boiling. But his best novels and stories, set in the English Midlands (the area he called 'the Five Towns', now Stoke-on-Trent), are masterpieces. They deal in a realistic way with the lives and aspirations of ordinary people (factory hands, shop assistants, housewives), but are full of disarming optimism and fantasy. Bennett's characters have ambitions; they travel, they read, they dream. Apart from the Five Towns novels his best-known works are two books originally written as magazine-serials: *The Card* (about a bouncy young man whose japes outrage provincial society but who ends up as mayor) and *The Grand Babylon Hotel*, a set of linked stories about the guests and staff in a luxury hotel.

THE OLD WIVES' TALE • *(1908)*
The lives of two sisters are contrasted: vivacious Sophia and steady Constance. Sophia feels constricted by life in the Five Towns, falls for a handsome wastrel and elopes with him to Paris, where he deserts her. Constance meanwhile marries a clerk in her father's shop, and settles to a life of bored domesticity. The novel charts the sisters' lives, and includes memorable scenes of the 1870 siege of Paris in the Franco-Prussian War. Its concluding section unites the sisters, now elderly, and shows, as their lives draw to a close, that those lives were all they had, that neither achieved anything or made any impact on the world.

The Five Towns novels are Anna of the Five Towns,

Strumpet City (set in pre-1914 Dublin); ▷Christina Stead, *The Beauties and Furies* (set in 1930s Paris); Colin MacInnes, *City of Spades* (set in racially divided 1950s London).

READ ON ▷

● *Clayhanger; Riceyman Steps.*
▶ ▷D.H. Lawrence, *The Rainbow.* ▷H.G. Wells, *Ann Veronica.* Theodore Dreiser, *Sister Carrie.* ▷Somerset Maugham, *Of Human Bondage.* ▷J.B. Priestley, *Angel Pavement.* Sherwood Anderson, *Winesburg, Ohio* is a set of stories echoing the feelings and lives of Bennett's characters in a small-town US setting.

The Old Wives' Tale, Clayhanger, Hilda Lessways, These Twain *and* The Roll Call. Riceyman Steps, *set in London, is grimmer and more Zolaesque.* Mr Prohack *is an entertainment, a good follow-up to* The Card. *Of Bennett's many other writings, particularly fascinating are his* Journals, *discussing such matters as his love of France, the meals he ate, the plays and novels he enjoyed, and above all his phenomenal day-to-day productivity.*

BENSON, E.F. (Edward Frederic) •
(1867–1940)
British novelist and non-fiction writer.

Although Benson wrote books of many kinds, he is best-known today for acid social comedies, and particularly for the 'Mapp and Lucia' series, televised with enormous success in the mid-1980s. His characters are well-to-do, middle-class Edwardians, whose chief interest in life is social one-upmanship. One's bridge-party, one's garden, one's paintings or one's recipes must simply outclass everyone else's, and if there is the slightest risk of failure, devious means must be employed.

MAPP AND LUCIA • *(1935)*
In previous books in the series, we have already met Lucia, the social queen of Riseholme, and Miss Mapp, who holds the same position in Tilling. Now Lucia moves to Tilling for the summer with her friend Georgie Pillson, rents Mapp's beloved house Mallards, and proceeds to upstage Mapp socially at every moment and in every way. The war between the ladies is fought at garden parties, poetry evenings, dinner-parties (at which Lucia's recipe Lobster à la Riseholme is a major weapon), and finally reaches its climax – one of Benson's most preposterous inventions – on an upturned table in the English Channel.

Benson's books include school stories, biographies, reminiscences, ghost stories (collected as Spook Stories *and* More Spook Stories*), and a shoal of comic novels, similar in themes and wit to the 'Lucia' books, including the 'Dodo' series and the (slightly) more serious* Mrs Ames *and* Secret Lives.

BIBLE: NEW TESTAMENT

▷Anthony Burgess, *The Kingdom of the Wicked*
Severia Huré, *I, Mary, Daughter of Israel*

READ ON ⟩

● *Queen Lucia*; *Paying Guests.*
▶ Tom Holt, *Lucia in Wartime* and *Lucia Triumphant* (sequels, as good as Benson at his best). Gabriel Chevalier, *Clochemerle*. Nancy Mitford, *Love in a Cold Climate*. Angela Thirkell, *Before Lunch.*

Pär Lagerkvist, *Barabbas*
George Moore, *The Brook Kerith*
▷Michèle Roberts, *The Wild Girl*
Henryk Sienkiewycz, *Quo Vadis?*
Frank Slaughter, *The Shoes of the Fisherman*

Ancient Rome (p 9); Bible: Old Testament (p 23)

BIBLE: OLD TESTAMENT

▷Joseph Heller, *God Knows*
▷Thomas Mann, *Joseph and his Brothers*
Jeanette Winterson, *Boating for Beginners*

Bible: New Testament (p 22); Other Peoples, Other
Times (p 186)

BINCHY, Maeve
Irish novelist.

Binchy's books are affectionate tapestries of the lives of
ordinary people, often in small Irish towns in the earlier
years of this century. 'Great' events happen offstage; the
spotlight is on birth, friendship, marriage, death and the
engrossing bustle of everyday life. Her style is gently satirical – village gossip turned into art – and her dialogue is
warm with the cadences of Irish speech. Her novels include *Light a Penny Candle*, *Dublin Four*, *Firefly Summer* and *Echoes* (1986), about a group of 1950s teenagers
growing up in a quiet seaside resort. *The Lilac Bus* (1986)
is a set of linked short stories about the passengers who
travel regularly on a small country bus.

READ ON ⟩

▶ Edna O'Brien, *The
Country Girls.*
Elizabeth North,
Worldly Goods. Rony
Robinson, *The Beano.*
Laurie Lee, *Cider With
Rosie* (nostalgic
memoirs of childhood
in a 1930s
Gloucestershire village,
of the English
countryside as it used
to be). Laura Ingalls
Wilder, *The Little
House on the Prairie*
(much less schmaltzy
than the TV series).
▷Eudora Welty, *Delta
Wedding.*

BLISH, James • *(1921–75)*
US novelist.

Blish used space-opera to discuss complex philosophical
and religious ideas. *A Case of Conscience* (1959), for example, sets born-again Christian Earth-scientists on a vast

READ ON ⟩

▶ ▷Frank Herbert, *Dune.*
▷Isaac Asimov,
Foundation. ▷J.G.

unexplored planet wondering whether the fact that they are human beings, God's supreme creation, gives them the right to exploit the planet's mineral wealth at the expense of the alien inhabitants, a lower order of existence; the book is part of the 'After Such Knowledge' tetralogy (the other volumes are *Black Easter*, *Doctor Mirabilis* and *The Day After Judgement*) in which Blish tried to work out a compromise between alchemy, black magic, religion and modern science. His best-known books are the 'Cities in Flight' novels, in which a mechanism is devised to spin whole sections of the Earth's surface into space, where their inhabitants eagerly or apprehensively set about reinventing their own lives. The series' protagonist is not a person but an entire community: Manhattan.

The 'Cities in Flight' novels are They Shall Have Stars, A Life for the Stars, Earthman Come Home *and* A Clash of Cymbals. *Blish's other books include* And All the Stars a Stage, Jack of Eagles *and* Midsummer Century. Anywhen *is a collection of short stories.*

BÖLL, Heinrich • *(1917–85)*
German novelist and non-fiction writer.

For decades after the second world war and the 'economic miracle' which followed it, German novelists hovered over their country like doctors examining a particularly interesting patient. How could any nation be so outwardly flourishing and seem so dead inside? Were such things as student riots in the 1960s or the urban terrorism of the 1970s isolated phenomena or symptoms of a deeper-rooted sickness? Böll, a Roman Catholic, linked the malaise of society with another kind of moral disintegration, the collapse of faith – but instead of preaching or hectoring he tried to alert his readers with bitter, saturnine irony. He is at his most savage in short stories and medium-length novels: *The Safety Net* (about terrorism), *The Lost Honour of Katherina Blum* (satirising the gutter press), *The Unguarded House* (scathing about miracles, economic or religious). Böll's longer books spread his rage more widely – and paradoxically, although this makes them more relaxed, as pacy and witty as ▷Bellow's, the urbane tone makes their messages even more unsettling.

GROUP PORTRAIT WITH LADY (Gruppenbild mit Dame) • *(1971)*
Böll takes a 'typical' German citizen of the post-war years – an inoffensive, dull woman in her 60s about whom the most fascinating information seems to be that she likes fresh rolls for breakfast – and tries to find out more about

Ballard, *The Burning World*. ▷Brian Aldiss, *The Helliconia Trilogy*.

READ ON ▷

● *Billiards at Half-past Nine* (a panoramic view of the last 50 years of German society, focussed on a single family); *The Clown* (a bleak study of one person's attempt to retain dignity and moral integrity, to say nothing of religious faith, in a society where such qualities are no longer valued).
▶ Robert Musil, *Young Törless*. Siegfried Lenz, *The Heritage*. ▷Saul Bellow, *Mr Sammler's Planet*. Nathalie Sarraute, *Portrait of an Unknown Man*. J.P. Marquand, *The Late George Apley*. Janet Hitchman, *Meeting for Burial*.

her by questioning her family, friends, neighbours, work-mates and old school-fellows. The method is familiar from TV documentary: a jigsaw puzzle of interlocking interviews, assembled to make a single picture. But two pictures in fact emerge: one of the woman herself and one of the teeming German society of which she is part. The book's style is brisk, witty and apparently uncontroversial, so that it is not till the end that we realise just what Böll is saying about Germany's moral plight.

Böll's other novels are And Where Were You, Adam?, Acquainted with the Night *and* Billiards at Half-past Nine. *His short stories are in* Absent Without Leave, Traveller, if you Come to Spa *and* Children are Civilians Too. What's To Become of the Boy? *is a brief, savage memoir of adolescence under the nazis;* Irish Journal *describes his stay in Ireland in the 1960s, and his affection for the Celtic, Catholic culture he found there.*

THE BOOKER PRIZE

In 1968 Booker International set up an annual prize for fiction by British and Commonwealth authors, intending it to be of major status, equal to such awards as the Prix Goncourt in France. Although the prize-money (currently £15,000) has long been overtaken by other British awards, the Booker competition still attracts more publicity than any other. Publishers submit promising titles each year, and a panel of judges makes a short list in September and selects a winner in October. The following list shows all the short-listed authors and titles so far, with winners' names in bold.

1969
    Barry England, *Figures in a Landscape*
    N. Mosley, *The Impossible Object*
▷Iris Murdoch, *The Nice and the Good*
▷**P.H. Newby, *Something to Answer For***
▷Muriel Spark, *The Public Image*
    G.M. Williams, *From Scenes Like These*

    1970
    A.L. Barker, *John Brown's Body*
▷Elizabeth Bowen, *Eva Trout*
▷Iris Murdoch, *Bruno's Dream*
▷**Bernice Rubens, *The Elected Member***
    William Trevor, *Mrs Eckdorff in O'Neill's Hotel*
    T. Wheeler, *The Conjunction*

    1971
    Thomas Kilroy, *The Big Chapel*
▷Doris Lessing, *Briefing for a Descent into Hell*
▷**V.S. Naipaul, *In a Free State***
▷Mordecai Richler, *St Urbain's Horseman*
    Derek Robinson, *Goshawk Squadron*

▷Elizabeth Taylor, *Mrs Palfrey at the Claremont*

1972
John Berger, G
▷Susan Hill, *Bird of Night*
▷Thomas Keneally, *The Chant of Jimmie Blacksmith*
David Storey, *Passmore*

1973
Beryl Bainbridge, *The Dressmaker*
▷**J.G. Farrell, *The Siege of Krishnapur***
Elizabeth Mavor, *The Green Equinox*

1974
▷Kingsley Amis, *Ending Up*
Beryl Bainbridge, *The Bottle Factory Outing*
▷**Nadine Gordimer, *The Conservationist***
Stanley Middleton, *Holiday*
▷C.P. Snow, *In Their Wisdom*

1975
▷**Ruth Prawer Jhabvala, *Heat and Dust***
▷Thomas Keneally, *Gossip from the Forest*

1976
André Brink, *An Instant in the Wind*
R.C. Hutchinson, *Rising*
Brian Moore, *The Doctor's Wife*
Julian Rathbone, *King Fisher Lives*
David Storey, *Saville*
William Trevor, *The Children of Dynmouth*

1977
Paul Bailey, *Peter Smart's Confessions*
Caroline Blackwood, *Great Granny Webster*
Jennifer Johnston, *Shadows on our Skin*
Penelope Lively, *The Road to Lichfield*
▷Barbara Pym, *Quartet in Autumn*
Paul Scott, *Staying On*

1978
▷Kingsley Amis, *Jake's Thing*
André Brink, *Rumours of Rain*
Penelope Fitzgerald, *The Bookshop*
Jane Gardam, *God on the Rocks*
▷**Iris Murdoch, *The Sea, The Sea***
▷Bernice Rubens, *A Five-year Sentence*

1979
Penelope Fitzgerald, *Offshore*
▷Thomas Keneally, *Confederates*
▷V.S. Naipaul, *A Bend in the River*
Julian Rathbone, *Joseph*
▷Fay Weldon, *Praxis*

1980
▷Anthony Burgess, *Earthly Powers*
Anita Desai, *Clear Light of Day*
▷**William Golding, *Rites of Passage***
▷Alice Munro, *The Beggar Maid*
Julia O'Faolain, *No Country for Young Men*
Barry Unsworth, *Pascali's Island*

J.L. Carr, *A Month in the Country*

1981
Molly Keane, *Good Behaviour*
▷Doris Lessing, *The Sirian Experiments*
Ian McEwan, *The Comfort of Strangers*
▷**Salman Rushdie, Midnight's Children**
Anne Schlee, *Rhine Journey*
▷Muriel Spark, *Loitering with Intent*
D.M. Thomas, *The White Hotel*

1982
John Arden, *Silence Among the Weapons*
William Boyd, *An Ice-cream War*
▷Lawrence Durrell, *Constance or Solitary Practices*
▷**Thomas Keneally, Schindler's Ark**
Alice Thomas Ellis, *The 27th Kingdom*
Timothy Mo, *Sour Sweet*

1983
▷Malcolm Bradbury, *Rates of Exchange*
J.M. Coetzee, Life & Times of Michael K
John Fuller, *Flying to Nowhere*
Anita Mason, *The Illusionist*
▷Salman Rushdie, *Shame*
▷Graham Swift, *Waterland*

1984
▷J.G. Ballard, *Empire of the Sun*
Julian Barnes, *Flaubert's Parrot*
▷**Anita Brookner, Hôtel du Lac**
Anita Desai, *In Custody*
Penelope Lively, *According to Mark*
David Lodge, *Small World*

1985
Peter Carey, *Illywhacker*
J.L. Carr, *The Battle of Pollocks Crossing*
▷**Keri Hulme, The Bone People**
▷Doris Lessing, *The Good Terrorist*
Jan Morris, *Last Letters from Hav*
▷Iris Murdoch, *The Good Apprentice*

1986
▷**Kingsley Amis, The Old Devils**
▷Margaret Atwood, *The Handmaid's Tale*
Paul Bailey, *Gabriel's Lament*
▷Robertson Davies, *What's Bred in the Bone*
▷Kazuo Ishiguro, *An Artist of the Floating World*
Timothy Mo, *An Insular Possession*

1987
▷Chinua Achebe, *Anthills of the Savannah*
Peter Ackroyd, *Chatterton*
Nina Bawden, *Circles of Deceit*
Penelope Lively, Moon Tiger
Brian Moore, *The Colour of Blood*
▷Iris Murdoch, *The Book and the Brotherhood*

BORGES, Jorge Luis • *(1899–1987)*

Argentinian short-story writer and poet.

Until the 1950s Borges worked as a librarian and was an admired poet – though, because his verse seems flat in translation, he was hardly known outside Spanish-speaking countries. But in the 1950s his 'fictions' began to appear in other languages, and his reputation spread worldwide. A 'fiction' is a short prose piece, ranging in length from a paragraph to a half a dozen pages. Some are short stories, in the manner of ▷Kipling, ▷Hemingway or ▷Kafka (whom Borges translated into Spanish). Others are tiny surrealist meditations, zen-like philosophical riddles or prose-poetry. A 20th-century writer produces a version of *Don Quixote* for modern times – and it is identical, word for word, to the original. (But is it any less real for all that?) A man meets a mysterious stranger by a riverside, and finds that the stranger is himself. A man writes about the terrifying prison which traps him – and only at the end reveals its name: the world.

LABYRINTHS • *(English edition 1962)*

This is a generous anthology of Borges' work, and gives the flavour particularly of the 'fictions'.

Borges' stories and fictions are in A Universal History of Infamy, Fictions, The Aleph, Dreamtigers, The Book of Sand *and* Doctor Brodie's Report. *His* Selected Poems *were published in English translation in 1972.*

BOWEN, Elizabeth • *(1899–1973)*

Irish novelist and short-story writer.

Although Bowen's themes were emotional – loneliness; longing for love; lack of communication – she wrote in a brisk and faintly eccentric style (italicising the most unlikely words, *for* example) which gives her stories an exhilarating feeling of detachment from the events and reactions they describe. She was especially skilful at evoking atmosphere in houses or locales: London streets and tube-stations during the second-world-war blitz become places of eerie fantasy rather than reality. Her concern, despite her characters' craving to preserve the social niceties, was to show 'life with the lid off' – and this, coupled with the unpredictability of her writing style, constantly edges her plots from actuality through dream to nightmare.

THE DEATH OF THE HEART • *(1938)*

Portia, a naive 16-year-old orphan (in a more modern

> **READ ON**

- *The Book of Imaginary Beings* (descriptions of 120 fanciful creatures from the weirder recesses of the world's imagination.
▶ ▷Gabriel García Márquez, *The Innocent Erendira*. Robert Coover, *Pricksongs and Descants*. Samuel Beckett, *More Pricks than Kicks*. ▷Italo Calvino, *Invisible Cities*. Michael Ayrton, *Fabrications*.
▶ **An unexpected parallel to Borges at his most surreal – so close at times that it seems like a send-up:** Woody Allen, *Without Feathers*.

> **READ ON**

- *The Heat of the Day; Eva Trout.*
▶ **To Bowen's novels:** ▷Henry James, *The Wings of the Dove*; ▷Angus Wilson, *The Middle Age of Mrs Eliot*; ▷Iris Murdoch, *The Sandcastle*. Peter Taylor, *A Summons to Memphis* sets scenes of similar emotional ambiguity in the US mid-west.
▶ **To Bowen's short stories:** ▷Elizabeth Taylor, *A Dedicated*

book she might be 12 or 13) goes to live with her stuffy half-brother and his brittle, insecure wife in fashionable 1930s London. Her innocence is in marked contrast to their world-weary sophistication, and they are as exasperated with her as she is with them. Then she falls in what she imagines to be love, and all parties are launched on an ever-bumpier emotional ride.

Bowen's other novels include The House in Paris, A World of Love *and* Eva Trout. *Her short stories are published in* Encounters, Ann Lee's, Joining Charles, The Cat Jumps *and the second-world-war collections* Look at All Those Roses *and* The Demon Lover.

BOYD, Martin • *(1893–1969)*
Australian novelist.

One of a large artistic family, Boyd originally trained as an architect, only taking up full-time writing in his 30s. He also spent much time in Europe, and writes in his autobiography of the pull between the cultural traditions of the Old World and the openness and opportunity of Australia. He turned all these themes and feelings into fiction. His principal characters are artistically sensitive people growing up in Australia, balancing the claims of family life against the need they feel to experience European art, culture and religion for themselves. He writes with malicious, ironical glee of large middle-class families, keeping up their pretensions and the façade of polite manners in what they feel is an exciting but barbarian environment. His best-known books are the 'Langton' tetralogy (1952–62): the 'biography' of Guy Langton and his extended family in the 80 years preceding the first world war. It centres on Guy's artistic and spiritual restlessness, but a major subsidiary theme is the gradual disintegration of a once tight-knit family as social opportunities in Australia increase and ties with the Old World grow less. The Langtons understand the past but have no sense of future opportunity; as Australia waxes, all they can do is wane.

The books in the Langton tetralogy are The Cardboard Crown, A Difficult Young Man, Outbreak of Love *and* When Blackbirds Sing. *Boyd's other novels include* Lucinda Brayford, Such Pleasure *and* The Montfords *(originally published under the pseudonym Martin Mills). His autobiographies* A Single Flame *and* Day of My Delights, *and the travel-book* Much Else in Italy, *interestingly reflect the main themes of his fiction.*

Man; ▷John Fowles, *The Ebony Tower.*

> READ ON ⟩

● *The Montfords.*
▶ **To the theme of the disintegrating family:** ▷Thomas Mann, *Buddenbrooks.*
▶ **To the Australian theme:** ▷Miles Franklin, *My Brilliant Career*; ▷H.H. Richardson, *The Fortunes of Richard Mahony.*
▶ **To the theme of young people uneasy with their cultural background:** ▷Ford Madox Ford, *Parade's End*; ▷Willa Cather, *My Antonia*; ▷J.D. Salinger, *The Catcher in the Rye.*

BRADBURY, Malcolm • *(born 1932)*
British novelist and screenwriter.

A university professor, Bradbury writes sharp satires on academic life. The form and style of his first two novels were straightforward, but from *The History Man* onwards he began using experimental methods: fragmenting the plots into short scenes like those of TV plays, writing in the present tense, incorporating footnotes, commentaries and asides. The feeling is that each book is a game, meant to amuse the author as well as the reader – a feature which sets Bradbury apart from all other 'campus' novelists.

THE HISTORY MAN • *(1975)*
The book – far funnier than the TV series it inspired – is set in a ghastly British 'new' university, all bare concrete and graffiti. Its hero is an equally abrasive 'new' academic, the sociologist Howard Kirk. Kirk thinks that sociology is the only study relevant to the modern world, and that it should be a vehicle for radical change. He also believes in sleeping with as many female staff and students as he can entice to bed. He preaches left-wing politics in his seminars, humiliates anyone he suspects of right-wing opinions (for example young men who wear ties and call him 'Sir'), organises sit-ins and strikes, and strides happily through the destabilised, quivering society he creates all round him.

Bradbury's other novels are Eating People is Wrong, Stepping Westward, *and (the most experimental)* Rates of Exchange. Cuts *is a long short story,* Mensonge *a send-up of current French lit-crit pretentiousness and* No, Not Bloomsbury *a collection of essays, articles and reviews. He has also written TV adaptations of his own and other people's books.*

BRADFORD, Barbara Taylor
British novelist.

Bradford's books – many set in the north of England – are stories of characterful young women who rise in the worlds of business and society despite all obstacles. Her best-known books are *A Woman of Substance* and *Hold the Dream*.

READ ON ▷

- *Stepping Westward* (about a naive English lecturer on an exchange visit to a liberal western US campus).
- ▶ **To *The History Man*:** ▷Mary McCarthy, *The Groves of Academe*; ▷Vladimir Nabokov, *Pnin*; ▷Randall Jarrell, *Pictures from an Institution*; John Barth, *The End of the Road*.
- ▶ **To *Stepping Westward*:** David Lodge, *Changing Places*. Michael Frayn, *Towards the End of the Morning* and Colin Douglas, *The Houseman's Tale* are 'campus' novels of a different kind, set not in universities but, respectively, in a newspaper office and a hospital.
- ▶ Tom Sharpe, *Wilt* and its glorious, tasteless sequels are campus farce rather than comedy, entertainment for its own gross sake without a whiff of satire.

READ ON ▷

- *Act of Will*.
- ▶ Nicola Thorne, *Where the Rivers Meet*. Audrey Howard, *Ambitions*. Pamela Oldfield, *The Gooding Girl*. ▷Judith Krantz, *Princess Daisy*.

BRENT OF BIN BIN: see FRANKLIN, Miles

BRONTË, Charlotte • *(1816–55)*
BRONTË, Emily • *(1818–48)*
British novelists.

Much has been made of the Brontës' claustrophobic life in the parsonage at Haworth in Yorkshire, and of the way they compensated for a restricted and stuffy daily routine by inventing wildly romantic stories. Their Haworth life was first described by a novelist (▷Gaskell), and is as evocative as any fiction of the time. In some ways it colours our opinion of their work: for example, if the third sister, Anne, had not been a Brontë, few people would nowadays remember her novels, which are pale shadows of her sister's books. But Charlotte and Emily need no biographical boosting. They were geniuses, with a (remarkably similar) fantastical imagination, a robust, melodramatic view of what a 'good story' ought to be, and a pre-Freudian understanding of the dark places of the soul. Their brooding landscapes and old, dark houses may have been drawn from life, but what they made of them was an original, elaborate and self-consistent world, as turbulent as dreams.

JANE EYRE • *(by Charlotte Brontë, 1847)*
The plot is a romantic extravaganza about a poor governess who falls in love with her employer Mr Rochester, is prevented from marrying him by the dark secret which shadows him, and only finds happiness on the last page, after a sequence of melodramatic and unlikely coincidences. The book's power is in its counterpointing of real and psychological events. We read about storms, fires, wild-eyed creatures gibbering in attics and branches tapping at the windows – but what we are really being shown is the turmoil in Jane's own soul, the maturing of a personality. This emotional progress, magnificently described, unifies the book and transmutes even its silliest events to gold.

WUTHERING HEIGHTS • *(by Emily Brontë, 1847)*
The story begins in the 1770s, when a rich Yorkshire landowner, Earnshaw, brings home a half-wild, sullen foundling he names Heathcliff. Heathcliff grows up alongside Earnshaw's own children, and falls in love with Cathy, the daughter. But he overhears her saying that she will never marry him because she is socially above him – and the rest of the novel deals with his elaborate revenge

> **READ ON** ▷

▶ **To Jane Eyre:** *Wuthering Heights.*
▶ **To Wuthering Heights:** *Jane Eyre.*
▶ **To *Jane Eyre:*** ▷Daphne Du Maurier, *Rebecca*; ▷Jean Rhys, *Wide Sargasso Sea*; ▷Margaret Mitchell, *Gone With the Wind*; George Douglas Brown, *The House With the Green Shutters.*
▶ **To *Wuthering Heights*:** R.D. Blackmore, *Lorna Doone*; ▷Thomas Hardy, *Tess of the d'Urbervilles*; ▷Iris Murdoch, *The Unicorn* (about the turbulent passions of a more modern heroine).

on her whole family and the way the emotional poison is eventually neutralised. As in *Jane Eyre*, desolate moorland and lonely, rain-lashed houses are used as symbols of the passions in the characters' hearts. Heathcliff, in particular, is depicted as if he were a genuine 'child of nature', the offspring not of human beings but of the monstrous mating of darkness, stone and storm.

All three sisters wrote Wordsworthy, nature-haunted poetry. Emily's only completed novel was Wuthering Heights; *Charlotte's were* Jane Eyre, The Professor *and* Villette; *Anne's were* Agnes Grey *and* The Tenant of Wildfell Hall.

BROOKNER, Anita
British novelist.

Brookner's novels are written in trim, witty prose, style for its own sake, a civilised delight. This exactly suits the characters of the people in her stories. They are middle-aged, upper-middle-class women (professors, librarians, novelists): well-off, well-tailored, well-organised and desperately lonely. Something has blighted their emotional lives, leaving them to order their comfortable, bleak existences as best they can, to fill their days. The books show us what brought them to their condition – usually the actions of others, husbands, parents or friends – and sometimes tell us how the problem is resolved. In 'well-made' stage and film dramas of the 1930s, women were always blinking back tears and bravely facing the future. Brookner's heroines, except that they have lost even the power to cry, try to do the same.

LOOK AT ME · (1983)
Frances Hinton, librarian at a medical research institute, lives a disciplined, unvarying existence which she compares wistfully with what she imagines to be the exuberant, exciting lives of the research workers and others who use the books. She is 'taken up' by one of the most brilliant men, dazzling as a comet, and by his emotionally extrovert wife. She falls in love, and imagines that she is loved in return. But what looks like being a sentimental education in fact teaches her only that all human beings are islands, and that unless we hoard our inner lives and treasure our privacy, we will lose even what peace of mind we have.

Brookner's other novels are A Start in Life, Providence, Hôtel du Lac, Family and Friends, A Misalliance *and* A

READ ON >

● *Hôtel du Lac.*
▶ Elizabeth Jane Howard, *Something in Disguise*. Edward Candy, *Scene Changing*. A.S. Byatt, *The Virgin in the Garden*. Jenny Diski, *Rainforest*. Susan Fromberg Shaeffer, *The Injured Party*.

Friend from England. *She is an expert on fine art, and has published books about the painters Watteau, Greuze and David.*

BUCHAN, John • *(1875–1940)*
British novelist.

Buchan's thrillers play virtuoso variations on the same basic plot. A stiff-upper-lipped hero (often Richard Hannay) discovers a conspiracy to End Civilisation as We Know It, and sets out single-handed, or with the help of a few trusted friends, to frustrate it. He is chased (often by the police as well as by the criminals), and wins through only by a combination of physical courage and absolute moral certainty. The pleasure of Buchan's novels is enhanced by the magnificently-described wild countryside he sets them in (usually the Scottish highlands or the plains of southern Africa), and by their splendid gallery of minor characters, the shopkeepers, tramps, local bobbies and landladies who help his heroes, often at enormous (if shrugged-off) personal risk.

THE THIRTY-NINE STEPS • *(1915)*
Richard Hannay, returning from South Africa, is told by a chance American acquaintance of a plot to invade England. Soon afterwards the American is killed and Hannay is framed for his murder. To escape two manhunts, one by the conspirators and the other by the police, he takes to the hills, and only after 300 pages of breathtaking peril and hair's-breadth escapes does he succeed in saving his country and clearing his name.

Buchan's other thrillers include Huntingtower, John MacNab *and* Witchwood *(all set in Scotland), and the Hannay books* Greenmantle, Mr Standfast *and* The Three Hostages. *He also wrote lively biographies (of ▷Scott, the emperor Augustus and Oliver Cromwell), and an autobiography,* Memory-Hold-the-Door.

BURGESS, Anthony • *(born 1917)*
British novelist and non- fiction writer.

Originally a composer, Burgess began writing books in his mid-30s, and since then has poured out literary works of every kind, from introductions to ▷Joyce (*Here Comes Everybody/Re Joyce*) to filmscripts, from opera libretti to book-reviews. Above all he has written novels, of a diversity few other 20th-century writers have ever equalled.

> **READ ON** ▷
>
> ● *Greenmantle; Mr Standfast; Prester John* (an African adventure as exciting and bizarre as anything by ▷H. Rider Haggard, whose *She* makes an excellent follow-up).
> ▶ Erskine Childers, *The Riddle of the Sands.* ▷Geoffrey Household, *Rogue Male.* ▷Ken Follett, *Storm Island/ The Key To Rebecca.* ▷Helen MacInnes, *The Snare of the Hunted.* Craig Thomas, *Firefox.* ▷Robert Ludlum, *The Gemini Contenders.*

> **READ ON** ▷
>
> ● *Earthly Powers* (a blockbuster embracing every kind of 20th-century 'evil', from homosexual betrayal to genocide, and the

They range from fictionalised biographies of Shakespeare (*Nothing Like the Sun*) and the early Christian missionaries (*The Kingdom of the Wicked*) to farce (the four Enderby stories, of which *Inside Mr Enderby* is the first and *Enderby's Dark Lady* is the funniest), from experimental novels (*The Napoleon Symphony*, about Napoleon, borrows its form from Beethoven's Eroica Symphony) to semi-autobiographical stories about expatriate Britons in the Far East (*The Malaysian Trilogy*). The literary demands of Burgess' books vary as widely as their contents: the way he finds a form and style to suit each new inspiration is one of the most brilliant features of his work.

A CLOCKWORK ORANGE • *(1962)*

In a grim future Britain, society is divided into the haves, who live in security-screened mansions in leafy countryside, and the have-nots, who swagger in gangs through the decaying cities, gorging themselves on violence. The book is narrated by the leader of one such gang, and is written in a private language, a mixture of standard English, cockney slang and Russian. (Burgess provides a glossary, but after a few pages the language is easy enough to follow, and its strangeness adds to the feeling of alienation which pervades the book.) The young man has committed a horrific crime, breaking into a house, beating up its owner and raping his wife, and the police are 'rehabilitating' him. His true 'crime', however, was not action but thought – he aspired to a way of life, of culture, from which his class and lack of money should have barred him – and Burgess leaves us wondering whether his 'cure' will work, since he is not a brute beast (as the authorities claim) but rather the individuality in human beings which society has chosen to repress.

Burgess' other novels include a reflection on what he sees as the death-throes of modern western civilisation, 1985, and a gentler, ▷Priestleyish book about provincial English life earlier this century, The Piano-players. *Little Wilson and Big God is autobiography, and* Urgent Copy *and* Homage to Qwert Yuiop *are collections of reviews and literary articles.*

Church's reluctance or inability to stand aside from it).

▶ **To *A Clockwork Orange:*** ▷Aldous Huxley, *Brave New World*; ▷Margaret Atwood, *The Handmaid's Tale*; ▷Russell Hoban, *Riddley Walker*.

▶ **To Burgess' historical novels:** John Hersey, *The Wall*; ▷Michèle Roberts, *The Wild Girl*.

▶ **To *The Malaysian Trilogy:*** ▷Paul Theroux, *Jungle Lovers*.

▶ **To the Enderby comedies:** David Lodge, *Small World*; ▷Peter De Vries, *Reuben, Reuben*.

C

CALVINO, Italo • *(1923–85)*
Italian novelist and short-story writer.

Calvino's first works followed the grim neo-realist tradition of the late 1940s, treating contemporary subjects in an unsparing, documentary way. But in the 1950s he decided to change his style, to write (as he put it) the kind of stories he himself might want to read. These were fantastic, surrealist tales, drawing on medieval legend, fairy stories, SF and the work of such 20th-century experimental writers as ▷Kafka and ▷Borges. The style is lucid and poetic; the events, however bizarre their starting-point, follow each other logically and persuasively; the overall effect is magical. In *Cosmicomics* huge space-beings play marbles with sub-atomic particles and take tea with one another as decorously as any Italian bourgeois family. The people in *The Castle of Crossed Destinies* are struck magically dumb, and have to tell each other stories using nothing but tarot cards. In *Invisible Cities* Marco Polo invents fantasy-cities to tickle the imagination of Kubla Khan. Calvino's wide-eyed, bizarre fantasy has been imitated but never surpassed; he is one of the most entrancing writers of the century.

OUR ANCESTORS • *(1951–9)*
This book contains a full-length novel (*The Baron in the Trees*) and two long stories. In *The Baron in the Trees* a boy abandons the ground for the treetops and – in one of Calvino's most sustained and lyrical tours-de-force – lives an entire, fulfilled life without ever coming down to earth. In *The Cloven Viscount* a medieval knight is split in two on the battlefield – and each half goes on living independently, one good, one bad, deprived of the link which made them a whole human being and gave them moral identity. In *The Non-Existent Knight* an empty suit of ar-

READ ON ▷

● *Invisible Cities*; *Cosmicomics*.
▶ John Gardner, *Vlemk the Box-painter* (a long medieval allegory, in the collection *The Art of Living and Other Stories*, which otherwise contains modern tales). ▷Thomas Mann, *The Holy Sinner*. T.H. White, *The Sword in the Stone*. Milan Kundera, *The Unbearable Lightness of Being*.
▶ **Good short-story follow-ups:** ▷Jorge Luis Borges, *Fictions*; Martin Amis, *Einstein's Monsters*; ▷Angela Carter, *The Bloody Chamber* (extraordinary post-Freudian, feminist reworkings of fairy tales).

mour takes on its own identity, fighting, discussing tactics, brawling – and forever yearning after the reality of life, the psychological and emotional fullness which it/he can never know.

Calvino's neo-realist books are The Path to the Nest of Spiders *(a novel) and* Adam, One Afternoon *(short stories). His fantasies are collected in* T Zero, Cosmicomics, Invisible Cities, Our Ancestors, The Castle of Crossed Destinies, Mr Palomar *and* The Watcher and Other Stories. Italian Folk-Tales *reworks traditional material in a similar, uniquely personal way.*

CAMUS, Albert • *(1913–60)*
French novelist and non-fiction writer.

READ ON >

Throughout his life, in newspaper articles, plays, essays and novels, Camus explored the position of what he called *l'homme revolté*, the rebel or misfit who feels out of tune with the spirit of the times. His characters recoil from the values of society. They believe that our innermost being is compromised by conformity, and that we can only liberate our true selves if we choose our own attitude to life, our day-to-day philosophy. Camus compared the human condition to that of Sisyphus in Greek myth, forever rolling a stone up a hill only to have it crash back down every time it reached the top – and said that the way to cope with this situation was to abandon ambition and concentrate on the here and now. But despite his uncompromising philosophy, his books are anything but difficult. His descriptions of sun-saturated Algeria (in *The Outsider*), rainy Amsterdam (in *The Fall*) or disease-ridden, rotting Oran (in *The Plague*) are fast-moving and evocative, and he shows the way inner desolation racks his heroes with such intensity that we sympathise with every instant of their predicament and long, like them, for them to break through into acceptance, into happiness.

● *The Fall.*
▶ ▷Saul Bellow, *The Victim.* ▷Hermann Hesse, *Rosshalde.* ▷William Golding, *The Spire.* Carlo Gébler, *Work and Play.* Simone de Beauvoir, *The Mandarins.* Paul Bowles, *The Sheltering Sky.*
▶ **More extrovert books, cloaking the philosophy in action and comedy respectively:** ▷Graham Greene, *A Burnt-out Case;* ▷Joseph Heller, *Something Happened.*

THE PLAGUE • *(1947)*
Plague ravages the Algerian town of Oran. Quarantined from the outside world, the citizens cope with their tragedy as best they can, either clinging to the outward forms of social life (petty city ordinances; the formalities of religion) or pathetically, helplessly suffering. (For Camus' original readers, the novel was an allegory of France under wartime nazi occupation.) At the heart of the story are Dr Rieux (the story-teller) and a group of other intellectuals. Each has different feelings about death, and for each of them the plague is not only a daily reality, an

external event which has to be endured, but a philosophical catalyst, forcing them to decide what they think about the world and their place in it.

As well as in novels, Camus set out his philosophy in two substantial essays, The Rebel *(L'homme révolté) and* The Myth of Sisyphus. *His plays are* Caligula, Cross Purpose, The Just Assassins *and* State of Siege *(a stage version of* The Plague*).* Exile and the Kingdom *collects short stories.*

CARR, Philippa • *(born 1906)*
British novelist.

'Philippa Carr' is one of the pseudonyms of ▷Eleanor Hibbert. She writes historical romances, showing the effect of great events on ordinary people's lives. Her best-known books are the *'Daughters of England' series*; other titles include *The Witch from the Sea, Sara Band of Two Sisters* and *Lament for a Lost Lover*.

READ ON ⟩

▶ Jane Aiken Hodge, *Judas Flowering.*
Juliette Benzoni, *'Catherine' series.*
Pamela Bennetts, *A Dragon for Edward.*

CARTER, Angela • *(born 1940)*
British novelist and non-fiction writer.

Carter's inspiration includes fairy tales, Jung's theory of the collective unconscious, horror movies and the fantasies of such writers as ▷Poe and ▷Shelley. Above all, she is concerned with female sexuality and with men's sexual predations on women. Her books range from Gothic reworkings of fairy tales (*The Bloody Chamber*) to such surrealist nightmares as *The Passion of New Eve* (see below). The novels begin with dream-images, and spiral quickly into fantasy. In the opening chapter of *The Magic Toyshop* (1967), for example, 15-year-old Melanie walks in a garden at night in her mother's wedding dress –a common, if none too reassuring dream. Soon afterwards, however, Melanie's parents die, she is fostered by a mad toymaker-uncle, and the book climaxes when she is forced to re-enact the myth of Leda and the Swan with a life-sized puppet-swan. At first sight such stories seem little more than an upmarket literary equivalent of the occult, sex-and-sadism shockers of ▷James Herbert or Stephen ▷King. But Carter's books are less titillating than psycho-political. They are nightmare-visions, designed to induce self-examination and to lead to change.

READ ON ⟩

● *Heroes and Villains.*
▶ D.M. Thomas, *The White Hotel.*
▷Margaret Atwood, *The Handmaid's Tale.*
Joanna Russ, *The Female Man.* Kathy Acker, *Blood and Guts in High School.* ▷Gore Vidal, *Myra Breckinridge.*

THE PASSION OF NEW EVE • *(1977)*
In a near-future USA where armies of blacks, feminists

and pubescent children are waging guerrilla war, the young man Evelyn hides in the California desert, only to be kidnapped by devotees of the multi-breasted, all-engulfing Earth Mother. She rapes him, castrates him and remakes him as a woman, Eve; the intention is to impregnate him/her with his own spilled sperm, to make her/him the parent of a second human race. But Eve escapes, trembling with fury at the outrage to her/his sexuality, and it is only after a series of even more nightmarish adventures that she is able at last to accept herself for what she is, to open herself to destiny.

Carter's other novels are Shadow Dance, Several Perceptions, Nights at the Circus, Heroes and Villains, Love *and* The Infernal Desire Machines of Dr Hoffman. *The* Sadeian Woman *is non-fiction, a study of the social and sexual potential of women.* Fireworks *collects short stories (among her most disturbing works), and* Nothing Sacred *collects essays and journalism.*

CATHER, Willa • *(1876–1947)*
US novelist.

Most of Cather's books are set in the south-western USA, and are about settlers (often European immigrants) coming to terms with the wilderness. But there is no Hollywood melodrama: her interests are in the contrast between civilised feelings and the wild natural environment, in psychological growth and change. In two characteristic books, *My Antonia* and *A Lost Lady*, the central female characters (the ones who change) are described by men who have watched them, and loved them, from a distance since childhood – a device which allowed Cather the objective, emotional distance from her characters which she preferred. This objectivity, and the elegance of her style, are two of the most enjoyable features of her books. Her sentences seem placid and unhurried: every event, every description seems to be given the same measured treatment. But nothing is extra. Every phrase has emotional or philosophical resonance, and after a few pages the reader is drawn into the narrative, hypnotised by nuance.

DEATH COMES FOR THE ARCHBISHOP • *(1927)*
Based on true events, and on diaries and letters by real people, this novel tells of two French Catholic missionaries to New Mexico in the second half of the 19th century. The book is partly about landscape, and contains magnificent descriptions of the desert. But it is mainly concerned with relationships: between the two priests, friends for

READ ON ⟩

● *Shadows on the Rock* (a similarly quiet book about the impact of the American wilderness on Europeans, this time 17th-century explorers in Quebec).
▶ Janet Lewis, *The Trial of Sören Kvist.*
▷Hermann Hesse, *Rosshalde.* George Moore, *The Brook Kerith* (about Joseph of Arimathea).
▷Patrick White, *A Fringe of Leaves.* Neil M. Gunn, *The Well at the World's End.*

many years, between the humans and their animals (who have to carry them on long, lonely desert journeys from one Christian settlement to another), and between the missionaries' ancient European culture and the stripped-to-essentials, 'primitive' habits of life and mind of their New Mexican flock. The book's title is not a promise of high drama. It refers to a Holbein painting, and suggested to Cather the feeling of frozen movement, of life arrested at the instant of recording, which she found in paintings and tried to recapture in her prose.

Two of Cather's novels, The Song of the Lark *and* Lucy Gayheart, *are about young women torn between the claims of family life and an artistic, musical career.* O Pioneers!, *like* My Antonia, *is about foreign immigrants settling in the wilderness. The main character of* The Professor's House *is a successful academic who suddenly feels that he has failed, that lack of danger (emotional, intellectual or physical) has blighted his life. Other novels are* One of Ours *and* My Mortal Enemy. Obscure Destinies *is a collection of short stories.*

CHANDLER, Raymond • *(1888–1959)*
US novelist.

In the 1930s Chandler (an ex-businessman and journalist) began writing gangster-stories for magazines, treating violence, prostitution and betrayal in the cynical, hard-boiled style popular in films of the time. His ambition was to replace the kind of detective novels then fashionable (stories of bizarre crimes solved by wildly eccentric detectives, distantly modelled on Sherlock Holmes: see ▷Christie; ▷Sayers) with books about realistic crimes, investigated in a plausible way by a detective who would be ordinary, with recognisable human hopes, fears and reactions. Philip Marlowe (Chandler's private-eye hero) is an honest, conscientious man who sweats, cowers and lusts just like anyone else. He narrates the stories himself, in a wisecracking, deadpan style – 'The next morning was bright, clear and sunny. I woke up with a motorman's glove in my mouth, drank two cups of coffee and went through the morning papers' – which has made two generations of literary critics fawn over Chandler, claiming him, somewhat snobbishly, as one of the few 'true novelists' in US crime fiction.

FAREWELL, MY LOVELY • *(1940)*
Marlowe, as often, is drifting with nothing particular to do when he is picked up (literally, by the scruff of the neck)

READ ON ⟩

● *The Big Sleep; The Lady in the Lake.*
▶ ▷Dashiell Hammett, *The Maltese Falcon.*
▷Ernest Hemingway, *To Have and Have Not.* Ross MacDonald, *The Drowning Pool.* John Milne, *Shadow Play* (set in the London underworld). James Hadley Chase, *No Orchids for Miss Blandish* is a sombre, bleak book, Chandler without the wisecracks. Greg MacDonald, *Fletch* is the first of a series starring a pleasingly farcical private eye, a would-be Marlowe who succeeds only in being himself.

by a muscle-bound ex-convict called Moose Malloy. From this simple event, as ripples spread on a pond, the story grows to take in a priceless necklace, kidnapping, blackmail and murder – and at its heart, like the still centre of a whirlwind, Marlowe slouches from clue to clue, a martyr to his own curiosity, pushing open every door and investigating each alleyway even though he knows, from long experience, that painful or nasty surprises are all he'll find.

Chandler's Marlowe novels are The Big Sleep, Farewell My Lovely, The High Window, The Lady in the Lake, The Little Sister, The Long Goodbye *and* Playback. Killer in the Rain *is a collection of short stories.*

CHEEVER, John • *(1912–82)*
US novelist and short-story writer.

Most of Cheever's stories appeared in the New Yorker between 1945 and 1975. The majority of his characters are prosperous New England commuters. They have beautiful houses in tidy neighbourhoods, their children go to good schools, and they can afford European holidays (often in Italy). But they are walking wounded: their emotions may be intact, but their hearts and consciences have been sliced away. They lacerate one another with sexual affairs, rows, petty-minded gossip and dispiriting, single-minded malice. The reason is that they believe that they are living in the American Dream – and by the day, by the minute, they find that it is a mirage. Cheever narrates their empty lives in sleek, ironic prose: his dialogue is particularly good at suggesting overtones of menace or longing in commonplace remarks.

THE STORIES • *(1978)*
This book of 61 stories contains all but a few teenage pieces. Most of the stories are set in commuter villages – fine examples are 'The Country Husband' or 'The Trouble of Marcie Flint' – but a few place their characters' wasted, tragic lives in lakeside summer homes (eg 'The Day the Pig Fell into the Well') or in a favourite Cheever location, Italy, where his people gape at the culture and civilisation they miss in their own drab lives. (Good examples are 'The Bella Lingua' and 'A Woman Without a Country'.)

Cheever's novels are The Wapshot Chronicle, The Wapshot Scandal, Bullet Park, Oh What A Paradise it Seems *and* Falconer *(on an uncharacteristic subject: the rehabili-*

READ ON ⟩

● Cheever's two Wapshot novels are set in the same world and among the same kind of bewildered characters as his stories. The Wapshot family, however, contains wonderful eccentrics, and the novels consequently spill into slapstick farce.
▶ **To Cheever's novels:** ▷John Updike, *The Centaur*; ▷Peter De Vries, *The Tunnel of Love*.
▶ **To the stories:** Peter Taylor, *Happy Families Are All Alike*; ▷Katherine Mansfield, *Bliss*; ▷L.P. Hartley, *The Killing Bottle*.

tation of a murderer in a 'correctional facility'). His story-collections are The Way Some People Live; The Enormous Radio; The Housebreaker of Shady Hill; Some People, Places and Things that will not Appear in my Next Novel; The Brigadier and the Golf Widow *and* The World of Apples.

CHEKHOV, Anton • *(1860–1904)*
Russian short-story writer and playwright.

Chekhov paid his way through medical school by writing short comic articles for magazines; in his mid-twenties he began publishing more elaborate pieces, and by the time he was 40 (and turning from stories to plays) he was considered one of the finest of all Russian prose-writers. Many of his stories are first-person monologues – he said that he was inspired by the sort of things people tell doctors during consultations, or penitents murmur at confession – and, like such monologues, they often reveal far more than the speaker intends. We hear symptoms, as it were, and from them diagnose a whole sick life. In other stories it is as if Chekhov were sitting beside us, drawing our attention to people moving about in the distance, and commenting in a quiet, compassionate way on their motives and feelings. Sympathetic detachment is the essence of his art: reading his stories (like watching his plays) is like looking through a window into other people's lives.

LADY WITH THE LITTLE DOG • *(1899)*
Chekhov's best-known story – perhaps because it seems exactly to match the ironical, tragi-comic mood of his plays – tells of two people who begin a casual holiday love-affair, find that they can't live without each other, and are then forced to do just that.

Chekhov's stories are published (by Oxford University Press) in a fine translation by Ronald Hingley, who catches every nuance of the original graceful style.

> READ ON

● Of Chekhov's plays, the nearest in mood to his stories are *Uncle Vanya* and *The Seagull*. (Michael Frayn's translations are recommended.)
► ▷Ivan Turgenev, *Sportsman's Sketches*.
Guy De Maupassant, *Miss Harriet*.
▷Katherine Mansfield, *In a German Pension*.
Seán O'Faoláin, *Foreign Affairs*.
▷Katherine Anne Porter, *The Leaning Tower*.

CHILDREN

▷David Cook, *Sunrising*
▷William Golding, *Lord of the Flies*
▷L.P. Hartley, *Eustace and Hilda*
Richard Hughes, *A High Wind in Jamaica*
Nancy Mitford, *The Blessing*
▷Marcel Proust, *Swann's Way* (part 1 of *Remembrance of Things Past*)

▷Mark Twain, *The Adventures of Tom Sawyer*

Adolescence (p 3)

CHRISTIE, Agatha • *(1890–1976)*
British novelist.

Ingenuity is the essence of Christie's detective stories. She confined herself largely to two detectives, pompous Poirot and elderly, inquisitive Miss Marple. Nowadays, as well as her plots, it is the period detail of her books which fascinates: her English villages, spa hotels, 1930s cruise-ships and above all country houses are caught (as Poirot might put it) like ze flies in ze amber. She chronicles a vanished pre-second-world-war, upper-middle-class Britain with an accuracy which is enhanced rather than diminished by the staginess of her characters and plots.

MURDER AT THE VICARAGE • *(1930)*
This typical Miss Marple story is set in a picture-postcard English village riven by gossip and inhabited by as unlikely a collection of eccentrics as even Christie ever threw together. Everyone could be guilty of murder, and Miss Marple's investigation is so gently persistent, so self-effacingly officious, that one trembles in case she ends up as victim rather than as sleuth.

MURDER IN MESOPOTAMIA • *(1936)*
A nurse goes to look after the neurotic wife of an archaeologist on a dig, and is thrown into the middle of intrigue, suspicion, rancorous insult and finally, inevitably, murder. At the end of it all Poirot applies his 'little grey cells' to unearthing means, motive and opportunity as painstakingly as an archaeologist trowelling treasure.

Among the best-known of Christie's 83 detective novels are The Murder of Roger Ackroyd, Ten Little Niggers/ Ten Little Indians/Then There Were None, Murder on the Orient Express *and* The Crooked House. *She also wrote stage plays (including* The Mousetrap), *an excellent second-world-war espionage thriller (*N or M), *and six romantic novels under the pseudonym Mary Westmacott.*

READ ON ▷

► To *Murder at the Vicarage: A Murder is Announced*;
► To *Murder in Mesopotamia: Death on the Nile*.
► Patricia Wentworth, *Miss Silver Investigates*. Gladys Mitchell, *Come Away, Death*. Dorothy Simpson, *The Night She Died*. Cyril Hare, *An Ill Wind*. The detective stories of Erle Stanley Gardner (eg *The Case of the Howling Dog*) and ▷Georges Simenon (eg *Maigret's Pipe*) describe a similar mixture of patient sleuthing and brilliant deduction; their settings (California and Paris) are as much part of their appeal as Christie's English villages and creepy country mansions are of hers.

CITIES: NEW WORLD
▷Saul Bellow, *Herzog* (Chicago)
Paul Gallico, *Mrs Harris in New York*
▷Mordecai Richler, *The Apprenticeship of Duddy Kravitz* (Montreal)
▷George Turner, *The Sea and Summer* (Melbourne, 1990)
▷Jerome Weidman, *Fourth Street East* (New York, 1920s)
Donald Westlake, *Gangway* (San Francisco)
▷Edith Wharton, *The Age of Innocence* (New York, 1880s)

CITIES: OLD WORLD

▷Marjorie Allingham, *The Tiger in the Smoke* (London)
▷Lawrence Durrell, *The Alexandria Quartet*
▷Mrs Gaskell, *Amos Barton* (Manchester)
▷Victor Hugo, *Notre Dame de Paris*
▷Christopher Isherwood, *Goodbye to Berlin*
John Lear, *Death in Leningrad*

CLARKE, Arthur C. (Arthur Charles) •
(born 1917)
British writer of novels, short stories and non-fiction.

Apart from ▷Asimov, Clarke is the best 'real' scientist among SF writers. His subject is space travel, and his 1940s and 1950s non-fiction books and articles predicted, in accurate detail, many things which have since happened, such as the invention of communications satellites, the first moon-landing and the development of laser space-weaponry. Like ▷Verne, he begins a fictional story with existing scientific fact or theory, and then extends it logically; even his wildest fantasies thus seem rooted in the possible. His main themes are the colonisation from Earth of other planets and visits to Earth by explorers from distant galaxies. His stories bustle with the detail of space-travel and setting up home in alien environments, and he is particularly interested in the psychological stress on people faced with the unknown, and with the relationship between human beings and high technology. These ideas outweigh sometimes wooden character-drawing and creaky plots: Clarke's stories are less interesting than his lively attitude to space and to the attempts of human beings to master it.

READ ON ⟩

● *Rendezvous with Rama* (as so often with Clarke, the straightforward development of a stunningly simple idea: that human beings land on and explore a planet which is a living, sentient being. A good, and psychologically more elaborate, follow-up to this is ▷Stanislaw Lem, *Solaris*.)
▶ ▷Jules Verne, *The First Men in the Moon*.
▷H.G. Wells, *The War of the Worlds*. ▷Robert Heinlein, *Have Space-suit, Will Travel*.
▷James Blish,

Agatha CHRISTIE

Julian SYMONS, THE END OF SOLOMON GRUNDY
(murder, obsession and madness in the English suburbs)

Friedrich DÜRRENMATT, THE PLEDGE
(maniacal child-killer stalks – and is stalked – across idyllic Swiss countryside)

Patricia HIGHSMITH, STRANGERS ON A TRAIN
(two men agree to commit 'perfect murder' for each other – and everything goes wrong)

PSYCHOLOGICAL CRIME

H.R.F. KEATING, FILMI, FILMI, INSPECTOR GHOTE
(mild Bombay police inspector; murder at the film studio)

POLICE PROCEDURAL

Lesley EGAN, CRIME AT CHRISTMAS
(no holiday for the men of Glendale Police Department, Los Angeles)

Nicholas FREELING, CASTANG'S CITY
(who gunned down Deputy Mayor of small French town?)

Rex STOUT, WHERE THERE'S A WILL
(orchid-loving, gourmet recluse; murderous family)

Dorothy L. SAYERS, THE NINE TAILORS
(lordly super-sleuth; death in a remote church tower)

DETECTIVES OF CHARACTER

Gladys MITCHELL, TWELVE HORSES AND THE HANGMAN'S NOOSE
(elderly, lizard-like Dame; death at the riding stables)

(one murderer, nine potential victims, all cooped up together – who is who?)

CRIME PUZZLES

Josephine **TEY, DAUGHTER OF TIME**
(hospitalised woman investigates 'crimes' of English King Richard III)

Carter **DICKENSON, THE RED WIDOW MURDERS**
(locked-room mystery in old, dark house)

Freeman Wills **CROFTS, DEATH OF A TRAIN**
(railway timetables; cast-iron alibis; Inspector French investigates)

Delano **AMES, CORPSE DIPLOMATIQUE**
(blackmail and murder in Brown's Hotel in Nice)

Cyril **HARE, WHEN THE WIND BLOWS**
*(murder in the Markshire Orchestral Society, where 'harmony' is
a word unknown)*

Pamela **BRANCH, MURDER'S LITTLE SISTER**
(who is trying to murder the bitchiest agony aunt in London?)

MURDER – WHERE?

PRIVATE SLEUTHING

A. Conan **DOYLE, THE HOUND OF THE BASKERVILLES**
(Sherlock Holmes and the fiend that stalks the moor)

Edmund **CRISPIN, THE MOVING TOYSHOP**
(Oxford poetry professor; death at a vanishing toyshop)

Harry **KEMELMAN, THURSDAY THE RABBI WALKED
OUT** *(Rabbi Small; murder of anti-semitic millionaire in Barnard's
Crossing, Massachusetts)*

THE SANDS OF MARS · *(1951)*

Martin Gibson, a world-famous writer of SF and on space-travel, is invited to make his first-ever real space journey, to report on a project for 'greening' Mars, making it fit for human habitation. The book is a straightforward account of Gibson's reactions to what he sees, and to the relationship between reality and his own writings. One might imagine that events since 1951 would have superceded Clarke's imaginings – but although some of the detail now seems old hat (for example Gibson's reactions to weightlessness), the meticulousness of other descriptions, especially of the way humans cope with daily life on Mars, still fascinates.

Clarke's short stories are admired: one, 'The Sentinel', is regularly claimed to be the finest SF story ever written. (It was the basis of the film 2001.) *A splendid selection is* The Nine Billion Names of God. *His novels include* Childhood's End, A Fall of Moondust *and* Imperial Earth.

Earthman Come Home (first of the 'Cities in Flight' series).

CLASSIC DETECTION

G.K. Chesterton, *The Innocence of Father Brown*
▷Michael Innes, *Stop Press*
▷P.D. James, *The Skull Beneath the Skin*
Harry Kemelman, *Tuesday the Rabbi saw Red*
Emma Lathen, *Banking on Death*
▷Ngaio Marsh, *Surfeit of Lampreys*
Gladys Mitchell, *Laurels are Poison*

Great Detectives (p 100); Murder Most Mind-Boggling (p 174); Police Procedural (p 192); Private Eyes (p 196)

COLETTE (Sidonie Gabrielle) · *(1873–1954)*
French novelist.

In the 1900s Colette's works were condemned as pornographic; in the 1970s she was claimed by the women's movement as one of the founders of feminism. The reason in each case is the same. Her themes are the awakening of sensual feelings in adolescence, the way in which young women first discover their sexual power, and the attempts by middle-aged people (of both sexes) to rejuvenate themselves by preying on innocence. Her stories are not explic-

READ ON ▷

● *A Lesson in Love* (La naissance du jour).
▶ Françoise Sagan, *Bonjour Tristesse*.
Edna O'Brien, *The Country Girls* (and its sequels *The Lonely Girl* and the magnificent *Girls in*

itly sexual, but she writes in an impressionistic style in which sun, flowers, insects, animals and the textures of skin, grass and clothes blur into a kind of drowsy, erotic reverie, a counterpart to the awakening feelings of her characters. Adult experience is always just ahead – and few of her young people notice, as the reader does, that every adult in Colette's books is a tragic figure, ineffectual or cynical. Youth, in the end, is the only worthwhile possession in life, and it is daily, hourly, squandered for experience.

THE RIPENING SEED (Le Blé en herbe) • *(1923)*

Colette's own favourite among her books, this tells of the relationship between two teenagers, Philippe and Vinca. They have been friends from childhood, and their families have spent the summer months every year together at the seaside. Now, in Vinca's sixteenth and Philippe's seventeenth year, the young people feel a new tension in their relationship –an anxiety about each other, and about themselves, which is not helped when Philippe is seduced by another, older summer visitor.

The most substantial of Colette's works is the 'Claudine' series of novels, about a young girl growing up in the early years of this century. Another pair of books, Chéri *and* The Last of Chéri, *is on a favourite theme, the corrupting effects of a young man's first sexual experience. Her other books, many based on her own experience and family, include* Sido, My Apprenticeship *and* The Tendrils of the Vine. *Her collected short stories were published in English in 1984.*

COMEDY THRILLERS

Delano Ames, *Murder, Maestro, Please*
▷Eric Ambler, *The Light of Day*
Pamela Branch, *The Wooden Overcoat*
▷Richard Condon, *Prizzi's Honour*
Greg MacDonald, *Fletch*
Jean Potts, *Go, Lovely Rose*
Andrew Taylor, *Caroline Type*
Donald Westlake, *A New York Dance*

COMPTON-BURNETT, Ivy • *(1884–1969)*
British novelist.

After a single false start (*Dolores*, an imitation of George ▷Eliot, later disowned), Compton-Burnett produced 19

Their Married Bliss). David Garnett, *Aspects of Love*. ▷Vladimir Nabokov, *Ada* and ▷André Gide, *The Immoralist*, though their purposes and plot-development are very different, catch the same sensual and poetic mood as Colette. ▷Carson McCullers, *The Member of the Wedding* is a harsher view of the awakening of a young girl to adult feelings. Charles Webb, *The Graduate* is a riotous send-up of the young man/older woman theme.

READ ON ⟩

▶ The uniqueness of Compton-Burnett's

comic novels in a uniquely bizarre, uncompromising style. Each book is set in a large late-Victorian or early-Edwardian household, ruled by a tyrant (one of the parents or some elderly, inflexible relative). Isolated by wealth from the outside world, the family members – often grown-up, middle-aged children – bicker, snub and plot against one another, powerless and embittered. There are family secrets to be revealed – incest, murder, insanity – and no member of the household, neither family nor servants, is a 'normal', unwarped human being. The books are written largely in dialogue, spectacularly wooden and artificial. Compton-Burnett's detractors find her novels unreadable; her fans think them hilarious.

Compton-Burnett's novels are Pastors and Masters, Brothers and Sisters, Men and Wives, More Women than Men, A House and its Head, Daughters and Sons, A Family and a Fortune, Parents and Children, Elders and Betters, Manservant and Maidservant, Two Worlds and their Ways, Darkness and Day, The Present and the Past, Mother and Son, A Father and his Fate, A Heritage and its History, The Mighty and their Fall, A God and his Gifts *and* The Last and the First.

CONDON, Richard • *(born 1915)*
US novelist.

Condon's black comedies treat horrifying matters – insanity, kidnapping, assassination – in a deadpan way, as if part of everyday experience. His characters live each moment with unflustered obsession, shopping, for example, for hand-grenades with the same matter-of-fact orderliness as for peaches or toothpaste. Condon is fascinated by wealth and power, and his books are set among politicians, financiers, mafia godfathers, generals and film-studio executives. It is a world in which power always corrupts, money never brings happiness and the devil always, delightfully, wins every trick.

ANY GOD WILL DO • *(1966)*
The hero, Francis Vollmer, is a bank executive in pre-1914 New York – and a maniac. Convinced that he is the unacknowledged son of a European aristocrat, he embezzles a fortune, learns French (and, in the process, the skills of cooking and acrobatic sex), changes his identity and sets out to find and claim his inheritance. Despite a wonderfully boring literal mind – he talks like an encyclopedia-entry on any subject, given only a trigger-word such as 'wine' or 'symphony' – he is irresistible to women, and his quest for identity is intertwined with a love-affair

style means that no other writers' works are truly similar. Stories of claustrophobic families, however, in artificial 'high styles' of their own and equally compulsive, are: Samuel Butler, *The Way of All Flesh* (a book which influenced Compton-Burnett herself); ▷Edith Wharton, *The Age of Innocence*; Jean Cocteau, *The Children of the Game* (Les enfants terribles); Molly Keane, *Good Behaviour;* ▷Mervyn Peake, *Titus Groan*.

READ ON ⟩

● *Prizzi's Honour*; *Prizzi's Family* (comedies about an upwardly-mobile mafia hit-man, a murderer with cultural aspirations).
▶ ▷Jerome Weidman, *Other People's Money*.
▷Thomas Mann, *Confessions of Felix Krull, Confidence Man*.
▷John Irving, *The Hotel New Hampshire*.

which might have brought him happiness if he had not, underneath all his suaveness, been as crazy as the man in every lunatic asylum who thinks himself Napoleon.

Condon's novels include The Whisper of the Axe, Arigato, The Vertical Smile, Mile High, The Manchurian Candidate *and* The Oldest Confession.

CONRAD, Joseph • *(1857–1924)*
Polish/British novelist.

Born in Poland, Conrad ran away to sea at 17 and ended up a captain in the merchant navy and a naturalised British subject. He retired from the sea at 37 and spent the rest of his life as a writer. There was at the time (1890s–1910s) a strong tradition of sea-stories, using the dangers and tensions of long voyages and the wonders of the worlds sailors visited as metaphors for human life. Most of this writing was straightforward adventure, with little subtlety; Conrad used its conventions for deeper literary ends. He was interested in 'driven' individuals, people whose psychology or circumstances force them to extreme behaviour, and the sea-story form exactly suited this idea. His books often begin as 'yarns', set in exotic locations and among the mixed (and mixed-up) human types who crew ocean-going ships. But before long psychology takes over, and the plot loses its straightforwardness and becomes an exploration of compulsion, obsession and neurosis.

HEART OF DARKNESS • *(from Youth, 1902)*
This 120-page story begins as a 'yarn': Marlow, a sea-captain, tells of a journey he once made up the Congo river to bring down a stranded steamer. He became fascinated by stories of an ivory-merchant, a white man called Kurtz who lived deep in the jungle and was said to have supernatural powers. Marlow set out to find Kurtz, and the journey took him deeper and deeper into the heart not only of the 'Dark Continent', but into the darkness of the human soul. (Francis Ford Coppola's 1970s film *Apocalypse Now* updated this story to the Vietnam War, making points about US colonialism as savage as Conrad's denunciation of the ivory-trade.)

Conrad's major novels are Lord Jim, The Nigger of the Narcissus, Nostromo, The Secret Agent *and* Under Western Eyes. *His short-story collections (an excellent introduction to his work) are* Tales of Unrest, Youth, Ty-

READ ON ▷

● *Typhoon* (which deals with corruption and exploitation of a different kind, this time using as its metaphor a passenger steamer caught in a typhoon in the China Sea); *The Secret Agent* (about the conflict between innocence and corruption among a group of terrorists in 1900s London).
▶ ▷Herman Melville, *Billy Budd, Foretopman*. ▷Graham Greene, *The Comedians*. Lionel Davidson, *Making Good Again*. B. Traven, *The Treasure of the Sierra Madre*. ▷Paul Theroux, *The Mosquito Coast*. John Kruse, *The Hour of the Lily*. ▷J.G. Ballard, *The Drowned World* is an SF novel of Conradian intensity.

phoon, A Set of Six, 'Twixt Land and Sea, Within the Tides *and* Tales of Hearsay.

COOK, David • *(born 1940)*
British novelist.

Cook's 1970s books were compassionate stories about the kind of people usually shunned by society (and by novelists): a depressive widow and a catamite in *Happy Endings*, a child molester in *Albert's Bridge*, a Downs Syndrome sufferer in *Walter*. The combination of clinical descriptions of awful events and warm-heartedness allowed him to take even greater risks in his next novels, *Winter Doves* (in which two inhabitants of a mental home, Walter and a would-be suicide, fall in love and run away to seek happiness together), and *Sunrising* (see below). Although Cook's early books seemed to place him with such British fictional horror novelists as Martin Amis, Ian McEwan or Iain Banks, the humanity and optimism of his work soon carried him far beyond the range of such contemporaries.

SUNRISING • *(1984)*
This book steps aside from the late-20th-century inadequates of Cook's other novels. It is set in the 1830s, and tells of three orphaned children who befriend each other and travel in search of a home. The descriptions of rural England, of the Oxford Goose Fair and especially of the London slums are as gripping as anything in ▷Dickens (but far less wordy), and the story is radiant with humanity. Despite the miseries and deprivation the children suffer, they find help and friendship, ordinary human decency, at every turn.

COOKSON, Catherine • *(born 1906)*
British novelist.

Cookson's romances are warm-hearted stories of 'ordinary people'. She sets most of them in the north-east of England (Tyneside) where she was born, and shows how her characters cope with the harsh conditions of 19th-century life in the area. Apart from her style, which is matter-of-fact, not moralising – it has learned lessons from 20th-century documentary – her books are in the unsentimental tradition of such great 'social' novels as those of ▷Mrs Gaskell or ▷George Eliot. She grouped many of her stories in series, in particular the 'Mary-Ann' books (beginning with *A Grand Man*) and the Mallen trilogy (*The Mal-*

READ ON ▷

● *Missing Persons* (an equally warm-hearted comedy about two elderly ladies who refuse to give in to old age. One sets up as a private detective, the other goes to find a lover and a new home in Tuscany).
▶ **To *Sunrising*:** ▷Charles Dickens, *Oliver Twist*; Richard Hughes, *A High Wind in Jamaica*; ▷J.G. Ballard, *Empire of the Sun*.
▶ **To *Missing Persons*:** Julian Barnes, *Staring at the Sun*.
▶ **To Cook's other books:** ▷Susan Hill, *I'm the King of the Castle*; Paul Bailey, *At the Jerusalem*; *Gabriel's Lament*.

READ ON ▷

▶ Catherine Gaskin, *Sarah Dane*. Marie Joseph, *Gemini Girls*, Danielle Steele, *The Promises*. ▷George Eliot, *The Mill on the Floss*. ▷Mrs Gaskell, *North and South*.

len Girl, *The Mallen Litter* and *The Mallen Streak*). The heroine of *Tilly Trotter*, *Tilly Trotter Wed* and *Tilly Trotter Widowed* (a characteristic series, written in the 1960s) is a poor but spirited girl in 1830s County Durham who becomes the mistress of the owner of the 'big house', emigrates to America when he dies, and returns in middle age to find happiness at last in her beloved native county.

COUNTRY HOUSES

Mazo de la Roche, *Jalna*
▷E.M. Forster, *Howards End*
▷Hermann Hesse, *Rosshalde*
▷Eudora Welty, *Delta Wedding*
▷Michael Innes, *Old Hall, New Hall*
▷Evelyn Waugh, *Brideshead Revisited*
▷P.G. Wodehouse, *Summer Lightning*

Old Dark Houses (p 183)

THE COUNTRYSIDE
(the implacability of nature)

Stella Gibbons, *Cold Comfort Farm*
▷Thomas Hardy, *The Woodlanders*
▷Geoffrey Household, *Rogue Male*
▷Paul Theroux, *The Black House*
Mary Webb, *Precious Bane*
▷Fay Weldon, *The Heart of England*
▷Edith Wharton, *Ethan Frome*

The Rhythm of Nature (p 204)

COX, Richard • *(born 1931)*
British novelist.

Cox was a defence correspondent, and is an expert on aerial warfare. His best-known thrillers (eg *The Time It Takes*, about mercenaries in central Africa) have a flying background, but everything he writes is enriched by his knowledge of modern weapons-systems and global politics.

READ ON ▷

▶ Ernest K. Gann, *The Aviator*. Spencer S. Dunmore, *The Sound of Wings*. ▷Frederick Forsyth, *The Dogs of War*.

CULTURE-CLASH
▷Chinua Achebe, *Things Fall Apart*
▷E.M. Forster, *A Passage to India*
  Brian Glanville, *Along the Arno*
▷William Golding, *The Inheritors*
▷Henry James, *The Europeans*
  Joseph Olshan, *A Warmer Season*
▷Evelyn Waugh, *The Loved One*
▷H.G. Wells, *Kipps*

D

DARK, Eleanor • *(born 1901)*
Australian novelist.

Dark's novels are psychological meditations like those of Virginia ▷Woolf, showing the movement of their characters' minds as they react to apparently ordinary events. The theme of *Prelude to Christopher* (1934) is that we are the prisoners of our past, that we carry the burden of previous actions and understandings – as Dark put it – the way snails carry their shells. *Sun Across the Sky* and *Waterway* each focus on a single day, during which a group of characters reaches a moment of self-realisation and psychological crisis which results in violent, tragic action. *Return to Coolami* (1936) is about the relationship of four people on a 300-mile drive through New South Wales; although the book is marvellously evocative of the Australian landscape (a recurring pleasure in Dark's work), the exploration is really of character not countryside and physical travelling is a metaphor for the journey of the soul. In the 1940s Dark applied similar techniques of psychological investigation to a historical subject, writing a novel-trilogy (*The Timeless Land*; *Storm of Time*; *No Barrier*) about the first European settlements in Australia. The counterpoint of lyrical descriptions of what (to the whites) was a virgin, beautiful land with analyses of the soul's turbulence caused by their amputation from their European culture and families gives these books extraordinary power; only ▷William Golding and ▷Patrick White so strikingly combine the epic and the intimate.

Dark's other novels are Slow Dawning, The Little Company *and the lighter* Lantana Lane, *the anecdotal story of a farming family in Queensland.*

READ ON ⟩

▶ **To Dark's psychological novels:** ▷Virginia Woolf, *The Waves*; ▷Nadine Gordimer, *The Conservationist*; ▷Anita Brookner, *A Misalliance*.
▶ **To the historical trilogy:** ▷William Golding, *Darkness Visible*; ▷Thomas Keneally, *The Playmaker*; ▷Patrick White, *Voss*; ▷William Faulkner, *Sartoris*.
▶ **To *Lantana Lane*:** ▷Miles Franklin (writing as 'Brent of Bin Bin'), *Up the Country*.

DAVIES, Robertson • *(born 1913)*
Canadian novelist, journalist and playwright.

The deceptively gentle, expansive tone of Davies' satires belies their extraordinary subject-matter: it is as if ▷Jane Austen had reworked ▷Rabelais. Davies' books are comedies of manners, many set in small university towns riven with gossip and pretension. *Tempest-tost* (1951) is about an amateur production of Shakespeare's *The Tempest* all but sabotaged by the unexpected, lacerating love of the middle-aged leading man for the girl who plays his daughter. *A Mixture of Frailties* (1958) describes the chain of bizarre events after a woman leaves money to educate a girl in the arts, unless and until the woman's son sires a male heir. In each novel of the 'Deptford trilogy' (1970–75) a different narrator tries to explain the circumstances leading up to the death of a man killed by a stone wrapped in a snowball. What each man does, however, is reveal his own tangled life-history and his bizarre enthusiasms (which range from medieval saints to Houdini, from the history of vaudeville to experiments into 'the collective unconscious').

THE REBEL ANGELS • *(1982)*
Alternate chapters of this story are told by Father Darcourt, a professor of Biblical Greek at a small Canadian university, and Ms Maria Magdalene Theotoky, a research student. The university is a quiet place, dedicated to placid scholarship and barbed common-room gossip. Ms Theotoky is researching Rabelais, and the plot suddenly erupts with priceless manuscripts, bizarre lusts and unsavoury accusations, devil-worship, scatology, and a storm of passion and deceit against which no grove of academe could stand unbowed. Davies is asking whether traditionalists (symbolised by the university Fathers) or 'rebel angels' (symbolised by a riotous gipsy family) are true guardians of the human soul. But he surrounds serious philosophical enquiry with a circus-parade of jokes, lists, parodies and slapstick. If Jane Austen rules his earlier books, in this one Rabelais is firmly, fruitily in charge.

The books in the 'Deptford trilogy' are Fifth Business, The Manticore *and* World of Wonders. *Davies's other novels include* Leaven of Malice *and* What's Bred in the Bone. *His humorous journalism is collected in* The Diary of Samuel Marchbanks, The Table Talk of Samuel Marchbanks *and* Marchbanks' Almanac, *and his plays include* A Jig for the Gipsy, Hunting Stuart *and the political satire* Question Time.

READ ON >

● *What's Bred in the Bone* (about a man who makes a fortune as an international conman, anti-nazi spy and art-forger, and about the horror of his stuffy, middle-class Canadian family when they discover the source of his – and their – riches, after his will is read).

▶ **To *Rebel Angels*:** ▷Randall Jarrell, *Pictures from an Institution*; ▷Anthony Burgess, *Enderby's Dark Lady*; Andrew Davies, *A Very Peculiar Practice*.

▶ **To *What's Bred in the Bone*:** ▷Laurence Sterne, *Tristram Shandy*; ▷Thomas Mann, *The Confessions of Felix Krull, Confidence Man*.

▶ **To Davies' work in general:** ▷John Irving, *The Hotel New Hampshire*; ▷Barbara Pym, *Quartet in Autumn*; Howard Jacobson, *Peeping Tom*.

DEEP SOUTH, USA

Harper Lee, *To Kill a Mocking Bird*
▷ Carson McCullers, *The Ballad of the Sad Café*
▷ Margaret Mitchell, *Gone With the Wind*
▷ Mark Twain, *The Adventures of Huckleberry Finn*
▷ Alice Walker, *The Color Purple*
▷ Eudora Welty, *Delta Wedding*
▷ Thomas Wolfe, *Look Homeward, Angel*

Places (p 191): US Small Town Life (p 246)

DEFOE, Daniel • *(1660–1731)*
British novelist and non-fiction writer.

A journalist, Defoe wrote over 500 essays, poems, political satires and other works, including a history of England, a handbook of good manners and a guide-book to Britain. In his 60s he began writing what he called 'romances': books which purported to be the autobiographies of people who had led unusual or adventurous lives (pirates, whores, treasure-hunters) but which were really fiction and among the earliest English novels. Apart from his characters' proneness to theological and philosophical reflection (eminently skippable), his books lack the ponderousness of later 18th-century fiction. His fast-moving, simple prose and his journalist's talent for description give his work a freshness which belies its age.

ROBINSON CRUSOE • *(1719)*
The germ of this story came from the autobiography of a real-life sailor, Alexander Selkirk, who was marooned on a desert island in 1704. As often in his works, Defoe was fascinated by the idea of the confrontation between civilisation and barbarism, in this case by how a 'modern' European, filled with the knowledge and aspirations of the Age of Reason, might cope if all the trappings of civilisation were stripped from him. Crusoe is allowed nothing but a few tools and other possessions saved from the shipwreck, and the resources of his own ingenuity. Later, after Crusoe has lived alone for 26 years, Defoe provides him with a companion, the 'savage' Friday, and so lets us see 'civilised' humanity through innocent, unsophisticated eyes.

Defoe's 'romances' include The Life and Adventures of Mr Duncan Campbell *(whose hero is a deaf-and-dumb conjurer),* Captain Singleton *(whose hero is a pirate),* Memoirs of a Cavalier *and* Memoirs of Captain George

READ ON ▷

● *The Farther Adventures of Robinson Crusoe.* Moll Flanders is a 'romance' of a similar kind, using the story of a woman forced by circumstances into crime to give a vivid picture of the thieves, prostitutes and highwaymen of the 18th-century English underworld, and of life in the convict settlements of Virginia.
▶ ▷Henry Fielding, *Tom Jones*. ▷William Golding, *Pincher Martin; Rites of Passage*. ▷Patrick White, *Tarr*. Michel Tournier, *The Other Friday* and Jane Gardam, *Crusoe's Daughter* play fascinating games with *Robinson Crusoe*'s themes and plot, Tournier by retelling the story from Friday's point of view, and Gardam by focussing on a reclusive girl

Carleton *(whose heroes are swashbuckling soldiers-of-fortune), and – more serious –* A Journal of the Plague Year, *a day-by-day, first-person account of life during the Great Plague of London in 1664.*

fixated on *Robinson Crusoe* who makes it her chief emotional resource. C.S. Lewis, *Out of the Silent Planet* is a similar novel of survival, set on the planet Mars, and J.M. Coetzee, *Foe* gives an alternative account of how *Robinson Crusoe* came to be written, and of the 'real' events which might have inspired it – Friday and Crusoe are the sole survivors from a wrecked slave-ship.

DE HAAN, Tom • *(born 1964)*
British novelist.

At one level, De Haan's *A Mirror for Princes* (1987) is a swaggering medieval tale, as crammed as a Breughel painting. Its setting is a glittering, barbarous feudal court. Its pages jostle with tyranny, intrigue, incest and delight in the earthier human pleasures. Its dialogue wastes no words, and the central element of its plot – the relationship between the poetry-loving third son of a tyrant and his hard-fighting, hard-wenching brothers while they wait for the old king to die – is hardly unfamiliar. But the book's title gives the game away: appearances are deceptive. *A Mirror for Princes* is set not in reality but in an imagined, timeless world of De Haan's own invention. The medieval detail, however fascinating, is no more important than the wimples and hautboys in religious paintings of the period. The book is a sustained meditation on power and love, a moral and philosophical allegory in the manner of ▷Hesse's *The Glass Bead Game*. The combination of this and red-blooded action is magnificently handled; *A Mirror for Princes*, De Haan's first novel, is a masterpiece.

▶ Pär Lagerkvist, *The Dwarf*. Helen Waddell, *Héloïse and Abelard*. ▷Thomas Mann, *The Holy Sinner*.

DEIGHTON, Len • *(born 1929)*
British novelist.

In the 1960s, fired by dislike of snobbish spy fantasies of the James Bond school, Deighton produced a series of books (beginning with *The IPCRESS File*) showing spies as ordinary human beings, functionaries of a ridiculous and

● *Goodbye Mickey Mouse* (a detailed, convincing – and, in its

READ ON
READ ON

outdated bureaucracy in which requisitions for paper-clips could take precedence over analyses of the danger of nuclear war. He devised for them a documentary, 'dossier' technique, flooding the text with lists, letters, memoranda, meeting-transcripts, diary-entries and technical notes – and went on to use it in a series of devastatingly authentic-seeming novels on non-spy subjects. Although his material is fictional, it reads like fact, like the transcript of a TV documentary which shows us people's thoughts and feelings as meticulously as what they do and say.

BOMBER • *(1970)*

In direct contrast to the stiff-upper-lip, jolly-good-show British war-films of the 1950s, Deighton gives a blunt, detailed idea of what it was probably like to prepare for and make an RAF bombing-raid in 1943. He is particularly interested in the tensions between service and civilian personnel, the class-divisions between officers and other ranks and the bumbling and paper-chasing which contrasted with, and sometimes jeopardised, the bravery of actual combat.

Deighton's spy-books include Funeral in Berlin, Horse Under Water, Spy Story *and the trilogy* Berlin Game, Moscow Set, London Match. *Close-up is a black satire on the film business. Only When I Larf is a comedy about confidence-tricksters. His 'dossier' novels include* SS-GB, *a nightmarish vision of what might have happened if Britain had lost the second world war and were now under nazi rule.*

implications for Western defence, horrifying – novel about USAF personnel manning a nuclear-weapons airfield in the UK).
► **To the spy-stories:** ▷John Le Carré, *The Spy Who Came in from the Cold*; Adam Hall, *The Quiller Memorandum*. (Hall also writes Deightonish war-stories under the name Elleston Trevor).
► **To Deighton's flying-stories:** Gavin Lyall, *Midnight Plus One*; Peter George, *Red Alert* (about the accidental triggering of the nuclear holocaust).

DEPRESSION AND PSYCHIATRY

▷Lisa Alther, *Other Women*
Paul Bailey, *Peter Smart's Confessions*
Roy Brown, *The Siblings*
Jonathan Kellerman, *Shrunken Heads*
▷Doris Lessing, *The Golden Notebook*
▷H.H. Richardson, *Maurice Guest*
▷J.D. Salinger, *Franny and Zooey*
▷Antonia White, *Beyond the Glass*

Madness (p 159); On the Edge of Sanity (p 183)

DE VRIES, Peter • *(born 1910)*
US novelist and journalist.

De Vries worked for the *New Yorker*, and his novels sa-
tirise a favourite target of that magazine, the upwardly-
mobile suburbanites he himself called 'globules of metro-
politan life'. His characters live in trim stockbroker villages on Long Island or in Connecticut. The husbands
commute into New York to work; the wives stay at home
to mind their beautiful houses, tend their lawn-sprinklers,
go to coffee mornings and PTA meetings and bore each
other to death. Evenings and weekends are given up to
self-improving parties (at which people read modern poetry and make bitchy remarks about each other's clothes)
and to furtive, desperate love-affairs. Most of De Vries'
books are first-person novels, and his narrators enliven
them with aphorisms, wisecracks, puns and parodies of
everything from TV commercials to the *Reader's Digest*.
It is an empty, panic-stricken society, pathetically narcissistic – but instead of merely sending it up, as many other
New Yorker writers and cartoonists do, De Vries shows it
with compassion as well as wit. His books may be slapstick, but they end in tears.

THE TUNNEL OF LOVE • *(1954)*
The story is told by Dick, the cartoons editor of a New
York magazine called *The Townsman*. He is happy in his
work and his marriage, but affects to be bored, constantly
making world-weary jokes which no one else appreciates,
and fantasising about a Maine hideaway called Moot Point
at which he woos beautiful women in the manner of Cary
Grant, Clark Gable or George Sanders. He and his wife
are asked to sponsor their neighbours as a suitable couple
to adopt a child – and the more Dick finds out about the
husband, a womanising cartoonist, the more he himself is
tangled in lust, deceit and sexual compromise.

De Vries' comic novels include Comfort Me with Apples,
Through the Fields of Clover, Reuben Reuben, Mrs Wal-
lop, I Hear America Swinging, Into Your Tent I'll Creep,
Sauce for the Goose, Madder Music *and* The Prick of
Noon. The Blood of the Lamb *is serious, about the death
of a child.*

DICKENS, Charles • *(1812–70)*
British novelist.

In his early 20s Dickens worked as a journalist, writing
reports of law court proceedings and Parliamentary de-

READ ON ▷

● *The Mackerel Plaza*;
*Let Me Count the
Ways.*
▶ ▷John Updike, *The
Witches of Eastwick.*
▷Iris Murdoch, *A
Severed Head.*
▷Kingsley Amis, *That
Uncertain Feeling.*
Martin Amis, *The
Rachel Papers.*
George Axelrod,
*Where Am I Now –
and Do I Need Me?*

READ ON ▷

● *Nicholas Nickleby*;
Oliver Twist.

bates, and short essays on the life and manners of the time (later collected as *Sketches by Boz*). It was not until the success of his first novel *Pickwick Papers*, when he was 25, that he made writing a full-time career. He composed large parts of his novels in dialogue, and was proud of his gift for showing character through speech alone; he also gave his minor characters (pot-boys, shop-customers, carters, oystermen, toddlers) turns of speech or physical eccentricities to make them instantly memorable – another theatrical technique. This character-vividness is matched by a sustained commentary on human nature and society: Dickens consistently savaged the humbug and petty-mindedness of the middle classes who bought his books, and said that human happiness comes not from law, religion, politics or social structures but from gratuitous, individual acts of kindness. In his later books, notably *Great Expectations* and *Our Mutual Friend*, savagery predominated over sentimentality to an extent rivalled only in ▷Zola.

DAVID COPPERFIELD · *(1849–50)*

Dickens' own favourite among his novels, this tells the story (in the first person, as if an autobiography) of a boy growing up: his unhappy childhood and adolescence, his first jobs and first love-affair, and the way he finally transmutes his experience into fiction and becomes a writer. As often in Dickens' books, subsidiary characters seem to steal the show: the grim Murdstones, the optimistic Micawbers, salt-of-the-earth Peggotty, feckless Steerforth and above all the viperish hypocrite Uriah Heep. But the book's chief interest is the developing character of Copperfield himself: apparently passive, at other people's mercy, he learns and grows by each experience, maturing before our eyes.

Dickens' novels, in order of publication, are Pickwick Papers, Oliver Twist, Nicholas Nickleby, The Old Curiosity Shop, Barnaby Rudge, Martin Chuzzlewit, Dombey and Son, David Copperfield, Bleak House, Hard Times, Little Dorrit, A Tale of Two Cities, Great Expectations, Our Mutual Friend *and* Edwin Drood. *His shorter works include* A Christmas Carol, A Child's History of England *and three collections of articles,* Sketches by Boz, American Notes *and* The Uncommercial Traveller.

DICKINSON, Peter · *(born 1927)*

British novelist and children's writer.

Although Dickinson's crime novels contain their quota of murders and clues, they centre on the unravelling of mysteries of a different kind. Each is set in a self-contained,

▶ Novels of 'growing up', using a biographical framework to give a picture (documentary, satirical or both at once) of society: ▷Henry Fielding, *Tom Jones*; ▷Somerset Maugham, *Of Human Bondage*; ▷Mark Twain, *Huckleberry Finn*; ▷James Joyce, *Portrait of the Artist as a Young Man*.
▶ **To Dickens' more savage social novels:** ▷Mrs Gaskell, *North and South*; ▷John Steinbeck, *The Grapes of Wrath*; ▷Patrick White, *Riders in the Chariot*.
▶ **To his more relaxed tableaux of human life:** ▷H.G. Wells, *Kipps*; ▷Angus Wilson, *Anglo-Saxon Attitudes*.

READ ON ▷

● *The Lively Dead.*
▶ **To Dickinson's crime-**

Charles DICTIONARY

Charles DICKENS

Victor HUGO, LES MISÉRABLES
(1820s France: honest man convicted to galleys escapes and rebuilds his life)

Anthony TROLLOPE, THE LAST CHRONICLE
OF BARSET
(1860s England: honest man wrongly accused of theft; student making his way in London)

Edith WHARTON, THE HOUSE OF MIRTH
(1880s New York heiress rejects ways of society to 'be herself')

J.B. PRIESTLEY, ANGEL PAVEMENT
(1920s London firm taken over, developed and ruined by confidence-trickster)

John O'HARA, THE LOCKWOOD CONCERN
(1930s Pennsylvania family becomes wealthy by violence, destroys itself)

James BALDWIN, GO, TELL IT ON THE MOUNTAIN
(1950s Harlem: son of slum family learns about sex, racism and born-again Christian love)

'DICKENSIAN' NOVELS:
BLEAK SIDE OF LIFE

David COOK, SUNRISING
(1830s England: three children rescued from degradation in rural and urban slums)

Mark TWAIN, THE ADVENTURES OF HUCKLEBERRY
FINN *(1860s Mississippi: boy's adolescence on river and in riverside communities)*

H.G. WELLS, THE HISTORY OF MR POLLY
(1890s England: middle-aged 'drop-out' has many adventures, finds happiness)

Thomas MANN, THE CONFESSIONS OF FELIX KRULL,
CONFIDENCE MAN *(1900s Europe: confidence-man's cheerful, amoral adventures among the bourgeoisie)*

Angus WILSON, THE MIDDLE AGE OF MRS ELIOT
(1950s widow travels world in search of happiness)

Saul BELLOW, THE ADVENTURES OF AUGIE MARCH
(1930s Chicago: zestful account of slum boy using his wits to make his way)

'DICKENSIAN' NOVELS:
CHEERFUL SIDE OF LIFE

*(dark childhood, miserable growing-up and eventual happiness
in 19th-century London)*

**LEARNING HOW TO BE
GROWN-UP**

William **THACKERAY, PENDENNIS**

(1840s London: after many escapades, young man finds literary success)

W. Somerset **MAUGHAM, OF HUMAN BONDAGE**

*(1890s London school days, Paris student life and eventual happiness
of lonely young man)*

Johann Wolfgang von **GOETHE, THE APPRENTICESHIP OF
WILHELM MEISTER**

*(1790s Europe: young man runs away to be an actor, experiences
real life, 'finds' himself)*

André **GIDE, THE COUNTERFEITERS**

(1920s Paris: young people growing up, initiated into life and love)

Mordecai **RICHLER, THE APPRENTICESHIP OF DUDDY
KRAVITZ**

(1930s Montreal: young man moves from rags to riches, loses his soul)

Lisa **ALTHER, KINFLICKS**

*(1960s USA: young woman learns about sex, love, feminism, protest-politics
and 'dropping out')*

bizarre society about which we long to learn more – and the further his detective investigates the crime, the deeper we are drawn into the surrounding atmosphere. *Sleep and His Brother* is set in a community of brain-damaged, psychically sensitive children, and the only being who knows the identity of the murderer is a 'talking' chimpanzee. *The Seals* is about a crazy religious community waiting for the apocalypse on a remote Scottish island. In *King and Joker* someone commits murder in a Buckingham Palace inhabited by an egalitarian, trendy-left royal family whose dark secrets give the book its fun. In later novels, Dickinson abandoned the crime format to explore wider themes, especially of identity. The mysteries in *A Summer in the Twenties*, *The Last House-Party* and *Hindsight*, for example, are not murders but long-forgotten love-affairs, betrayals and family secrets whose effects stain the lives of the present generation.

SKIN DEEP • *(1968)*

A tribe of people from Papua New Guinea lives in a terraced house in London, carrying out stone-age rituals in the attics. Their chief is murdered, and the community begins to fall apart. Superintendent Pibble must not only find the murderer, but reassure the tribespeople – and to do that he must try to enter their minds and understand their culture.

Dickinson's adult novels include A Pride of Heroes, The Lizard in the Cup, The Poison Oracle, The Lively Dead *and* One Foot in the Grave. *He has also written children's books:* Tulku, Annerton Pit *and an SF trilogy,* The Changes.

DONALDSON, Stephen • *(born 1947)*
US novelist.

Donaldson's major work, the 2600-page Thomas Covenant series (1977–84), is adventure-fantasy inspired by – and as good as – ▷Tolkien's *The Lord of the Rings*. Thomas Covenant, a leper, is transported to a distant country in the grip of the evil Lord Foul. He finds that his wedding-ring is a powerful magic talisman, but is at first reluctant to use it because he believes himself psychologically tainted by his illness – in fact he wonders if the Land and its plight are not fantasies of his own sick mind. The novels chart his spiritual agonising, his recruitment of a band of helpers and followers, and his epic battles against Lord Foul.

novels: ▷Michael Innes, *The Daffodil Affair*; H.R.F. Keating, *Death and the Visiting Firemen*; Gladys Mitchell, *The Twenty-third Man*.

▶ **To his non-crime books:** Macdonald Harris, *The Balloonist*; Bamber Gascoigne, *The Heyday*; ▷John Irving, *The World According to Garp*.

> **READ ON**

▶ ▷David Eddings, *Pawn of Prophecy* (first of the Belgariad quintet). Jack Vance, *Lyonesse*. R.A. MacAvoy, *Damiano*.

The Thomas Covenant books are Lord Foul's Bane, The Illearth War, The Power That Preserves, The Wounded Land, The One Tree, White Gold Wielder *and the brief* Gildenfire.

DONLEAVY, J.P. (James Patrick) •
(born 1926)
Irish novelist.

Beginning with *The Ginger Man* (1955), Donleavy has written a series of bawdy, boozy 'biographies', like shaggy-dog stories reworked by ▷Joyce. Nothing much happens to his heroes: they wander amiably through life, spending much time in bed and even more in pubs, and endlessly, riotously reflecting on the meaning of life and love. His other novels include *A Singular Man, The Beastly Beatitudes of Balthazar B, The Destinies of Darcy Dancer, Gentleman,* and *Are You Listening, Rabbi Löw?.*

DOSTOEVSKI, Fyodor • *(1821–81)*
Russian novelist.

Dostoevski admired ▷Balzac and ▷Dickens, and set out to describe Russian characters and society in a similar way, creating atmosphere by a series of vivid evocations (verbal snapshots) of everything from people's skin and clothes to the texture of furniture or the gleam of rain on cobble-stones. His characters are a gallery of 'types', particularly strong on the destitute, the suffering and the inadequate. He was fascinated by people driven to extreme behaviour by despair or lack of external moral guidance, such as the teaching of his own Christian faith. Raskolnikov, the central character of *Crime and Punishment,* makes himself a moral outsider by committing murder. Myshkin in *The Idiot* is so tormented by the thought of his own inadequacy that he becomes the imbecile he thinks he is. Every member of the Karamazov family (in *The Brothers Karamazov*) is morally tainted, and only the youngest, a novice monk, is able to wrestle with his own evil nature and win. If Dostoevski had been a 20th-century writer, his pessimistic view of human existence might have led him to surrealist black comedy (see ▷Kafka); as it was, the psychological intensity of his books is closer to stage tragedy (*King Lear* or *Medea*, say) than to prose fiction, and has a similar all-engulfing power.

CRIME AND PUNISHMENT • *(1866)*
Raskolnikov, a student, driven to neurotic frenzy by his

READ ON ▷

▶ Flann O'Brien, *At Swim-Two-Birds.* ▷John Kennedy Toole, *A Confederacy of Dunces.* Robert Coover, *Pricksongs and Descants* (short stories).

READ ON ▷

● *The Idiot; The Brothers Karamazov.*
▶ ▷Victor Hugo, *Les misérables.* ▷Nathaniel Hawthorne, *The Scarlet Letter.* ▷Joseph Conrad, *Under Western Eyes.* ▷Albert Camus, *The Fall* (La chute). ▷Vladimir Nabokov, *Despair.* ▷Georges Simenon, *Act of Passion.* ▷François Mauriac, *The Nest of Vipers* (Le nœud de vipères). Paul Bailey, *A Distant Likeness* reverses one of the themes of *Crime and Punishment*: obsession with a crime triggers self-condemnation and madness not in the criminal but in the investigating officer.

powerlessness to change the injustice of the world, decides to demonstrate the freedom of his soul by a single gratuitous act: murder. Instead of being liberated, however, he is enslaved by his own guilt-feelings, and the book describes, in a remorseless and clinical way, the disintegration of his personality. The part of his 'conscience' is embodied in Inspector Petrovich, who harries him like a Fury from ancient myth, goading and cajoling him to admit his guilt and so to purge his soul.

Dostoevski's other books include Notes From the House of the Dead *(based on his own prison-camp experiences: he was a political dissident),* Winter Notes on Summer Experiences *(a horrified account of the degenerate Europe he found while visiting the London World Exhibition of 1862), and the novels* Notes from Underground, The Gambler *and* The Possessed.

DOYLE, Arthur Conan • *(1859–1930)*
British writer of novels, short stories and non-fiction.

A doctor with very few patients, Doyle began writing to improve his income. His main interest was military history, and he regarded his historical novels (eg *The White Company*, the story of a band of 14th-century knight-errants, or the Brigadier Gerard books, set during the Napoleonic Wars) as his best work. His Sherlock Holmes stories were meant as potboilers, and throughout his life he claimed (while still going on writing them) to be embarrassed by their success. The Holmes stories were published by *Strand Magazine* in the UK and by *Harper's* in the USA; these papers also serialised Doyle's Professor Challenger novels (beginning with *The Lost World*), about a flamboyant scientific genius and explorer, a blend of the heroes of ▷Verne and ▷Rider Haggard.

THE MEMOIRS OF SHERLOCK HOLMES • *(1893)*
In each of the 11 stories in this collection, Holmes is presented with a problem which seems insoluble – at least so far as his friend and chronicler Dr Watson can see – and solves it by a mixture of dazzling deductive reasoning and melodramatic adventure. He is a master of disguise, an expert shot and boxer, a drug-taker, a neurotic introvert, a plausible liar who uses every trick to trap his suspects – and Doyle's style has a single-mindedness, an obsessiveness, which perfectly suits both Holmes' character and the mysteries he is set to solve.

Doyle's Holmes books are the novels A Study in Scarlet,

<table>
<tr><td>READ ON ▷</td></tr>
</table>

● *The Case Book of Sherlock Holmes.*
▶ Nicholas Meyer, *The Seven-per-cent Solution* (one of the most convincing of many Holmes stories by others since Doyle went out of copyright). G.K. Chesterton, *The Father Brown Stories.* Gladys Mitchell, *Twelve Horses and the Hangman's Noose.* John Dickson Carr, *The Emperor's Snuff Box.*

The Sign of Four, The Hound of the Baskervilles *and* The Valley of Fear, *and the short-story collections* Adventures of Sherlock Holmes, The Return of Sherlock Holmes, His Last Bow *and* The Case Book of Sherlock Holmes. *The Challenger books include* The Poison Belt *and* The Land of Mist, *and Doyle's historical novels, apart from those mentioned, include* Micah Clarke *(set during the Monmouth Rebellion of 1685 and its bloody aftermath).*

DRABBLE, Margaret • *(born 1939)*
British novelist and non- fiction writer.

An admirer of ▷Eliot and ▷Bennett, Drabble has updated their fictional ideas to the present day. Her books are crammed with the detail of everyday lives – fetching children from school, making gravy, taking inter-city trains, washing tights – and are about 'ordinary' people: housewives, librarians, teachers, midwives. But Drabble, like Eliot and Bennett, is also interested in intellectual ideas, in describing the spirit of the times as well as their domestic detail. Without being feminist, her books centre on women's experience. They tell us how middle-class girls of the late 1950s felt about their lives, how they went on in the 1960s to balance marriage, motherhood and careers, and how they coped in the 1970s and 1980s with teenage children and rocky marriages. It is fiction so honest that it seems almost like autobiography: every one of Drabble's women shares an outlook, a tone of voice, which sounds (rightly or wrongly) like the author's own.

THE RADIANT WAY • *(1987)*
The lives of three women of similar age (late 40s) and background (educated middle-class) are contrasted, in a brilliantly-evoked mid-1980s Britain. All were born in the north of England; Liz has moved south and made a career as a Harley Street psychiatrist; her sister has stayed at home to look after their senile mother; Alix and her husband, failing to make a success in London, are returning north to regenerate their lives. The characters' contrasting experience, and their middle-aged views of the way their younger ambitions have worked out, match the political and social feelings Drabble sees as typical of Britain in the 1980s, when the young adults of the flower-power generation are just beginning to feel that life has passed them by.

Drabble's novels are The Garrick Year, The Millstone, Jerusalem the Golden, The Waterfall, The Realms of

READ ON ⟩

● *The Garrick Year* (a moving study, set in the 1960s, of a woman trying to manage both marriage, to a rising actor, and the claims of her own career).
▶ Penelope Mortimer, *The Pumpkin Eater*. Deborah Moggach, *Close to Home*. ▷Margaret Atwood, *The Edible Woman*. Joan Didion, *A Book of Common Prayer*. Mary Flanagan, *Trust*.
▶ **Earlier books foreshadowing Drabble's concerns:** ▷George Eliot, *Middlemarch*; ▷Arnold Bennett, *Hilda Lessways*; ▷Virginia Woolf, *Mrs Dalloway*.

Gold, The Ice Age *and* The Radiant Way. *She has also written biographies of Wordsworth and Bennett.*

DREAMING SPIRES
(books set in Cambridge and Oxford Universities)

▷Max Beerbohm, *Zuleika Dobson*
  Glyn Daniel, *The Cambridge Murders*
  Alan Judd, *The Noonday Devil*
▷Barbara Pym, *Crampton Hodnett*
▷Dorothy L. Sayers, *Gaudy Night*
▷Tom Sharpe, *Porterhouse Blue*
▷C.P. Snow, *The Affair*

Higher (?) Education (p 118)

DUMAS, Alexandre • *(1802–70)*
French writer of novels, plays short stories and non-fiction.

In his 20s Dumas worked as a civil service clerk; it was not until he was 29 that he was able to take up writing full-time. From then till his death, working with a team of assistants, he poured out over 250 plays, novels, essays, books on history, travel and cooking and no less than 22 volumes of memoirs. He was one of the most popular authors of his century, and the genre he specialised in, swashbuckling historical romance, was a favourite for 120 years, a forerunner of both modern spy stories and fantasy.

THE THREE MUSKETEERS • *(1844–5)*
At the beginning of the 17th century d'Artagnan, a young country squire, goes to Paris to seek adventure. He makes friends with three of the King's musketeers (by the unusual method of challenging each of them to a duel on the same day) and the four become inseparable. D'Artagnan is accepted for royal service, and the musketeers throw themselves into the political intrigues centring on weak king Louis, his unhappy queen and her arch-enemies Cardinal Richelieu and the seductive, treacherous Milady. The story involves stolen jewels, masquerades, bluff and double bluff, and the musketeers gallop the length and breadth of France, duelling, drinking, wenching and making a thousand skin-of-the-teeth escapes. Although the book's style is old-fashioned, its breathless plot, its good humour and above all the wisecracking, bantering friendship between the four central characters, give it irresistible

READ ON ▷

● Dumas continued the Musketeers' adventures in *Twenty Years After*, *The Vicomte of Bragelonne* and *The Man in the Iron Mask*.
▶ **Swashbuckling stories:** Rafael Sabatini, *Captain Blood*; Jeffery Farnol, *The Broad Highway*; Stanley J. Weyman, *Gentleman of France*; Baroness Orczy, *The Scarlet Pimpernel*.
▶ **The idea of buddies united against the world is repeated, in a similar tongue-in-cheek way, in** ▷Len Deighton, *Only When I Larf* (about 1960s conmen) and Donald Westlake, *Gangway!* (about 1860s San Francisco crooks).

gusto. After a few dozen pages of acclimatisation, it may prove hard to put it down.

Although Dumas was best-known – and is now best-re-membered – for his Musketeers adventures, he wrote fine novels set in other periods, notably The Queen's Necklace *and* The Countess of Charny *(both of which take place during the French Revolution) and* The Count of Monte Cristo, *about a man falsely imprisoned for helping the de-feated Napoleon, who escapes, discovers hidden treasure and proceeds to hunt down the people who betrayed him.*

DU MAURIER, Daphne • *(born 1907)*
British novelist and non-fiction writer.

Although Du Maurier wrote novels and stories of many kinds, she is best known for a series of atmospheric romances set in the English West Country (Cornwall, Devon and Somerset) and drawing on the moorland land-scape and seafaring associations of the area. In her best-loved book, *Rebecca* (1938), a girl marries an enigmatic young widower and goes to be mistress of his large coun-try house Manderley, only to find it haunted by the mys-tery of his first wife's death. Solving that mystery (against the wishes of the sinister housekeeper Mrs Danvers) is the only way to bring happiness to the young girl (who is un-named) and peace to her tormented husband – and the search leads her into a psychological labyrinth as threaten-ing as the corridors of the dark old house itself.

Du Maurier's romances include Jamaica Inn, French-man's Creek, My Cousin Rachel *and* Mary Anne. *Her other novels include* The King's General, The Parasites, The Glassblowers *and* The House on the Strand. *The Ap-ple Tree/Kiss Me Again Stranger,* The Breaking Point *and* Early Stories *are collections of short stories. She also wrote plays, biographies (of her family, Branwell Brontë and Francis Drake) and an autobiography,* The Shaping of a Writer/Myself When Young.

DUNNETT, Dorothy • *(born 1923)*
British novelist.

Dunnett is best-known for two enormous historical sagas, swashbuckling romances set in the 15th and 16th centu-ries. The hero of the 'Lymond' books is a Scottish soldier of fortune whose adventures take him as far as Malta, the Ottoman Empire and Russia (where he serves in the army

READ ON

► Jane Gardam, *Crusoe's Daughter.* ▷Charlotte Brontë, *Jane Eyre.* Susan Howatch, *Penmarric.* ▷Frank Yerby, *A Woman Called Fancy.* Catherine Darby, *Rowan Garth.*

READ ON

► Reay Tannahill, *The World, the Flesh and the Devil.* ▷Tom De Haan, *A Mirror for Princes.* ▷Jean Plaidy, of Ivan the Terrible). Back home, he becomes the protector of the infant Mary Queen of Scots and is embroiled in the religious and political intrigues of the English Tudor court. A second series (beginning with *Niccolò Rising* and continuing with *The Spring of the Ram*) is in progress. It is the story of an equally charming adventurer, this time set in Renaissance Italy (Florence at the time of the Medicis and Savonarola) and Germany (during the religious wars triggered by Martin Luther's condemnation of the Roman Catholic Church). Dunnett's other books include *King Hereafter*, a novel about the historical Macbeth, King of Scotland, and a series of romantic thrillers set in the present day, all of whose titles – at least in the UK editions – include the name 'Dolly'. (These were originally published under the pseudonym Dorothy Halliday.)

The Lymond books, in order, are The Game of Kings, Queen's Play, The Disorderly Knights, Pawn in Frankincense, The Ringed Castle *and* Checkmate. *The 'Dolly' books are* Dolly and the Singing Bird/The Photogenic Soprano, Dolly and the Cookie Bird/Murder in the Round, Dolly and the Doctor Bird/Match for a Murderer, Dolly and the Starry Bird/Murder in Focus *and* Dolly and the Nanny Bird.

DURRELL, Lawrence • *(born 1912)*
British writer of novels, poems and non-fiction.

Durrell has lived most of his life out of Britain, in Greece, Egypt and France. As well as fiction, he has written poetry and half a dozen non-fiction books about Greek islands: they are among his most enjoyable work, allowing scope for the impressionistic descriptions of landscape and character and the ruminations on love and life which sometimes clog his novels. In his fiction, he uses experimental forms, constantly varying each story's structure and standpoint; this sets up a dialogue between writer and reader, a feeling of collaboration, which is one of the most exhilarating aspects of his work.

THE ALEXANDRIA QUARTET • *(1957–60)*
Each book in the quartet, *Justine, Balthazar, Mountolive* and *Clea*, tells us part of the story: they give different viewpoints of the same events, and it is not till the end that every motive, every action, every twist of character becomes clear. The people are a group of friends and lovers, English, Greek and Egyptian, living in the turmoil of late-1930s Alexandria. At the centre is Darley, a teacher

READ ON

The Plantagenet Prelude and its sequels: the Plantagenet Saga. Frans Bengtsson, *The Long Ships* (set in Viking times). ▷R.L. Stevenson, *Kidnapped* and its sequels (set in 18th-century Scotland, during the Jacobite uprisings).

● *Tunc* and *Numquam* (a pair of Siamese-twin novels) are similarly dreamlike, setting bizarre events and characters in a blur of countries and climaxing magnificently, if unexpectedly, under the dome of St Paul's Cathedral, London.
▶ Stuart Evans, *Centres of Ritual* (and its sequels: the 'Windmill Hill' sequence). ▷Nathanael West, *The Dream Life of Balso Snell*. D.M. Thomas, *Birthstone*. ▷Olivia Manning, *The Balkan*

and would-be writer who observes events, partakes, but cannot explain. A main 'character' is the city of Alexandria itself. Durrell/Darley pretends to be giving accurate pictures of its souks, bars, palaces, brothels and crumbling embassies, but it is a dream-city, a fantasy-land where reality is subjective and events are only what you make of them.

As well as The Alexandria Quartet, *Durrell's novels include* The Black Book, The Dark Labyrinth/Cefalù *and the five-novel 'Avignon quincunx',* Monsieur, Livia, Constance, Sebastian *and* Quinx. *His* Collected Poems *are published, and* Antrobus Complete *is a collection of satirical stort stories about diplomats, like TV sitcom frozen on the page. His island books include* Prospero's Cell *(about Corfu, also the subject of his brother Gerald's* My Family and Other Animals*)*, Reflections on a Marine Venus *(about Rhodes) and* Bitter Lemons *(about Cyprus).*

Trilogy (set in Bucharest and Athens during the second world war); *The Levant Trilogy* (set in Cairo).

E

EDDINGS, David • *(born 1931)*
US novelist.

After one modern adventure story, *High Hunt*, Eddings concentrated on fantasy. His best-known work is the 'Belgariad quintet' (1982–4), a ▷Tolkien-influenced saga of good and evil, magic and mysticism – but laced, unlike *The Lord of the Rings*, with a strong sense of the absurd. The books in the series are *Pawn of Prophecy*, *Queen of Sorcery*, *Magician's Gambit*, *Castle of Wizardry* and *Enchanter's Endgame*. Eddings is currently writing a second series, further adventures of his hero Garion, who begins as a scullion, graduates to be sorcerer's apprentice and ends up a fully-fledged wizard.

> **READ ON** ▷
>
> ▶ Alan Dean Foster, *Spellsinger*. ▷Piers Anthony, *A Spell for Chameleon*. T.H. White, *The Once and Future King*. ▷J.R.R. Tolkien, *Lord of the Rings*.

ELIOT, George • *(1819–80)*
British novelist.

'George Eliot' was the pen-name of Marian Evans, a farm-manager's daughter. She grew up in the stifling provincial pieties of middle-class Victorian England, but after her father's death became an atheist and freethinker, travelled abroad and set up home in London. She was at the heart of the liberal intellectual circles of her time: a supporter of Darwin, an admirer of ▷William Morris and other early socialists. A similar receptivity to new ideas and disdain for convention mark her novels. They deal with the kind of moral issues (such as whether a 'good life' can be lived without religion, or if sexual happiness is essential to a successful marriage) which were rarely discussed in polite Victorian company and were even less common in literature. At the same time her books teem with realistic detail of provincial society, minutely observed. The combination of exact documentation of beha-

> **READ ON** ▷
>
> ● *The Mill on the Floss* (about a brother and sister who are idyllically happy together as children, grow apart in adult life, and are finally, tragically reunited).
> ▶ **Matching Eliot's concern for the individual stifled by society:** ▷Gustave Flaubert, *Madame Bovary*; ▷Mrs Gaskell, *North and South*; ▷Thomas Hardy, *Jude the Obscure*; Benjamin

viour and character with unashamed discussion of ideas normally left unspoken was a heady one: she was one of the most widely read authors of her day.

MIDDLEMARCH · *(1871–2)*

Two people try to break free from the petty-minded boredom of the English provincial town of Middlemarch. Dorothea Brooke marries because of intellectual infatuation, only to find that her husband (an elderly scholar) is a domestic tyrant. Tertius Lydgate, a doctor struggling to introduce new medical ideas in a society which is deeply suspicious of them, marries for love, only to find that his wife's brainless following of fashion destroys his bank-balance, his self-confidence and his social position.

Apart from Romola, *set in 15th-century Florence, all Eliot's novels have 19th-century English locations and characters. Her first book,* Scenes from Clerical Life, *contains three mid-length stories; it and the short novel* Silas Marner *(about a freethinking country weaver tormented for his beliefs and for a crime he did not commit) are the most accessible of all her works. Her full-length novels are* Adam Bede, The Mill on the Floss, Felix Holt, Middlemarch *and* Daniel Deronda.

Disraeli, *Sybil.*
▶ **To *Daniel Deronda*:** ▷Henry James, *Portrait of a Lady*; Janet Lewis, *The Trial of Sören Kvist.*
▶ **Contemporary books combining social observation with 'issues' in an Eliotish way, though their styles are entirely different:** ▷Margaret Drabble, *The Millstone*; ▷Katharine Anne Porter, *Pale Horse, Pale Rider*; Winifred Holtby, *South Riding*; Simone De Beauvoir, *The Mandarins.*

F

FAMILIES: ALL-ENGULFING

▷Anita Brookner, *Family and Friends*
▷Angela Carter, *The Magic Toyshop*
▷William Faulkner, *The Sound and the Fury*
▷John Galsworthy, *The Forsyte Saga*
  Irene Handl, *The Sioux*
▷François Mauriac, *The Nest of Vipers*
▷Christina Stead, *The Man Who Loved Children*

Families: Eccentric (p 72); Families: Many Generations (p 72)

FAMILIES: ECCENTRIC

  H.E. Bates, *The Darling Buds of May*
▷Ivy Compton-Burnett, *A House and its Head*
▷John Irving, *The Hotel New Hampshire*
  Nancy Mitford, *The Pursuit of Love*
▷Vladimir Nabokov, *Ada*
  Peter Tinniswood, *A Touch of Daniel*
▷Virginia Woolf, *To the Lighthouse*

Families: All-engulfing (p 72); Families: Many Generations (p 72); Parents and Children (p 187)

FAMILIES: MANY GENERATIONS

▷Isabel Allende, *The House of the Spirits*

▷Gabriel García Márquez, *One Hundred Years of Solitude*
▷Winston Graham, *Poldark*
▷Thomas Mann, *Buddenbrooks*
▷Maisie Mosco, *Almonds and Raisins*
 Richard Peck, *This Company of Women*
▷I.B. Singer, *The Family Moskat*
 Nicola Thorne, *A Place in the Sun*
 Jan Webster, *Collier's Row*

Families: All-engulfing (p 72); Families: Eccentric (p 72)

FANTASY ADVENTURE

▷Stephen Donaldson, *'Thomas Covenant' series*
▷A. Conan Doyle, *The Lost World*
▷David Eddings, *'Belgariad' quintet*
 C.S. Lewis, *Out of the Silent Planet*
 Terry Pratchett, *The Colour of Magic*
▷J.R.R. Tolkien, *Lord of the Rings*
▷Jules Verne, *Journey to the Centre of the Earth*
 Patricia Wrightson, *The Ice is Coming*

Fantasy Societies (p 73); High Adventure (p 117)

FANTASY SOCIETIES

▷Tom De Haan, *A Mirror for Princes*
 Michael Frayn, *Sweet Dreams*
▷Ursula Le Guin, *Malafrena*
▷Anne McCaffrey, *Dragonflight*
▷Robert Silverberg, *Lord Valentine's Castle*
▷Jonathan Swift, *Gulliver's Travels*
▷H.G. Wells, *The Time Machine*
 T.H. White, *The Once and Future King*

Future Societies (p 86)

FARMER, Philip José • *(born 1918)*
US novelist.

Each of Farmer's SF novels is the exploration of a single, brilliantly surreal initial idea: in *Dayworld*, for example, that the world's overpopulation leads to each human being

READ ON

● *Jesus on Mars.*
▶ ▷Michael Moorcock, *Warlord of the Air.*

being allowed one day per week of 'life' and having to spend the other six in cold storage. His best-known work is the 'Riverworld' series (1972–80; the individual titles are *To Your Scattered Bodies Go*; *The Fabulous Riverboat*; *The Dark Design*; *The Magic Labyrinth*; *Gods of Riverworld*.) Riverworld is a planet on which every human being ever born, from the dawn of history to beyond the present day, has been reborn in the far future as part of a psychological experiment. The series tells how three people, Samuel Clemens (alias ▷Mark Twain), Richard Burton (translator of the *Kama Sutra*) and Alice Hargreaves (née Liddell: the inspiration for *Alice In Wonderland*) explore Riverworld and try to discover the nature and purpose of the experiment of which they – to say nothing of King John of England, plotting a political coup – are part.

▷Frank Herbert, *The Dosadi Experiment*.
▷Isaac Asimov, *Foundation*.

FARRELL, J.G. (James Gordon) •
(1935–79)
British novelist.

After three contemporary novels, including *The Lung* (1965, based on his own experience), about the onset of polio, Farrell took all his themes from history. *Troubles* (1970), set in Ireland after the first world war, is a barbed account of the Irish freedom-struggle against the English, and draws uncomfortable parallels with the present-day situation in Northern Ireland. *The Siege of Krishnapur* (1973), equally vitriolic and farcical – its tone is close at times to ▷Heller's *Catch-22* – is set in 1850s India, during the so-called 'Mutiny'. *The Singapore Grip* (1978) is a blockbuster about the Japanese capture of Malaysia in the second world war – for Farrell, the beginning of Britain's eclipse as a global power. Taken together, the three books are an indictment of Britain's attitude towards its empire: not so much thuggishness as boneheaded indifference, the unconcern of those who never imagine that others might resent their rule.

> **READ ON**

▶ To *Troubles*: Liam O'Flaherty: *The Informer*; Bernard MacLaverty, *Cal*.
▶ To *The Siege of Krishnapur*: ▷John Masters, *Nightrunners of Bengal*; Idries Shah, *Kara Kush*.
▶ To *The Singapore Grip*: ▷J.G. Ballard, *Empire of the Sun*; Timothy Mo, *An Insular Possession*.

FAULKNER, William • *(1897–1962)*
US novelist and short-story writer.

Faulkner's work deals obsessively with a single theme: the moral degeneracy of the US Deep South. His characters are the descendants of the cotton barons of the time before the Civil War, and of the slaves who worked for them. The whites live in crumbling mansions, dress in finery handed down from previous generations and bolster their sagging self-esteem with snobbery, racism and drink. The

> **READ ON**

● *Sartoris* (about the family of a Southern Civil War general coming to terms with defeat); *Intruder in the Dust* (a comparatively sunny book about an blacks either fawn, as if slavery had never been abolished, or seethe in decaying slums on the edge of town. The air itself seems tainted: despair, lust, introversion and murder clog people's minds. It is a society without hope or comfort, and Faulkner describes it in a series of moral horror stories, compulsive and merciless.

THE SOUND AND THE FURY • *(1929)*

The novel's theme is how moral decadence overwhelms two generations of the white Compson family. We see a brother and sister, Caddy and Quentin, growing up as bright, happy adolescents, full of hope for the future, only to fall victims to the family taint and spiral into incest, nymphomania and suicide. One of their brothers, Jason, a morose bully, succeeds his father as head of the family and becomes a miser and a tyrant; their other brother Benjy has a mental age of two. In the second half of the book we see the corruption threatening to engulf Caddy's and Quentin's incestuous daughter, and her attempts to break free from the family curse. Large sections of the book are told as first-person narratives, by Caddy, Jason, Quentin and – eerily, a tour de force of writing, demanding concentration in the reader –the idiot Benjy. A final strand of claustrophobia is added by the Compsons' negro servants: watching, always-present, like the chorus of a particularly fraught Greek tragedy.

Faulkner's short stories are in two fat volumes, Collected Stories *and* Uncollected Stories. *His main Southern novels, a series set in the imaginary Yoknapatawpha County, Mississippi, are* Sartoris, Absalom, Absalom!, The Unvanquished *and the trilogy* The Hamlet, The Town *and* The Mansion. *His other books include* Intruder in the Dust, The Sound and the Fury, Light in August, The Rievers *and two books in experimental styles,* As I Lay Dying *and* Requiem for a Nun.

FIELDING, Henry • *(1707–54)*
British novelist and playwright.

Fielding's first successes were with satirical stage comedies: *Rape upon Rape* (a farce) and *The Tragedy of Tom Thumb* (a parody of melodramatic tragedy). But his plays were too political for the authorities, who closed them down. He turned to fiction, announcing that he meant to write an English equivalent of *Don Quixote*. His books are life-stories, involving charming young people in a series of escapades as they journey from country-house to inn, from farmyard to theatre-box, from law-court to bedroom,

adolescent awakening to adulthood).

▶ **Good Deep South follow-ups:** ▷Carson McCullers, *The Ballad of the Sad Café*; William Styron, *Lie Down in Darkness*; Harper Lee, *To Kill a Mocking Bird*; Tenessee Williams, *Short Stories*.

▶ **More cheerful:** ▷Eudora Welty, *Delta Wedding*; Calder Willingham, *Eternal Fire*.

▶ **Good follow-ups on the theme of the degenerate, collapsing family:** ▷Thomas Mann, *Buddenbrooks*; Giuseppi Tomaso di Lampedusa, *The Leopard*; ▷Ivy Compton-Burnett, *Mothers and Sons*.

▶ **Good stylistic follow-ups:** ▷James Joyce, *Ulysses*; ▷Virginia Woolf, *To the Lighthouse*.

READ ON ⟩

● *Joseph Andrews* (a parody of the heroine-in-moral-danger novels of ▷Samuel Richardson, the story of a young man so beautiful that every woman he meets longs to entice him into bed, and so innocent that gathering experience and outwitting would-be predators at every step. Fielding's novels are long and leisurely: it is as if he is taking a stroll through English society, high and low, and everything he sees or hears reminds him of an anecdote, genial, unhurried and preposterous.

TOM JONES • *(1749)*

Tom Jones is a foundling brought up by kindly Squire Allworthy. He is a personable, amorous young man, and his immorality finally makes Allworthy send him into the world to seek his fortune. The novel tells Tom's adventures, in and out of bed, as he wanders through England enjoying life as it comes, torn by the thought of his true-love Sophia Western, but still ready to be seduced by every pretty girl he meets. The story is told in short chapters, like extended anecdotes, and Fielding keeps breaking off to address the reader directly, telling jokes, pointing morals and commenting on the life and manners of the time.

Fielding's other novels are Joseph Andrews *and* Amelia. *A Journey from This World to the Next and The Life and Death of Jonathan Wild the Great are short, savage satires: the second, for example, treats a notorious, real-life highwayman as if he were an epic hero.* Journal of a Voyage to Lisbon *is a fascinating travel-diary about crossing the Bay of Biscay in a leaky, storm-tossed ship.*

he notices neither this nor the more dangerous pitfalls of his path through life).

▶ Bob Coleman, *The Later Adventures of Tom Jones* (a 1986 sequel to *Tom Jones*, taking Tom to colonial America, where he is embroiled not only in love-affairs but in the War of Independence). Apuleius, *The Golden Ass* (in the ▷Robert Graves translation). Miguel de Cervantes Saavedra, *Don Quixote.* ▷Daniel Defoe, *Moll Flanders.* ▷Laurence Sterne, *Tristram Shandy.*

▶ **Later books in a similarly relaxed, satirical and biographical vein:** ▷H.G. Wells, *Kipps*; ▷Thomas Mann, *Confessions of Felix Krull*; ▷Mary McCarthy, *Birds of America*; ▷Saul Bellow, *The Adventures of Augie March.*

THE FILM BUSINESS

Dirk Bogarde, *West of Sunset*
▷Len Deighton, *Close-up*
▷Peter De Vries, *The Prick of Noon*
H.R.F. Keating, *Filmi, Filmi, Inspector Ghote*
▷Frederic Raphael, *California Time*
Terry Southern, *Blue Movie*
▷Nathanael West, *The Day of the Locust*
Donald Westlake, *Who Stole Sassi Manoon?*

FITZGERALD, F. Scott (Francis Scott) •
(1896–1940)
US novelist and short-story writer.

In the USA of the 1920s the earnestness which had been needed to win the first world war was replaced by giddy exhilaration. Jazz, bootleg liquor, drugs and sex seemed to be not merely pleasures, but symbols of a new, liberated age – and the fact that that age was clearly doomed, that the dancing would end in tears, gave every party, every spending-spree, an edge of extra excitement, as if people were roller-skating on the brink of the abyss. Fitzgerald, rich, handsome, athletic and talented, not only wrote about this doomed high society, but was one of its leaders. In the 1930s, when the inevitable reckoning came – the Great Depression was parallelled in Fitzgerald's life by his wife's madness and his own alcoholism and bankruptcy – his books not unnaturally turned sour and sad. But his 1920s stories and novels told the legend of the 'jazz age' with such glittering force that it is easy, now, to believe that all America, and not just a few thousand sophisticates, lived like that.

THE GREAT GATSBY • *(1925)*
In a millionaire community on Long Island, the enigmatic bachelor Gatsby gives huge all-night parties at his mansion, orgies of dancing, drugs and sex, the season's most fashionable events. His fascinated neighbour, the book's narrator Nick Carraway, makes friends with him and begins unravelling the secrets of his personality. Carraway's intervention triggers revelations about Gatsby's criminal past, and a love-affair between Gatsby and the wife of a wealthy oaf, Tom Buchanan; these in turn lead to further tragedy. At the end of the book Carraway sits alone outside Gatsby's deserted house, reflecting on the emptiness of the lives he has just described.

Fitzgerald's 1920s novels are This Side of Paradise, The Beautiful and Damned *and* The Great Gatsby. Tender is the Night, *bitterly autobiographical, describes the life of an alcoholic writer and his insane wife on the French Riviera, and the unfinished* The Last Tycoon *is a satire on the Hollywood for which he wrote rubbish to earn money in his last desperate months of life.* Tales of the Jazz Age *and* Taps at Reveille *are collections of short stories.*

READ ON ▷

● *The Beautiful and Damned* (about the doomed marriage of two bright young things, leaders of jazz-age society: a book given ferocious ironical point for today's readers by what we know of the decay to come in Fitzgerald's own marriage).

▶ ▷Evelyn Waugh, *Vile Bodies.* ▷Anthony Powell, *Afternoon Men.* Anita Loos, *Gentlemen Prefer Blondes.* Ronald Firbank, *Valmouth.* Vita Sackville West, *The Edwardians.* Andrew Sinclair, *The Breaking of Bumbo.* Martin Amis, *Success* applies Fitzgerald's tone of hopeless, cynical black farce to a much later 'doomed' generation: our own, and ▷William Thackeray, *Vanity Fair* takes a similar view of 19th-century English middle-class society.

FLAUBERT, Gustave • *(1821–80)*
French novelist.

Many of Flaubert's contemporary writers – even such 'realists' as ▷Balzac and ▷Dickens – believed that 'fiction' involved larger-than-life characters, events or emotions. Flaubert's ambition, by contrast, was to hold up a mirror to ordinary people in humdrum situations, to take the boring events of commonplace lives and make them interesting. He also avoided heightened language, wit, irony and the other devices novelists used to enliven their narrative. He worked to make his prose evenly-paced and unobtrusive, taking its tensions and climaxes from the flow of events themselves. In modern times, similar techniques have been used in 'fly-on-the-wall' TV documentaries, where a camera-crew records unscripted scenes from daily life.

MADAME BOVARY • *(1857)*
Emma, a romantic and foolish young woman, dreams of being swept away on clouds of ecstasy, either by a handsome lover or into the arms of the Church. She marries a small-town doctor, and finds the routine of provincial life stifling and unfulfilling. She tries to bring excitement into her life by flirting, and is gradually trapped in pathetic and grubby love-affairs, stealing from her husband to pay for her ever more eccentric whims. In the end, destroyed by her inability to live up to her own dreams, she kills herself – and everyone else's life goes on as if she had never existed.

Flaubert's novels of ordinary French life are Madame Bovary, Sentimental Education *(L'Éducation sentimentale) and the unfinished* Bouvard and Pécuchet. Salammbô *applies the same techniques to a story of the Carthage of Hannibal's time, to bizarre effect, as if an archaeological treatise had been jumbled up with the script for a Hollywood epic film.* The Temptation of St Anthony *seeks to describe all the temptations, of flesh, spirit and will,· which might assail a devout Catholic believer;* Three Stories *contains 'A Simple Heart', one of the most moving of all Flaubert's works.*

FLEMING, Ian • *(1908–64)*
British novelist.

Fleming's James Bond books are like comic strips for adults: Bond is a super-hero who saves the world from spectacularly nasty, psychopathic master-criminals. Bond

READON >

● *Sentimental Education* (about a young man who tries, like Emma Bovary, to spice his boring life with grand passions, and fails. A secondary strand in the book is the political situation leading up to the 1848 revolution – something as busy and sterile, in Flaubert's opinion, as his hero's attempts to find meaning in existence).
▶ ▷Italo Svevo, *A Life.* ▷Arnold Bennett, *Hilda Lessways.* ▷Joseph Heller, *Something Happened.* ▷Elizabeth Taylor, *A Wreath of Roses.* ▷Iris Murdoch, *Under the Net.* ▷R.K. Narayan, *The English Teacher,* though set in a society (provincial India) and a period (the 1950s) remote from *Madame Bovary,* and less than a quarter as long, magnificently matches Flaubert's insight into the way that the joys and sorrows of small lives, no less than large, can tear the heart.

READON >

● *From Russia With Love.*
▶ In the 1960s, until

wins through by a mixture of supreme physical prowess and bizarre, Batmanish technology which turns every fountain-pen into a two-way radio and every watch or shoe-lace into an arsenal of deadly weapons. Adult tastes are catered for less by psychological insight or intellectual depth than by frequent sex-scenes (Bond, as well as everything else, is a super-stud) and by laconic, hardboiled wit. In everything but plot – over-the-top technology, larky dialogue, high-gloss violence – the Bond films give the exact flavour of Fleming's books.

GOLDFINGER • *(1959)*

Auric Goldfinger has two obsessions: gold and power. He plans to smash the vaults of Fort Knox with a nuclear missile and use the stolen gold to finance world domination. Only Bond can stop him – and the book shows in deadpan, second-by-second detail how he does it.

Other Bond novels include Moonraker, Thunderball, From Russia With Love, Diamonds are Forever, Dr No, On Her Majesty's Secret Service, You Only Live Twice *and* The Man With the Golden Gun. Octopussy *is a collection of short stories.*

▷Deighton and ▷Le Carré took the spy-story in a different direction, there were a million Bond imitations and spoofs, of which some of the jolliest are by John Gardner, Fleming's official successor as chronicler of Bond. Leslie Charteris, *The Saint Goes On,* and his other 1930s Saint books, share Fleming's blend of fast action and affable wit.

► **More recent follow-ups:** ▷Robert Ludlum, *The Matarese Circle*; Joe Poyer, *The Chinese Agenda.*

FOLLETT, Ken • *(born 1949)*
British novelist.

Follett's novels are fast-action thrillers, many with industrial-espionage or wartime themes. His books include *The Bear Raid* (about stock-market espionage), *Storm Island/ The Key to Rebecca* (a fight for survival on an uninhabited island during the second world war) and *The Man from St Petersburg* (about the secret negotiations between the powers before the first world war, and moving, with biting social relevance, from scenes set in the London slums to the whispers and backstabbings of an opulent Imperial court).

READ ON ▷

► Palma Harcourt, *A Matter of Conscience.* Clive Egleton, *Troika.* George Markstein, *Soul Hunters.*

FORD, Ford Madox • *(1873–1939)*
British novelist and non-fiction writer.

Although Ford produced books of all kinds, from biographies to historical novels (*The Fifth Queen*, a Tudor trilogy), he is best remembered for *Parade's End* and *The Good Soldier. The Good Soldier* (1915) is a ▷Jamesian story about two couples who meet in a German hotel and become emotionally and sexually entwined, with devastating results for both themselves and the innocent young ward of one of them. The four novels of *Parade's End*

READ ON ▷

► Vita Sackville-West, *The Edwardians.* Isabel Colegate, *The Shooting Party.* ▷C.P. Snow, *Strangers and Brothers.* ▷Kazuo Ishiguro, *An Artist of The Floating World*

(1924–8) tell how a country landowner, a young man rooted in the social and moral attitudes of the past, is forced by experience (as an officer in the first world war and as a reluctant participant in the freer sexual atmosphere of the post-war years) to slough off the skin of Victorian morality and come to terms, a dozen years later than everyone else, with 20th-century values.

(setting the 'coming-to-terms' theme in post-war Japan). Lynne Reid Banks, *Casualties* (set in present-day Holland, among survivors of wartime nazi persecution). Richard Aldington, *The Hero*. Frank Swinnerton *(Nocturne; Young Felix; Harvest Comedy)* and Elizabeth M. Roberts *(The Time of Man; My Heart and My Flesh)* are novelists much like Ford, and almost equally neglected.

FORESTER, C.S. (Cecil Scott) •
(1899–1966)
British novelist.

Forester is best-known for his 'Hornblower' novels, about a career officer in the British navy of Nelson's time. The books are rich in the detail of life on wooden fighting ships, and the historical background is meticulous; Forester however gives Hornblower 20th-century sensibilities (he is for example sickened by floggings and horrified by the brutality of war) which both flesh him out as a character and draw the reader into the story. The Hornblower series has overshadowed Forester's other books, which include two superb novels set during the Napoleonic Wars (*Death to the French*; *The Gun*), the psychological crime stories *Payment Deferred* and *Plain Murder*, and the comedy-thriller *The African Queen*, memorably filmed in the 1950s with Katharine Hepburn and Humphrey Bogart.

BROWN ON RESOLUTION • *(1929)*
This tense thriller is about a man captured by an enemy ship during the first world war and taken to the remote island of Resolution, where he escapes and tries, single-handed, to hinder the refitting of the warship before he himself can be tracked down and killed.

The core of the Hornblower series is a trilogy of books (The Happy Return, Flying Colours, Ship of the Line) *often published together as* Captain Horatio Hornblower. *Other books in the series fill in details of Hornblower's*

> **READ ON**

● *The African Queen* (about a prissy missionary and a rough-diamond ship's captain who take a leaky old boat full of dynamite downriver in second-world-war Africa to blow up an enemy convoy – and fall in love on the way).
▶ **To Forester's thrillers:** ▷Geoffrey Household, *Watcher in the Shadows*; ▷Graham Greene, *A Gun for Sale/This Gun for Hire*.
▶ **To the Hornblower books:** Bernard Cornwell, *Sharpe's Honour* (one of a series about an army officer at the time of the Peninsular War); Alexander Kent, *Richard Bolitho*,

career, tracing his adventures over a quarter of a century. Typical titles are Mr Midshipman Hornblower, Hornblower and the Atropos, Hornblower in the West Indies *and* Lord Hornblower.

FORSTER, E.M. (Edward Morgan) •
(1879–1970)
British novelist.

All Forster's novels were written in the 1900s (though *A Passage to India* was not published until 1924), and all are concerned with the crippling emotional reticence he considered typical of the Edwardian age. Outwardly extrovert and competent, the Edwardians (Forster thought) were afraid of intimacy. They replaced it with 'manners', and often even members of the same family, even husbands and wives, were inhibited from showing towards each other the kind of genuine feelings they revealed towards God, the flag or their pampered pets. Forster's plots all turn on the disastrous results of emotional inexperience, of people blundering about in each other's sensibilities. In *Where Angels Fear to Tread* an Edwardian family's inability to believe that an Italian can have true paternal feelings for his baby leads to a doomed expedition to Italy to kidnap the child. In *Howards End* a note from one friend to another, confessing love (in fact one snatched kiss in a garden) leads to a hurricane of emotional misunderstanding and disapproval which involves a dozen people and three generations. The central character in *The Longest Journey* tries to 'connect' emotionally with his newly-discovered, no-good step-brother, and in the process destroys first his marriage and then himself. Forster, himself an emotional introvert (a self-deprecating homosexual), offers no solutions. But few writers have better described the problem: his intuition for emotional nuance and his compelling characterisation (especially of women), give his books fascination despite their narrow focus.

Midshipman (Kent also writes modern naval adventures under his real name, Douglas Reeman: a good example is *Winged Escort*). George Macdonald Fraser, *Flashman* and its sequels turn the whole idea splendidly upside-down, telling us the outrageous grown-up career of the caddish bully from *Tom Brown's Schooldays*.

READ ON >

● *A Room With a View* (about the emotional awakening of a snobbish English girl visiting Italy for the first time and realising that there is a real world beyond Edwardian English convention).
▶ **To *A Passage to India*:** ▷Ruth Prawer Jhabvala, *Heat and Dust*; Paul Scott, *The Raj Quartet*; M.M. Kaye, *The Far Pavilions*.
▶ **To Forster's work in general:** ▷Henry James, *The Wings of the Dove*; ▷Marcel Proust, *Within a Budding Grove* (the second part of *Remembrance of Things Past*); ▷L.P. Hartley, *The Go-Between*; ▷Somerset Maugham, *East and West*.

E.M. FORSTER

A PASSAGE TO INDIA *(1910s English girl*
confused by experience of the Raj)

Rudyard **KIPLING, KIM**
(adventures of Anglo-Indian boy in heyday of Raj)

Timothy **MO, AN INSULAR POSSESSION**
(Blockbusting novel about English imperialism in Hong Kong)

James **BLISH, A CASE OF CONSCIENCE**
*(should mineral-rich planet be exploited at expense of native inhabitants'
life and culture?)*

Kingsley **AMIS, RUSSIAN HIDE AND SEEK**
(life in Orwellian Britain, part of Russian 'evil empire')

IMPERIALISM, GOOD AND BAD

R.K. **NARAYAN, THE VENDOR OF SWEETS**
(devout Hindu in rural India dismayed by son's 'progressive' ways)

V.S. **NAIPAUL, A HOUSE FOR MR BISWAS**
*(Indian Hindu in Jamaica caught between dependence on his wife's all-
engulfing family and his longing to lead his own life)*

L.P. **HARTLEY, THE GO-BETWEEN**
*(small boy in 1910s England carries love-messages, emotions he
only dimly understands)*

CONFUSED EMOTIONS

Willa **CATHER, MY ANTONIA**
*(daughter of 19th-century Bohemian immigrants growing
up in rural Nebraska)*

Paul **THEROUX, FONG AND THE INDIANS**
(Indian shopkeeper struggling to survive in rural, tribal Africa)

Ruth Prawer **JHABVALA, HEAT AND DUST**
(Englishwoman contrasts modern India with her aunt's 1920s experience)

Henry **JAMES, THE AMBASSADORS**
*(Rich 1900s Americans take 'culture' to Europe, find it more civilised
than they expected)*

BETWEEN TWO WORLDS

John **LE CARRÉ, THE PERFECT SPY**
(memoirs of elderly double agent, trying to discover where his loyalty lies)

James **CLAVELL, SHÔGUN**
(American becomes samurai in 17th-century Japan)

Paul **SCOTT, STAYING ON**
(plight of English in India after independence)

Peter **VANSITTART, THREE SIX SEVEN**
*(Romanised Britons watching advance of barbarism after 4th century collapse
of Roman power)*

TWILIGHT OF EMPIRE

P.H. **NEWBY, THE PICNIC AT SAKKARA**
(English teacher in 1950s Egypt confused by collapse of British Empire)

Morris **WEST, THE AMBASSADOR**
(US ambassador in Vietnam, appalled by his country's actions there)

Gerald **SEYMOUR, FIELD OF BLOOD**
(undercover SAS officer hunts IRA suspect in present-day Belfast)

A PASSAGE TO INDIA · *(1924)*

Adela Quested leaves for India to get to know her fiancé Ronny before she marries him. Her openness of manner, and especially the way she treats Indians as equals, offends the stuffy British community. For her part, she is overwhelmed by India, and her stupefaction leads her to a moment of mental confusion during which she accuses an Indian friend, Dr Aziz, of molesting her on a visit to the Malabar Caves. In court, oppressed by the certainty of the English that Aziz must be guilty, she reruns the events at Malabar in her mind, and suddenly recants. Her behaviour has, however, made apparent the unbridgeable gulf between Indians and English under the Raj, not to mention the lack of communication between 'free spirits' such as herself and her more hidebound contemporaries.

Forster's other fiction includes the novel Maurice *(about a homosexual friendship; written in the 1910s but not published until the 1970s) and three collections of short stories,* Celestial Omnibus, The Eternal Moment *and* The Life to Come.

▶ **Fascinating books showing culture-clash going the other way** (people used to 'abroad' being discomforted by contemporary Britain): ▷Paul Theroux, *The Black House*; ▷P.H. Newby, *Leaning in the Wind.*

FORSYTH, Frederick · *(born 1938)*
British novelist.

Forsyth worked as a BBC reporter and a war correspondent, and his thrillers are as immediate and waffle-free as good news-stories. They often include real people and events; only the hair-trigger tension of his plots makes actuality look tame. In *The Odessa File* (1972), for example, a journalist covering the hunt for a war-criminal uncovers a nazi arms-smuggling conspiracy to help Arab terrorists in Israel. The details are fiction, but the story is as fresh as this morning's news.

Forsyth's novels are The Day of the Jackal, The Devil's Alternative, The Fourth Protocol *and* The Dogs of War. The Shepherd *is a short novel;* No Comebacks *collects short stories.*

> READ ON

▶ Walter Wager, *Telefon.* ▷Ted Allbeury, *The Crossing.* Daniel Easterman, *The Seventh Sanctuary.*

FOWLES, John · *(born 1926)*
British novelist.

Obsession and delusion are Fowles' main themes. The deranged hero of *The Collector* 'collects' a pretty girl as one might a butterfly. The heroes of *Daniel Martin* and *Mantissa* are authors deserted by the Muse, one a screenwriter corrupted by success, the other a novelist undergoing crea-

> READ ON

● *The Magus* (revised version): about a man trying obsessively to find out if what he thinks he experiences tive therapy at the hands (and other parts) of a seductive, feminist goddess. *A Maggot*, set in the 18th century, re-works a real-life murder investigation to take in erotic obsession, witchcraft, religious mania and flying saucers. Fowles further blurs the boundary between 'truth' and 'fiction' by using experimental techniques. He shifts between past and present, makes authorial asides and comments, and gives us two, three or half a dozen alternative versions of the same events. As with ▷Durrell, this experimentalism is coupled with ornate prose (sometimes in brilliant imitation of 18th and 19th century styles); few modern best-selling writers offer such a packed experience.

THE FRENCH LIEUTENANT'S WOMAN • *(1969)*

The book's heart is a straightforward 19th-century story about the obsessive love-affair between a rich man and an outcast, the 'French Lieutenant's Woman' of the title. They meet in the seaside town of Lyme Regis; their affair scandalises society; she runs away; he pursues her. Fowles' prose, likewise, is for much of the time straightforward and solid in the 19th-century manner. But he also plays games with the reader. He keeps interrupting the story to tell us things about Lyme Regis (home of Mary Anning the fossil-collector), Darwin, Freudian psychology and the social customs of Victorian London. He claims that he has no idea what will happen next, that this is the characters' story, not his. He supplies alternative endings, so that we can choose our own. These devices give the book an unexpectedness in marked contrast to its sober 19th-century heart – it is as if someone reading us ▷Eliot or ▷Thackeray kept breaking off to perform conjuring tricks.

Apart from novels, Fowles has published a story-collection, The Ebony Tower, *and* The Aristos, *a set of philosophical meditations.*

FRANCIS, Dick • *(born 1920)*
British novelist.

Francis writes brilliantly-paced, characterful thrillers, most of them about blackmail, fraud and revenge among jockeys, owners, trainers, bookies and others involved in the racing business. In *Break In* (1986), for example, champion steeplechaser Kit Fielding sets out to discover why someone is trying to ruin his brother-in-law, the trainer Bobby Allardeck – and at once himself becomes the target of newspaper smears, bribery, entrapment and attempted murder.

is real or fantasy. Much of it involves magic, and takes place on a mysterious Greek island – or seems to, for our perception of 'truth' and 'fiction' is as shifting as the character's.

▶ To *The French Lieutenant's Woman*: John Barth, *The Sotweed Factor*; John Berger, *G*; ▷William Golding, *Rites of Passage*; Thornton Wilder, *The Bridge of San Luis Rey*.

▶ To *The Magus*: ▷Lawrence Durrell, *The Dark Labyrinth/ Cefalù*; D.M. Thomas, *The White Hotel*.

> READ ON >

▶ Grant Adamson, *Wild Justice*. ▷Jeffrey Archer, *A Matter of Honour*. Nicholas Freeling, *The Dresden Green*.

Francis' novels include Dead Cert, Blood Sport, Forfeit, Bonecrack, Slay-Ride, Risk, Whip Hand *and* Proof. The Sport of Queens *is autobiography, fascinating about his own racing days.*

FRANKLIN, Miles • *(1879–1954)*
Australian novelist.

'Miles Franklin' was one of the pseudonyms of Stella Miles Franklin. She wrote optimistic tales of pioneer farming life in Australia, in a cheerful, bustling style; her novels are like literary patchwork quilts. Under the name Miles Franklin she is best-known for *My Brilliant Career* (1901), its sequel *My Career Goes Bung* (1946) – the story of a breathlessly enthusiastic adolescent, Sybylla Melvyn, as she learns about life, the arts and love on outback farms and in the big city – and *All That Swagger* (1936), a more serious panorama of outback life. Under a second pseudonym, 'Brent of Bin Bin', Franklin published six lighter novels on the same lines, 'snapshots of ordinary life' modelled on the writings of ▷Mark Twain. Their titles are *Up the Country, Ten Creeks Run, Back to Bool Bool, Cockatoos, Prelude to Waking,* and *Gentlemen at Gyang Gyang.* One editor (Carmen Callil) called her an 'unsophisticated genius', prone to 'ebullient outpourings'; the description is exact.

Franklin's other books under her own name include the novels Some Everyday Folk and Dawn, Old Blastus of Bandicoot *and* Bring the Monkey *and the autobiographical memoir* Childhood at Brindabella. *Under the pseudonym 'Mrs Ogniblat l'Artsau' she published one novel,* The Net of Circumstance.

FREEMANTLE, Brian • *(born 1936)*
British novelist.

As well as his own name, Freemantle uses the pseudonyms Richard Gant and Leslie Street. His books include thrillers (*Goodbye to an Old Friend; Face Me When You Walk Away*) and a series of spoof spy-stories (eg *Clap Hands, Here Comes Charlie*) featuring the amiable down-and-out Charlie Muffin, whose past life and whose character are as fascinating as the missions he undertakes.

READ ON ▷

▶ ▷Mark Twain, *The Adventures of Tom Sawyer.* H.E. Bates, *The Darling Buds of May.* Betty MacDonald, *The Egg and I.* Laura Ingalls Wilder, *The Little House on the Prairie.*

▶ **Exactly matching Franklin's bouncy, happy style, though its theme and location are entirely different:** ▷Jerome K. Jerome, *Three Men in a Boat.*

READ ON ▷

▶ ▷Len Deighton, *Horse Under Water.* Roy Lewis, *A Certain Blindness.* Sara Woods, *Cry Guilty.* John Wainwright, *All On a Summer's Day.*

FRIENDS (?) AND NEIGHBOURS
(gossip; bitchiness; one-up-manship)
▷E.F. Benson, *Mapp and Lucia*
▷Peter De Vries, *The Mackerel Plaza*
▷Mrs Gaskell, *Cranford*
▷Sinclair Lewis, *Main Street*
▷Barbara Pym, *A Glass of Blessings*
▷John Updike, *Couples*

The Human Comedy (p 124)

FUTURE SOCIETIES

▷Margaret Atwood, *The Handmaid's Tale*
▷Angela Carter, *The Passion of New Eve*
▷Robert Graves, *Seven Days in New Crete*
▷Aldous Huxley, *Brave New World*
▷Walter M. Miller, *A Canticle for Leibowitz*
▷William Morris, *News from Nowhere*
▷George Orwell, *1984*
▷George Turner, *The Sea and Summer*
▷John Wyndham, *The Chrysalids*

Fantasy Societies (p 73)

G

GALSWORTHY, John • *(1867–1933)*
British novelist and playwright.

In the 1960s an adaptation of Galsworthy's *The Forsyte Saga* was the most popular British TV series ever shown till then. It spawned a thousand imitations – series and books about rich families quarrelling over multi-million pound businesses and living wretched private lives have become a genre in themselves. Some critics say that this is unfair to Galsworthy, who was regarded as a heavyweight writer in his day (of plays as well as novels). But although he intended his first Forsyte book (*The Man of Property*) as a serious novel, as soon as the Forsytes became popular he quite happily extended it into a saga, adding another dozen novels and short stories.

THE FORSYTE SAGA • *(1922)*
This contains three novels and two short stories. Its subject is the way money-making and commercial endeavour atrophy the emotions. Three generations of Forsytes are morally tainted by their family's business success, in particular Soames and his unhappy wife Irene. Every boardroom victory is balanced by a bedroom defeat; children inherit not only wealth, but the poisoned character which goes with it. There is more than a whiff of Victorian moralising about it all: in Galsworthy the bad always end unhappily (and so do the good). But unlike many later family-business sagas, his books offer three-dimensional characters, and he is particularly good at showing the ebb and flow of relationships between the sexes. *To Let*, the third volume of the saga, a Romeo and Juliet story with a devastating final twist, is a fine example of this, one of Galsworthy's most satisfying books.

Apart from the Forsyte books (two trilogies – The Forsyte

> **READ ON**

● *A Modern Comedy.*
▶ ▷Anthony Trollope, *Can You Forgive Her?* (and its sequels: the 'Palliser' family saga). ▷Thomas Mann, *Buddenbrooks* (an equally withering, but jollier, account of the decline of a powerful mercantile family). ▷C.P. Snow, *The Conscience of the Rich* (a moving study of the son of a family dynasty at odds with his parents). ▷Henry James, *The Spoils of Poynton* (a study of property as 'the middle-class deity'). ▷Christina Stead, *House of All Nations.*
▶ **Of the dozens of family-business blockbusters which followed the TV success of *The Forsyte Saga,* the juiciest are** Harold Robbins, *The Adventurers*; ▷Judith Krantz, *Princess Daisy*

Saga; A Modern Comedy – *and the short-story collections* Four Forsyte Stories *and* On Forsyte Change*), Galsworthy's novels include* The Island Pharisee, Fraternity *and the trilogy* End of the Chapter, *a saga about the Charwell family (cousins of the Forsytes).*

GASKELL, Mrs (Elizabeth Cleghorn) •
(1810–65)
British novelist.

For a century after her death, Gaskell was chiefly remembered for a biography of her friend ▷Charlotte Brontë, and for *Cranford*, a gently malicious book about middle-class life in a provincial town. (It reads like a collaboration between ▷Austen and ▷Trollope, without being quite as good as either.) But she was actually a novelist of a far tougher kind. She was a friend of ▷Dickens and ▷Eliot, and shared their interest in social themes, particularly the way men treat women and the plight of the urban poor. She lived in Manchester, and wrote pungently about life among the 'dark Satanic mills' (as Blake had called them) which her southern readers had till then imagined were figments of the revolutionary imagination. Her novels were discussed in Parliament and led to social reform, a result which greatly pleased her. They survive today less as social documents than as powerful stories of people struggling against their environment or the indifference of others.

MARY BARTON • *(1848)*
Mary's father is a mill-hand employed by the unfeeling Henry Carson. He is also a staunch fighter for workers' rights. When the mill-owners ignore their workers' requests for better treatment, the men decide to murder Carson as a warning to his class, and nominate Barton to fire the gun. Mary's beloved Jem Wilson is arrested for the crime, and Mary has to face the agony of proving his innocence by incriminating her father.

Gaskell's novels Ruth, Cousin Phyllis *and* Wives and Daughters *concern the relationship between the sexes.* Sylvia's Lovers, *an unsmiling tale set in 18th-century Whitby, is about a man snatched by the press gang.* Mary Barton *and* North and South *are about class war.* Lois the Witch, *a long short story, is set during the Salem witch-hunts of the 17th century.*

and ▷Barbara Taylor Bradford, *A Woman of Substance.*

READ ON ⟩

● *North and South* (in which a southern minister goes to preach God's word in a northern mill-town, and his wife and daughter become involved in the class-struggle – a concern greatly complicated when the daughter falls in love with a mill-owner's son).

▶ ▷Charlotte Brontë, *Shirley.* ▷Charles Dickens, *Hard Times.* ▷Émile Zola, *Germinal.* ▷Arnold Bennett, *Clayhanger.* ▷D.H. Lawrence, *Sons and Lovers.* ▷Jack London, *The People of the Abyss* (about slum life), David Storey, *Radcliffe* and Upton Sinclair, *The Jungle* carry Gaskell's themes into the 20th century.

▶ Lewis Grassic Gibbon, *A Scots Quair* (partly in Scots dialect, but comprehensible) is a saga of three generations coping with harsh conditions, on West highland crofts and in industrial Glasgow during the 1920s General Strike.

GIDE, André • *(1861–1951)*

French novelist, poet and non-fiction writer.

In Plato's dialogues, Socrates tries to reach the core of a philosophical argument by elimination: each wrong assumption, each false trail is considered and rejected until what is left is 'truth'. Gide admired Plato – his favourite among his own works was *Corydon*, a set of four Platonic dialogues discussing homosexuality – and he used Socrates' methods in his fiction. His heroes seek the truth about themselves, the core of their being, and they do it by considering and rejecting all religious, social, sexual and intellectual conventions. Sometimes a quest results in the happiness of self-knowledge, but often the young men – Gide was not over-interested in young women – find, when they reach the core of themselves, that there is nothing there at all. Gide's contemporaries found his moral stripteases shocking, and condemned him as a pornographer; nowadays the most striking thing about his books is their spare, limpid style, which makes even more startling the things they say.

THE IMMORALIST • *(1902)*

Michel, a young intellectual, nearly dies of tuberculosis, and his brush with death changes his character. He rejects his former convention-ridden life in favour of living each moment for itself, of doing exactly what he pleases. As his personality flowers, that of his beloved wife begins to wither, leaving him to agonise over whether his actions have led to psychic liberation or to a surrender to selfishness.

Gide's other fiction includes Strait is the Gate *(La porte étroite),* The Vatican Cellars, Isabelle, The Pastoral Symphony *(La Symphonie pastorale) and* The Counterfeiters. *His non-fiction works on similar themes include* If it Die *(Si le grain ne meurt),* Et nunc manet in te/Madeleine *and* Journals.

GOETHE, Johann Wolfgang von •
(1749–1832)

German writer of novels, poems, plays and non-fiction.

Goethe's genius expressed itself in restless intellectual en-

---

> **READ ON**

● *Strait is the Gate*; *The Pastoral Symphony*. *The Vatican Cellars* is a more extrovert, ironic romp involving murder, the kidnapping of the Pope and a frantic chase across Europe. *The Counterfeiters* is about a group of secondary schoolboys in Paris, their adolescent friendships and the adults who initiate them into grown-up life.

▶ **To Gide's short, philosophical books:** ▷Hermann Hesse, *Peter Camenzind*; Joris-Karl Huysmans, *Against Nature*; Frederick Rolfe, *The Desire and Pursuit of the Whole*; ▷Aldous Huxley, *Eyeless in Gaza*.

▶ **To** *The Counterfeiters*: ▷Colette, *A Lesson in Love*; ▷Marcel Proust, *Cities of the Plain* (the fourth part of *Remembrance of Things Past*).

▶ **More modern books on Gidean themes:** ▷Iris Murdoch, *The Flight from the Enchanter*; Ian McEwan, *The Comfort of Strangers*.

> **READ ON**

● *The Travels of Wilhelm Meister* takes Meister

ergy: he never heard an idea without wanting to develop it. He took the nearest convenient form – Shakespearean or Greek tragedy, letters, biography – and crammed it with philosophical and political reflections, discussions and suggestions. During his lifetime he was regarded as an innovator, forming European thought; by hindsight he seems rather to have caught ideas in the air – humanism, romanticism, political libertarianism – expanded them and given them wide circulation. Like Shakespeare, he distilled the spirit of his age – and this feeling, the sense that in reading him we are communing with the 18th and early 19th centuries at their sanest and most stimulating, is one of the main pleasures of his work.

THE APPRENTICESHIP OF WILHELM MEISTER •
(1796)

This enormously long, leisurely novel is the spiritual and moral 'biography' of Wilhelm Meister. As a young man, fascinated by the stage (and by Marianne, an actress), he gives up his business career and runs away to join an acting company. He takes part enthusiastically in their lives, and observes both their sorrows (symbolised by the brutal treatment of Mignon by her trapeze-artist 'protector') and their triumphs (symbolised by a production of Hamlet in which he takes part). He decides that this life – 'the world' – is not for him, and leaves. In the castle of Lothario he experiences both earthly pleasures ('the flesh') and religious conversion ('the spirit') and rejects them. Finally, matured by all his experiences, he decides to devote his life to education, to passing on all he knows, 'the balance that makes a human being', to his young son.

Goethe is best-known for his poetry, and for such plays as Egmont, Iphigenie in Tauris, Götz von Berlichingen/Ironhand *and* Faust. *Apart from* Wilhelm Meister, *his novels are* The Sorrows of Young Werther *and* Elective Affinities.

and his son on a ramble through Europe. They sample every kind of human society, and their experiences make this book a reflection on 'manners' and politics, just as *The Apprenticeship of Wilhelm Meister* dealt with individual human personality. *The Sorrows of Young Werther*, in letter-form, tells the story of a young man tormented by love for his friend's fiancée. *Elective Affinities* is a heartless, amoral book (anticipating ▷Gide) about a married couple each of whom has a love-affair.

▶ **To Wilhelm Meister:** ▷Miguel de Cervantes Saavedra: *Don Quixote.* ▷Thomas Mann, *The Magic Mountain.*

▶ **To *Elective Affinities*:** ▷George Eliot, *Daniel Deronda*; ▷Christina Stead, *The Man Who Loved Children.*

▶ **To *The Sorrows of Young Werther*:** ▷Hermann Hesse, *Gertrud.* Thomas Love Peacock, *Nightmare Abbey* sends up the 'Werther syndrome', the idea that the only way to be a true romantic hero, or a creative artist, is to tell the world every detail of the anguish in your soul.

GOGOL, Nikolai Vasilevich • *(1809–52)*
Russian writer of novels, short stories and plays.

The despair which seems to hover over much Russian fiction was replaced in Gogol by hilarity: he was a 20th-century surrealist ahead of his time, a forerunner of ▷Kafka and Ionesco. His best-known work, the stage-farce *The Government Inspector*, is about a confidence trickster mistaken for a high official by a village of pompous fools. In one of his stories a nose takes on a malign, satirical life independent of its owner's will; in another a man saves for years to buy a new coat, only to be mugged and robbed the first time he wears it. Gogol's preferred form was the short story: he was terrified of writer's block. He struggled for a dozen years to finish his one long book, *Dead Souls*, and in 1852, convinced by a religious adviser that the second (unpublished) half of the book was 'sinful' and that if he went on writing he would go to hell, he burned the manuscript and fasted until he died.

DEAD SOULS • *(1842)*
In 19th-century Russia landowners estimated their wealth not only by the acres they owned, but also by the number of their serfs, or slaves. Chichikov, a confidence-trickster, realises that serfs who die between official censuses are not legally dead until the next census, and so still count as property. He travels the length and breadth of Russia, buying 'dead souls' from landowners, and becomes – on paper at least – one of the wealthiest men in the country. Gogol uses this simple story as the basis for a set of farcical character-studies: he saw the book as a portrait-gallery of contemporary Russia, and filled it with short, self-contained comic episodes. He also wrote, with ironical pointedness, that Chichikov's journey stands for the journey of every human being through life: we move on, never sure of what is coming next, relieved each time that whatever it was we did, we got away with it.

Gogol's most surreal short stories are 'Diary of a Madman', 'Nevski Prospekt', 'The Portrait', 'The Nose *and* The Overcoat'. *His collections* Evenings on a Farm, Mirgorod *and* Arabesques *are more farce than surrealism, short sketches about tongue-tied suitors, credulous peasants and feather-headed, pretty girls.*

GOLDING, William • *(born 1911)*
British novelist.

From his first novel (*Lord of the Flies*, 1954, about choir-

READ ON ▷

▶ Gogol's sinister brilliance is matched in the short stories of ▷Kafka, Saki and Roald Dahl; his gentler comic stories are like ▷Chekhov's.
▶ **Good follow-ups to Dead Souls:** Ivan Goncharov, *Oblomov* (about a man so alienated from the world that he decides to spend the rest of his life in bed); ▷Franz Kafka, *America*; ▷Jaroslav Hašek, *The Good Soldier Švejk*; Bernard Malamud, *The Fixer*; Miguel de Cervantes Saavedra, *Don Quixote*.

READ ON ▷

● *The Inheritors* (a

LORD OF THE FLIES (*choirboys lost on desert island revert to satanic evil, humanity's dark side*)

Daniel **DEFOE, ROBINSON CRUSOE**
(*18th-century shipwrecked sailor builds new life on desert island*)

Jonathan **SWIFT, GULLIVER'S TRAVELS**
(*18th-century sailor tries to teach European 'culture' in fantasy lands he visits*)

James Vance **MARSHALL, WALKABOUT**
(*English children marooned in Australian outback, taught survival by Aboriginal boy*)

SURVIVING

Susan **HILL, I'M THE KING OF THE CASTLE**
(*devil-child, jealous of rival, torments the life from him*)

Stephen **KING, CARRIE**
(*bullied girl in junior high school uses Devil's power to take revenge*)

EVIL AND CHILDREN

John **WYNDHAM, THE MIDWICH CUCKOOS**
(*alien race seeks to capture England by breeding race of hyper-intelligent, soulless children*)

Henry **JAMES, THE TURN OF THE SCREW**
(*neurotic governess tries to protect two innocent charges against half-sensed, wholly evil ghosts*)

Fay **WELDON, THE HEART OF ENGLAND**
(*evil forces in Glastonbury countryside interfere with yuppie lives*)

John **UPDIKE, THE WITCHES OF EASTWICK**
(*bored Connecticut housewives play with witchcraft — and raise the Devil*)

THE DEVIL

James **BLISH, BLACK EASTER**
(*nuclear scientist enlists Devil's help in bringing about Armageddon*)

Patrick **WHITE, VOSS**
(*half-crazy explorer leads doomed 19th-century expedition into heart of Australia*)

Joseph **CONRAD, HEART OF DARKNESS**
(*African jungle used as metaphor for the evil in humanity*)

THE WILDERNESS

C.S. **LEWIS, PERELANDRA**
(*battle for survival — and against unrelenting evil — on the empty planet Venus*)

Brian **MOORE, THE BLACK ROBE**
(*17th-century Jesuit among 17th-century Indians: bloody, hopeless culture-clash*)

boys reverting to savagery after being marooned on a desert island) onwards, Golding has explored the dark side of human nature. He believes that homo sapiens is corrupt, that we destroy more than we create, that we are devilish without redemption. But instead of baldly stating this philosophy, he dresses it in allegories of the most unusual and fantastical kind. He pictures the devil engulfing not only choirboys on an island, but also (in other novels) a drowning sailor, a tribe of neanderthal people, the dean of a medieval cathedral, a boy growing up in 1960s Britain, and a group of 18th-century people sailing towards Australia. He evokes these situations with absolute conviction: few writers are better at suggesting the feel, taste, smell and sound of things, the texture of experience.

THE SPIRE • *(1964)*

Inspired by a vision, medieval Dean Jocelin commissions for his cathedral a 400-foot spire. He intends it as proof of human aspiration towards God; his enemies see it as a symbol of vanity, the devil's work; the master-builder points out that as the cathedral's foundations are inadequate, the tower will bring the whole building crashing down. Jocelin over-rides all objections, the work proceeds – Golding gives fascinating, vertigo-inducing detail of medieval building techniques – and the higher the spire rises the more people are destroyed. In the end the struggle between God and the devil takes over Jocelin's own self. In truly medieval manner, his brain and body become a battleground, and the issue moves from the tower to questions of his own moral integrity and saintliness.

Golding's novels are Lord of the Flies, Pincher Martin, Free Fall, The Spire, The Pyramid, Darkness Visible, Rites of Passage *and its sequel* Close Quarters, *and* The Paper Men. The Scorpion God *is a collection of three long stories, one based on his stage-comedy* The Brass Butterfly, *about a crazy inventor trying to interest a decadent Roman ruler of Egypt in steam power.*

brilliantly-imagined story of the coming of homo sapiens, seen from the standpoint of the gentle ape-people they exterminate).
▶ ▷Hermann Hesse, *Narziss and Goldmund* (which parallels both the good/evil theme and the medieval craft-background of *The Spire*). John Barth, *Giles Goat-boy* (a fantasy, partly satirical, about a professor who brings a child up with no company but goats, trying to avoid contaminating him with human original sin). ▷Anthony Burgess, *Earthly Powers*. Umberto Eco, *The Name of the Rose*.

GOOD AND EVIL
(the Devil at large)

Mikhail Bulgakov, *The Master and Margharita*
▷John Fowles, *A Maggot*
▷Stephen King, *Carrie*
Ian McEwan, *The Comfort of Strangers*
Neville Shulman, *Exit of a Dragonfly*
▷I.B. Singer, *Satan in Goray*
▷John Updike, *The Witches of Eastwick*

▷Fay Weldon, *The Life and Loves of a She-Devil*

Something Nasty . . . (p 224)

GORDIMER, Nadine • *(1923)*
South African novelist and short-story writer.

Gordimer makes life in South Africa (and especially among the tormented liberal whites who are her main characters) an objective background for subjective choice. Her concerns are the diversity of human nature, and the way our moral and psychological personality is revealed in what we do. She also, magnificently, evokes the vastness and beauty of Africa. Like other South African writers (notably Alan Paton and Laurens van der Post). she gives the continent a kind of mystical identity; its indigenous inhabitants understand this completely, but it gives the incoming whites (who can only dimly perceive it) an unsettling sense of their own inadequacy, as if they are made second-class citizens not by other people's laws but by the very place they live in.

A SPORT OF NATURE • *(1987)*
From adolescence rich, white Hillela is dominated by politics and sex, and combines the two: sex is a source of power, politics give orgasmic satisfaction. She is attracted by, and attracts, powerful men of all professions and races – and progressively moves out of the orbit of whites to a leading position in the black revolutionary movement. The book ends with the success of the revolution, the establishment of majority rule – and with doubts sown in the reader's mind about Hillela herself. Has she really identified as wholly with the blacks as she hoped, or does she remain the 'sport of nature', or freak, of the book's title?

Gordimer's other novels are The Lying Days, A World of Strangers, Occasion for Loving, The Late Bourgeois World, A Guest of Honour, Burger's Daughter, The Conservationist *and* July's People. *Her story-collections include* Not For Publication, Livingstone's Companions *and* A Soldier's Embrace.

READ ON ▷

● *The Late Bourgeois World* (a grim study of white liberals in a police state. Max, tortured into betraying his friends, commits suicide, and Liz (his divorced wife) is left to choose between continuing in bourgeois complacency, doing nothing about the situation but wring her hands, and joining the black revolutionary movement).
▶ André Brink, *Rumours of Rain* (about redneck Afrikanerdom). J.M. Coetzee, *In the Heart of the Country*. David Caute, *News From Nowhere* (about a liberal journalist covering the events which led to the establishment of Zimbabwe). ▷Isabel Allende, *Of Love and Shadows*. ▷John Le Carré, *The Little Drummer Girl*. Alan Paton, *Cry, the Beloved Country* (a moving book about ancient Zulu culture and the discord brought by invading whites; it is mirrored, from a different point of view, by ▷Chinua Achebe, *Things Fall Apart*).

GORKY, Maxim • *(1868–1936)*
Russian writer of novels, short stories and plays.

'Gorky' (bitter) is the pen name of Aleksei Maksimovich Peshkov – and in view of his childhood, few names could have been more appropriate. He was left to fend for himself at the age of eight, and spent his childhood as a barge-hand, washer-up, thief, beggar, tramp and journalist. This 'apprenticeship', as he called it, affected the style and content of his writing. He saw himself as a colleague and heir of ▷Dostoevsky and ▷Tolstoy, and aimed to write the same kind of panoramic, allegorical works as theirs. But whereas their world was that of landowners and the bourgeoisie, his was one of serfs, vagabonds, criminals and other members of what he called society's 'lower depths'. He despised the middle class, and wrote with contempt of their dependence on money, gentility and religion, the very forces which were destroying them. His preoccupations led him to friendship with Lenin, and to enthusiastic support for the 1917 revolution. Many of his post-1917 books are grandiose and propagandist, and his revolutionary sympathies have diminished his reputation in capitalist countries. But his early work places him squarely in the company of the great 19th-century writers he admired.

FOMA GORDEEV • *(1899)*
Foma, the son of an illiterate barge-owner who has made a fortune conveying goods on the Volga, has been brought up in his godfather's cultured, bourgeois home. His father tries to take him into the business, to educate him in the ways of the world, and for a time Foma thrives. But when the old man dies and he inherits, his head is turned and he lives a life of increasing debauchery, ending up as a lunatic and a drunkard. He is a man without identity: he takes on the moral colouring of the society around him, and is destroyed.

Gorky is known for plays (such as The Lower Depths *and* Smug Citizens*) as well as for prose fiction. His novels include* Mother, Foma Gordeev, The Artamonov Affair, The Life of Klim Samgin *and the post-revolutionary tetralogy* Bystander, The Magnet, Other Fires *and* The Spectre. *His short stories are headed by* 'Twenty-six Men and a Girl', *which normally gives its name to collections. His best-known work, in or out of the USSR, is the autobiographical trilogy* My Childhood, My Apprenticeship *and* My Universities.

READ ON ▷

● *Yegor Bulitchev and Others* (a black comedy about a dying merchant fawned on by hypocrites who anticipate rich pickings when he dies). *My Childhood* (the first volume of Gorky's autobiography, a scalding account of his life as a barge-hand, the background to Foma Gordeev).
▶ ▷Fyodor Dostoevsky, *The Gambler* (a harsh account of aristocratic folly and obsession in Tsarist Russia, the kind of decadence Gorky vociferously denounced). Jean Genet, *Querelle of Brest* (the story of a boy's brutal upbringing among criminals and gansters in France between the two world wars). ▷Jerome Weidman, *I Can Get It For You Wholesale* (about a young man making his way by guile in the business world of post-Depression New York – and the moral disintegration of character which is the price he pays).

GRAHAM, Winston • *(born 1911)*
British novelist.

Although Graham has written books of many kinds, from historical romances to thrillers, he is best-known for the brooding, atmospheric 'Poldark' saga, about feuding families in 18th and 19th century Cornwall. The first Poldark book was *Ross Poldark/Renegade*, and the series includes *Demelza*, *Jeremy Poldark*, *Warleggan/The Last Gamble* and *The Black Moon*. Graham's best-known thriller is *Greek Fire*.

READ ON ▷

▶ ▷Emily Brontë, *Wuthering Heights*. Arthur Quiller-Couch('Q'), *Troy Town*. ▷Daphne Du Maurier, *My Cousin Rachel*. R.D. Blackmore, *Lorna Doone*.

GRASS, Günter • *(born 1927)*
German writer of novels, plays and non-fiction.

In his twenties Grass worked as a graphic artist, stage designer and jazz musician; he took up writing full-time only after his novel *The Tin Drum* was a best-seller, when he was 32. Politics are the main subject of his books: he grapples with what has happened in Germany over the last half-century, and what is happening now. He uses a framework of absurdity, blending real events with wild black fantasy, collapsing history (so that time is like a well from which you draw not systematically but at random), and making his characters allegorical figures like the people in cartoons. The leading character in *The Tin Drum* (1959), for example, symbolising the German people, is a child who chooses to stop growing at the age of three, and who spends forty years banging a toy drum and giggling as the procession of nazism and post-war reconstruction passes by. For Grass, the human condition is 'absurd': not only ridiculous but morally and philosophically out of focus. His books offer no solutions, but they point out the problems with enormous, malicious glee.

THE FLOUNDER • *(1977)*
The wife and husband from a Grimm fairy-tale move through the entire history of the human race, popping up in this period or that, playing each role by the conventions of its time, and endlessly, affably arguing about gender dominance. They are aided or hindered by a talking fish from the same fairy-tale: it takes now her side, now his. Finally the fish is ordered to defend itself before a late 20th-century feminist tribunal, and the whole male/female business is thrashed out in a hearing as preposterous as the trial in Alice in Wonderland. The fact that this book is about sexual rather than German politics makes it one of Grass's most accessible novels to non-German readers, and it is also wonderfully enlivened with puns, poems, satires

READ ON ▷

▶ *The Tin Drum* is the most accessible of the 'Danzig' novels, and although its theme (nazism) gives it a harsher tone than *The Flounder*, it is equally hilarious and bizarre.

▶ **Other books similarly reinventing the human race, tossing all human knowledge and invention into a single fantastic melting-pot:**
▷Thornton Wilder, *The Eighth Day*; ▷Kurt Vonnegut, *Galápagos*; ▷J.G. Ballard, *The Unlimited Dream Company*; ▷Michèle Roberts, *The Book of Mrs Noah*.

and recipes. The pleasures of human life have not had such a going-over since ▷Rabelais.

Grass's other novels include the 'Danzig trilogy' (The Tin Drum, Dog Years and Local Anaesthetic), From the Diary of a Snail, Cat and Mouse, The Meeting at Telgte, Headbirths and The Rat.

GRAVES, Robert • *(1895–1985)*
British novelist, poet and non-fiction writer.

Graves' main interests were myth and poetry. He wrote a best-selling version of the Greek myths, a controversial account of the Bible stories as myth, and *The White Goddess* (1948–52), a study of poetic inspiration. Throughout his life he composed poetry (much of it autobiographical), and his love-poems in particular are much admired. He claimed that his novels were potboilers, written to finance 'real' work, but their quality and craftsmanship belie this description. Most are historical, reimagining characters of the past – from the author of the *Odyssey* to Jesus – as people with markedly 20th-century sensibilities, able to view the events of their own lives, as it were, with hindsight. His books are like psychological documentaries, as if we are looking directly into his characters' minds.

I, CLAUDIUS • *(1934)*
This novel and its sequel *Claudius the God* purport to be the autobiography of the fourth Roman emperor. A spastic and an epileptic, he is regarded by everyone as a fool and ignored; he thus survives the myriad political and dynastic intrigues of the first 50 years of the Roman empire, the reigns of his three dangerous predecessors. He is finally made emperor himself, in a palace coup – and proceeds to rule with a blend of wisdom, guile and ruthlessness which he describes with fascinated relish. The story ends – typically for Graves – with a real document, an account by a Roman satirist of the 'Pumpkinification of Claudius', the arrival of the stammering, limping fool of an emperor in Olympus, home of the gods and of his own terrifying, deified relatives.

Graves' other novels include Count Belisarius *(set in 6th-century Byzantium),* Sergeant Lamb of the Ninth *and* Proceed, Sergeant Lamb *(about the American War of Independence),* Wife to Mr Milton *(set in Puritan England, and written in a brilliant pastiche of 17th-century prose),* Homer's Daughter *(set in prehistoric Greece), and* King Jesus *(about the life and death of Christ).* Seven Days in

READ ON ▷

● *The Golden Fleece/ Hercules My Shipmate* (a novelised account of the expedition of Jason and the Argonauts to find the Golden Fleece, with ingenious, rational explanations of such magic events as the escape from the Clashing Rocks, the yoking of bronze bulls and the sowing of serpents' teeth).

▶ **To *I, Claudius*:** ▷Mary Renault, *The King Must Die*; Marguerite Yourcenar, *Memoirs of Hadrian*; Naomi Mitchison, *The Corn King and the Spring Queen*; Joan Grant, *Winged Pharaoh*.

▶ **Classical works, close to Graves for exuberance of imagination:** Herodotus, *Histories*; Petronius, *Satyricon*.

▶ **Books of similar gusto, on non-classical subjects:** Frederick Rolfe, *Hadrian the Seventh* (about a waspish inadequate – not even a priest – who is elected Pope); Augusto Roa Bastos, *I The Supreme* (the fantasy-

Robert **GRAVES**

Norman **MAILER, ANCIENT EVENINGS**
(memories of chief minister of warrior-pharaoh Rameses II)

Gore **VIDAL, CREATION**
('memoirs' of Persian diplomat who knew Socrates, Buddha and Confucius)

Joan **GRANT, WINGED PHARAOH**
(Grant describes her own previous existence in ancient Egypt)

Joseph **HELLER, GOD KNOWS**
('memoirs' of Old Testament King David)

Marguerite **YOURCENAR, MEMOIRS OF HADRIAN**
(reflections of 14th Roman Emperor and philosopher)

Hilda **DOOLITTLE ('H.D.'), HEDYLUS**
(Samos, 3rd century BC: ex-courtesan, lover and poet-son meditate delicately on life, love, the arts and politics)

John **ARDEN, SILENCE AMONG THE WEAPONS**
('memoirs' of actor's agent mixed up with Roman dictator Sulla in 1st century BC)

Peter **VANSITTART, THREE SIX SEVEN**
(twilight of Roman Britain, late 4th century)

Anthony **BURGESS, THE KINGDOM OF THE WICKED**
(Luke, Paul and other early Christian missionaries)

(4th Roman Emperor's 'memoirs' of his bloodthirsty forebears)

Henry **TREECE, MEDEA**
(powerful evocation of myth-witch, scorned wife who murdered her children)

Mary **RENAULT, THE MASK OF APOLLO**
('memoirs' of actor-spy in 4th century BC Greece)

Peter **GREEN, ACHILLES HIS ARMOUR**
(Alcibiades, the Oscar Wilde of ancient Athens)

Mario **VARGAS LLOSA, THE WAR OF THE END OF THE WORLD** *(19th-century South American religious community, communist, waiting for the Apocalypse)*

Augusto Roa **BASTOS, I, THE SUPREME**
('memoirs' of Francia, 19th-century dictator of Paraguay)

Gabriel García **MÁRQUEZ, THE AUTUMN OF THE PATRIARCH** *(deathbed monologue of fanatical, deranged South American dictator)*

Nicholas **MONSARRAT, RUNNING PROUD**
(one of Columbus' sailors shipwrecked in New World, is taken for a god)

Carlos **FUENTES, TERRA NOSTRA**
('memoirs' of Philip II of Spain, in deranged old age)

Stephen **MARLOWE, THE MEMOIRS OF CHRISTOPHER COLUMBUS** *(early disappointments and ironic triumph of unscrupulous adventurer-explorer)*

New Crete *is an urbane future-fantasy, and* Goodbye to All That *is autobiography, moving from a tormented account of Graves' time as an officer in the first world war to malicious glimpses of Oxford life and the literary London of the 1920s.*

autobiography of a 19th-century Paraguayan dictator deranged by power); ▷Gore Vidal, *Kalki* (about an insane Vietnam veteran who imagines himself Kalki, the last avatar of the god Vishnu whose coming will end the present cycle of human existence).

GREAT DETECTIVES

John Dickson Carr, *Death Watch*
▷Agatha Christie, *Death on the Nile*
▷A. Conan Doyle, *The Hound of the Baskervilles*
▷Dorothy L. Sayers, *Murder Must Advertise*
▷Georges Simenon, *Inquest on Bouvet*
Rex Stout, *Plot it Yourself/Murder in Style*

GREENE, Graham • *(born 1904)*
British writer of novels, plays and non-fiction.

In the 1930s Greene wrote several thrillers influenced by ▷Buchan and by action-films of the time: they include *Stamboul Train* (set on the Orient Express), *A Gun for Sale/This Gun for Sale* (about the manhunt for a political assassin) and *The Confidential Agent* (about left-wing politics in a right-wing state). This work culminated in atmospheric filmscripts, of which the best (later novelised) was *The Third Man*. But thrillers – and, later, comedies such as *Our Man in Havana*, *Travels With My Aunt* and *Monsignor Quixote* – always took second place, at least in Greene's own estimation, to his Catholic novels. These are all concerned with people tormented by their own moral failure and by the longing for God's forgiveness. The settings are often the tropics; the political situations are unstable; the heroes are second-rank functionaries despised by their superiors. Two novels, *Brighton Rock* (1938, about a petty criminal in 1930s Brighton) and *The Human Factor* (1978, about the minor-public-school loyalties and betrayals of the British Intelligence Services), set similar searches for grace in a soulless, down-at-heel

> **READ ON**

● *The Power and the Glory* (a lacerating story, set in Mexico during a left-wing revolution, about a drunken, self-hating priest who struggles against his own fear and the persecution of the revolutionaries to take God to the peasants).
▶ 'Psychic thrillers', similarly showing people driven to the edge of breakdown and beyond, by circumstances, their surroundings or consciousness of their own moral failings:

Britain. Despite the Catholic overtones of these books, which non-believers may find unconvincing, Greene's plots are fascinating, and his evocation of character and place is marvellous.

THE HEART OF THE MATTER · (1948)

Scobie, Captain of Police in a God-forsaken African colony during the second world war, is a decent, honest man. His wife Louise, tormented by memories of their dead daughter and by her own isolation from the rest of the British community, begs him to send her away to South Africa – and because of a mixture of pity for her misery and anguish at his inability to make her happy, he breaks police rules and borrows money from a suspected diamond-smuggler. From that lapse onwards, everything Scobie does ends in disaster, and there is nothing he can do but watch himself, appalled but helpless, as he plunges remorselessly towards damnation.

Greene's other novels include The End of the Affair, The Quiet American, A Burnt-out Case, The Comedians, The Honorary Consul *and* Doctor Fischer of Geneva. *His short stories (many of them 'comedies of the sexual life', as he called them) are collected in* Twenty-one Stories *and* May We Borrow Your Husband? *He has also written travel books and plays.*

▷Malcolm Lowry, *Under the Volcano*; ▷Joseph Conrad, *Nostromo*; B. Traven, *The Treasure of the Sierra Madre*; ▷Georges Simenon, *The Stain on the Snow*.
► **Short stories:**
▷Somerset Maugham, *Creatures of Circumstance*; ▷Ernest Hemingway, *Men Without Women*.

GROWING UP: TEENAGERS

  Lynne Reid Banks, *The Writing on the Wall*
▷Elizabeth Bowen, *The Death of the Heart*
▷Willa Cather, *The Song of the Lark*
▷Charles Dickens, *David Copperfield*
▷André Gide, *The Counterfeiters*
▷Rose Macaulay, *They Were Defeated*
▷Mary McCarthy, *Birds of America*
▷Iris Murdoch, *The Flight from the Enchanter*
▷J.D. Salinger, *The Catcher in the Rye*

Adolescence (p 3); Children (p 41); Families: All-engulfing (p 72); Growing Up: Young Adults (p 101)

GROWING UP: YOUNG ADULTS

▷Lisa Alther, *Kinflicks*
▷Ford Madox Ford, *Parade's End*
▷Johann Wolfgang von Goethe, *The Apprenticeship of*

Wilhelm Meister
▷Nadine Gordimer, *A Sport of Nature*
▷Marcel Proust, *Within a Budding Grove* (part 2 of
  Remembrance of Things Past)
▷Philip Roth, *Goodbye, Columbus*
  Charles Webb, *The Graduate*

Growing Up: Teenagers (p 101); 'Only Connect'
(p 183); Perplexed by Life (p 190)

H

HAGGARD, H. Rider (Henry Rider) •
(1856–1925)
British novelist.

Haggard's novels are adventure fantasies set in wildly exotic locations: the geysers and glaciers of Iceland (*Erik Brighteyes*), the South American jungle (*Montezuma's Daughter*) or – most commonly of all – Darkest Africa, a continent of the imagination as fabulous as the setting of Sindbad's adventures in *The Arabian Nights*. In *King Solomon's Mines* (1885), Haggard's best-known book, Allan Quatermaine leads a safari in search of the fabulous treasure beyond Africa's Solomon Mountains, a treasure which has already claimed a thousand lives. Desert heat, jungle, hostile warrior-tribes and ice-caves in the mountains must all be faced, to say nothing of black magic, cannibalism and the guile and treachery of members of Quatermaine's own party. Hokum? The best.

> **READ ON** ▷
>
> ● *She; Allan Quatermaine; Ayesha: The Return of She.*
> ▶ ▷John Buchan, *Prester John*. ▷A. Conan Doyle, *The Lost World*. James Hilton, *Lost Horizon*. ▷Wilbur Smith, *Shout at the Devil*. Edgar Rice Burroughs, *A Princess of Mars*.

HAILEY, Arthur • *(born 1920)*
British/Canadian novelist.

Hailey's books are well-researched, fast-paced adventures set not in jungles or jet-set ski-resorts but in the no less exotic surroundings of a luxury hotel (*Hotel*), an international airport (*Airport*), the US government (*In High Places*) or Wall Street (*The Moneychangers*). In all of them, the fascination is as much in the detail of the location as in action: his books are fly-on-the-wall documentary, thriller and soap opera rolled into one. The hero of *Overload* (1979), a power-company executive, claims that his employers' greed and carelessness will lead to a breakdown of the entire electrical network of California. He becomes involved with ecological fringe-groups, citizen-pro-

> **READ ON** ▷
>
> ▶ Burton Wohl, *The China Syndrome*. John Trenhaile, *The Mahjong Spies*. Paul Gallico, *The Poseidon Adventure*.

tection societies, terrorists, big-business troubleshooters and muck-raking newspaper-reporters – and as the novel pounds towards its climax, he is proved to have been a truer prophet of disaster than even he suspected.

HAMMETT, Dashiell • *(1894–1961)*
US writer of novels, short stories and screenplays.

A former private detective, Hammett wrote stories and serials for pulp magazines, and later became a Hollywood scriptwriter. He perfected the 'private eye' story, in which kidnappings, thefts and murders are investigated by laconic, wisecracking individuals who are always just on the side of the angels and just one step ahead of the police. His best-known detectives are Sam Spade (made famous by Humphrey Bogart), the urbane Nick Charles (made famous in William Powell's 'Thin Man' films) and 'The Continental Op'. Hammett's novels are *The Dain Curse*, *Red Harvest*, *The Maltese Falcon*, *The Glass Key* and *The Thin Man*; his story-collections include *The Continental Op*, *A Man Called Spade* and *A Man Called Thin*.

READ ON ▷

▶ ▷Raymond Chandler, *The Lady in the Lake*. James M. Cain, *No Orchids for Miss Blandish*. Ross Macdonald, *The Drowning Pool*. Peter Coffin, *The Search for My Great Uncle's Head*. Andrew Bergman, *The Big Kissoff of 1944*. ▷Norman Mailer, *Tough Guys Don't Dance*.

HARDY, Thomas • *(1840–1928)*
British novelist and poet.

As a young man Hardy worked as an ecclesiastical architect, sketching and surveying country churches. This work intensified his love of the old ways of the countryside, patterns of life and customs which dated from feudal times. This is the background to his novels (which are all set in south-western England, the ancient kingdom of Wessex). He describes the minutiae of farming and village life with the exactness of a museum curator, and his characters' habits of mind are rooted in the ebb and flow of the seasons, in the unending cycle of tending for their animals and caring for the land. Life is unhurried but inexorable: Hardy's people are owned by their environment. They are also subject to a range of violent passions and emotions – Hardy thought of human beings as the playthings of destiny – and the placid continuum of existence is the setting for such irrational psychological forces as jealousy, intolerance and revenge. Hardy's bleakness and pessimism were much criticised, and in 1895 he gave up novels to concentrate on poetry. Paradoxically, for all the sombreness of their events, his novels are valued now mainly for their feeling of the harmony between human beings and nature: a kind of rural innocence which has

READ ON ▷

● *The Mayor of Casterbridge*; *Tess of the d'Urbervilles*.
▶ **Books on similar themes, in a similar style:** ▷George Eliot, *Adam Bede*; ▷Mrs Gaskell, *Ruth*; ▷Edith Wharton, *Ethan Frome*; Melvyn Bragg, *The Hired Man*.
▶ **Further away in period or manner, but equally atmospheric:** ▷John Fowles, *The French Lieutenant's Woman*; ▷Sigrid Undset, *Kristin Lavransdatter*; Oliver Onions, *The Story of Ragged Robyn*.

long since disappeared.

FAR FROM THE MADDING CROWD • *(1874)*

The shepherd Gabriel Oak works for Bathsheba Everdene, and loves her. Bathsheba's head is turned by dashing Sergeant Troy, who marries her and then deserts her, letting her believe that he is dead. Bathsheba now agrees to marry Boldwood, a yeoman farmer, unimaginative and dull, who has secretly loved her for years. Then Troy comes back and claims his wife – provoking a crisis and the resolution of the uneasy relationship between Oak and Bathsheba which has simmered all this time.

Hardy's other novels include Under the Greenwood Tree, A Pair of Blue Eyes, The Return of the Native, The Trumpet-Major, The Mayor of Casterbridge, The Woodlanders, Tess of the d'Urbervilles *and* Jude the Obscure. *He wrote an epic drama set during the Napoleonic Wars,* The Dynasts, *and several books of poetry including* Satires of Circumstance, Moments of Vision *and* Winter Words.

HARRISON, Harry • *(born 1925)*
US novelist and short-story writer.

Although Harrison has written serious SF (eg the fast-moving adventure-series *Deathworld I*, *Deathworld II* and *Deathworld III*), he is best-known for farce, and especially for his books about the Stainless Steel Rat. In a future where technology has made crime all but redundant, James Bolivar di Griz, the Stainless Steel Rat, is a spectacular exception to the rule. He sees himself as a public benefactor, keeping the police on their toes, giving employment to insurance clerks and bringing colour and excitement to TV newscasts. In the first book of the series, *The Stainless Steel Rat*, the galactic police decide that the only way to cope with him is to recruit him and send him to catch the lovely interplanetary criminal Angelina.

The Stainless Steel Rat books include The Stainless Steel Rat's Revenge, The Stainless Steel Rat Saves the World, The Stainless Steel Rat Wants You! *and* The Stainless Steel Rat for President. *Harrison's other novels include* Planet of the Damned, Make Room! Make Room!, Star Smashers of the Galaxy Rangers, Skyfall, Great Balls of Fire *and* Mechanismo. Two Tales and Eight Tomorrows, Prime Number *and* One Step from Earth *are collections of short stories.*

READ ON ⟩

● *The Technicolor Time Machine.*
▶ ▷Kurt Vonnegut, *Cat's Cradle.* Robert Sheckley, *The Status Civilization.* Jack Trevor Story, *Morag's Flying Fortress.*

HARTLEY, L.P. (Leslie Poles) •
(1895–1972)
British novelist and short-story writer.

An admirer of ▷James and ▷Forster, Hartley wrote a dozen decorous, restrained novels about emotional deprivation and the way childhood experience shadows a person's whole existence. His best-known books are the 'Eustace and Hilda' trilogy (*The Shrimp and the Anemone, The Sixth Heaven* and *Eustace and Hilda*, 1944–7, about a brother and sister whose emotional interdependence, innocent-seeming when they are children, blights their later lives, and *The Go-Between* (1953), about a boy on holiday during an idyllic Edwardian summer. Carrying messages between two doomed lovers (the daughter of the 'big house' and a tenant farmer), he is emotionally crippled by the passions he senses but hardly understands. *Facial Justice* (1960) is an uncharacteristic but fascinating book, a future-fantasy set in a drab post-nuclear world where there is no fear, no pain, no unkindness – and no room for individuality or emotion.

Hartley's other main novels are The Boat, A Perfect Woman, The Hireling *and* The Brickfield. *His short-story collections include* The Killing Bottle *and* The Travelling Grave.

READ ON ▷

▶ ▷Henry James, *What Maisie Knew.* ▷Anita Brookner, *Hôtel du Lac.* ▷Edith Wharton, *The Age of Innocence.* ▷Elizabeth Bowen, *The Death of the Heart.* Jane Gardam, *A Long Way from Verona.* Philip Larkin, *Jill.*

HAŠEK, Jaroslav • *(1883-1923)*
Czech novelist and journalist.

Hašek spent most of his youth as a dropout and a half-baked political activist (for which, for six months, he was imprisoned by the Russians as a spy). He served, reluctantly, in the first world war, was invalided out and became a satirical journalist. His masterpiece, the 700-page comic novel *The Good Soldier Švejk*, makes hilarious use of all his early experiences. Švejk is the town drunk, a dog-catcher, who is conscripted into the Austrian army as the lowliest of privates. A moon-faced, brainless lump, he obeys every fatuous order and follows every regulation to the letter. The book follows his farcical army career, during which he rises to the dizzy heights of chaplain's batman, takes part in the first world war and sees the first skirmishes of the Russian revolution. He understands nothing of what is going on: food, drink and staying out of trouble are all that interest him. Hašek uses Švejk's blankness like a mirror, showing up officers, politicians and bureaucrats for the fools they are. His nihilistic, iconoclastic farce was quite remarkably ahead of its time. *The*

READ ON ▷

▶ ▷François Rabelais, *Gargantua* is the nearest match for Hašek's farcical gusto, and Von Grimmelshausen, *Simplex Simplicissimus* is about a Middle Ages precursor of Švejk. Of more modern books, Eric Linklater, *Private Angelo* is a genial satire on the second world war; Thomas Berger, *Reinhart in Love* is a similarly light-hearted novel about a Švejkish US 'little man'. ▷Thomas

Good Soldier Švejk was banned, or available only in censored form, for over 40 years. It was not until the 1970s, when Absurd Drama and novels like ▷Heller's *Catch-22* had taught us not to take ourselves or our 'betters' so seriously, that it came at last into its own, was published complete, and was recognised as a satirical masterwork in the class of *Gargantua* or ▷Gogol's *Dead Souls*.

All earlier English translations of The Good Soldier Švejk *have been outclassed by Cecil Parrott's, written in the 1970s. Parrott has also published a selection of Hašek's lunatic journalism,* Jaroslav Hašek: the Red Commissar.

HAWTHORNE, Nathaniel • *(1804–64)*
US novelist.

Hawthorne was a descendant of William Hawthorne, one of the Pilgrim Fathers and a notable religious bigot – something which embarrassed Hawthorne himself, as he was a free-thinker, a believer in social equality and a dabbler in the utopian idealism of the mid-1800s USA. Although there was enough family money to pay for his university education, he was forced to earn a living thereafter, and did so as a customs officer, part-time publisher's editor and a newspaper contributor. Much of his early writing was excellent but minor – examples are the short-story collections *Twice-told Tales* and *Mosses from an Old Manse*, for adults, and *A Wonder Book* and *Tanglewood Tales*, sensitive retellings of Greek myth for children. He was triggered into greatness by discovering, in an old chest in Salem, Massachusetts, documents about his family's part in the Salem witchhunts of the mid 17th-century. Soon afterwards, he wrote *The Scarlet Letter* (1850), a novel about intolerance and humbug among the first Puritan settlers in the USA. Hester Prynne has spent two years in Boston, waiting for her elderly husband to join her from England. In the meantime she has borne a love-child, Pearl, and the Puritans pillory her and brand her an adulteress, making her wear the scarlet letter 'A' embroidered on her clothes. Her husband arrives, discovers that her secret lover is a minister of the church, and mercilessly persecutes him for refusing to admit his guilt. Hester's husband and lover pursue their enmity to the end; they ignore Hester herself, who in the meantime lives an unobtrusive but truly Christian life helping the neighbours who once ill-treated her.

Mann, *The Confessions of Felix Krull, Confidence Man* about a confidence-trickster travelling the spas and luxury hotels of Europe in the 1900s, though it lacks Hašek's devastating view of war and politics, exactly parallels his wide-eyed, amiable style.

READ ON ▷

● *The House of the Seven Gables* (a similarly remorseless novel about a New England family cursed for generations because of their forebears' persecution of an innocent man for witchcraft). *The Blithedale Romance* (a satire, based on Hawthorne's own experience, about life in a Massachusetts utopian community).
▶ ▷Aldous Huxley, *The Devils of Loudon*.
▷I.B. Singer, *Satan in Goray* (set in a medieval community of Polish Jews torn apart by the appearance of a false Messiah).
André Brink, *Rumours of Rain* (about ignorance and intolerance in present-day South Africa).
Robert Coover, *The Origin of the Brunists* (a fascist allegory about the growth of a ruthless religious sect).

HEINLEIN, Robert • *(born 1907)*
US novelist.

Of all SF novelists, Heinlein has always had a most dazzling variety and range, without ever sacrificing literary
quality or exuberance of imagination. In the 1940s and
1950s his books were ▷Wellsian, ▷Vernian stories of
space exploration and the colonisation of distant planets –
still satisfying nowadays for their style and plots, even
though much of their science has been overtaken by
events. In the 1960s he won a cult hippy following when
his book *Stranger in a Strange Land* seemed to be advo-
cating a mystical union of humankind brought about by
flower power, free love and hallucinatory drugs. His
1970s and 1980s books were ironical farces, akin to the
bleakly hilarious fantasies of ▷Joseph Heller and ▷Kurt
Vonnegut. His best known novels, the heart of his
achievement, are a series of independent but linked books
about Lazarus Long, a man who has the ability to live
forever, and who ends up as a kind of universal patriarch:
everyone in existence is one of his descendants. Heinlein
explores the personal and social problems of such a person, stirring in exotic and fascinating plot ideas. In *Time
Enough for Love* (1973), for example, Lazarus Long,
bored with life and contemplating suicide, is distracted by
being allowed to try the forbidden experience of time-
travel: he goes back to 1917, fights in the first world war,
meets himself as a six-year-old and falls in love with his
own mother.

Other books including Lazarus Long are Methuselah's
Children, Number of the Beast *and* The Cat Who Walks
Through Walls. *Heinlein's other novels include* I Will
Fear No Evil, The Day After Tomorrow *and* Job. *His
short stories, including such classics as 'The Man Who
Sold the Moon' and 'The Green Hills of Earth', are in the
two-volume omnibus* The Past Through Tomorrow.

HELLER, Joseph • *(born 1923)*
US novelist.

Throughout the 1950s, the escalation of the nuclear arms
race produced in many people a feeling of desperate impo-
tence. Faced with imminent apocalypse, the only possible
option seemed to be hysterical, cynical laughter. By the
early 1960s this mood was common in plays, comedians'
routines, cartoons and satirical magazines, and Heller's
first novel *Catch-22* expressed it perfectly. On the surface
a wild farce about airmen in the second world war, it

READ ON

● *Job* (a Bible-inspired
story of a human being
tormented by a
practical-joking,
malicious God and
finally befriended by
the Devil).
▶ ▷Isaac Asimov,
Foundation. ▷Philip
José Farmer,
Riverworld. ▷Kurt
Vonnegut, *Galápagos*.

READ ON

● All Heller's novels
centre on characters
who are trapped.
Something Happened
(1974) shows a man in
thrall to his own
boringness; the main
character of *Good as
Gold* (1979) is

shows human beings as both trapped in a detestable destiny and paradoxically liberated, by the absence of hope or choice, to do exactly as they please, to turn reality into fantasy. Until *Catch-22*, this had been a theme for serious novels (for example those of ▷Camus, ▷Sartre or ▷Hemingway); Heller made it comedy, leading a trend which has since spread from the arts into our general attitude to both our 'leaders' and the way we live.

CATCH-22 • *(1961)*

A group of US bomber-pilots is stationed on a Mediterranean island during the second world war. Every time a man thinks he has flown his quota of bombing-missions, high command doubles the number. There is no escape, and the reason is Catch-22: if you're sane enough to ask to be grounded because what you're doing is crazy, you're sane enough to fly. For all its bleak philosophy, *Catch-22* is brilliantly funny, particularly in its deadpan reporting of the lunatic, gung-ho US top brass, of Milo Minderbinder's extension to infinity of the rules of free-market enterprise (profiteering on everything from eggs to his comrades' lives), and of such pitiful victims of destiny as Major Major Major, a man haunted by his name. Robert Altman's film *M*A*S*H*, and the dazzling TV series which followed it, caught an exactly similar mood; *Catch-22* is like all *M*A*S*H*'s most ludicrous, lacerating scenes gathered into one glorious, agonising whole.

Heller's other novels are Something Happened, Good as Gold *and* God Knows. No Laughing Matter *is non-fiction, a blackly funny account of Heller's recovery from near-fatal illness.*

HEMINGWAY, Ernest • *(1898-1961)*
US novelist and short-story writer.

Few great writers provoke such love/hate reactions as Hemingway: it seems impossible to read him without judging him. The reason is that although he wrote some of the most evocative, persuasive prose of the century – as direct and compelling as a journalist's reports – many people find his subject-matter repellent. He believed that creatures, including human beings, are at their noblest when fighting for survival, and his novels and stories are therefore about boxing, big-game hunting, deep-sea fishing, bull-fighting and above all war. Hemingway himself realised that his macho philosophy belonged more to the Middle Ages than the 20th century, and most of his books are tinged with failure. His heroes rarely succeed in 'proving' themselves, their wars are futile, the emphasis is on

oppressed by his New York Jewish family and by hatred of Henry Kissinger; in *God Knows* (1984) the Old Testament King David is shackled by knowledge of the world's whole future history, and by his relationship with a wisecracking, cynical and unhelpful God. ('Where does it say nice?' asks God. 'Where does it say I have to be nice?').

▶ ▷Jaroslav Hašek, *The Good Soldier Švejk.* ▷Wyndham Lewis , *Childermass.* ▷Philip Roth, *Portnoy's Complaint.*

READ ON ⟩

● *The Old Man and the Sea* describes a duel to the death between the old Cuban fisherman Santiago and a gigantic marlin, the biggest fish he has ever tried to catch in his life. The book is short, and concentrates on Santiago, struggling not only with the marlin but against his own failing powers,

Joseph HELLER

Len **DEIGHTON, BOMBER**
(meticulous planning for a bombing-run over Germany in World War II)

Neville **SHUTE, LANDFALL**
(breakdown of young pilot who sinks 'one of ours' by mistake)

Stephen **CRANE, THE RED BADGE OF COURAGE**
*(young volunteer horrified but exhilarated by battle conditions
in American Civil War)*

WAR IS HELL

Andrew **SINCLAIR, GOG**
*(giant from past washed up in Scotland, travels to London, horrified at
20th-century 'civilisation')*

IT'S A MAD, MAD WORLD

Günter **GRASS, THE TIN DRUM**
(nazism as an insane circus-parade watched by a gleeful, baby-brained adult)

Budd **SCHULBERG, WHAT MAKES SAMMY RUN?**
(Sammy claws his way to the top; scum always floats)

Richard **CONDON, MILE HIGH**
(US power politics; a farcical orgy of sex, drugs, blackmail and murder)

Jerzy **KOSINSKI, BEING THERE**
(lame-brain gardener taken for political guru and saint)

Terry **SOUTHERN, CANDY**
(virgin innocent abroad – neither innocent nor virgin for long)

(lunacy of war; USAF bomber base on fantasy mediterranean island in World War II)

Mario **VARGAS LLOSA, THE CITY AND THE DOGS; THE TIME OF THE HERO**
(farcical tragedy of young cadets in 1950s Peruvian military academy)

Norman **MAILER, THE NAKED AND THE DEAD**
(World War II US conscripts brutalised by conditions of service on a hopeless Pacific mission)

ANTI-WAR NOVELS

Erich Maria **REMARQUE, ALL QUIET ON THE WESTERN FRONT**
(lives of four young men disrupted and ruined by brutality of World War I trench warfare)

Richard **HOOKER, M*A*S*H**
(US doctors in Korea fighting insane conditions, boredom and gung-ho top brass)

CRAZINESS OF COMMAND

Leslie **THOMAS, THE VIRGIN SOLDIERS**
(over-sexed, bewildered British conscripts in Far East)

Thomas **PYNCHON, GRAVITY'S RAINBOW**
(what is top secret World War II establishment for? What is meaning of life? Should war (and sex) not be more fun that this?)

Jaroslav **HAŠEK, THE GOOD SOLDIER ŠVEJK**
(World War I batman obeys every order, believes every lie, keeps out of trouble)

Herman **WOUK, THE CAINE MUTINY**
(crew court-martialled for mutinying against insane World War II minesweeper captain)

Peter **GEORGE, RED ALERT**
(chain of command follies and failures triggers World War III)

pain, despair and death. But the dream remains, and is Hemingway's own dream. He spent his leisure time in exactly the activities he describes –precise details of how to fight bulls, hunt big game, box or fish are what he does best – and in 1961, feeling too old and sick to continue, he shot himself.

A FAREWELL TO ARMS • *(1929)*

A US ambulance driver in Italy during the first world war is wounded and taken to hospital, where he falls in love with an English nurse. While he convalesces. the couple are deliriously happy, but then he is commanded back to the front. She tells him that she is pregnant, and they decide that their only course is 'a farewell to arms', escaping from the war to neutral Switzerland.

Hemingway's other novels are The Torrents of Spring, The Sun Also Rises/Fiesta *(which includes a superb description of bull-running during the festival at Pamplona),* Death in the Afternoon *(about bull-fighting),* The Green Hills of Africa, To Have and Have Not, For Whom the Bell Tolls *(set during the Spanish civil war),* Across the River and Into the Trees *and* The Old Man and the Sea. *Several unrevised, unfinished books were published posthumously: the best-known is the novel* Islands in the Stream. *His short-story collections include* In Our Time, Men Without Women *and* Winner Take Nothing.

HERBERT, Frank • *(1920–86)*
US novelist.

Herbert's work is dominated by the 2000-page (6-novel) 'Dune' series (1965–85), an SF epic whose scope and complexity dwarf all rivals. Dune is a desert planet, inhabited by gigantic sand-worms which produce mélange, a substance which inhibits aging and gives knowledge of the past and future. The saga (each of whose novels is self-contained) tells how Paul Atreides inherits Dune, has to win it from his enemies and then colonise it. It describes the 'greening' of a planet where water is the most precious of all commodities, and recounts the wars between the Atreides family and other interests (especially the powerful Bene Gesserit sisterhood, which is dedicated to harnessing the pure power of thought and so dispensing with science and technology). The books are partly a swaggering multi-generation saga, the apotheosis of space-opera, and partly a detailed and moving account of the inter-relationship between the colonists and their planet. The effort of controlling but not destroying the environment produces in them a feeling of near-mystic communion with natural

and kept going only by determination and a lifetime's skill.
▶ ▷Graham Greene, *The Power and the Glory*. ▷Norman Mailer, *The Naked and the Dead*. ▷George Orwell, *Homage to Catalonia*. ▷Jack London, *The Sea-wolf*. Hammond Innes, *Campbell's Kingdom*. Alistair Maclean, *The Guns of Navarone*.

READ ON ▷

▶ **Good SF follow-ups:** ▷Brian Aldiss, *Helliconia Spring* and its sequels; ▷Ursula Le Guin, *The Left Hand of Darkness*.
▶ **Good non-SF follow-ups:** Frans Bengtsson, *The Long Ships* (about Vikings exploring the surface of our own planet); Jean M. Auel, *Earth Children* (a saga of the distant past, about human beings learning to control their environment and discovering ways of civilisation); Nicholas Monsarrat, *Running*

forces which contrasts strongly with the snarling and bickering of their relations with one another.

The first Dune trilogy is Dune, Dune Messiah *and* Children of Dune; *the second is* God Emperor of Dune, Heretics of Dune *and* Chapterhouse of Dune. *Herbert's many other books, space-opera on a less exalted level, include* The Dragon in the Sea, The Whipping Star, The Dosadi Experiment, The Green Brain *and* The Saratoga Barrier.

Proud (about one of Columbus' sailors shipwrecked and forced, by the tribe who find him, to invent himself as a godlike personality, with deeds to match).
National Lampoon, *Doon* is a splendid send-up of all Herbert's ideas – replacing mélange, for example, with a wonder-drug called Coke.

HERBERT, James • *(born 1943)*
British novelist.

Herbert's supernatural chillers, among the most frightening in the business, include *The Dark*, *The Domain*, *The Fog*, *The Rats*, *Shrine*, *The Spear*, *The Survivor*, *Sepulchre* and *Moon* (about a boy on an island who dreams of a sadistic, supernatural creature – at the same time as it dreams of him).

▶ ▷Stephen King, *It*.
Margaret Bingley,
Devil's Child. Dean R.
Koontz, *Whispers*.
▷H.G. Wells, *The Island of Doctor Moreau*.

HESSE, Hermann • *(1877-1962)*
German/Swiss novelist and non-fiction writer.

A poet and mystic, Hesse was influenced by Jung's ideas of the unconscious and the collective unconscious, and later by Buddhist philosophy. His most famous mystical novel, *The Glass Bead Game/Magister Ludi* (Das Glasperlenspiel), is about a future utopia where all questions about life, morality and personality are covered by a monastic philosophical system centred on a zen-like game involving coloured beads and an abacus. Hesse's reputation for gentle, philosophical woolliness has obscured his true worth. His novels before *The Glass Bead Game* are spare, moving accounts of how people in psychological turmoil reach peace with themselves, either through their own efforts or with the help of friends and loved ones. He is something of a special taste, but few writers' works so reward their devotees.

ROSSHALDE • *(1914)*
Veraguth, a world-renowned painter, is suffering creative block. His marriage is breaking down, and he and his wife

● *Gertrud* (1910, the story of a tragic love-triangle between a girl and two young men who are close friends).
Steppenwolf (1927) and *Narziss and Goldmund* (1930) are both about the divided self. In *Steppenwolf* a middle-aged recluse has given in to the negative, hopeless side of his nature, and is 'brought back' by the spiritual energy of three young people who may be dream-figures, projections of

stay together out of love for Rosshalde, their beautiful country estate, and devotion to their young son Pierre. Veraguth's problems seem beyond cure – until unexpected tragedy forces him to come to terms with himself, and so to find peace at last.

Hesse's major novels are Gertrud, Peter Camenzind, Under the Wheel/The Prodigy, Siddhartha *(about Buddha),* Steppenwolf, Narziss and Goldmund *and* The Glass Bead Game. *He also published shorter, more mystical fiction (*Knulp; Klingsor's Last Summer*), poetry, short stories, essays and letters.*

his subconscious. In *Narziss and Goldmund* (set in medieval Europe, with a background of monastic and craft-guild life) the conflict between flesh and spirit is symbolised by the two main characters, close friends, one carnal, one spiritual.

► **To *Rosshalde*:** ▷André Gide, *The Pastoral Symphony* (*La symphonie pastorale*).

► **To *The Glass Bead Game*:** ▷Tom De Haan, *A Mirror for Princes*.

► **To *Narziss and Goldmund*:** Georges Bernanos, *Diary of a Country Priest* (about the battle between flesh and spirit in a priest's soul).

► **To *Steppenwolf*:** D.M. Thomas, *The White Hotel*.

► **To Hesse's work in general:** ▷Heinrich Böll, *The Clown*; ▷Kazuo Ishiguro, *An Artist of the Floating World*.

HEYER, Georgette • *(1902–74)*
British novelist.

Apart from a handful of detective stories (eg *Envious Casca; Detection Unlimited*), all Heyer's novels are historical. Some centre on real events (*The Infamous Army*, for example, is about the battle of Waterloo); others, notably *Beauvallet* (1929), *The Tollgate* (1954) and *The Unknown Ajax* (1959), are heady tales of smugglers, highwaymen and other members of the 18th-century underworld. The bulk of her books are light-hearted, frothy romances. A hero and heroine who detest or distrust one another are thrown together by circumstances

READ ON ⟩

► **To the novels based on real events:** Margaret Irwin, *Young Bess* (first of a trilogy about Queen Elizabeth I of England); ▷Jean Plaidy, *The Spanish Bridegroom*.

► **To the adventure novels:** ▷Daphne Du

and fall in love. Often she 'tames' him or he 'tames' her; sometimes masquerade (such as posing as lady's maids or cads) is involved. Heyer's knowledge of Regency ways was exhaustive: every garment, vehicle, gesture and turn of phrase seems exactly and delightfully right. Her novels are fast-moving, uncomplicated entertainment. She perfected the Regency genre, and within it she is unsurpassed.

Heyer's best-known romances are The Masqueraders, These Old Shades, Devil's Cub, Regency Buck, Friday's Child, The Foundling, The Grand Sophy, Bath Tangle, Sprig Muslin *and* Cotillion. Pistols for Two *contains short stories.*

HIBBERT, Eleanor • *(born 1906)*
British novelist.

Hibbert wrote all her books under pseudonyms: Eleanor Burford ▷Philippa Carr, Elbur Ford, ▷Victoria Holt, Kathleen Kellow, ▷Jean Plaidy and Ellalice Tate.

HIGGINS, Jack • *(born 1929)*
British novelist.

'Jack Higgins' is one of the pseudonyms of Henry Patterson, who also writes thrillers as Martin Fallon, James Graham, Hugh Marlow and Harry Patterson. The Higgins books are pacy, violent and full of character. They include *The Last Place God Made*, *A Prayer for the Dying*, *The Eagle Has Landed* (imagining Britain under SS rule), *Hell is Always Today*, *The Dark Side of the Street* and *Solo* (in which a concert pianist, fleeing from the police, kills an assassin's daughter by accident – a mistake which must be punished).

Maurier, *Jamaica Inn*; Jane Aiken Hodge, *Rebel Heiress*; ▷Mary Stewart, *This Rough Magic* (set in modern Greece).

▶ **To the romances:** ▷Jane Austen, *Mansfield Park*; Sheila Walsh, *The Rose Domino*: Clare Darcy, *Eugenia*; Bob Coleman, *The Further Adventures of Tom Jones.*

> **READ ON** >

▶ ▷Len Deighton, *Berlin Game*. Alexander Fullerton, *Regenesis*. Colin Forbes, *Terminal*. Gerald Seymour, *Kingfisher*.

HIGH ADVENTURE

▷Desmond Bagley, *The Golden Keel*
▷Alexandre Dumas, *The Three Musketeers*
▷H. Rider Haggard, *King Solomon's Mines*
▷Anthony Hope, *The Prisoner of Zenda*
  Hammond Innes, *Campbell's Kingdom*
  Rafael Sabatini, *Captain Blood*
▷Wilbur Smith, *Shout at the Devil*
  B. Traven, *The Treasure of the Sierra Madre*

Georgette HEYER

Clare **DARCY, ELYZA**
(plain girl disguises herself as boy to find romance)

Caroline **COURTNEY, DUCHESS IN DISGUISE**
(spurned wife disguises herself to win husband's love)

Jane **AUSTEN, SENSE AND SENSIBILITY**
(love-affairs of two sisters; sensible Elinor and impulsive, romantic Marianne)

Joan **AIKEN, MANSFIELD REVISITED**
(spirited girl 'tames' brother-in-law's snobbish family)

REGENCY ENGLAND

COMEDY OF MANNERS

Henry **FIELDING, TOM JONES**
(escapades of foundling wandering 18th-century England to find truth about himself)

P.G. **WODEHOUSE, BILL THE CONQUEROR**
(Percy Pilbeam's havoc-strewn career as editor of 'Society Spice')

Iris **MURDOCH, A SEVERED HEAD**
(sexual merry-go-round in 'swinging' 1960s London)

Mary **WESLEY, THE VACILLATIONS OF POPPY CAREWE** *(rich heiress reviews young men in her life to find the 'best' – i.e. least obviously eligible – husband. Love intervenes.)*

Mary **STEWART, NINE COACHES WAITING**
(English governess in France, caught in family feud, saves charges from death, finds love)

Helen **MACINNES, RIDE A PALE HORSE**
(US journalist at Prague conference approached by would-be defector)

ROMANTIC MYSTERY

Anne **BRIDGE, THE GINGER GRIFFIN**
(intrigue and unhappiness in pre-Revolutionary China)

Jane Aiken **HODGE, POLONAISE**
(love and politics in 1810s Poland, caught between Russia and Napoleon)

(dislike turns to love in Regency English high society)

PERIOD ROMANCE

Norah **LOFTS, THE BRITTLE GLASS**
(independent girl grows up in 18th-century Fens, a place of smugglers, gipsies and highwaymen)

T.N. **MURARI, TAJ**
(love of Indian Shah Jahan and his wife, for whom he built the Taj Mahal)

Kathleen **WINSOR, FOREVER AMBER**
(love and adventure in 17th-century, Restoration England)

Rosalind **LAKER, WHAT THE HEART KEEPS**
(two immigrants to 1900s USA fall in love, make life together in Wild West and early Hollywood)

M.M. **KAYE, THE FAR PAVILIONS**
(love across the races in dying days of British Raj in India)

Margaret **PEMBERTON, NEVER LEAVE ME**
(successful Californian looks back on doomed wartime love-affair with German officer, when she works for French Resistance)

Caroline **FIRESIDE, GOODBYE AGAIN**
(will heroine sacrifice glamorous film career for love?)

Erich **SEGAL, LOVE STORY**
(two college students fall idyllically, tragically, in love)

20TH-CENTURY ROMANCE

Action Thrillers (p 2); Agents and Double Agents (p 3); Terrorists/Freedom Fighters (p 234)

HIGHER (?) EDUCATION

▷Robertson Davies, *The Rebel Angels*
▷J.P. Donleavy, *The Ginger Man*
  Richard Gordon, *Doctor in the House*
  Howard Jacobson, *Coming from Behind*
▷Randall Jarrell, *Pictures from an Institution*
▷Alison Lurie, *The War Between the Tates*
▷Mary McCarthy, *The Groves of Academe*
▷Tom Sharpe, *Wilt*

Dreaming Spires (p 66)

HIGHSMITH, Patricia • *(born 1921)*
US novelist and short-story writer.

Except for *The People Who Knock on the Door* (1982, about the disintegration of an 'ordinary' US family whose father becomes a born-again Christian) Highsmith's books are all psychological thrillers. They show the planning and commission of horribly convincing, 'everyday' crimes, and the way murder erodes the murderer's moral identity. Few writers screw tension so tight in such functional, unemotional prose. Highsmith's most chilling insight is how close the criminally insane can be to people just like ourselves.

RIPLEY'S GAME • *(1974)*
Ripley, who appears in several Highsmith books, is a charming American psychopath who lives in France. In this book, out of boredom, he sets up circumstances to snare an entirely innocent man into committing murder. But the murder-victim is a mafia boss, and soon assassins begin to hunt down both Ripley and his dupe. The plot is exciting, but Highsmith's main concern is the comparison between Ripley's icy amorality and the conscience-racked flailings of the man he corrupts.

Other Ripley books are The Talented Mr Ripley, Ripley Under Ground *and* The Boy Who Followed Ripley. *High-smith's other novels include* Strangers on a Train, The Two Faces of January, The Story Teller/A Suspension of Mercy, The Tremor of Forgery, Edith's Diary *and* Found

READ ON ▷

● The central character of *The Glass Cell* (a typical non-Ripley book) is a man released from prison after six years during which his character has been brutalised and his moral integrity destroyed. Tormented by the possibility of his wife's unfaithfulness, he sets out to discover the truth.
▶ Julian Symons, *The Man Who Killed Himself.* ▷Georges Simenon, *The Hatter's Ghosts.* Greg MacDonald, *Running Scared.* ▷Ruth Rendell, *Live Flesh.* ▷P.D. James, *The Skull Beneath the Skin.* Celia Fremlin, *Appointment with Yesterday; Don't Go to Sleep in the Dark*

in the Street. The Snailwatcher/Eleven, The Animal-lover's Book of Beastly Murder, The Black House, Mermaids on the Golf Course *and* Tales of Natural and Unnatural Catastrophes *contain short stories.*

HILL, Reginald • *(born 1936)*
British novelist.

Hill writes thrillers and adventure stories under the pseudonyms Dick Morland (*Heart Clock*), ▷Patrick Ruell and Charles Underhill (*Captain Fantom*). Under his own name he writes affable, joky detective stories, featuring slobbish Inspector Dalziel and his bushy-tailed, over-eager assistant Pascoe. Hill's books include *A Clubbable Woman, An Advancement of Learning, A Fairly Dangerous Thing, A Very Good Hater* and the cheekily-named *Another Death in Venice.*

HILL, Susan • *(born 1942)*
British writer of novels, short stories and non-fiction.

Except for *The Woman in Black*, a ghost-story in classic 19th-century style, all Hill's novels and stories are about predatory emotional relationships. One partner (spouse, friend, lover or acquaintance) can only survive by engulfing the other, and the process is agonising and deliberate, an erosion of spirit without hope or help. Her least bleak book is *In the Springtime of the Year* (1974), in which a young woman devastated by the death of her husband is rescued from despair by the tranquil daily round of country life. Hill's themes may be sombre, but she writes with delicacy and compassion: in the end, the tears we shed are for the human condition itself, a predicament which is like a third partner in the stories, a malign presence feasting on victims and predators alike.

I'M THE KING OF THE CASTLE • *(1970)*
Mr Hooper, a lonely widower, invites Mrs Kingshaw to be housekeeper of his large Victorian mansion. He hopes that his ten-year-old son and hers will become friends. But the boy Hooper resents Kingshaw's invasion of his psychological kingdom, and torments him. The psychopathic child, possessed by the devil, was a familiar figure in pulp fiction and films of the 1970s (a good example is the 'Omen' film series); Hill turns the same subject into art.

Hill's other main novels are A Change for the Better, Gentleman and Ladies, Strange Meeting *and* The Bird of

(short stories).

> **READ ON** ⟩

▶ Colin Watson, *One Man's Meat*. Joyce Porter, *Who the Hell Was Sylvia?*. Ira Wallach, *The Absence of a Cello*.

> **READ ON** ⟩

● *The Bird of Night*
▶ **To *I'm the King of the Castle:*** ▷Henry James, *The Turn of the Screw*; ▷John Wyndham, *Chocky*; ▷William Golding, *Lord of the Flies*.
▶ **To *In the Springtime of the Year:*** Penelope Lively, *Perfect Happiness*. Hill's grim compassion, and her unblinking descriptions of the desolation of the soul, are matched in ▷Carson McCullers, *Reflections in a Golden Eye*; James Agee, *A Death in the Family* and ▷John Updike, *The Centaur*.

Night, *a sombre book about a manic-depressive artist and the friend who tries to help him.* The Albatross *and* A Bit of Singing and Dancing *contain short stories.*

HISTORICAL ADVENTURE

Peter Carter, *The Black Lamp*
Bernard Cornwell, *Sharpe's Regiment*
Frederick Couens, *Gnur Bodi*
▷C.S. Forester, *Mr Midshipman Hornblower*
George Macdonald Fraser, *Flashman*
▷Homer, *Odyssey*
▷R.L. Stevenson, *Kidnapped*

Action Thrillers (p 2); Agents and Double Agents (p 3); High Adventure (p 117)

HOBAN, Russell • *(born 1925)*
US/British novelist.

Hoban first made his name with children's books and with *Turtle Diary* (1976), a novel about two lonely people drawn together by their ambition to return the turtles from the London Zoo to the sea. His chief fame, however, is for *Riddley Walker* (1980). This is a future-fantasy, set in England generations after the nuclear holocaust. The society is primitive – making fire is still a problem, never mind organising the rule of law – and the survivors are haunted by memories of the time before the bomb. Rags of old culture, technology and morality flap in their minds, as inexplicable and as powerful as myth. Their language, similarly – the one the book is written in – is shredded, reconstituted English: words coalesce, grammar has collapsed, new metaphors sprout like weeds. Although this style is difficult at first, it becomes perfectly comprehensible after a few pages, and before long the broken, patched-together words begin to seem like poetry, as Riddley, the story-teller, struggles to find ways to describe the pictures inside his mind.

READ ON >

● *The Lion of Boaz-Jachin and Jachin-Boaz; The Medusa Frequency.*
▶ ▷William Golding, *Pincher Martin.*
▷George Turner, *Vaneglory.* ▷Anthony Burgess, *A Clockwork Orange.* Robie Macauley, *A Secret History of Time to Come.*

HOLT, Victoria • *(born 1906)*
British novelist.

'Victoria Holt' is one of the pseudonyms of ▷Eleanor Hibbert. She writes romantic mystery and suspense. In *Secret for a Nightingale*, for example, a 19th-century

READ ON >

▶ ▷Norah Lofts, *The Wayside Tavern.*
Naomi Jacob,

English girl marries for love in India, and finds out only after her return to England that her husband has not told her everything about himself.

Holt's two dozen other books include Mistress of Mellyn, The Bride of Pendorric, The Shivering Sands, Lord of the Far Islands *and* My Enemy the Queen.

HOMER • *(c 9th century BC)*
Greek epic poet.

Although Homer's *Odyssey* was composed to be de-claimed, section by section, at royal feasts, the depth of its character-drawing and its psychological perception transcend such fragmented performances: in a good prose translation (such as E.V. Rieu's) it is as complex and fas-cinating as any modern novel. Its plot, taken from Greek myth, recounts Odysseus' supernatural adventures on his way home from the Trojan War and his epic battle with the suitors who have plagued his wife Penelope during his absence. But it is also the story of Odysseus' own devel-opment, of the way his experiences mould and mature his personality. Each of his encounters – with the flesh-eating giant Polyphemus, the Lotus-eaters, the Sirens, the seduc-tress Calypso, Circe, Nausicaa – changes him, teaches him more about himself, until he is ready to prove himself to his enemies, his people and his patient wife. The *Iliad*, similarly, uses the framework of myth (the quarrel be-tween Achilles and Hector during the Trojan War) to dis-cuss such themes as ambition, pride, courage, the place of destiny in human lives and the glory and futility of war.

'Gollantz' saga.
Cynthia Harrod-Eagles,
'Dynasty' series.
Caroline Courtney,
Guardian of the Heart.
Sarah Woodhouse,
The Indian Widow.

READ ON ⟩

▶ **Modern novels drawing on Greek myth:** ▷Robert Graves, *The Golden Fleece/Hercules My Shipmate*; *Homer's Daughter* (a fantasy about the events leading up the composition of the *Odyssey*); ▷Mary Renault, *The King Must Die*; Henry Treece, *Electra.*

▶ **Books using Homeric style or themes:** Virgil, *Aeneid* (a patriotic Roman epic about the defeated Trojans' voyage to found a new home in Italy); Petronius, *Satyricon* (a parody of the Odyssey set among the pimps, prostitutes, hermaphrodites, fake prophets and sybarites of a fantasy ancient Rome); Miguel de Cervantes Saavedra, *Don Quixote*; ▷Lev Tolstoy, *War and Peace*. The theme of Odysseus' self-discovery, and each individual adventure in turn, inspired ▷James Joyce, *Ulysses.*

HOPE, Anthony • *(1863–1933)*
British novelist.

In *The Prisoner of Zenda* (1894) Hope invented the 'Ruritanian' adventure-story, a colourful escapist yarn set in some fantasy foreign kingdom. Rudolf Rassendyl, an upper-class Englishman on holiday in the middle European country of Ruritania, is astonished to find that he is an exact double of the king, and even more surprised when the king is kidnapped just before his coronation, and Rassendyl is asked to impersonate him. As the story proceeds, the kidnappers (the king's ambitious brother and his henchman Rupert of Hentzau, the finest swordsman in Ruritania) try to foil the coronation-plans, and Rassendyl (who has meanwhile fallen in love with Flavia, the future queen) breaks into Zenda Castle to rescue the imprisoned king. The novel has been filmed a dozen times, and has inspired one of the cinema's favourite clichés: two men, one debonair, one saturnine, duelling up and down the steps of an ancient castle, slicing candles in half, parrying thrusts with three-legged stools and matching each rapier-thrust with a dazzling shaft of wit.

> **READ ON** ▷

> ● *Rupert of Hentzau* (the sequel); *Sophy of Kravonia*.
> ▶ Jane Barry, *The Conscience of the King*. Marjorie Bowen, *The Viper of Milan*. Rafael Sabatini, *Captain Blood*. ▷A. Conan Doyle, *The White Company*. P.C. Wren, *Beau Geste*. ▷John Buchan, *John MacNab*. ▷Robert Ludlum, *The Parsifal Mosaic*.

HOUSEHOLD, Geoffrey • *(born 1909)*
British novelist.

Household's thrillers follow squarely in the steps of ▷Buchan, pitting single individuals against the might of sinister corporations, political groups or foreigners, and letting them win by persistence, guts and an invincibly late-Edwardian code of gentlemanly behaviour. Many of his heroes are themselves hunted, and have to 'hole up' either in seedy urban lodgings or in the countryside, where they live by the survival strategies of a commando training manual. The mixture of boys' comic-strip yarns and adult terror is common in English thrillers; in Household's hands it is unsurpassed.

Household's best-known books are Rogue Male, Rogue Justice, The High Place, A Rough Shoot, A Time to Kill, Watcher in the Shadows *and* The Courtesy of Death.

> **READ ON** ▷

> ▶ John Welcome, *Run for Cover*. ▷Graham Greene, *A Gun for Sale/This Gun for Hire*. Hugh McCutcheon, *A Hot Wind from Hell*. James Graham, *A Game for Heroes*. William Haggard, *Closed Circuit*. ▷Peter Dickinson, *The Seals*.

HOWATCH, Susan • *(born 1940)*
British novelist.

After a number of atmospheric romances (*The Dark Shore, The Waiting Sands, April's Grave, The Devil on Lammas Night*), Howatch made a second reputation with

> **READ ON** ▷

> ▶ Jean Stubbs, *Kits Hill*. Mary Pearce, *The Appletree Saga*.

multi-generation family sagas, setting internal rivalries and alliances against the background of historical events. Her books include *Cashelmara*, *The Rich Are Different* and *Penmarric* (the story of a British family from Victorian times to the second world war).

HUGO, Victor • *(1802–85)*
French novelist, poet and playwright.

Although Hugo was principally a poet and dramatist, he is also remembered for four panoramic historical novels. *Notre Dame de Paris* (1831), set in medieval times, is about the beautiful foundling Esmeralda, the men who try to seduce her, and the deformed Quasimodo, bell-ringer at Notre Dame cathedral, who loves her. The book's detail of Parisian low life is matched in *Les misérables* (1862), about a noble-hearted convict and the corrupt policeman who persecutes him. *The Toilers of the Sea* (1866) allegorises the eternal struggle between human beings and nature into a story of Guernsey fishermen, fighting both the elements and each other. *Ninety-three* (1873) is about royalist resistance in the French Revolution. Hugo's novels are long and prone to philosophising, but they make up for it by the energy of their plots, the melodramatic attraction of their characters – not for nothing is the Hunchback of Notre Dame a Hollywood favourite – and the extraordinary feeling they give that every event, every story, is just one glimpse of the teeming anthill of human life.

HULME, Keri • *(born 1947)*
New Zealand novelist and short-story writer.

Hulme's first novel *The Bone People* was the outsider which won the Booker Prize for 1985. It counterpoints the story of a woman's attemps to 'thaw' an autistic child with an extended reflection on Maori legend and culture. For Hulme, the Maoris are like disabled people in a fit society, and she invests their presence and their culture with the resonance of myth. Her prose-style is uncompromising and experimental, full of fragmented dialogue, stream-of-consciousness narrative and abrupt shifts in time and place. In 1987 *The Bone People* was followed by *The Windeater (Te Kaihau)*, a collection of short stories writ-

Jessica Stirling, *The Spoiled Earth.*

READ ON ▷

▶ **To *Notre Dame de Paris*:** Alessandro Manzoni, *The Betrothed* (I promessi sposi).
▶ **To *Les misérables*:** Heinrich Mann, *The Blue Angel/Small Town Tyrant.*
▶ **To *The Toilers of the Sea*:** ▷Charles Dickens, *Hard Times.*
▶ **To *Ninety-three*:** ▷Alexander Solzhenitsyn, *August, 1914.*
▶ **To the more swaggering elements of Hugo's style:** ▷Lew Wallace, *Ben Hur;* ▷Alexandre Dumas, *The Man in the Iron Mask*; Mika Waltari, *Sinuhe the Egyptian.*

READ ON ▷

▶ Ian Wedde, *Symme's Hole.* Bruce Chatwin, *The Songlines.* Kathy Acker, *Blood and Guts in High School.* Sheila Watson, *The Double Hook.* Amos Tutuola, *Pauper, Brawler and Slanderer.*

ten over the previous decade. They share the preoccupations, themes and style of *The Bone People* – with an added ingredient, radical feminism – but their shortness makes them easier to read, an excellent introduction to Hulme's work. Despite, or perhaps because of, Hulme's stylistic experiments, the impact of these stories is both overwhelming and unforgettable.

THE HUMAN COMEDY

▷Jane Austen, *Pride and Prejudice*
▷John Cheever, *The Wapshot Chronicle*
▷Peter De Vries, *The Tunnel of Love*
  David Lodge, *The British Museum is Falling Down*
▷Alison Lurie, *Real People*
▷Barbara Pym, *A Glass of Blessings*
▷William Thackeray, *Vanity Fair*
  Angela Thirkell, *High Rising*
▷H.G. Wells, *Tono-Bungay*

Dreaming Spires (p 66); Friends (?) and Neighbours (p 86); Higher (?) Education (p 118)

HUNTER, Evan • *(born 1926)*
US novelist.

Hunter writes under his own name and under the pseudonyms ▷Ed McBain, Richard Marsten (*Rocket to Luna*; *Vanishing Ladies*) and Hunt Collins (*Cut Me In*). As Hunter he has written children's books, plays, screenplays (notably *The Birds*, for Hitchcock), tough novels of New York life (eg *The Blackboard Jungle*, 1954, about an idealistic teacher in a slum high school), and thrillers, many of them agreeably laced with farce. His books (many of them filmed) include *Buddwing*, *The Paper Dragon*, *Last Summer*, *Nobody Knew They Were There*, *Hail to the Chief*, *Where There's Smoke* and *Every Little Crook and Nanny*.

READ ON ▷

▶ Donald Westlake, *The Mercenaries.* ▷Richard Condon, *Prizzi's Honour.* Colin Dunne, *Black Ice.*

HUXLEY, Aldous • *(1894–1963)*
British novelist and non-fiction writer.

Huxley's early books were glittering satires on 1920s intellectual and upper-class life, accounts of preposterous conversations at country-house costume parties and in

READ ON ▷

● *Ape and Essence* (about a California-dwelling group of

such unlikely meeting-places as publishers' offices or the Egyptian Room at the British Museum. His characters are intelligent, creative, fascinating and empty; haunted by the pointlessness of existence, they pass their time flirting, gossiping, swapping philosophical ideas and planning all kinds of japes and pranks. In the 1930s, beginning with *Brave New World*, he changed his approach. Instead of focussing his satire on a single section of British society, he turned on the human race at large, and wrote a series of increasingly bitter books demolishing all our ambitions to make a better society by science, philosophy, religion, socialism or (in the late 1950s, at the germination-stage of flower-power) hallucinatory drugs. His books are a witty, cold dazzle of ideas; enjoyable as you read them, they leave an acid aftertaste.

BRAVE NEW WORLD • *(1932)*

In a soulless future world, genetic engineering programmes people from birth for their status in society, and removes all aggressive or unproductive instincts. Individuality, creativity and personality are sacrificed in the causes of material prosperity, good health and freedom from anxiety. Only a small group of 'savages' – people like us – survives, in a community in New Mexico, and one of them escapes and is brought into the 'real world', with tragic results. As in all his novels, Huxley tells this tale soberly and without comment: the flatness of his prose brilliantly intensifies the horror of what he is saying. Nothing truly terrible happens – and that is the most terrible thing of all.

In chronological order, Huxley's novels are Crome Yellow, Antic Hay, Those Barren Leaves, Point Counter Point, Brave New World, Eyeless in Gaza, After Many a Summer, Time Must Have a Stop, Ape and Essence, The Genius and the Goddess *and* Island. Limbo, Mortal Coils, The Little Mexican, Two or Three Graces *and* Brief Candles *collect short stories, all of them early.*

survivors from the nuclear holocaust, primitives visited by a horror-struck scientist from New Zealand).

▶ **To Huxley's social satires:** ▷F. Scott Fitzgerald, *The Beautiful and Damned* (from the 1920s); ▷Anthony Powell, *Venusberg* (from the 1930s); Martin Amis, *Money* (from the 1980s).

▶ **To *Ape and Essence*:** ▷Paul Theroux, *O-Zone.*

▶ **To Huxley's later books:** Frederick Pohl and C.M. Kornbluth, *The Space Merchants;* ▷L.P. Hartley, *Facial Justice;* Michael Frayn, *Sweet Dreams.*

I

INDIA

▷J.G. Farrell, *The Siege of Krishnapur*
  Valerie Fitzgerald, *Zemindar*
▷E.M. Forster, *A Passage to India*
▷Ruth Prawer Jhabvala, *Heat and Dust*
▷Rudyard Kipling, *Kim*
  T.N. Murari, *Taj*
▷R.K. Narayan, *The Vendor of Sweets*
▷Salman Rushdie, *Midnight's Children*

INNES, Michael • *(born 1906)*
British novelist.

'Michael Innes' is the pseudonym of the Oxford don J.I.M. Stewart. His 50 detective novels set bizarre puzzles in the unhurried world of Oxford colleges, English country houses, fine art auction-rooms and elegant Tuscan villas. Well-bred, exquisitely educated people cheat, lie and kill without ruffling a hair and with a well-turned quotation always on their lips. The blend of privilege and nastiness is brilliant, and the pace of Innes' writing enhances it. When brutality happens it is fast, unexpected and breathtaking; when Innes' detectives Appleby or Honeybath investigate the speed is gentle and unflustered, allowing plenty of time to savour every epigram, every devious conversational nuance, every glass of port. Stewart's novels and stories under his own name use similar locations, the same placid style and an even more twinkly-eyed cultural affectation, but instead of murders they concern such gentler matters as friendship (especially between old and young), family feuds, love-affairs and unexpected inheritances.

READ ON ⟩

● *The Daffodil Affair*; *From London Far*.
▶ **To Innes' detective stories at their larkiest:** Edmund Crispin, *The Moving Toyshop*; Rex Stout, *Too Many Cooks*; Carter Dickson, *The Ten Teacups*; Gladys Mitchell, *Laurels Are Poison*.
▶ **To J.I.M. Stewart's novels:** ▷C.P. Snow, *The Masters*; ▷Anthony Powell, *Afternoon Men*.

OPERATION PAX/PAPER THUNDERBOLT · *(1951)*
In a private clinic in the quiet Oxford countryside something extremely sinister – brainwashing? conditioning by
drugs? plotting world domination? – is going on. A petty
criminal, kidnapped by the experimenters as a human
guinea-pig, escapes and hides in Oxford, where the action
at once involves East European refugees, eccentric dons,
the pupils of a prep school for especially brainy boys, and
John Appleby's pretty young sister Jane. The investigation
climaxes in the 'stacks' of the Bodleian Library, a pile of
eight million books in a cavernous vault under Radcliffe
Square.

*Innes' earlier novels (more convoluted and fantastical
than his later books) include* Death at the President's
Lodgings, Lament for a Maker, Appleby on Ararat, The
Weight of the Evidence, A Night of Errors *and* The
Journeying Boy. *At the heart of Stewart's books is a quin-
tet of novels of Oxford life,* The Gaudy, Young Patullo, A
Memorial Service, The Madonna of the Astrolabe *and*
Full Term. Myself and Michael Innes *is J.I.M. Stewart's*
autobiography.

INTO THE WILDERNESS

▷Willa Cather, *Death Comes for the Archbishop*
▷Joseph Conrad, *Heart of Darkness*
  Fenimore Cooper, *The Last of the Mohicans*
▷Eleanor Dark, *The Timeless Land*
  Brian Moore, *Black Robe*
▷Paul Theroux, *The Mosquito Coast*
▷Patrick White, *Voss*

IRVING, John · *(born 1942)*
US novelist.

At first glance, Irving's novels seem little more than surreal black comedies, magic realism exported from South
to North America. In fact, nothing that happens in his
books is unbelievable: his tales may lose nothing in the
telling, but they are always plausible. The main characters
of *Setting Free the Bears* plot to release the inmates of the
Vienna Zoo. The hero of *The World According to Garp* is
a writer whose creativity is only triggered when terrible
things happen to the women he loves. The family in *The*

READ ON

● *The World According
to Garp.*
▶ ▷Salman Rushdie,
Midnight's Children.
Richard Brautigan,
*Trout Fishing in
America.* ▷Russell
Hoban, *Turtle Diary.*
Gerald H. Morris,

Hotel New Hampshire turns a derelict girls' school into a hotel (complete with dancing bear), and later, when business falls off, moves to Austria where the hotels are smaller, the bears are cleverer, and terrorists are threatening to take over the Vienna Opera. Irving, in his deadpan way, constantly implies – and who can deny it? – that there is nothing eccentric here, that he is recording the bizarreness of life itself.

THE CIDER HOUSE RULES • *(1985)*

Homer Wells, brought up in a rural Maine orphanage and abortion clinic run by the saintly ether-addict Dr Larch, struggles against his destiny, which is to become a gynaecologist and take his mentor's place. He runs away, becomes the manager of a cider-farm, falls in love with his best friend's wife and lives a life of confused obscurity – but he constantly feels the pull back to the clinic and to Melony, a homicidal feminist who hero-worships him and is waiting her chance to murder him.

Irving's other novels are The Water-Method Man *and* The 158-Pound Marriage.

ISHERWOOD, Christopher • *(1904–86)*
British/US writer of novels, screenplays and non-fiction.

Isherwood was a university teacher in California, a writer of plays, films and non-fiction books (chiefly autobiographical or on Hindu mysticism). His novels and stories are all based on personal experience. The best-known (*Mr Norris Changes Trains/The Last of Mr Norris*, 1935; *Goodbye to Berlin*, 1939; *The Berlin Stories*, 1946) are set in 1930s Berlin, a seedy, decadent city haunted by German defeat in the first world war and by the gathering power of nazism. They are first person stories, told by a naive young language teacher amused, perplexed and vaguely terrified by the human tragi-comedy he reports. They have been filmed, made into a stage-play (*I Am a Camera*) and a hit musical (*Cabaret*). In a similarly rueful vein, Isherwood's novel *A Single Man* (1964) describes the emptily busy life of a lonely homosexual teaching English literature at a US university.

ISHIGURO, Kazuo • *(born 1954)*
Japanese/British novelist.

Ishiguro was educated in England and writes in English. His books are gentle, poetic studies of the effects on pre-

Doves and Silk Handkerchieves. Jack Trevor Story, *Morag's Flying Fortress*.

READ ON ⟩

● *Prater Violet*; *A Meeting by the River*.
▶ ▷Ruth Prawer Jhabvala, *Heat and Dust*. ▷Mary McCarthy, *Birds of America*. Michael Frayn, *The Russian Interpreter*. Francis King, *The Custom House*. ▷Angus Wilson, *Setting the World on Fire*.

READ ON ⟩

▶ ▷R.K. Narayan, *The English Teacher/*

sent-day Japanese of earlier 20th-century events. The central character of *A Pale View of Hills* (1982), a middle-aged woman living in England, is driven by her daughter's suicide to a prolonged reverie about her own childhood in Nagasaki, and her attempt to rebuild her life and her emotional relationships after the city's atomic destruction in 1945. Oni, the elderly protagonist of *An Artist of the Floating World* (1986), was a prominent propagandist for Japanese militarism in the 1930s, and now, in his own 60s, has to come to terms with the collapse of his professional life, his ostracism by younger colleagues, and the way his own children's moral values, typical of the new Japan, seem to deny everything he ever believed in or affirmed.

Grateful to Life and Death. ▷Willa Cather, *The Professor's House.* ▷Graham Greene, *The Quiet American.*

J

JAGGER, Brenda • *(1937–86)*
British novelist.

Jagger wrote historical romances, many of them in series and most set in Yorkshire. Her books include the trilogy *Clouded Hills, Flint and Roses* and *Sleeping Sword*, and *A Song Twice Over* (1985, about two early Victorian women, one poor, one rich, who fall in love with the same man).

JAMES, Henry • *(1843–1916)*
US/British novelist and short-story writer.

As well as novels, James wrote plays, essays, travel-books, literary criticism and a dozen volumes of short stories. In his fiction he returned again and again to the same theme: the conflict between decadence and innocence. James identified decadence with the 'old culture' of Europe, and innocence with the late 19th-century USA; his books often involve visitors from one continent experiencing and coming to terms with the other. Because he was not religious – he was brought up as a rationalist – the moral struggle of his plots is usually less between overt 'good' and 'evil' than between different standards and manners, and he also liked to tease out every strand of meaning in a situation, to explain and theorise about his characters' motives and the possible outcome of each choice they make. Untangling this, especially in his last three, most intricately stylised novels (*The Wings of the Dove, The Ambassadors* and *The Golden Bowl*), is one of the chief pleasures of his work.

THE WINGS OF THE DOVE • *(1902)*
Kate Croy lives with her snobbish aunt, who plans to

READ ON ▷

▶ ▷Maeve Binchy, *Light a Penny Candle*. Alice Adams, *Superior Women*. ▷Georgette Heyer, *False Colours*.

READ ON ▷

● *Portrait of a Lady* (about the moral and social consequences of a young American's decision to settle in England and Italy); *The Ambassadors* (a long, ironical novel about how Europe changes a group of Americans, young and middle-aged, rich and poor, friends and strangers).
▶ ▷Marcel Proust, *Swann's Way* (part I of *Remembrance of Things Past*). ▷E.M. Forster, *A Room with a View*. ▷Edith Wharton, *The Reef*. ▷Muriel Spark, *The Mandelbaum Gate*.

make a 'great' marriage for her. But Kate is secretly engaged to a penniless journalist, Merton Densher. Millie Theale, a young, rich American, visits Kate's aunt to be introduced to London society, and becomes Kate's friend. Millie is frail, and it is soon apparent that she is dying. She goes to Venice, where she welcomes all her friends in a decaying palazzo on the Grand Canal. Kate persuades Merton to try and comfort Millie's last months by pretending that he loves her; Kate hopes that Millie will then leave money to Merton which will enable them to marry. So everyone will be happy. But another of Millie's suitors, the unprincipled Lord Mark, tells Millie of Merton's and Kate's secret engagement – a revelation which brings tragedy to all three principal characters.

James' other novels include Daisy Miller, Portrait of a Lady, Washington Square, The Bostonians, The Spoils of Poynton *and* The Tragic Muse. *Of his 100 short stories and novellas, the best-known are* The Turn of the Screw *(about two children haunted by a sinister dead couple),* The Real Thing *and* The Lesson of the Master.

JAMES, P.D. (Phyllis Dorothy) ·
(born 1920)
British novelist.

Although James is often described as the 1980s 'Queen of Crime', ▷Agatha Christie's heir, she is more like a cross between ▷Sayers and ▷Highsmith. The crimes in her books are brutal, are committed by deranged, psychopathic people, and are described in chilling, unblinking prose as objective as a forensic report. Her detective, Adam Dalgliesh, is a poet and aesthete, combining brilliant detective instincts with a liberal conscience and a dandyish distaste for what he does. Although the books at first seem long and leisurely, James racks tension inexorably tighter until her dénouement: not a cosy Christieish explanation round the library fire, but a scene of pathological, cathartic violence.

A TASTE FOR DEATH · *(1986)*
A lonely spinster, taking flowers to decorate her local church, finds the throat-cut corpses of a tramp, Harry Mack, and a prominent Tory MP, Sir Paul Berowne. Berowne has been the subject of recent slanderous accusations, and Dalgliesh's investigation must begin by deciding whether he was murdered or committed suicide after killing Mack. The story gradually sucks in various members of Berowne's large and mutually hostile family, his servants and his mistress – and as well as showing us this,

▷Stendhal, *Scarlet and Black.* ▷Elizabeth Bowen, *Eva Trout.*

> **READ ON**

● *Death of an Expert Witness.*
▶ ▷Ngaio Marsh, *Surfeit of Lampreys.* ▷Marjorie Allingham, *The Tiger in the Smoke.* ▷Patricia Highsmith, *Ripley Under Ground.* ▷Ruth Rendell, *A Sleeping Life.* Margaret Millar, *Mermaid.*

and describing the police work in exact, unhurried detail, the book also concerns itself with the lives and preoccupations of Dalgliesh's assistants, especially Inspector Kate Miskin, the newest member of the team.

James' other novels are Cover Her Face, A Mind to Murder, Unnatural Causes, Shroud for a Nightingale, An Unsuitable Job for a Woman, The Black Tower, Innocent Blood *and* The Skull Beneath the Skin.

JANSSON, Tove • *(born 1917)*
Finnish novelist and children's writer.

Jansson is best-known for her 'Moomin' books for children: humorous fantasies about gentle balloon-creatures with magic powers. *The Summer Book* (1972), for adults, is a short, beautiful novel about a young child's relationship with her grandmother. The two of them quietly investigate their world – much of the book takes place on a peaceful island in the Gulf of Finland where the family are spending the summer – and share their feelings. They have two kinds of innocence: the child's freshness and the grandmother's paring-down of a lifetime's experience. The mood is placid and evocative, and for all its shortness the book is one of the half-dozen most poetic evocations of childhood composed this century.

JARRELL, Randall • *(1914–65)*
US poet, children's writer and novelist.

Jarrell's main fame is for poetry and a well-loved children's book, *The Animal Family* (1965). His only adult novel, *Pictures from an Institution* (1954), is one of the funniest of all campus comedies. It takes place in a progressive women's college in the 1950s. The girls are dewy-eyed innocents, passionate for life and learning; the faculty-members are wild eccentrics, whether they be Dr Rosenblum the advanced Austrian composer, Jerrold and Flo Whittaker the hippie sociologists, Gertrude the experimental novelist (and her down-trodden husband and greatest fan Sidney) or President Robbins himself, formerly an Olympic swimmer and now a fundraising superman. There is no real plot: the book runs through one eventful year, and the fun is in Jarrell's mixture of malice, magnificent one-liners and affection for even his most absurd characters.

READ ON ▷

● *Sun City.*
▶ **Childhood memoirs of similar poetic intensity:** Laurie Lee, *Cider With Rosie*; Flora Thompson, *Lark Rise to Candleford*; W.H. Hudson, *Far Away and Long Ago*; ▷Vladimir Nabokov, *Speak, Memory*; Gerald Durrell, *My Family and Other Animals.*

READ ON ▷

▶ D.J. Enright, *Academic Year.* ▷Anthony Burgess, *Enderby's Dark Lady.* ▷Kingsley Amis, *Lucky Jim.* Robertson Davies, *The Rebel Angels.*

JEROME, Jerome K. (Klapka) •
(1859–1927)
British novelist and journalist.

Jerome, an actor, wrote humorous pieces while waiting to go on stage; after the success of *Three Men in a Boat* in 1889 he became a full-time writer. *Three Men in a Boat* is the story of a boating holiday on the Thames undertaken by three London clerks (to say nothing of the dog). The book's deadpan humour – what Jerome calls its 'hopeless and incurable veracity' – depends on magnifying life's small problems (such as opening a tin without a tin-opener, or being in the same house as a courting couple without embarrassing them) to epic proportions, and on losing no opportunity for reflections on life, liberty, the pursuit of happiness, and the heroes' invincible conviction that middle-class Victorian young Britons, such as themselves, are the goal to which all human evolution has been tending.

JHABVALA, Ruth Prawer • *(born 1927)*
British novelist and screenwriter.

In a series of placid, gently ironical novels and screenplays (beginning with *Shakespeare Wallah* (1965), for the Merchant-Ivory partnership), Jhabvala has become a main European chronicler of India since the Raj. She is less interested in public events than in emotions, and particularly in the interface between two mutually uncomprehending cultures, Indian and European. In her best-known book, *Heat And Dust* (1975, filmed 1983), a young Englishwoman visits modern India to find out about her aunt's unhappy love-affair there 60 years before. The story cuts between the two periods, contrasting the modern character's apparently sophisticated racial and cultural awareness with the aunt's naivety and immaturity, and making points about attitudes (of Indians towards the English and vice versa) both during the Raj and in our own day.

Jhabvala's novels include To Whom She Will, The Nature of Passion, Esmond in India, The Householder, Get Ready for Battle, A Backward Glance, A New Dominion, Three Continents *and* In Search of Love and Beauty *(set in the USA, and influenced by her experience scripting* ▷Henry James' The Europeans *for Merchant-Ivory). Like* Birds Like Fishes, A Stronger Climate, An Experience of India, Out of India *and* How I Became a Holy Mother *are collections of short stories.*

READ ON ⟩

● *Three Men on a Bummel*; *My Life and Times* (autobiography).
▶ George and Weedon Grossmith, *The Diary of a Nobody.* ▷Max Beerbohm, *Zuleika Dobson.* A.G. Macdonell, *England, Their England.* Stephen Leacock, *Literary Lapses.* Giovanni Guareschi, *The House that Nino Built.*

READ ON ⟩

● *Esmond in India.*
▶ ▷E.M. Forster, *A Passage to India.* Paul Scott, *Staying On.* Rabinadrath Tagore, *The Home and the World.* Anita Desai, *Games at Twilight* (stories).

JONG, Erica • *(born 1942)*
US novelist and poet.

Although Jong is primarily a poet, she became world-famous for two bleak prose satires on our contemporary obsession with sex. The novels are the autobiography of
Isadora. In *Fear of Flying* (1974) she spends her time
cock-hunting: the Holy Grail, she tells us, is the 'zipless
fuck', sex without commitment, and she searches for it in
locker-rooms, on trains and planes, on beaches, in hotel
rooms and wherever else multiple orgasms beckon. In
How to Save Your Own Life (1978) she has fame and
wealth (as the author of a best-selling dirty book), and
walks the treadmill of personal appearances, tours and the
jetset life while still (metaphorically and literally) unzip-
ping every man in sight. But by now the sex is even more
mechanical; the pleasure is no smaller but lasts less long,
and Isadora is increasingly obsessed by the void in her
own life where love should be. Jong's novels have sold
because of their frequent, explicit descriptions of sexual
coupling – no position is left untried – and because they
were at the forefront of the battle to have women's sexuality treated as openly as men's. But they also, chiefly, sa-
tirise contemporary US life and values. The zipless fuck is
a metaphor for instant gratification of every kind, and the
books' insistent theme is that there is much, much more to
life.

*Serenissima is a fantasy about a woman transported back
in time to 16th-century Venice, where she has a passionate affair with a young English playwright and poet who
later immortalises her as 'the dark lady'. Jong's poetry-
collections include* Fruits and Vegetables, Half-Lives,
Loveroot, Here Comes *and* At the Edge of the Body.

JOYCE, James • *(1882–1941)*
Irish novelist and short-story writer.

Although Joyce settled in Italy at 27, and spent the rest of
his life there, he never left the Ireland of his memory: his
work is a ceaseless exploration of Irish scenery, education, history, religion, habits of thought and patterns of
daily life. His early writings – the short stories in *Dubliners* (1914) and the novel *Portrait of the Artist as a
Young Man* (1915), based on his own school and university life – are stylistically straightforward. They are also
notable for precise evocation of sensation and atmosphere.
By giving a mosaic of tiny impressions (the feel of
wooden desks in a schoolroom, the taste of mud on a

> **READ ON** ▷

▶ ▷Lisa Alther, *Kinflicks*.
Marilyn French, *The
Women's Room.*
▷Jean Rhys, *Good
Morning, Midnight.*

> **READ ON** ▷

▶ Ralph Ellison, *Invisible
Man.* ▷Malcolm Lowry,
Under the Volcano.
▷Thomas Wolfe, *Look
Homeward, Angel.*
▷Virginia Woolf, *Mrs
Dalloway.* ▷John
Kennedy Toole, *A
Confederacy of
Dunces* is a kind of
comic Ulysses, set in
New Orleans, and both

rugby field, the smell of gas-lamps in student digs) Joyce builds up a detailed picture which is both factually and emotionally compelling. (▷Proust used a similar idea in the childhood sections of *Remembrance of Things Past*.) In his two long novels, *Ulysses* (1922) and *Finnegans Wake* (1939), Joyce developed this mosaic structure further: *Ulysses* relates the events of a single day, *Finnegans Wake* a man's thoughts and dreams during a single night. Parts of these books are stream-of-consciousness monologues, a tumble of apparently unrelated sentences threading a path through the maze of one person's mind. Joyce often seems to be collapsing language itself: syntax splits apart; words blur into one another; each page is a kaleidoscope of puns, parodies, half-quotations, snatches of song and snippets from half a dozen languages. Some people find this style unreadable; for others it is endlessly rewarding, a mesmeric impression of the jumble of thought itself.

ULYSSES · *(1922)*

The book follows two people, Leopold Bloom and Stephen Dedalus, from dawn to midnight on a single day in Dublin in 1904. At one level what they do is ordinary: they shave, go to the privy, eat, drink, argue in bars, go to a funeral, borrow money, flirt with girls on a beach, visit Dublin's red-light area. But Joyce also shows us their thoughts, the fragmentary responses and impressions evoked by each real incident. The book ends with a 60-page 'interior monologue', the inconsequential, erotic reverie of Bloom's wife Molly as she lies beside him, drifting into sleep.

Joyce's works are Dubliners*;* Portrait of the Artist as a Young Man *(based on an earlier, unfinished novel,* Stephen Hero*, which has also been published);* Ulysses*;* Finnegans Wake*; Chamber Music and Pomes Penyeach (poetry).*

Joyce's experimental writing and the whole concept of Irishness are spectactularly sent up in Flann O'Brien, *At Swim-Two-Birds*.

James JOYCE

IRELAND

James **PLUNKETT, STRUMPET CITY**
(Dublin life and troubles – of all kinds – before World War I)

Molly **KEANE, GOOD BEHAVIOUR**
(large Anglo-Irish family collapsing under its own eccentricity)

Flann **O'BRIEN, AT SWIM-TWO-BIRDS**
(homosexual biographer doing research, finds himself being engulfed by his subject and by memories of his own past life)

SELF-DISCOVERY

Virginia **WOOLF, MRS DALLOWAY**
(middle-class Englishwoman preparing for dinner-party reviews –and reveals – her whole existence and inner self)

Marcel **PROUST, THE GUERMANTES WAY**
(Part III of Remembrance of Things Past *– the effects of death – of love and the death of the beloved)*

Iris **MURDOCH, THE SANDCASTLE**
(middle-aged schoolmaster, besotted with young artist, finds his whole life toppling round his ears)

Joseph **HELLER, SOMETHING HAPPENED**
(empty man, New York business executive, reviews the reasons for the failure of his career and family life)

John **FOWLES, THE MAGUS**
(man seeks true meaning of experience: is our life as real as it seems, or a series of illusions – and if illusion, how well-disposed is the illusionist?)

(journey of self-discovery on single Dublin day in 1904)

'JOYCEAN' NOVELS:

**BIG, EXPERIMENTAL,
ALL-ENCOMPASSING**

Alexander **THEROUX, D'ARCONVILLE'S CAT**
(jilted by sophomore lover, D'Arconville leaves US Deep South to 'find himself' in Venice)

John **BARTH, GILES GOAT-BOY**
(US professor tries to bring up child free of original sin)

Salman **RUSHDIE, MIDNIGHT'S CHILDREN**
(Saleem and family, 'handcuffed to India', experience the 80-year evolution of independence and self-renewal)

Laurence **STERNE, TRISTRAM SHANDY**
('autobiography' of 18th-century English gentleman turns into the longest, richest shaggy-dog story ever told)

Italo **SVEVO, THE CONFESSIONS OF ZENO**
(explaining to his psychiatrist why he can't give up smoking, Zeno tells the tale of his extraordinary, inadequate existence)

Joyce **CARY, THE HORSE'S MOUTH**
(eccentric artist determines to live bohemian existence, boozy and bawdy, reinventing his own character from day to day)

John Kennedy **TOOLE, A CONFEDERACY OF DUNCES**
(self-confessed genius bestrides New Orleans like an anarchic, flatulent colossus, finds it too small to accommodate his appetite for mischief)

Anthony **BURGESS, EARTHLY POWERS**
('memoirs' of aged homosexual novelist, who has been at heart of all human betrayal and bitchiness since the 20th century began)

Robertson **DAVIES, WHAT'S BRED IN THE BONE**
(odyssey of art-forger, thief and conman, as discovered from his will)

Saul **BELLOW, HUMBOLDT'S GIFT**
(Chicago)

J. D. **SALINGER, THE CATCHER IN THE RYE**
(New York)

Lawrence **DURRELL, THE ALEXANDRIA QUARTET**

Eleanor **DARK, WATERWAY**
(Sydney)

CITIES

K

KAFKA, Franz • *(1883-1924)*
Czech novelist and short-story writer.

In the 1920s and 1930s people regarded Kafka as an un-smiling neurotic who depicted the human condition as a bureaucratic hell without explanation or compassion: 'Kafkaesque' was a synonym for 'nightmarish'. Kafka, by contrast, always regarded himself as a humorist, in the line of such surrealist East European jokers as ▷Gogol. Each of his novels and stories develops a single idea to ludicrous, logical-illogical extremes. In 'Metamorphosis' a man has to cope with the fact that he has turned into a gigantic beetle overnight. The prison-camp commander of 'In the Penal Colony' is so eager to show off a newly-invented punishment-machine that he turns it on himself. In 'The Burrow' a creature designs a defence-system of underground tunnels so complex and so perfect that it be-comes the whole meaning of existence: it engulfs its own creator. The central figure of *The Trial (Der Prozess)* is arrested one morning although he has done nothing wrong, spends the book trying to discover the charges against him, and is finally executed without explanation. It is easy to treat such tales as psychological or political allegories. But it is also possible to read them as jokes, grimly funny anecdotes invented just for the hell of it. Perhaps keeping his face straight was Kafka's best trick of all.

THE CASTLE (Das Schloss) • *(1926)*
An ordinary, unremarkable man, K, arrives in a strange town to take up the post of Land Surveyor. He finds that no one is expecting him, that the town and the castle which dominates it are a labyrinthine bureaucracy where everyone is responsible only for passing the buck to some-one else, and each favour done, each door opened, leads

READ ON ▷

● *The Trial*; *America* (the story of a naive young German who goes to the USA thinking that its streets are paved with gold, and goes on believing it despite being cheated and betrayed by everyone he meets).
▶ **Echoing Kafka's humour:** ▷Jaroslav Hašek, *The Good Soldier Švejk*; ▷Joseph Heller, *Catch-22*; ▷Nathanael West, *The Dream Life of Balso Snell*; Joe Orton, *Head to Toe*.
▶ **Echoing the idea of a 'Kafkaesque', nightmare society:** Rex Warner, *The Aerodrome*; Alasdair Gray, *Lanark*; Max Frisch, *I'm Not Stiller*; ▷George Orwell, *1984*.

only to more confusion. K's efforts to reach the heart of the mystery, to be given some official confirmation of his existence, are doomed, hilarious and have the logic not of reality but of a very bad dream indeed.

Kafka's novels are The Trial, The Castle *and* America. *Of the many collections of his stories, the best is* Kafka's Shorter Works, *translated by* Malcolm Pasley.

KENEALLY, Thomas • *(born 1935)*
Australian novelist and playwright.

Although Keneally has written books on many subjects, including the partly-autobiographical *Three Cheers for the Paraclete* (1968), about a young Roman Catholic losing his faith, he is best-known for 'faction': powerful fictional treatments of the issues and personalities behind real events. Apart from *Blood Red, Sister Rose* (1974), about Joan of Arc, his books are set in comparatively recent times, usually at decisive moments in the history of a people or continent – and Keneally gets under the skin of the participants, showing how great events happen for what are usually far smaller and more personal reasons (a quarrel; a cold in the head) than the awareness of grand political or strategic trends which historians would suggest. He is not, however, a 'historical' novelist, simply telling tales about the past. His concentration on issues gives his stories universal resonance: we are constantly shown the relevance of the events he describes to our present-day situation or attitudes. His best-known books are *The Chant of Jimmie Blacksmith* (1971, about racial confrontation in 19th-century Australia), *Gossip from the Forest* (1973, set during the 1918 Armistice negotiations), *Confederates* (1979, about Stonewall Jackson's campaigns in the American civil war) and *The Playmaker* (1987, see below).

SCHINDLER'S ARK • *(1982)*
Schindler is a bragging, boozing opportunist who makes a fortune in Poland during the second-world-war German occupation, buying up the businesses of dispossessed Jews. We read about his black-market deals, his backslapping relationship with the authorities, his parties and his mistresses – and gradually discover that his lifestyle is a façade, that his true activity is saving thousands of Jews from the gas-chambers.

Keneally's other novels include A Dutiful Daughter, Bring Larks and Heroes *(set in 19th-century New South Wales),* Season in Purgatory *(about Tito and the Yugoslavian par-*

READ ON ▷

● *The Playmaker* (in which convicts transported to 18th-century New South Wales, under the guidance of a confused, would-be liberal army lieutenant, rehearse and perform – of all things – Farquhar's Restoration comedy *The Recruiting Officer*).
▶ E.L. Doctorow, *The Book of Daniel*. Lionel Davidson, *Making Good Again*. William Styron, *Sophie's Choice*.

Thomas KENEALLY

E.L. DOCTOROW, THE BOOK OF DANIEL
(lives of children of US immigrants executed for espionage)

John FOWLES, A MAGGOT
(witchcraft, murder and possible UFOs in 18th-century England)

Tony WEEKS-PEARSON, DODO
(extermination of dodo brings culture-shock to native inhabitants of idyllic Pacific island)

Frederick FORSYTH, THE DAY OF THE JACKAL
(plot to assassinate General de Gaulle of France)

Martin Cruz SMITH, STALLION GATE
(Mexican magic versus development of first atomic bomb)

NOVELS ARISING FROM REAL EVENTS

Bruce CHATWIN, THE SONG LINES
(writer travels modern Australia, investigating Aboriginal sacred places)

William GOLDING, CLOSE QUARTERS
(life on 1790s convict-ship sailing from England to Australia)

THE AUSTRALIAN PAST

Eleanor DARK, THE TIMELESS LAND
(first white settlers in Australia)

Patrick WHITE, A FRINGE OF LEAVES
(shipwrecked 1910s woman learns survival by assimilating Aborigine culture)

Nathaniel HAWTHORNE, THE SCARLET LETTER
(religious hysteria and persecution in Puritan New England)

Chinua ACHEBE, THINGS FALL APART
(Nigerian tribal life, the rhythms of civilisation, disrupted by coming of white missionaries)

FRONTIERS OF CIVILISATION

Brian MOORE, BLACK ROBE
(Jesuit priest in 17th-century Huron Indian country: irreconcilable culture-clash)

(1780s Australia: English officer guides convicts through production of a Restoration comedy)

CONVICTS

Victor **HUGO, LES MISÉRABLES**
(19th-century France: honest man wrongly convicted to the galleys tries to rehabilitate himself)

Alexander **SOLZHENITSYN, ONE DAY IN THE LIFE OF IVAN DENISOVICH**
(20th-century USSR: unsparing account of life in labour-camp for dissidents)

Charles **DICKENS, LITTLE DORRIT**
(19th-century England: corrupting effects of money, and life in the Marshalsea Debtors' Prison)

John **CHEEVER, FALCONER**
(20th-century USA: life in 'correctional facility' as experienced by mentally unstable, middle-class wife-murderer)

PLAYS AND PLAY ACTORS

Robertson **DAVIES, TEMPEST-TOST**
(amateurs in 1950s Canadian university town)

Paul **BAILEY, PETER SMART'S CONFESSIONS**
(testimony of unsuccessful, mentally unstable actor)

Virginia **WOOLF, BETWEEN THE ACTS**
(thoughts and feelings of everyone involved in village historical pageant)

Roger **LANGRIGG, THERE'S A PORPOISE CLOSE BEHIND US** *(sour success of 'bright young things' on 1930s London stage)*

AUSTRALIAN LIFE: THE FUNNY SIDE

Elizabeth **JOLLEY, THE FUNNY SIDE**

Peter **CAREY, ILLYWHACKER**

Howard **JACOBSON, REDBACK**

tisans during and after the second world war), A Victim
of the Aurora, A Family Madness, Passenger *and* The
Cut-Rate Kingdom. *He has also written films, stage
plays, children's books and a fascinating account of his
travels in Australia,* Outback.

KING, Stephen • *(born 1946)*
US novelist.

King writes horror-stories: tales of obsession, insanity and
the supernatural made even more terrifying by the ordinary US suburbs, schools and factories where they take
place. His books (many made into blockbuster films) are
*The Dead Zone, Carrie, Salem's Lot, Firestarter, The
Shining, The Stand, Christine, Pet Sematary, Cujo, It* and
Misery (1987), about a best-selling author kidnapped by a
maniac. *Night Shift* and *Skeleton Crew* are collections of
ghoulish short stories. King also writes as *Richard Bachman* (whose *Thinner*, about a man tormented by a gipsy's
curse, is not for readers who find it hard to sleep).

> **READ ON** ⟩

▶ **To King's novels:**
▷James Herbert,
Sepulchre; Richard
Matheson, *The
Shrinking Man*; ▷Ruth
Rendell, *Live Flesh* –
and, from an earlier
generation, ▷H.G.
Wells, *The Island of
Doctor Moreau.*
▶ **To his short stories:**
▷Edgar Allan Poe,
*Tales of Mystery and
Imagination*; ▷Patricia
Highsmith, *Mermaids
on the Golf Course*;
Roald Dahl, *Kiss, Kiss*;
▷Angela Carter,
Fireworks.

KIPLING, Rudyard • *(1865–1936)*
British short-story writer and poet.

Kipling learned his craft working for English-language
newspapers in India in the 1880s. He wrote reports, stories and poems about the British soldiers and administra-
tors, their servants and the snake-charmers, fortune-tellers
and other characters of the towns they lived in. Later, during the Boer War, he worked as a correspondent in South
Africa, where he was a friend of Cecil Rhodes. Under the
circumstances, it would have been hard for him not to reflect the imperialist attitudes of his age, first sunny confidence and then the jingoistic panic which overtook it in
late Victorian times. But he is a more rewarding writer
than this suggests. His sympathies were always with sub-
ordinates – with private soldiers rather than generals, servants rather than employers, children rather than adults.
He wrote well about all three: his stories for and about
children, in particular, are magnificent. Something like
half of each collection – most books contain both stories

> **READ ON** ⟩

● *Plain Tales from the
Hills*; *Debits and
Credits.*
▶ **To Kipling's stories
about children:**
▷Katherine Mansfield,
*Bliss and Other
Stories.*
▶ **To his stories about
colonial adults:**
▷Somerset Maugham,
Orientations; the short
stories of Noël
Coward. ▷John
Masters, *Nightrunners
of Bengal,* and ▷J.G.
Farrell, *The Siege of*

and poems – is nowadays hard to take, not least where he writes in baby-talk (as in the *Just-So Stories*, O best-beloved) or uses funny spellings to evoke Cockney or Irish speech. But every archness is balanced by a gem of insight or sensitivity. In this, too, he was characteristic of his time.

KIM • *(1901)*

This episodic novel is the story of a British orphan brought up as a beggar in Lahore, who becomes first the disciple of a wandering Buddhist priest and then an agent of the British secret service. He travels throughout India, and Kipling uses his adventures as a framework for descriptions of everyday scenes and characters, of 'such a river of life as nowhere else exists in the world'.

Kipling's collections include Barrack-room Ballads, The Seven Seas *and* The Years Between *(verse),* Soldiers Three *(stories), and the mixed prose-and-verse collections* Many Inventions, Traffics and Discoveries, A Diversity of Creatures *and* Debits and Credits. *His novels are* The Light That Failed *and* Captains Courageous, *and his children's books include the* Just-so Stories, *the* Jungle Book, Puck of Pook's Hill *and the public-school yarn* Stalky and Co. Something of Myself *is a guarded autobiography.*

KOSINSKI, Jerzy • *(born 1933)*
Polish/US novelist and non-fiction writer.

Kosinski settled in the USA in his 20s, and all his fiction is in English. He writes of contemporary life with horrified disdain, as if he were a being from an alien planet describing some bizarre and repulsive civilisation – indeed, the SF of such writers as ▷Moorcock or ▷Vonnegut is the closest parallel to his experimental, fantastical style. His best-known book (because of the Peter Sellers film made from it) is *Being There* (1971), about a non-person, a man of miniscule intelligence whose ideas are received entirely from television or from gardening, and whose monosyllabic mutterings are taken by all around him as profound moral and political philosophy. Chance (the hero) ends up as adviser to the US president, and we are left uncomfortably wondering if he may not also be the only sane person in a lunatic society. Kosinski's other novels also centre on outsiders. The central character of *The Painted Bird* (1965) is a swarthy orphaned child in peasant Poland, regarded by everyone as an alien (a Jew or a gipsy) and rejected. The hero of *The Devil Tree* (1973) is a young man isolated from society both by im-

Krishnapur, about the 1857 Indian 'Mutiny', match Kipling's insight into the heyday of the Raj.

▷ READ ON ▷

● *Steps* (the random thoughts and conversations of a youth growing up in a country he hates and from which he is planning to emigrate as soon as chance allows).
▶ ▷Michael Moorcock, *The English Assassin.* Milan Kundera, *The Book of Laughter and Forgetting.* ▷Saul Bellow, *Mr Sammler's Planet.* Patrick McGinley, *The Trick of the Ga Bolga.* ▷I.B. Singer's short stories, although their subjects are entirely unlike

mense inherited wealth – he could buy and sell whole countries – and by his own adolescent fantasy that he is the only person in the world obsessed by sex. In *Cockpit* (1975) and *Blind Date* (1977) the central characters are secret agents isolated from the real world not only by their trade but by their own burgeoning, uncommunicated thoughts.

Kosinski's, share his feeling that the world is a terrifying, alien environment in which human beings survive – if they do survive – only by chance or because of their own uncompromisingly lateral stance to life.

KRANTZ, Judith
US novelist.

In the 1970s Krantz took the 'novel of affairs' genre (big-business as sex; sex as big business) perfected a generation earlier by such writers as Harold Robbins, and refurbished it for modern tastes. The businesses of which she writes are multi-national corporations; the wealth is megabucks; the sex is as near pornography as respectable publishers will print. Only the morality remains the same: non-existent. Krantz's books (*Princess Daisy*; *Scruples*; *Mistral's Daughter*; *I'll Take Manhattan*) are like dirtied-up versions of such TV soaps as *Dallas* or *Dynasty*: superb escapism.

READ ON ⟩

▶ Shirley Conran, *Lace*. Jackie Collins, *Lucky*. Sally Quinn, *Regrets Only*. Sidney Sheldon, *Bloodlines*.

L

LARGER THAN LIFE

Peter Carey, *Illywhacker*
▷Robertson Davies, *What's Bred in the Bone*
Howard Jacobson, *Redback*
▷Robert Nye, *Falstaff*
Petronius, *Satyricon*
▷François Rabelais, *Gargantua*
▷Laurence Sterne, *Tristram Shandy*

LAWRENCE, D.H. (David Herbert) •
(1885-1930)
British writer of novels, short stories, plays and poems.

For 70 years Lawrence's radicalism has outraged as many people as it has enthralled. He thought that every matter of concern to human beings, and moral and ethical issues in particular, could be settled by rational discussion, if people would only be honest about themselves. His novels deal with such matters as female emancipation, the class struggle, atheism, sexual liberation and pacifism – not explicitly but as part of an ongoing advocacy of nakedness, of people at their best when stripped of inhibition and convention. Lawrence regarded his plain speaking as a way of shedding light in dark corners, a return to the innocence of the Garden of Eden; his enemies thought it shocking. Nowadays, when his rawness seems less threatening, his books stand up not only for moral earnestness – they read at times like humourless, secular sermons – but for their acute presentation of people and society in turmoil, of attitudes to life which the second world war and the dawn of the nuclear age have made seem unimaginably remote.

READ ON ▷

● *The Rainbow*.
▶ ▷George Eliot, *Middlemarch*.
▷Thomas Hardy, *Jude the Obscure* (especially close to *Women in Love* in its treatment of tensions between the sexes). David Storey, *Radcliffe*. Melvyn Bragg, *The Maid of Buttermere*. ▷Thomas Wolfe, *Look Homeward, Angel*. Henry Roth, *Call It Sleep*. ▷James Baldwin, *Go Tell it on the Mountain*.

SONS AND LOVERS · *(1913)*

Paul Morel is the son of ill-matched parents, an ex-school-teacher and an illiterate, alcoholic miner. Morel's mother is determined to help her son escape from the physical grind and intellectual atrophy of pit-village life and fulfil his ambition to be a writer. Her love for him is, however, a force for darkness not liberation. It inhibits both his self-discovery and his relationship with other people (especially the young farm-girl Jessie, who encourages his writing), and it is only when he breaks free of his mother – a protracted, agonising process, a second birth – that he is able to fulfil the destiny she has planned for him.

Lawrence's other novels include The Rainbow *and its sequel* Women in Love, Aaron's Rod, Kangaroo, The Plumed Serpent *and* Lady Chatterley's Lover. *He also published poems, travel books (eg* Sea and Sardinia; Mornings in Mexico), *plays, books on history and literature, and collections of short stories (eg* England, My England; The Woman Who Rode Away).

LE CARRÉ, John · *(born 1931)*

British novelist.

For over a century, writers from ▷Verne to ▷Fleming depicted espionage as a swashbuckling, Robin Hood activity with clear rules, absolute moral standards and a penchant for flamboyance. But in the 1960s this view changed. The Cuban missile crisis all but led to world annihilation; the Berlin Wall was built; a series of well-publicised defections revealed that spies were secretive, unremarkable men, morally hesitant and trapped by their own profession. Betrayal, not derring-do, was their stock-in-trade; east, west, north, south, they were as indistinguishable as civil service clerks. This is the atmosphere of Le Carré's books. His characters are not James Bonds, swaggering forth to smash conspiracies of global domination; in dark back streets and rainy woods they nibble away at one another's loyalties, hardly even certain of their own. It is a world of remorseless moral erosion, and Le Carré chillingly shows how it functions entirely for itself, inward-looking and self-perpetuating, with minimal relevance to real life. Since he began writing, every real-life spy-scandal, every revelation of how the 'intelligence' community works, seems to prove his accuracy – unless spies themselves have come to believe the legend he spins.

THE QUEST FOR KARLA · *(1974–80)*

This trilogy (*Tinker Tailor Soldier Spy, The Honourable*

READ ON ⟩

● *A Small Town in Germany; A Perfect Spy.*
▶ **To the spy-stories:** ▷Ruth Rendell, *Talking to Strange Men;* ▷Graham Greene, *The Human Factor;* John Lear, *Death in Leningrad.* Julian Semyonov, *Tass is Authorized to Announce* is a cold-war spy-story seen from the Russian side.

▶ **To** *The Naive and Sentimental Lover:* ▷John Fowles, *Daniel Martin;* ▷Frederic Raphael, *April, June and November.*
▶ **To** *The Little Drummer Girl;* ▷Doris Lessing, *The Good Terrorist.*

John LE CARRÉ

THE PERFECT SPY *('autobiography' of upper-echelon British spy — and double-agent)*

Robert **LUDLUM, THE PARSIFAL MOSAIC**
(can 'burnt-out' agent's secret knowledge prevent World War III?)

John **LEAR, DEATH IN LENINGRAD**
(ex-spy Ashweald revels in Leningrad — but there is a price to pay)

John **TRENHAILE, THE MAHJONG SPIES**
(can Chinese Intelligence stop KGB destabilising Hong Kong?)

Ted **ALLEBURY, THE SECRET WHISPERS**
(double agent escaping from eastern to western Europe)

Martin Cruz **SMITH, STALLION GATE**
(can Mexican folk magic halt 1945 race to develop atomic bomb?)

Michael **MOLLOY, THE KID FROM RIGA**
(can SAS officer give up his career for love? In the meantime . . .)

Walter **WAGER, TELEFON**
(brainwashed assassins, 'sleepers', await trigger phone-calls to terrorise USA)

Jack **HIGGINS, CONFESSIONAL**
(KGB agent sent to Belfast to stir things up)

Ian **FLEMING, DOCTOR NO**
(super-agent 007 outwits psychopathic master-criminal)

Len **DEIGHTON, HORSE UNDER WATER**
(drugs, spies, master-criminals, all boiled together in Marrakesh)

Eric **AMBLER, THE MASK OF DIMITRIOS/COFFIN FOR DIMITRIOS** *(hero tracks down elusive, deadly master-criminal)*

Philip **MACDONALD, THE LIST OF ADRIAN MESSENGER**
(10 people on list, marked for death. What is the link — and can they be saved in time?)

A. J. **QUINNELL, IN THE NAME OF THE FATHER**
(who is killing off ageing world leaders, one by one?)

Schoolboy and *Smiley's People*) is about the British Intelligence 'circus', and particularly the role played in it by a senior official, George Smiley. His task is to investigate double agents, 'moles', inside the service, while safeguarding his own position and keeping warily in touch with contacts and rivals in the eastern bloc. His enquiries uncover treacheries and compromises extending back over two generations: the corrupt, Kafkaesque 'Circus', with its links to Oxbridge, the public schools, clubland and government, is a cancer at the throat of British life, and Smiley is interested less in curing it than in a complex damage-limitation exercise.

Le Carré's other spy-books are The Spy Who Came in from the Cold, The Looking Glass War, A Small Town in Germany *and* A Perfect Spy. *His other books are the detective stories* Call for the Dead *and* A Murder of Quality, The Naive and Sentimental Lover *(about a bored middle-aged man given the chance to reconstruct his life) and* The Little Drummer Girl *(about a young idealist in the Middle East who turns to terrorism).*

LE GUIN, Ursula • *(born 1929)*
US novelist.

Le Guin made her name writing space opera (the 'League of All Worlds' series), and the prize-winning 'Earthsea' trilogy for children. In the late 1960s and 1970s she broadened her scope, using the framework of alternative-world fantasy to discuss social, ecological and political themes. Although many of her books are still technically SF, set in the future and on other planets, she also lets people from the past and the present break through into magical kingdoms whose values and customs are ironical variations on our own. *The Word for World is Forest* (1976) takes place on a planet covered in forests and inhabited (literally) by 'little green people', who shepherd the trees and spend their lives in placid meditation. Then earthpeople come to harvest the trees, treat the locals as mindless and worthless and force them to learn to fight for their way of life. *The Left Hand of Darkness* (1969) is a poetic description of Winterworld, of how people cope with life in an utterly hostile natural environment. The hero of *Malafrena* (1980) is a landowner's son who becomes a revolutionary leader in a world in which the political ferment of post-Napoleonic Europe is blended with the religious outlook of Germany in Luther's time and the psychological and ecological concerns of the late 20th century; although science and technology are unfailingly medieval, in all other respects time on Earth has become a

> **READ ON**

● *The Left Hand of Darkness.*
▶ ▷Tom De Haan, *A Mirror for Princes.*
▷Stephen Donaldson, *Lord Foul's Bane* (first in the 'Chronicles of Thomas Covenant' series). Ian Watson, *The Gardens of Delight.* C.S. Lewis, *Perelandra.*

continuum, has ceased to be sequential.

THRESHOLD · *(1980)*

The time is the present. Hugh, a supermarket checkout operator, crosses the freeway into a wood and finds himself in another realm, with its own time, its own laws and its own haunting reality, a world away (literally) from his own constricted and unhappy life. He meets a girl who has also broken through, and their explorations lead to a journey, a fight against nameless evil, and the inner peace which will sustain them when they return to everyday reality.

Le Guin's other novels include Rocannon's World, Planet of Exile, City of Illusions, The Lathe of Heaven *and* The Dispossessed. The Wind's Twelve Quarters *and* Orsinian Tales *have collections of short stories.* The Earthsea trilogy *(as magical as her adult fantasies, but with a child as hero) is* A Wizard of Earthsea, The Tombs of Atuan *and* The Farthest Shore.

LEHMANN, Rosamond · *(born 1901)*
British novelist.

The ideas behind Lehmann's novels were strengthened by reading Jung and by psychic research after her daughter's death in the 1950s. She believes that we are not alone, that each person is part of a greater whole: the experience and knowledge of all human beings who have ever existed. We can enter into that experience, make use of it, during the rites of passage from one stage of existence to another –birth, adolescence, marriage, death – when the subconscious is particularly receptive. Lehmann's heroines are people on the brink of self-discovery; they are either innocents or victims of life, and the novels describe, in a lucid way far removed from the exoticism and mysticism of their events, how self-knowledge is achieved and how it changes the heroine's life, for bad or good.

THE BALLAD AND THE SOURCE · *(1944)*

Ten-year-old Rebecca, picking bluebells in the garden of the old house beside the churchyard, is invited inside by the owner, Mrs Jardine, who knew Rebecca's grandmother and becomes Rebecca's friend. Rebecca listens enthralled to Mrs Jardine's tales of 'the old days' – and the more terrible the stories (they are accounts of passion, adultery, betrayal and hatred in Mrs Jardine's own young life), the more Rebecca is ensnared. Mrs Jardine is not so much like a witch casting a spell – though this is how

READ ON ▷

● In *A Sea-Grape Tree* (the sequel to *The Ballad and the Source*) Rebecca, now grown-up and betrayed by men exactly as Mrs Jardine had been, goes to a Caribbean island to sort out her life and is affected not only by the people she meets there but by spirit-visitors from her past, including Mrs Jardine herself.
▶ ▷Rose Macaulay, *The World My Wilderness*. ▷Iris Murdoch, *The Philosopher's Pupil*. ▷Virginia Woolf, *Mrs Dalloway*. ▷Alison Lurie, *Imaginary Friends*. Rebecca West, *The Thinking Reed*. Jane Gardam, *Crusoe's Daughter*.

Rebecca's alarmed mother sees her – as a Sibyl from the remote past, revealing the true nature of human emotional existence.

Lehmann's other novels are Dusty Answer, Invitation to the Waltz *and its sequel* The Weather in the Streets, The Echoing Grove *and* A Sea-Grape Tree. The Gipsy's Baby *collects short stories, and* The Swan in the Evening *is an autobiographical memoir centring on her reactions to her daughter's death.*

LEM, Stanislaw • *(born 1921)*
Polish novelist.

Lem's novels are ▷Kafkaesque SF, a blend of black humour and psychological mysticism. His best-known books are *The Cyberiad, His Master's Voice, The Invincible, One Human Minute, Fiasco* and – thanks to Tarkovsky's mesmeric film – *Solaris* (1961), about astronauts trapped on a planet which is a thinking organism, able to sense the nerve-impulses of living beings which land on it, and then make clones.

READ ON ▷

● *The Futurological Congress* (a spoof of his own work).
▶ ▷Robert Silverberg, *Tom O'Bedlam*. Jack Vance, *The Blue World*. Robert Irwin, *The Arabian Nightmare*.

LESSING, Doris • *(born 1919)*
British novelist and non-fiction writer.

Lessing was brought up in Rhodesia (now Zimbabwe), but her involvement in progressive politics made it an uncomfortable place to live, and she moved to London in 1949. In the same year she published her first novel, *The Grass is Singing*, about relationships between the races, and followed it in 1952 with the semi-autobiographical *Martha Quest*, the first in a five-book series (the other volumes, published over the next 17 years, are *A Proper Marriage, A Ripple from the Storm, Landlocked* and *The Four-gated City*). The sequence took her heroine from girlhood to marriage in white Rhodesia, from political virginity to radical activiso, from Africa to London, from youth to age. Martha becomes a feminist; she samples and rejects the 'swinging sixties'; she tries religion and mysticism; she watches, and reports on, the last hours of the human race as we writhe towards the apocalypse. The books are in a straightforward 'as-told-to' style: they have the power of documentary rather than fiction. Two other Lessing novels, *The Golden Notebook* (1962, about an unhappy writer coming to terms with herself as a person and with her place in a male-dominated society) and *Briefing for a Descent into Hell* (1971, about nervous breakdown), have

READ ON ▷

▶ Margaret Laurence, *A Jest of God*. ▷Patrick White, *The Solid Mandala*. ▷Margaret Drabble, *Jerusalem the Golden*. Stanley Middleton, *Harris' Requiem*. Marilyn French, *The Women's Room*. Simone de Beauvoir, *She Came to Stay*. ▷H.H. Richardson, *The Fortunes of Richard Mahony*.

similar intensity. Lessing's (Jungian) psychological interests, and her fascination with Sufi mysticism, influence much of her other work, especially the five-volume sequence 'Canopus in Argus' (1979–83), which uses an SF format to explore ideas not so much of outer as of inner space, the alternative realities inside the mind.

The 'Canopus in Argus' novels are Shikasta; The Marriage Between Zones Three, Four and Five; The Sirian Experiments; The Making of the Representatives for Planet 8 *and* Documents Relating to the Sentimental Agents in the Volyen Empire. *Lessing's other fiction includes the novels* Memoirs of a Survivor, The Summons before the Dark *and* The Good Terrorist, *and the short-story collections* The Habit of Loving, A Man and Two Women *and* African Stories.

LEWIS, Sinclair • *(1885-1951)*
US novelist.

In the 1920s Lewis won prizes for a series of satirical novels on aspects of US life. They are exhaustively researched, and use a fly-on-the-wall technique, reporting actions and speech in an objective-seeming way which conceals Lewis' own devastating authorial point of view. His theme was that the more honest, the more naive people seem, the more they are concealing humbug, and he was especially scathing about the US middle and professional classes. *Main Street* (1920) and *Babbitt* (1922) are slices of life in typical middle US towns: gossip-ridden, bigoted, censorious and unimaginative. *Dodsworth* (1929) is about a wimpish rich businessman trying to discover his soul (and put new life into his flagging marriage) by travelling in Europe. *Arrowsmith* (1925) is a comparatively serious study of a young doctor interested in bacteriological research. *Elmer Gantry* (1927), perhaps the most relevant of Lewis' books today, is about a religious charlatan, a born-again preacher who uses his charms to seduce women and embezzle money.

The best of Lewis' other novels – his later work tends slackly to repeat former themes – are It Can't Happen Here *(about fascism in the late 1930s USA) and* Gideon Planish *(a savage satire about big business and philanthropy).*

READ ON ▷

▶ **To the satires:**
Hamilton Basso, *The View from Pompey's Head*; ▷John Updike, *Rabbit, Run*; ▷Jerome Weidman, *The Centre of the Action*; ▷Thornton Wilder, *Heaven's My Destination*; ▷Heinrich Böll, *Billiards at Half-past Nine*; ▷Saul Bellow, *Mr Sammler's Planet.*
▶ **To Arrowsmith:** ▷C.P. Snow, *The Search.*

LEWIS, Wyndham • *(1882-1957)*
British writer and artist.

Lewis spent his life outraging the bourgeoisie, first as a wild avant-garde artist and then as a fiercely opinionated essayist on art and politics, a member of Mosley's British fascist party and an outspoken Hitler-supporter. His novels were prancing satires in the manner of ▷Huxley or ▷Waugh. *Tarr* (1918) and *The Apes of God* (1930) send up art-snobs and the dealers and phoney artists who prey on them. *The Revenge for Love* (1937) is about society people playing at politics but understanding nothing of a real tragedy (the Spanish Civil War) going on under their noses. The hero of *Self-condemned* (1954), a middle-aged professor tired of European life, retreats to a Canadian hotel, only to find it fuller of frauds and fools than the world he has left. Lewis' most stinging satire is the trilogy *The Human Age* (1928–55). It is about Armageddon, and shows the Day of Judgement not in lofty Christian terms but as a dusty, sweaty carnival, human beings prancing or shuffling to their doom at the whim of a cackling, deformed Showman – the gatekeeper of eternity is not St Peter but Mr Punch.

READ ON ▷

▶ **To the satires:** Richard Aldington, *Seven Against Reeves*; ▷Anthony Powell, *What's Become of Waring?*; ▷Aldous Huxley, *Antic Hay*; Julian Symons, *The Immaterial Murder Case.*
▶ **To Lewis' more apocalyptic comedies:** Joyce Cary, *The Horse's Mouth*; ▷Patrick White, *The Twyborn Affair*; Stuart Evans, *The Caves of Alienation.*

LOFTS, Norah • *(1904–86)*
British novelist.

Lofts wrote historical romances, many set in East Anglia. *The Brittle Glass* (1942) is typical: the story of Sorrel Kingabay, the red-haired, independent daughter of a Norfolk trader in the early 1700s, when smugglers and highwaymen still roamed the English Fens.

Lofts' other novels include many set in romantic or sinister old houses: The Town House, The House at Old Vine, The House at Sunset, Gad's Hall, Haunted House. *Her other romances include* Jassy *and* Day of the Butterfly, *and her thrillers (written under the name Peter Curtis) are* Dead March in Three Keys, Lady Living Alone *and* The Devil's Own.

READ ON ▷

▶ Oliver Onions, *The Story of Ragged Robyn.* ▷Daphne Du Maurier, *Jamaica Inn.* Sarah Woodhouse, *Daughter of the Sea.*

LONDON, Jack • *(1879–1916)*
US novelist, short-story and non-fiction writer.

In his teens London worked as a docker, a seal-hunter, an oyster pirate (stealing from other fishermen's oyster-beds) and a customs officer; he also tramped across the United States and took part in the Klondike Gold Rush. At 19 he

READ ON ▷

● *White Fang* (a mirror-image of *The Call of the Wild*: the story of a wild dog drawn to the settled down to writing, aiming to produce 1000 words a day, and began turning out he-man articles and short stories, heavy on adventure and light on character. His human beings (most of them fur-trappers, gold-miners or fishermen) take a two-fisted approach to life. Brutality rules, and survival is only guaranteed until someone stronger or brighter comes along. However blinkered London's view of life – he managed, at the same time, to be a fervent socialist and a fascist convinced that fair-haired, blue-eyed Aryans were the master-race – he wrote of it with breath-taking, blood-hammering effectiveness. His descriptions of fights, and of men battling against enormous natural hazards, set a model which many tough-guy writers have imitated, but none surpassed.

CALL OF THE WILD • *(1903)*

Buck, a St Bernard dog, is stolen from his home in California and taken to the Klondike as a sledge-dog. He passes from owner to owner, each more brutal than the last, until he finds kindness at the hands of John Thornton. But Thornton is killed, Buck's last link with human beings is broken and he escapes to the wild and becomes the leader of a wild-pack.

London's novels include Before Adam *(about the prehistoric ancestors of homo sapiens),* The Sea-wolf *(a* ▷*Conradian account of the struggle between a brutal sea-captain and the city couple he kidnaps) and* The Iron Heel *(a story of the future, recounting the struggle of a group of urban guerrillas to overthrow a dictatorship which has overrun Chicago). His story-collections include* Children of the Frost, The Road, When God Laughs, The Strength of the Strong *and* Island Tales. John Barleycorn *is an autobiographical novel about a writer battling alcoholism.*

LOWRY, Malcolm • *(1909–57)*
British novelist.

Lowry began experimenting with drugs and drink at Cambridge, and by the time he was 20 he was irretrievably addicted. He spent the rest of his life bumming across the world, in rehabilitation clinics, or in self-imposed isolation while he struggled to turn his experiences into fiction. The only novel published during his lifetime – it took him 30 years to write it – was *Under the Volcano* (1947). This tells of the last two days in the life of an alcoholic British consul in revolution-torn Mexico, and intertwines memory, dream and reality in the manner of ▷Joyce's *Ulysses.*

human race, who is betrayed and ill-treated by every owner – the description of his life as a fighting-dog is particularly harrowing – until he ends up at last with a master he can trust).

▶ To *The Call of the Wild:* Richard Adams, *The Plague Dogs;* Romain Gary, *White Dog;* ▷H.G. Wells, *The Island of Doctor Moreau.*

▶ To London's books about humans: ▷Ernest Hemingway, *The Old Man and the Sea; To Have and Have Not;* ▷Maxim Gorky, *Foma Gordeev;* ▷Joseph Conrad, *Typhoon.*

▶ To his short stories: Ring Lardner, *Round Up: the Stories/ Collected Short Stories.*

READ ON

● *Lunar Caustic; Dark as the Grave Wherein My Friend is Laid* (about a boozy, doom-ridden tour of Mexico).
▶ ▷Joseph Conrad, *Heart of Darkness.*
▷F. Scott Fitzgerald, *Tender is the Night.*
▷Fyodor Dostoevsky, *The Idiot.* ▷Lawrence

Durrell, *The Black
Book.*

LUDLUM, Robert • *(born 1927)*
US novelist.

Ludlum also writes as Jonathan Ryder (*The Cry of the
Halidon*; *The Rhineman Exchange*). His thrillers (many
based on real-life incidents) are suspenseful, tough-talking
and racy: they include *The Scarlatti Inheritance*, *The
Gemini Contenders*, *The Matarese Circle*, *The Osterman
Weekend* and *The Parsifal Mosaic* (1982, in which a
burnt-out, 'disposable' agent holds the knowledge, without realising it, which will prevent a madman code-named
Parsifal from triggering world war three).

READ ON ⟩

▶ Allen Drury, *The
Roads of Earth.* Fred
Taylor, *Walking
Shadows* (set among
German officers during
the second world war).
▷John Le Carré, *A
Perfect Spy.*

LURIE, Alison • *(born 1926)*
US novelist.

Lurie's streamlined, ivy-league prose, her effortless blend
of farce and irony, and the bitchy elegance of her plots
link her to such classy US contemporaries as Mary Mc-
Carthy, John Updike or Philip Roth – and she has the unsettling ability to lay the human condition bare for our pity
even as she sends it up. The people in her novels are all
terribly nice: well-educated, well-off, well-dressed, liberal
and compassionate. Their lives are like placid pools – and
into each of them Lurie drops the acid of discontent (usually something to do with sex) and invites us to smile as
the water seethes. Her funniest books are set on university
campuses: *Love and Friendship* (1962) is about two people trapped in an affair (and what everyone else thinks
about it); *The War Between the Tates* (1974) shows the
gradual collapse of a 'perfect' marriage under threat from
a combination of adultery and student politics. The heroine of *Imaginary Friends* (1967), finding reality emotionally unfulfilling, seeks to reinvent her personality by
psychic experimentation. The narrator of *Only Children*
(1979) is a child, who reports on the sexual imbroglios of
the adults around her with a wide-eyed gravity which
arises less from innocence than from a precocious understanding not only of what is going on but of the sort of
butter-won't-melt-in-my-mouth cuteness adults expect
from little girls.

READ ON ⟩

● *The War Between the
Tates.*
▶ **To *Foreign Affairs*:**
▷Mary McCarthy, *The
Company She Keeps*;
Joan Didion, *A Book
of Common Prayer*;
▷Philip Roth, *The
Professor of Desire.*
▶ **To *The War Between
the Tates*:** Susan
Fromberg Shaeffer,
The Injured Party.
▶ **To *Love and
Friendship*:** David
Lodge, *Small World.*
▶ **To *Only Children*:**
▷Henry James, *What
Maisie Knew.*
▶ **To Lurie's work in
general:** ▷Anita
Brookner, *Look at Me*;
Alice Thomas Ellis,
The Birds of the Air.

FOREIGN AFFAIRS • *(1984)*
Three Americans are visiting England: Vinnie, a 54-year-
old professor, Fred, a hunky young academic, and Chuck,
a middle-aged, none-too-bright businessman on a package

tour. The novel shows Vinnie's attempts to bring into the two men's lives the same kind of decorous, unflustered order she herself enjoys – and the way her own values crumple under the strain of real emotion.

Lurie's other novels are Real People, *a comedy about artists coping with inspirational blocks and sexual passion in a 'creative colony', and* A Nowhere City, *a serious book about a woman trying to cope with unfocussed psychological panic.*

Alison LURIE

Randall JARRELL, PICTURES FROM AN INSTITUTION
(send-up of life in 'progressive' US women's university, 1950s)

Mary MCCARTHY, THE GROVES OF ACADEME
(political satire: protest-movement when university president tries to sack incompetent lecturer)

Malcolm BRADBURY, STEPPING WESTWARD
(naive Englishman takes up post on 'liberated' Californian campus)

Vladimir NABOKOV, PAIN
(sad Russian émigré tries to adjust to US university ways, while clinging to culture of 'old country')

US CAMPUS LIFE

Franz KAFKA, AMERICA
(innocent young German immigrant discovers fantasy-land)

William BOYD, STARS AND BARS
(shy Englishman plunged into fast-lane US business life)

Peter DE VRIES, REUBEN, REUBEN
(boozy, hard-wenching poet cuts a swathe through crackerbarrel Massachusetts community)

Evelyn WAUGH, THE LOVED ONE
(the US funeral business will never seem the same again)

John UPDIKE, BECH, A BOOK
(problems of US author: family, publishers, fans, lecture-audiences, reporters, writer's block . . .)

UNCOMFORTABLE IN AMERICA

(tragi-comic collapse of 'civilised' marriage on 'liberal' US university campus)

ACADEMIC FOLLIES

David **LODGE**, **SMALL WORLD**
(international conference-circuit)

Robertson **DAVIES**, **THE REBEL ANGELS**
(Canadian Rabelais – researcher raises the Devil)

Kingsley **AMIS**, **LUCKY JIM**
(1950s English culture-snobbery in small-town university)

Howard **JACOBSON**, **COMING FROM BEHIND**
(English provincial and polytechnic life – as in 'you don't have to be mad to work here, but it helps')

Max **BEERBOHM**, **ZULEIKA DOBSON**
(life and love among 1910s Oxford dreaming spires)

J.B. **PRIESTLEY**, **LOW NOTES ON A HIGH LEVEL**
(classical music snobs at 1950s BBC – who will get first performance of famous Scandinavian composer's latest symphony?)

Paul **BRYERS**, **COMING FIRST**
(trendy TV producer works hard not to be male chauvinist)

Hilary **MANTEL**, **VACANT POSSESSION**
(rollercoaster black satire: 'madwoman' drives yuppie English family crazy)

Patrick **DENNIS**, **AUNTIE MAME**
(high society – conventional and bizarre – 1950s USA: eccentric aunt takes over 'education' of shy orphan nephew)

NON-ACADEMIC FOLLIES

M

MACAULAY, Rose • *(1881–1958)*
British novelist.

In the 1920s Macaulay wrote deadpan satires, giving the impression that the British Isles were a rest-home for incurable eccentrics. *Potterism* attacks the gutter press. *Crewe Train* sends up publishing. *Told by an Idiot* features a clergyman who tries on new beliefs – Agnosticism, Anglicanism, Catholicism, Christian Socialism, Dissent, Ethicalism and Unitarianism – like shirts. Unlike many satirists of the time, who treated their characters like puppets, Macaulay always wrote of her people with rueful sympathy, however withering her wit about the foolish things they did. In the 1930s, beginning with *They Were Defeated* (see below), she began to concentrate on the sympathetic side of her art, writing about people (young girls especially) who are racked by the need to choose between the life of the mind and that of the flesh: their intellectual or spiritual ambitions are ambushed by sexual infatuation. The second world war, and a succession of private misfortunes, made Macaulay give up novel-writing for a dozen years, but she returned triumphantly in her mid-70s with *The World My Wilderness* (about a confused girl trying to discover her psychological identity after the second world war) and a riotous, malicious romp about love (sacred and profane), *The Towers of Trebizond*.

THEY WERE DEFEATED • *(1932)*
In 17th-century, Puritan England, Dr Conybeare is determined to educate his 15-year-old daughter Julian as if she were a man. The girl takes lessons from Robert Herrick, rector of the parish, until Herrick is driven out for sheltering an old woman accused of witchcraft. Julian goes to Cambridge, where she has private coaching from the don John Cleveland. Cleveland, however, is more interested in

---

READ ON ▷

● *The Towers of Trebizond.*
▶ **To the satires:** Compton Mackenzie, *Vestal Fire*; Nancy Mitford, *Love in a Cold Climate*; ▷Muriel Spark, *The Ballad of Peckham Rye*.
▶ **To *They Were Defeated*:** ▷Robert Graves, *Wife to Mr Milton*.
▶ **To Macaulay's work in general:** ▷Willa Cather, *The Song of the Lark*; ▷Elizabeth Bowen, *The Death of the Heart*; A.S. Byatt, *The Virgin in the Garden*.

her virginity than in her mind, and seduces her – and she
finds herself as entranced by sex as by the heady religious
and intellectual atmosphere of Cambridge. Then her
brother finds out about the seduction, and tragedy ensues.

Macaulay's other novels include (from the 1920s) Dangerous Ages, Orphan Island, Keeping Up Appearances *and*
Staying with Relations, *and (from the 1930s)* I Would be
Private *and* No Man's Wit. *She also wrote poetry, essays
on literature and religion, and a book combining travel,
archaeology and autobiography,* The Pleasure of Ruins.

MADNESS

▷Richard Condon, *Any God Will Do*
  Margaret Forster, *The Bride of Lowther Fell*
▷Susan Hill, *The Bird of Night*
  Ken Kesey, *One Flew Over the Cuckoo's Nest*
  Sylvia Plath, *The Bell Jar*
▷Jean Rhys, *Good Morning, Midnight*
▷Evelyn Waugh, *The Ordeal of Gilbert Pinfold*

Depression and Psychiatry (p 57); On the Edge of
Sanity (p 183)

MAILER, Norman • *(born 1923)*
US writer.

As well as novels, Mailer has published both non-fiction
(eg *Marilyn*, about Marilyn Monroe) and 'faction', a
blend of real events and fiction (eg *The Executioner's
Song*, 1979, an examination of the character and crimes of
the murderer Gary Gilmore). Most of his novels are set in
the present day, and deal with a single theme: maleness.
He regards violence and competitiveness as essential com-
ponents of masculinity, related to sexual potency – and
claims, further, that capitalist society will only succeed if
it models itself on the aggressive, cocky male. The world
being what it is, Mailer is often forced – like ▷Hem-
ingway before him – to describe the failure of these
macho fantasies, and because so many of his books are
about the failure of the American dream, despair gives his
writing stinging political relevance. *The Naked and the
Dead* (1948) is about the brutalisation of a group of bewildered young airmen in the second world war. In *Why Are
We in Vietnam?* (1967), a savage Hemingway parody, a
man takes his son on a bear-hunt as an 18th birthday cele-

READ ON

▶ **To Mailer's
contemporary fiction:**
▷Ernest Hemingway,
*For Whom the Bell
Tolls*; ▷John Cheever,
Falconer; Henri de
Montherlant, *The
Bullfighters*; William
Styron, *The Long
March*.
▶ **To *Ancient Evenings*:**
James Clavell,
Shôgun; L.P. Myers,
The Near and the Far;
▷Thomas Mann,
*Joseph and His
Brothers*.

bration, and this quintessential US manhood-ritual is linked, in a devastating final paragraph, with the mindless, gung-ho crowing of the gook-slaughtering US army in Vietnam, to which the boy will be drafted now that he is adult. *An American Dream* (1965), an equally pungent satire, shows a man at the end of his tether who commits murder and then tries to cudgel from his increasingly insane mind the reasons why his country should have conditioned him to kill, why someone else's violent death should be the outcome of the American dream.

ANCIENT EVENINGS • *(1983)*

Pharaoh Rameses IX of Egypt, perplexed by his failure as a ruler, asks his minister Menenhetet to think back to a former existence as charioteer to the great warrior pharaoh Rameses II, and to explain the secrets of Rameses' success. Menenhetet's account is the bulk of the book, a dazzling description of a society dependent on belief in magic and on a (not unconnected) view of its own powers of rejuvenation, of constantly being able to deconstruct and reconstruct its past.

A good sampler of Mailer's work is Advertisements for Myself, *an anthology of his early writings with a fascinating autobiographical commentary. His other novels include* Barbary Shore, The Deer Park *and the thriller* Tough Guys Don't Dance.

MANN, Thomas • *(1875–1955)*
German novelist and non-fiction writer.

Although Mann was not a political writer, the themes of his work reflect northern European politics of the last 100 years. His first great novel, *Buddenbrooks* (1901), shows the decline of a powerful German industrial family over three decades – and although it is superficially a Forsyte-like family saga, its strength comes from the persistent impression that the Buddenbrooks are characteristic of the decadent 'old Germany' as a whole. The hero of *The Magic Mountain* (1924) spends much of the book learning about Europe's moral, artistic and philosophical heritage – and then goes to fight in the first world war. In *Joseph and His Brothers* (1933–43), based on the Bible and written under the shadow of nazism, Joseph, the figure symbolising progress, is a plausible rogue, a Hitler-figure, and his brothers, symbolising barbarism, are as gullible as they are honest. The composer-hero of *Doctor Faustus* (1947) can unlock his creativity only by entering ever deeper into the morass of his own mind, and by accepting

READ ON ▷

● *Buddenbrooks; The Confessions of Felix Krull, Confidence Man.*
▶ **To *The Magic Mountain*:** ▷Johann Wolfgang von Goethe, *The Apprenticeship of Wilhelm Meister*; Robert Musil, *The Man Without Qualities.*
▶ **To *Buddenbrooks*:** ▷I.B. Singer, *The Family Moskat*; ▷Honoré de Balzac, *Cousin Bette.*
▶ **To *Joseph and His Brothers*:** ▷Gustave Flaubert, *Salammbô.*
▶ **To *Dr Faustus*:**

that to be 'ordinary' is to opt not for cultural calm but for chaos. The con-man central character of *The Confessions of Felix Krull, Confidence Man* (1954), Mann's only comic novel, preys on the expectations of those who still believe in the old rules of religion, society and politics.

THE MAGIC MOUNTAIN (Der Zauberberg) • *(1924)*

Castorp, a rich, unimaginative young man, spends seven years in a Swiss TB sanatorium. The sanatorium is full of endlessly talkative intellectuals, who educate Castorp in music, philosophy, art and literature. The book shows him growing in both knowledge and moral stature, until at last he is cured both of TB and of the greater disease (in Mann's eyes) of ignorant complacency. As the novel ends, however, he strides out to fight in the first world war – and Mann invites us, in the light of hindsight, to ponder his probable fate and that of the European culture he has so laboriously acquired.

Mann's shorter works include Mario the Magician *(about demonic possession),* Death in Venice *(Tod in Venedig) (about a dying writer galvanised by longing for a beautiful boy),* Lotte in Weimar *(a historical novel about the young ▷Goethe), and* The Holy Sinner *(a beautiful – and poker-faced, despite the ridiculousness of its events – retelling of a medieval religious legend involving incest, communion with angels and magical transformations).* Stories of a Lifetime *is a collection of short stories.*

MANNING, Olivia • *(1908–80)*
British novelist.

Manning is best known for the 6-novel sequence *Fortunes of War* (*The Balkan Trilogy*, 1960–65 and *The Levant Trilogy*, 1977–80). The central characters, Guy and Harriet Pringle, are English expatriates during the early years of the second world war. They settle in Bucharest, where Guy teaches English; then, as the Axis powers advance, they move to Athens and from there to Cairo, where they 'hole up' during the desert campaign of 1942. Like the rest of Manning's characters, English, Middle Eastern or European, the Pringles dwell on the fringes, not at the centre, of great events; their lives are bounded by bread-shortages, electricity-cuts and squabbles over status. The civilisation which bred them is collapsing, and they are themselves symbols of its decadence: they are effete and powerless, able only to run before events. None the less, Harriet's character does contain the seeds of change. When she marries Guy she is an unawakened personality, a genteel 1930s 'English rose'. Events draw from her

---

Hermann Broch, *The Death of Virgil*; ▷Susan Hill, *The Bird of Night*.
► **To *Death in Venice*:** ▷Hermann Hesse, *Peter Camenzind*.
► **To *The Holy Sinner*:** Hilda Doolittle ('H.D.'), *Hedylus*.

READ ON

► ▷Elizabeth Bowen, *The Heat of the Day*. Jennifer Johnston, *The Captains and the Kings*. Isabel Colegate, *The Shooting Party*. ▷Evelyn Waugh, *Sword of Honour*.

emotional and intellectual strength she never knew she had – and the effects are to alienate the rest of the stuffy British community and to put stress on her marriage to Guy, an honourable, unimaginative man trapped in pre-war attitudes. He wanted a wife who was a companion not an equal, a pupil not a friend; although he is the same age as Harriet, he is as typical of the 'old' generation as she is of the 'new'. None of this is openly declared. At first sight Manning seems to be offering no more than a series of artless anecdotes about the muddle and horror of life in exotic cities engulfed by war. It is not till the mosaic is complete that her underlying scheme becomes apparent: the description of a whole culture in a state of unwished-for, panic-stricken change.

The novels in The Balkan Trilogy *are* The Great Fortune, The Spoilt City *and* Friends and Heroes; *those in* The Levant Trilogy *are* The Danger Tree, The Battle Lost and Won *and* The Sum of Things. *Manning's other novels are* Artist Among the Missing, School for Love, A Different Face, The Doves of Venus, The Play Room *and* The Rain Forest. Growing Up *and* A Romantic Hero *are collections of short stories.*

MANSFIELD, Katherine • *(1888–1923)*
New Zealand short-story writer.

Mansfield went to London at 14, and spent the rest of her life in Europe. When she wrote of New Zealand it was either with childhood nostalgia (for example in 'Prelude' and 'At The Bay') or with distaste for the lives its adults led in the outback ('Ole Underwood'; 'The Woman at the Store') or in dingily genteel suburbs ('Her First Ball'; 'How Pearl Button was Kidnapped'). She admired ▷Chekhov's stories, and sought to write the same kind of innocent-seeming anecdotes distilling single moments of human folly or aspiration. Many of her stories are about small children. In 'Sixpence', for example, she describes a little boy's sudden inexplicable naughtiness, and the guilt his father feels when he beats him; in 'The Little Girl', she shows a young child's feelings for her father. Her favourite characters were shallow, silly and desperate people: an unemployable film-extra ('Pictures'), a snob-bish mother and her unmarried daughters ('The Garden-party'), a hen-pecked singing-teacher ('Mr Reginald Peacock's Day'), expatriates on the continent ('The Man Without a Temperament'; 'Je ne parle pas français'). She polished and refined her prose, often spending months on a single story – and the feeling of craftsmanship in her

READ ON ▷

▶ ▷Anton Chekhov, *The Lady With the Little Dog and Other Stories.* ▷John Cheever, *Collected Stories.* Jean Stafford, *Collected Stories.* William Saroyan, *Best Stories of Saroyan.* ▷Elizabeth Bowen, *The Dream Lover.* Dorothy Parker, *Here Lies.*

work, of slightly self-conscious artistry, greatly enhances the impression she seeks to give, that tragedies are not diminished because the lives they affect are small.

Mansfield's story-collections are In A German Pension, Bliss, The Garden Party, The Dove's Nest *and* Something Childish. *Her* Journals *give fascinating glimpses both of her character and of the events and conversations which she drew on in her work.*

MÁRQUEZ, Gabriel García • *(born 1928)*
Colombian novelist and short-story writer.

READ ON ▷

▶ ▷Salman Rushdie, *Shame.* ▷Isabel Allende, *The House of the Spirits.* Carlos Fuentes, *The Old Gringo.* ▷Virginia Woolf, *Orlando.* ▷Italo Calvino, *Our Ancestors.* Gerald H. Morris, *Doves and Silk Handkerchieves.*

In Márquez' invented South American town of Macondo, a place isolated from the outside world, 'magic realism' rules: there is no distinction between magic and reality. At one level, life is perfectly ordinary: people are born, grow up, work, cook, feud and gossip. But there is a second, irrational and surrealist plane to ordinary existence. The Macondans (unless they murder each other for reasons of politics, sex or family honour) live for 100, 150, 200 years. Although they are as innocent of 'real' knowledge as children – they think ice miraculous and they are amazed to hear that the world is round – they know the secrets of alchemy, converse with ghosts, remember Cortez or Drake as 'uncles'. Macondo is a rough-and-tumble Eden, a paradise where instinct rules and nothing is impossible – and Márquez spends his time either describing its enchantment or detailing the savage results when people from the outside world (jackbooted generals; con-men; lawyers; bishops) break through to 'civilise' it. For Márquez, Macondo stands for the whole of South America, and his stories are barbed political allegories. But he seldom lets this overwhelm the books. Instead of hectoring, he opens his eyes wide, puts his tongue in his cheek and tells us wonders.

ONE HUNDRED YEARS OF SOLITUDE • *(1967)*
As Colonel Aurelio Buendia faces the firing squad, the whole history of his family flashes before his eyes. They begin as poor peasants, in a one-roomed hut on the edge of a swamp. They proliferate like tendrils on a vine: Aureliano himself has 17 sons, all called Aureliano. The family-members absorb knowledge, people and property until they and Macondo seem indissoluble. Finally, led by Aureliano senior, they defend the old, innocent values against invasion by a government which wants to impose the same laws in Macondo as everywhere else, and the dynasty disappears from reality, living on only in fantasy,

as a memory of how human beings were before the whole world changed.

Márquez' other novels are No One Writes to the Colonel, In Evil Hour, Chronicle of a Death Foretold *and* The Autumn of the Patriarch *(the stream-of-consciousness monologue of a dying dictator). His short stories are collected in* Leaf-storm and other Stories, Big Mama's Funeral *and* Innocent Erendira and other Stories.

MARSH, Ngaio • *(1899–1982)*
New Zealand novelist.

Few writers use 'classic' detective-story ingredients as magnificently as Marsh. Her murder-methods are ingenious and unexpected. Her locations are fascinating: backstage (and onstage) at theatres; during a village-hall concert; in the shearing-shed of a sheep-farm; at a top-level diplomatic reception. Her characters are exotic and her detection is scrupulously fair, with every clue appearing to the reader at the same time as to Alleyn, Marsh's urbane and hawk-eyed sleuth. Above all, her books move at a furious pace, fuelled by her effervescent glee at the follies of humankind.

FINAL CURTAIN • *(1947)*
Shortly after the second world war, Agatha Troy (Alleyn's artist wife) is persuaded to spend a week painting the portrait of Sir Henry Ancred, a distinguished actor now retired. She goes to his country mansion, and finds it a lowering old house in the best whodunnit tradition. One wing has been taken over by an evacuated prep school, and the rest is filled with eccentric relatives who have been plunged into twittering alarm by the arrival of Sir Henry's young, vulgar and nubile mistress, who may just become his wife and cut the rest of the family off from their inheritance. Sittings for the painting proceed – Sir Henry is costumed as for his most famous role, Macbeth – and are interrupted first by a series of unpleasant practical jokes, and then by the old man's murder. Scotland Yard must be called in, and Alleyn arrives back from war-service just in time to take the case and sort out the murderer from half a dozen candidates, each with a cast-iron alibi and a very good reason for wishing Sir Henry dead.

Marsh's three dozen novels include Hand in Glove, Died in the Wool, Clutch of Constables, Vintage Murder, Spinsters in Jeopardy, Surfeit of Lampreys, Black as He's Painted *and* Death in Ecstasy. Black Beech and Honey-

READ ON

● *Enter a Murderer; Overture to Death.*
▶ ▷Marjorie Allingham, *The Beckoning Lady.* H.R.F. Keating, *Zen There Was Murder.* Emma Lathen, *When in Greece.* Jean Potts, *Go, Lovely Rose.* ▷Peter Dickinson, *The Poison Oracle.*

dew is an autobiography, especially interesting on her childhood and her fascination with theatre.

MASTERS, John • *(born 1914)*
British novelist.

Masters, an army officer in India, wrote a series of books setting fictional characters in the context of real historical events. The Raj background and the interplay between two incompatible cultures are brilliantly evoked, and the foreground action is fast, thrilling and plausible. The best-known books in the sequence are *Nightrunners of Bengal* (1951), set during the Indian 'Mutiny', and *Bhowani Junction* (1954), about the plot to blow up a train during the struggle for independence.

Masters' other books include Far, Far the Mountain Peak, The Road Past Mandalay, The Breaking Strain, Thunder at Sunset *and* The Himalayan Concerto.

> **READ ON**

▶ **Equally sensitive to India and its history during the last 150 years:** Paul Scott, *The Raj Quartet*; ▷J.G. Farrell, *The Siege of Krishnapur.*
▶ **Similar books, about different periods and continents:** James Clavell, *Shôgun* (set in 17th-century Japan); ▷Robert Graves, *Sergeant Lamb of the Ninth* and ▷Gore Vidal, *1776* (both about the American War of Independence); ▷C.S. Forester, *The Gun* (set in the Peninsular War); Timothy Mo, *An Insular Possession* (about the British and Hong Kong).

MAUGHAM, W. Somerset (William) •
(1874–1965)
British writer of novels, short stories and plays.

A tireless traveller (especially in the Far East), Maugham wrote hundreds of short stories based on anecdotes he heard or scenes he observed en route. Many of them were later filmed: 'Rain', for example (about a missionary on a cruise-liner in Samoa struggling to reform a prostitute, and losing his own soul in the process), was made half a dozen times. Maugham's novels used true experience in a similar way, shaping it and drawing out its meaning but keeping close to real events. *Liza of Lambeth* (1897) is about a London slum girl tormented by her neighbours for conceiving a bastard child. *Of Human Bondage* (1915) is the story of an orphan, bullied at school because he has a club foot, who struggles to find happiness as an adult, is

> **READ ON**

▶ **To *Liza of Lambeth*:** ▷Émile Zola, *The Boozer* (L'Assommoir).
▶ **To *Of Human Bondage*:** ▷C.P. Snow, *Strangers and Brothers*; ▷Jerome Weidman, *Fourth Street East.*
▶ **To *The Moon and Sixpence*:** Joyce Cary, *The Horse's Mouth.*
▶ **To *Cakes and Ale*:** ▷Rose Macaulay, *Crewe Train*; ▷J.B.

ravaged by love for a worthless woman, and settles at last to become a country doctor. The stockbroker hero of *The Moon and Sixpence* (1919) gives up career, wife and family to become a painter in the South Seas, as Gauguin did. *Cakes and Ale* (1930) is an acid satire about the 1930s London literary world; Maugham avoided libel suits only by claiming that every writer it pilloried was just another aspect of himself.

Maugham's other novels include The Trembling of a Leaf, The Casuarina Tree, The Razor's Edge *and* Catalina. *His* Complete Short Stories *and* Collected Plays *(from 1907–32 he wrote two dozen successful plays, mainly comedies) were published in the 1950s. A* Writer's Notebook *and* The Summing Up *give fascinating insights into the balance between his life and work.*

MAURIAC, François • *(1885–1970)*
French novelist.

Mauriac's books, all set among rich families in the Bordeaux wine country at the start of this century, are based on Roman Catholic doctrines of guilt and repentance. They show people tormented by conscience (often quite justified: his characters include murderers, embezzlers, adulterers and family tyrants). Some are never challenged; others are outcasts, reviled by neighbours and relatives as unpleasant as they are themselves. A few repent, and the move from moral darkness to light irradiates their souls. The quest for redemption is, however, always left to the individual: no one is saved against his or her own will. Despite the religious starting-point of Mauriac's books, they are anything but churchy: they are psychological case-studies rather than religious tracts. Like ancient Greek tragedy, his work can seem remorselessly gloomy – and it has a similar hypnotic power.

THE NEST OF VIPERS (Le nœud de vipères) • *(1932)*
The book is the confession of a dying man, trying to explain to his grown-up children how his wife's infidelity, many years before, shrivelled his soul and led him to hate both her and them. For 30 years he has plotted to rob them of their inheritance, taking pleasure in the prospect of their distress when he dies and leaves them penniless. Then his wife unexpectedly dies, and he begins a reassessment of his moral situation, and a painful process of rehabilitation.

Mauriac's other novels include Thérèse Desqueyroux *(a*

Priestley, *The Image Men.*

▶ **To the short stories:** Guy De Maupassant, *Boule de Suif*; ▷R.L. Stevenson, *Island Nights' Entertainment*; ▷Rudyard Kipling, *Wee Willie Winkie*; ▷Paul Theroux, *World's End.*

READ ON ⟩

▶ ▷Carson McCullers, *Reflections in a Golden Eye.* ▷Graham Greene, *Brighton Rock.* Theodore Dreiser, *Sister Carrie.* ▷Patricia Highsmith, *The People Who Knock on the Door.* John Hergesheimer, *The Three Black Pennies.*

▶ The idea of the stifling, overbearing family is sent up in ▷Ivy Compton-Burnett, *Brothers and Sisters* and ▷Tom Sharpe, *Ancestral Vices.*

chilly investigation of the mind of a woman who has poisoned her husband), Genetrix *(about a young couple whose love is blighted by the man's monstrous, possessive mother),* The Desert of Love *(in which a father and son fall in love with the same woman), and* The Woman of the Pharisees *(about religious bigotry, and the way the middle-aged resent the young).*

McBAIN, Ed • *(born 1926)*
US novelist.

'Ed McBain' is one of the pseudonyms of ▷Evan Hunter. He writes fast, tough police-procedurals set in New York; many of them (including the 87th Precinct series) are woven out of several simultaneous investigations, in the manner of such TV series as *Hill Street Blues.* McBain also describes the private lives of his hard-talking, streetwise cops: this humanises the violence. His books include *Cop Hater, Give the Boys a Great Big Hand, Calypso* and *Eighty Million Eyes.*

> **READ ON**

▶ Chester Himes, *Blind Man With a Pistol.* Dell Shannon, *Date With Death.* Lesley Egan, *The Hunters and the Hunted.* Joseph Wambaugh, *The Choirboys.* Martin Cruz Smith, *Gorky Park* is an intriguing variation on the formula: a police-procedural set in Moscow and involving corruption and departmental infighting in the Kremlin itself.

McCAFFREY, Anne • *(born 1926)*
US novelist.

Although McCaffrey has written novels, romances, a thriller and books on music and cookery, she is best-known for SF (often, eg in *The Crystal Singer*, with a musical background) and fantasy. Her most substantial work is the 'Pern' sequence of novels. Pern is a distant, medieval world where the élite ride and telepathically control – or are controlled by –dragons; the dragons are the only beings which can destroy Thread, a devastating space-virus which would otherwise engulf all other life. The series details the fragile balance of society on Pern, and in particular the symbiosis – by turns comic, tragic and movingly poetic – between humans and dragons on which all life depends.

The Pern books (self-contained but linked) are Dragon-flight, Dragonquest, The White Dragon, Dragonsong, Dragonsinger, Dragondrums *and* Moreta. *McCaffrey's other SF books include* The Ship Who Sang, Restoree *and*

> **READ ON**

● *The Crystal Singer.*
▶ ▷Piers Anthony, *Vicinity Cluster.* ▷Robert Heinlein, *Glory Road.* ▷Ursula Le Guin, *The Word for World is Forest.*

Dinosaur Planet. Get off the Unicorn *is a collection of short stories.*

McCARTHY, Mary • *(born 1912)*
US novelist and non-fiction writer.

As well as novels, McCarthy has published books on Venice and Florence, political essays (especially on the US involvement in Vietnam) and an admired – and fictionalised – autobiography, *Memoirs of a Catholic Girlhood.* (She set the record straight in 1987 with the more factual *How I Grew.*) Each of her half-dozen novels simultaneously discusses and satirises major issues of its day. The heroine of *The Company She Keeps*, from the 1940s, tries to reconcile being a free spirit with her longing to find Mr Right. *The Group*, a 1960s best-seller, is about eight women making their way in society and demanding equal shares in the sexual and social revolution. The hero of *Birds of America* (1971) is a naive young American in Europe, worrying himself sick over small matters like dirty toilet-bowls, and over such large ones as ecological balance, the awfulness of US package-tourists and the fact that no one in Europe seems to share America's high opinion of itself. In *Cannibals and Missionaries* (1980) a group of wealthy, cultured people is held hostage by terrorists. One US critic (Brady Nordland) called *Birds of America* 'sweet, funny and very clever'; the description fits all McCarthy's work.

THE GROVES OF ACADEME • *(1952)*
Henry Mulcahy is an inefficient, unreliable teacher in the English Department of Jocelyn College. He is also a married man with children, and a left-wing activist. The President of the College decides not to renew Mulcahy's tenure, and the department immediately starts politicking in Mulcahy's defence. The book's once-topical background (it was published during the anti-left witch-hunts of Senator Joe McCarthy – no relation of Mary McCarthy, and certainly no soul-mate) has faded, leaving a sparkling, malicious campus comedy in which everyone gets their due come-uppance; the final irony, discomforting Mulcahy's woolly liberal colleagues, is particularly neat.

McCarthy's other novels are The Oasis/A Source of Embarrassment *and* A Charmed Life. Cast a Cold Eye *is a collection of short stories.*

READ ON ▷

● *Birds of America.*
▶ To *The Groves of Academe:* D.J. Enright, *Academic Year*; Howard Jacobson, *Coming from Behind.*
▶ To *The Group:* Rona Jaffe, *Class Reunion* (and its sequel *Mazes and Monsters*).
▶ To **McCarthy's novels generally:** Alice Thomas Ellis, *The Other Side of the Fire*; A.N. Wilson, *The Sweets of Pimlico*; ▷Frederic Raphael, *The Graduate Wife*; ▷Alison Lurie, *The War Between the Tates.*

McCULLERS, Carson • *(1917–53)*
US novelist.

Reading McCullers is like visiting a freak-show: her characters are repulsive but fascinating, kin to the more macabre human figures in modern pop and horror videos. The hero of *The Heart is a Lonely Hunter* (1940) is a deaf-mute, distracted by his inability to communicate either his sensitivity or his generosity of spirit. The awkward, ugly heroine of *The Ballad of the Sad Café* (1951) runs a haven in the Georgia swamps for tramps, lunatics and other social misfits – and her world is shattered when she falls in love with a malign homosexual dwarf. *Reflections in a Golden Eye* (1941) describes boredom and sexual obsession among the wives in a wartime army camp. *Clock Without Hands* is about racism. Only in one book, *The Member of the Wedding*, does McCullers transcend such nightmarish imaginings. Her heroine is a young adolescent in a household bustling with preparations for a wedding: fascinated but totally ignorant about what is going on, she feels as locked out of 'real' (ie adult) society as the freaks and emotional cripples of McCullers' other books.

> **READ ON** ▷
>
> ▶ **To McCullers' more freakish books:** Ian McEwan, *The Comfort of Strangers*; Iain Banks, *The Wasp Factory*; Deborah Moggach, *Porky*; Paul Bailey, *At The Jerusalem*; ▷Émile Zola, *Nana*.
> ▶ **To *The Member of the Wedding*:** ▷Eudora Welty, *Delta Wedding*; ▷Katherine Anne Porter, *The Leaning Tower* (short stories).

MELVILLE, Herman • *(1819–91)*
US novelist.

As a teenager, Melville educated himself by reading the Bible, Shakespeare, Milton and Sir Thomas Browne. He served at sea until he was 23, and later worked as a customs officer. His books take their style from the grand literature he read, and their stories from his own seafaring adventures or from travellers' tales. His novels are long, and read at times as if Genesis or Job had been revised to include whaling, smuggling, shipwreck and naval war. But their epic thought and style easily match the magnificence of the books which influenced him.

MOBY-DICK • *(1851)*
Moby Dick is a huge sperm-whale, and the novel tells of Captain Ahab's obsessive attempts to hunt it down and kill it. Melville's whaling-lore is exhaustive, his action-scenes are breath-taking, and he gives an unforgettable picture of Ahab: lonely, driven, daunting as an Old Testament patriarch, a fitting adversary for the monster he has vowed to kill.

Melville's other novels include Typee *and* Omoo, *based on his own experiences after being shipwrecked among cannibals in Polynesia;* Redburn: his First Voyage; *White-*

> **READ ON** ▷
>
> ▶ ▷Nathaniel Hawthorne, *The Scarlet Letter*. ▷Victor Hugo, *Toilers of the Sea*. ▷Joseph Conrad, *The Nigger of the Narcissus*.
> ▶ **Novels about dark obsessions of other kinds:** ▷Thomas Mann, *Doctor Faustus*; ▷Norman Mailer, *An American Dream*; ▷John Fowles, *The Collector*.

jacket, or The World in a Man-o'-War; *the bitter satire* The Confidence Man *and* Billy Budd, *the story of an inarticulate young sailor who kills a sadistic petty officer.*

THE MIDDLE AGES

▷Italo Calvino, *Our Ancestors*
  Umberto Eco, *The Name of the Rose*
▷William Golding, *The Spire*
▷Victor Hugo, *Notre Dame de Paris*
  Pär Lagerkvist, *The Dwarf*
▷Thomas Mann, *The Holy Sinner*
▷Jean Plaidy, *The Bastard King*
  Helen Waddell, *Peter Abelard*

Other Peoples, Other Times (p 186); Renaissance Europe (p 201)

MILLER, Walter M. • *(born 1922)*
US novelist.

In Miller's best-known novel, *A Canticle for Leibowitz* (1960), the human race has survived the nuclear holocaust (or 'Great Fallout') at the expense of having to retrace its steps towards civilisation. In the twelfth century of the new era, the curators of knowledge are a group of monks, the Blessed Order of Leibowitz. They pore over their sacred writings, Leibowitz's jottings and research-notes, and try to turn what they read into actuality. Their experiments – which even they view with alarm, tampering with powers beyond their comprehension – will (we know from hindsight) parallel the discoveries of alchemists and scientists from our own time, repeating the cycle which led to the Great Fallout in the first place. In the meantime, in all ignorance, the monks are just making their first experiments with electricity.

> READ ON ⟩

● *The Darfsteller.*
▶ ▷Russell Hoban, *Riddley Walker.*
  ▷James Blish, *Black Easter.* Bamber Gascoigne, *Cod Strewth* (a similar, but comic story: the surviving book is not science but scraps of ▷Rabelais).

MITCHELL, Margaret • *(1900–49)*
US novelist.

Gone with the Wind, Mitchell's only book (published in 1936; filmed three years later with Clark Gable and Vivien Leigh) was aptly described in its day as 'the greatest love-story ever told'. In Atlanta, Georgia, at the outbreak of the 1860s American civil war, Scarlett O'Hara

> READ ON ⟩

▶ ▷Boris Pasternak, *Doctor Zhivago.*
  ▷Daphne Du Maurier, *Rebecca.* Colleen McCullough, *The Thorn*

falls in love with Ashley Wilkes, the foppish son of a neighbouring plantation-owner, only to discover that he is having an affair with her sister. Heartbroken, she turns to other men, including the cynical, rakish Rhett Butler. The civil war proceeds, the South loses, Atlanta is burned and Scarlett's beautiful house, Tara, is plundered. The devastation of war mirrors the suffering in her heart. She tells Rhett of her hopeless love for Ashley, Rhett leaves her (with a blunt 'Frankly, my dear, I don't give a damn'), and she realises that he was really the man she loved all the time.

MONEY

▷John Galsworthy, *The Forsyte Saga*
  Brian Glanville, *The Financiers*
▷Maxim Gorky, *Yegor Bulitchev and Others*
▷Judith Krantz, *Scruples*
  Emma Lathen, *Banking on Death*
▷Christina Stead, *House of All Nations*
▷Jerome Weidman, *A Family Fortune*
  Donald Westlake, *Bank Shot*

MOORCOCK, Michael • *(born 1939)*
British novelist.

In the 1960s Moorcock edited the SF magazine New Worlds, pioneering and encouraging 'new wave' writing. The underlying ideas of this are traditional: time-travel, space-opera, sword-and-sorcery. But the literary style is freewheeling, psychedelic, experimental and poetic. Moorcock's own 'new wave' work is at its peak in his Jerry Cornelius books (eg *The English Assassin*; *The Final Programme*), which are less straightforward novels than firework displays of ideas, magical mystery tours round one man's overheated brain. In later books Moorcock returned to a more sober style, still crammed with ideas but much easier to read. Many of his novels offer alternative versions of the present (*Warlord of the Air*, for example, imagines a 20th century where the first world war never happened and the old 19th century empires, British, Austrian, Russian and German, are still jockeying for power). Others (*Gloriana*; *The Jewel in the Skull*) are satires about societies which are dark and decadent perversions of our own. A good starting-point to his multifarious, dazzling work is the 1970s series 'Dancers at the End of Time' (*An*

Birds. M.M. Kaye, *The Far Pavilions.*

> READ ON

● *The Jewel in the Skull.*
▶ ▷Robert Heinlein, *Number of the Beast.* Robert E. Vardeman and Victor Milan, *The War of Powers.* ▷J.G. Ballard, *The Day of Creation.* ▷Robert Silverberg, *Tom O'Bedlam.*

Alien Heat, The Hollow Lands, The End of All Songs and a cluster of less closely related novels). The time is the very last days of the universe. The few hundred surviving members of the human race control vast energies: anything desired can be obtained by twisting a 'power ring'. Jerek Cornelian (the last human being ever to be born, an avatar of Jerry Cornelius from the earlier novels) falls in love with a strait-laced Victorian time-traveller, Mrs Amelia Underwood. He follows her back in time, and is promptly stranded in the slums of Victorian London: a typical Moorcock idea, allowing him to collapse history, fantasy, social comment and literary parody – Cornelian gives ▷H.G. Wells the idea for The Time Machine – into a single mesmeric and unpredictable experience.

Many of Moorcock's novels are grouped in series: The Chronicles of the Black Sword, The High History of the Runestaff, The Chronicles of Castle Brass, The Books of Corum, The History of the Eternal Champion. *His single novels include* The Ice Schooner, Breakfast in the Ruins *and* Condition of Muzak. The Singing Citadel, Voyage on a Dark Ship *and* The Time Dweller *are collections of short stories.*

MOORHOUSE, Frank • *(born 1938)*
Australian short-story writer.

Moorhouse's stories are character-sketches: he is less interested in plot than in showing states of feeling, emotion and (particularly) psychological disturbance. His complex style (short scenes, jump-cut as in films; dialogue with little indication of who is speaking; no distinction between the description of thoughts and actions, the subjective and the objective), quickly builds up a sense of randomness, of disorientation. Some of his 1960s stories were published in girlie magazines, and their sexual explicitness was considered shocking at the time. His collections are *Futility and Other Animals* (1969, anthropologist's reports on the 'urban tribe' of small-town Australia), *The American Baby* (1972, parodying Australia's infatuation with US culture), *Conference-ville* (1976, set among university students and teachers), *Tales of Mystery and Romance* and *The Everlasting Secret Family and Other Secrets*, both about the obsessions and rituals of 'ordinary' family life.

READ ON ▷

▶ Robert Coover, *Pricksongs and Descants.* ▷J.D. Salinger, *Nine Stories/ For Esmé, with Love and Squalor.* ▷Keri Hulme, *The Windeater.* Anaïs Nin, *Under a Glass Bell.* Richard Brautigan, *Willard and His Bowling Trophy* (novel).

MORRIS, William • *(1834–96)*
British craftsman and writer.

At the end of his life Morris (hitherto an artist, designer and philosopher) turned to fiction, writing historical novels and two future-fantasies, *A Dream of John Ball* (1888) and *News From Nowhere* (1891). *News from Nowhere* has the distinction of being one of the very few fantasies to predict a happy future for the human race. Its hero drifts off to sleep during a political meeting in the 1890s, and wakes up to find that he has been transported 60 years forwards in time, and that every socialist dream has been fulfilled. The worker's paradise exists: war, fear, disease and poverty have been eradicated, along with money, prisons and politicians. Everyone is equal, and the harmony between human beings and their environment (the banks of the Thames) is as perfect as it was in Eden before the arrival of the Serpent. Morris' vision is poetic rather than sickly-sweet, and he writes without a twitch of irony. Whatever our hindsight-programmed cynicism a century later, *News from Nowhere* is still a fascinating and remarkable read. If its optimism had been based on Christian rather than humanist beliefs, it might be universally recognised as a major work of visionary literature – which is exactly what it is.

Morris' historical novels (influenced by Icelandic sagas and northern European legends such as Beowulf) include The House of the Wolfings, The Wood Beyond the World *and* The Sundering Flood.

MOSCO, Maisie
British novelist.

Mosco, a prolific romantic novelist, is best-known for the saga of a Jewish family, refugees from early 20th-century European pogroms, who make a new home in northern England. Her detail of Manchester slum existence in the first half of this century, and of the closeness of Jewish family and community life, is particularly admired. The books in the sequence (all written in the 1980s) are *Almonds and Raisins*, *Scattered Seed* and *Children's Children*.

READ ON ▷

● *A Dream of John Ball.*
▶ ▷Robert Graves, *Seven Days in New Crete*. Sarah Scott, *Millenium Hall*.
▷Hermann Hesse, *The Glass Bead Game*. Michael Frayn, *Sweet Dreams* (a satire on exactly the kind of liberal-socialist paradise Morris describes – but literal: Frayn's leading character is exploring Heaven itself).

READ ON ▷

▶ Thomas Armstrong, *The Crowther Chronicles*. Claire Rayner, *'Performers' series*. ▷Bernice Rubens, *The Brothers*. ▷Mrs Gaskell, *Mary Barton* and *North and South* give an earlier, even robuster, view of life in industrial Manchester.

MUNRO, Alice • *(born 1931)*
Canadian short-story writer.

Many of Munro's stories are set in the villages and small towns of British Columbia and Ontario, places she depicts as genteel, culturally negligible and bigoted, stagnant since the days of the Model T Ford. Many of her characters are young people of spirit (usually women or girls), stretching the bounds of this environment. Although her themes are modern – feminism, for example – her careful descriptions of the streets, houses, rooms and clothes of her people give the stories a strong nostalgic appeal. She is like one of the gentler Southern US writers (▷Eudora Welty, say) transported north.

Munro's story-collections include Lives of Girls and Women, Something I've Been Meaning to Tell You, The Moons of Jupiter *and* Who Do You Think You Are?/The Beggar Maid, *in which the stories are linked to form an episodic novel.*

READ ON ⟩

▶ ▷Eudora Welty, *The Golden Apples.*
▷Katherine Mansfield, *The Dove's Nest and Other Stories.*
Sherwood Anderson, *Winesburg, Ohio.* Edna O'Brien, *A Scandalous Woman and Other Stories.*

MURDER MOST MIND-BOGGLING

John Franklin Bardin, *Devil Take the Blue-Tail Fly*
Edmund Crispin, *The Moving Toyshop*
▷Peter Dickinson, *The Lively Dead*
Umberto Eco, *The Name of the Rose*
H.R.F. Keating, *A Rush on the Ultimate*
Cameron McCabe, *The Face on the Cutting-room Floor*
Josephine Tey, *The Singing Sands*

Classic Detection (p 46); Great Detectives (p 100); Private Eyes (p 196)

MURDOCH, Iris • *(born 1919)*
Irish/British novelist and philosopher.

The subject of Murdoch's two dozen novels is personal politics: the ebb and flow of relationships, the way we manipulate others and are ourselves manipulated. The time is now; the people are middle-class, professional, usually from the English Home Counties – and they are all bizarre, possessed by a demon which blurs reality and dream into a single, mesmeric state. Seduction, mysticism and moral disintegration are favourite themes, and the in-

READ ON ⟩

● *The Book and the Brotherhood.*
▶ ▷Mary McCarthy, *A Charmed Life.* Alice Thomas Ellis, *The 27th Kingdom.* D.M. Thomas, *Birthstone.* Mary Flanagan, *Trust.*

Iris MURDOCH

An Unofficial Rose *(nine people, all looking for love; nine intertwined, entangled lives)*

Anita **BROOKNER, A Misalliance**
(divorced woman, keeping up façade of busy, fulfilled existence, is troubled by chaotic emotional life of people she meets)

Jenni **DISKI, Rainforest**
(professor tries to stop intellectual meticulousness destroying emotional life)

Bernice **RUBENS, Our Father**
(archaeologist's meeting with God in Sahara triggers a search of her past and the relationship between her charismatic, enigmatic parents)

Susan **HILL, In the Springtime of the Year**
(young widow 'rehabilitated' from grief by calm rhythms of country life)

Jane **GARDAM, Crusoe's Daughter**
(Robinson Crusoe gives lonely woman purpose in life and grasp on sanity)

D.M. **THOMAS, The White Hotel**
(case-history of disturbed woman, erotic and violent, reflects nightmarish psychic experience of all 20th-century humanity)

WOMEN ALONE

Lisa St Aubin de **TERAN, The Bay of Silence**
(apparently happy, successful film actress haunted by schizophrenia)

Lawrence **DURRELL, The Dark Labyrinth/Cefalù**
(group of tourists enter Cretan labyrinth in search of psychic identity – and each quest is unexpectedly fulfilled)

Virginia **WOOLF, To the Lighthouse**
(thoughts and memories of large close family on holiday: projected day-trip to a lighthouse focuses each of their lives)

SEARCHING FOR SELF

Eleanor **DARK, Return to Coolami**
(four people motoring in Australian outback discover themselves)

Christopher **ISHERWOOD, A Meeting By the River**
(two brothers, estranged and 'lost', find Buddhism, true love and tranquility of soul)

Hermann **HESSE, Steppenwolf**
(lonely middle-aged recluse 'rehabilitated' spiritually by three mystical, possibly fantasy young people)

Olivia **MANNING, The Rain Forest**
(young couple, psychically 'lost', seek solace on magical, sinister tropical island)

Paul **THEROUX, The Mosquito Coast**
(tired of US civilisation, man takes family 'back to nature' in Ecuadorian jungle)

Rosamond **LEHMANN, A Sea-Grape Tree**
(deserted wife seeks spiritual and psychic reassurance on Caribbean island)

Patrick **WHITE, Voss**
(explorers 'find' themselves by trekking across Australia; at home in Sydney, girl waits breathlessly for news)

Isabel **ALLENDE, The House of the Spirits**
(Trueba family women, over four generations, order their lives by magic, fantasy and psychic communion rather than as their patriarch ordains)

Angus **WILSON, The Middle Age of Mrs Eliot**
(widow seeks happiness by surrendering to impulse, going on haphazard Far Eastern odyssey)

LURE OF THE EXOTIC

nocent late adolescent (whose effect on other people's lives is often devastating) is a standard character.

THE BELL · *(1958)*

Should we live our lives by the conventions of society or moment by moment, defining ourselves by our own changing moods and enthusiasms? This question perplexes every character in *The Bell*: all are waiting for a sudden inspiration or discovery which will define their existence, show them how they should behave. The setting is a lay community housed in a former convent, a refuge for an eccentric collection of inmates whose peace is disturbed by the mechanics of replacing the convent bell and by the arrival of two amoral 'innocents', Dora and Toby. *The Bell* was popular in the hippie 1960s, and still seems to catch the wide-eyed, distracted mood of those times. But its story and characters are fascinating and its images (for example that of the nude, startlingly white-bodied Toby diving, like a fallen angel, into the murky convent lake to investigate a sunken bell) are as disturbing as they are unforgettable.

Murdoch's other novels include The Flight from the Enchanter, The Sandcastle, A Severed Head, The Red and the Green, The Time of the Angels, The Sea, The Sea *and* The Book and the Brotherhood.

MUSIC

▷Anthony Burgess, *The Piano Players*
▷Willa Cather, *The Song of the Lark*
▷Hermann Hesse, *Gertrud*
  Jack Higgins, *Solo*
▷Thomas Mann, *Doctor Faustus*
▷H.H. Richardson, *The Getting of Wisdom*
  Joseph Skvorecky, *Dvořák in Love*

Irene Handl, *The Sioux*.

N

NABOKOV, Vladimir • *(1899–1977)*
Russian/US novelist and short-story writer.

Nabokov wrote in Russian until 1940, when he settled in the USA; thereafter, he worked in English, and also translated and revised his earlier works. He was fascinated by language, and his books are firework displays of wit, purple-prose descriptions, ironical asides and multi-lingual puns: for his admirers, style is a major pleasure of his work. Several of his novels take the form of teasing 'biographies', revealing as much about their dogged biographers as their subjects. The hero of *The Defence* (1929) is a chess-champion, crippled emotionally both by his profession and by his feeling of identity with the whole Russian cultural tradition. The heroes of *The Real Life of Sebastian Knight* (1941) and *Look at the Harlequins!* (1974) play ironical games with their would-be biographers: the more they seem to reveal themselves, the more elusive they become. *Pnin* (1957) is a sad comedy about an accident-prone Russian professor at a US university, trying to keep the customs of the Old Country in a baffling new environment. *Invitation to a Beheading* (1935) and *Bend Sinister* (1947), Nabokov's most political books, are stories of oppression and nightmare in harsh totalitarian regimes. *Despair* (1934) is a dream-like psychological thriller about a man who hunts down and murders his double, only to find that he has destroyed himself. Humbert Humbert, the tragi-comic hero of *Lolita* (1955), is led by sexual infatuation for a twelve-year-old girl into a farcical kidnapping, a flight from the police through the motels and diners of grubby middle America, and finally to murder. The book's tone of obsessive erotic reverie is repeated in *Ada* (1969), about an incestuous love-affair between two rich, spoiled people in a mysterious country midway between 19th-century Russia and the 1930s USA.

READ ON >

● *Pnin*.
▶ **To Nabokov's elegant, games-playing style:** ▷Muriel Spark, *The Abbess of Crewe*; John Barth, *Giles Goat-boy*; ▷Frederic Raphael, *California Time*; Julian Barnes, *Flaubert's Parrot*.
▶ **To his darker novels:** ▷Franz Kafka, *The Trial*; ▷Jerzy Kosinski, *The Painted Bird*; Martin Amis, *Success*.
▶ **To his short stories:** Richard Barthelme, *City Life*.

PALE FIRE · *(1962)*

Few novels can ever have had such an original form: a 999-line poem with introduction and commentary. The poet is an exiled Eastern European king; the commentator is a fool who fantasises that he is the real heir to the throne, and that he is writing under the shadow of an assassination-plot. The effect is as if ▷Anthony Hope had beefed up someone's PhD thesis: *Pale Fire* is funny, clever – and, despite its bizarre form, a delightfully easy read.

Nabokov's other novels include King, Queen, Knave; Glory; Camera Obscura/Laughter in the Dark *and* The Gift. Nabokov's Dozen, Nabokov's Quartet, A Russian Beauty, Tyrants Destroyed *and* Details of a Sunset *are short-story collections.* Speak, Memory *is a poetic account of his privileged, pre-Revolutionary Russian childhood.*

NAIPAUL, V.S. (Vidiadhar Surajprasad)
(born 1932)
Trinidadian novelist and non-fiction writer.

A Trinidadian Indian who settled in England in his early 20s, Naipaul identifies exclusively with none of these three communities, and has written about all of them. His early novels (culminating in *A House for Mr Biswas*) were gentle tragi-comedies, but from the late 1960s onwards his books grew darker. He wrote savage non-fiction about the West Indies, India, South America and the Middle East, a mixture of travel and harsh political and social analysis, and his novels dealt with totalitarian oppression and despair. *In a Free State* is about cultural alienation: its central characters are an Indian servant in Washington, a Trinidadian in racist London and two whites in a fanatical black-power Africa. *Guerrillas* is set in a Caribbean dictatorship, *A Bend in the River* in a 'new' African country, emerging from centuries of colonial exploitation into a corrupt, Orwellian state. For most of the 1980s Naipaul wrote no fiction, but in 1987 he published *The Enigma of Arrival*, synthesising most of his earlier themes. Its hero, a Trinidadian writer living near Salisbury, reflects ruefully on the passing of 'old England' and the breakdown of the existing order of things.

A HOUSE FOR MR BISWAS · *(1961)*
Mr Biswas is a free spirit shackled by circumstance. He is

READ ON ▷

● *The Mystic Masseur.*
▶ **To the social comedies:** ▷R.K. Narayan, *Mr Sampath/ The Printer of Malgudi*; Amos Tutuola, *The Palm-wine Drinkard*; Timothy Mo, *Sour Sweet.*
▶ **To Naipaul's political novels:** ▷Joseph Conrad, *Nostromo*; Christopher Hope, *Black Swan.*

a poor Hindu in Trinidad, an educated man among illiterates, a good-natured soul who irritates everyone. He marries into an enormous extended family, the Tulsis, and spends the next 20 years trying to avoid being engulfed by their lifestyle, which he finds vulgar and ridiculous. The conflict – critics see it as an allegory about the absorption of political or ethnic minorities – is chiefly expressed in comedy. Mr Biswas is desperate to escape from the Tulsis' rambling mansion, thronged with disapproving relatives; his ambition is to live decently with his family in a home of his own. Although he succeeds, the book ends ironically and tragically: his victory, the vindication of all he stands for, turns to ashes even as he savours it.

Naipaul's other novels include The Suffrage of Elvira, Mr Stone and the Knights Companion *and* The Mimic Men. *His non-fiction books include* The Middle Passage *(on the West Indies and South America),* An Area of Darkness *and* India: a Wounded Civilisation *(two studies, a decade apart, of Indian life and politics) and* Among Believers: an Islamic Journey. The Overcrowded Barracoon *is a collection of essays and articles;* Miguel Street *and* A Flag on the Island *are collections of short stories.*

NARAYAN, R.K. (Rasipuran Krishnaswami) • *(born 1907)*
Indian novelist.

Narayan's stories are set in the imaginary southern Indian town of Malgudi, or in the villages and farms of the nearby Mempi Hills. His characters are shopkeepers, peasant farmers, craftsmen, priests, money-lenders, teachers and housewives, and his theme is the way Hindu belief sustains them in the face of the bewildering or ridiculous events of daily life. Many of his books are comedies. In *The Maneater of Malgudi* (1961) a demented taxidermist works on a series of creatures of ever-increasing size until, to universal panic, he suggests killing and stuffing the town's sacred elephant. The narrator of *A Tiger for Malgudi* (1983) is a worldly-wise tiger who becomes a circus performer, a film star and a travelling guru. *The Painter of Signs* (1976) recounts the farcical relationship between Raman, an ambitious but under-employed sign-painter, and Daisy from the Family Planning Centre, a New Woman whose life is dedicated not to love-affairs but to preventing over-population. Other books replace knockabout with gentler, more bitter-sweet scenes from the human comedy. *The English Teacher/Grateful to Life and Death* (1945) is a beautiful story about a husband

READ ON >

● *The Financial Expert.*
▶ Rabinadrath Tagore, *The Home and the World.* Anita Desai, *The Clear Light of Day.* S.N. Ghose, *And Gazelles Leaping.* ▷Kazuo Ishiguro, *An Artist of the Floating World.* ▷Tove Jansson, *The Summer Book.* Giovanni Guareschi, *The Little World of Don Camillo* (short stories).

coping with grief after the death of his beloved wife. In *The Guide* (1958) a pushy young man sets himself up as a tourist-guide, becomes the manager of a brainless dancer, and finally finds fulfilment not in any such secular enterprise but as a prophet.

THE VENDOR OF SWEETS • *(1967)*

The sweet-manufacturer Jagan is a devout Hindu, a follower of Gandhi. He lives an austere, uncomplicated and self-sufficient life. Then his wastrel son Mali arrives from Delhi with a non-Indian wife and a scheme for enriching himself by marketing a machine for writing novels. Mali and his wife take up residence in Jagan's house, and the old man is torn between love for his son, exasperation, and distress at the contrast between what Mali is doing (which he claims to be in the spirit of the 'new India') and the beliefs and rituals which have sustained Jagan all his life.

Narayan's other novels include Swami and Friends *and* The Bachelor of Arts *(which with* The English Teacher *form a trilogy),* Mr Sampath/The Printer of Malgudi, The Financial Expert *and* The Talkative Man. A Horse and Two Goats, An Astrologer's Day, Lawley Road *and* Malgudi Days *are short-story collections;* My Days *is a placid autobiography.*

NEWBY, P.H. (Percy Howard) • *(born 1918)*
British novelist.

The people in Newby's satires have neither the power nor the will to influence events. They are content to let things happen – and those things are unpredictable, dreamlike and bizarre. *Leaning in the Wind* (1986), set in the leafy English countryside, treats its characters like pieces in a surreal board-game. The protagonists are an insurance man who is also a poet, and the daughter of a nazi couple who emigrated to Cincinatti; he loves her, but she loves a Kenyan white settler who may or may not be descended from Shakespeare's sister. The plot revolves with remorseless, inconsequential logic round hauntings, forged manuscripts, betrayals and adulteries – and when the climax of the book demands a rabbit from the hat, out pops Idi Amin, that unlikeliest of conjurer's props.

Newby's other novels include A Journey to the Interior, Picnic at Sakkara, A Season in England, Revolution and Roses, A Guest and his Going, Something to Answer For *and* A Lot to Ask. Ten Miles from Anywhere *is a collection of short stories.*

READ ON ⟩

▶ Michael Frayn, *The Russian Interpreter.*
▷Alison Lurie, *Foreign Affairs.* ▷Evelyn Waugh, *Scoop.*

NEWSPAPERS

▷Heinrich Böll, *The Lost Honour of Katherina Blum*
Max Davidson, *Wellington Blue*
Michael Frayn, *Towards the End of the Morning*
George Gissing, *New Grub Street*
▷Rose Macaulay, *Potterism*
▷William Thackeray, *Pendennis*
▷Evelyn Waugh, *Scoop*

NINETEENTH-CENTURY ENGLAND

Caryl Brahms and S.J. Simon, *Don't, Mr Disraeli*
Richard Cobbold, *Margaret Catchpole*
▷David Cook, *Sunrising*
▷Charles Dickens, *Hard Times*
▷John Fowles, *The French Lieutenant's Woman*
George and Weedon Grossmith, *The Diary of a Nobody*
▷William Thackeray, *Pendennis*
▷Anthony Trollope, *The Warden*

NYE, Robert • *(born 1939)*
British writer of novels and children's books.

As well as novels, Nye has written prize-winning children's books and poetry. His best-known adult novel, *Falstaff* (1976), is the autobiography of Shakespeare's fat knight, written as a series of two-or-three-page meditations on such subjects as 'Honour', 'Sherry Sack' and 'Sir John Falstaff's Prick'. Falstaff feels that he has been comprehensively betrayed – by his times, by his family, by his king and above all by his own aging flesh. He looks back on the successes (and excesses) of his life, reshaping awkward facts and warming himself on the memory of gargantuan meals, orgies, pranks and confidence tricks. Nye's wonderful flights of language are sometimes his own, sometimes shameless Shakespeare-borrowings, and his view of late Middle Ages life as a glorious, uninhibited romp – 'eat, drink, fuck, for tomorrow we die' – is swaggering and seductive, so long as you can stay the pace.

> READ ON >

● *Merlin*; *The Voyage of the Destiny*.
▶ ▷François Rabelais, *Gargantua*. Petronius, *Satyricon*. Bamber Gascoigne, *Cod Strewth*. Stephen Marlowe, *The Memoirs of Christopher Columbus*. ▷John Kennedy Toole, *A Confederacy of Dunces*.

O

OGNIBLAT L'ARTSAU, MRS: see Franklin, Miles

O'HARA, John • *(1905–1970)*
US novelist and short-story writer.

In 18 novels and no less than 374 short stories, O'Hara created a one-person archive of US life and thought in the first half of this century. He wrote of ordinary middle Americans coping with financial, social, religious and family crises. Many of his stories are told in the first person or in the form of letters, and are strong on irony, revealing the teller's mind or attitudes despite the words he or she uses. The prevailing mood is desperation. O'Hara's people feel that their lives and their country are like monsters out of control; all that can be done is to try to live a decent life, and even that ambition is ambushed by poverty, drink, sex, ambition or politics. This concentration on the darker side of life sometimes leads, in O'Hara's longer books, to melodrama: they deal in a soap-opera style with such issues as abortion, alcoholism or incest. His short stories, by contrast, are well-controlled, single anecdotes, remarkable for their restraint.

O'Hara's story-collections include Files on Parade, Here's O'Hara, The Great Short Stories of O'Hara, 49 Stories, The O'Hara Generation *and* Pal Joey *(which he, Rodgers and Hart made into a successful musical, about an amoral, cynical 1930s night-club owner). His novels include* BUtterfield 8, Ten North Frederick, A Rage to Live *and* The Lockwood Concern.

> READ ON

▶ **To O'Hara's novels:** Ellen Glasgow, *The Sheltered Life*; Jean Stafford, *Boston Adventure*; John Braine, *Room at the Top*; Alberto Moravia, *The Woman of Rome*; Joyce Carol Oates, *Do With Me What You Will*.

▶ **To O'Hara's short stories:** Sherwood Anderson, *Winesburg, Ohio*; Ring Lardner, *You Know Me, Al*; Peter Taylor, *The Old Forest*; V.S. Pritchett, *When My Girl Comes Home*.

OLD AGE

▷Kingsley Amis, *Ending Up*
▷Honoré de Balzac, *Old Goriot*
 Julian Barnes, *Staring at the Sun*
▷David Cook, *Missing Persons*
▷Tove Jansson, *Sun City*
▷Muriel Spark, *Memento Mori*

OLD DARK HOUSES

▷Jane Austen, *Northanger Abbey*
 Robert Bloch, *Psycho*
▷Charlotte Brontë, *Jane Eyre*
▷Daphne Du Maurier, *Rebecca*
 Dinah Lampitt, *Sutton Place*
▷Mervyn Peake, *Gormenghast*
 Horace Walpole, *The Castle of Otranto*

Country Houses (p 51)

'ONLY CONNECT'
(people emotionally ill-at-ease)

▷Anita Brookner, *Look at Me*
▷George Eliot, *Middlemarch*
▷Gustave Flaubert, *Madame Bovary*
▷E.M. Forster, *Howards End*
▷Rosamond Lehmann, *The Ballad and the Source*
▷Mary McCarthy, *The Company She Keeps*
▷John Updike, *Marry Me*

Against the Stream (p 3); Perplexed by Life (p 190)

ON THE EDGE OF SANITY

▷Djuna Barnes, *Nightwood*
▷Lawrence Durrell, *The Dark Labyrinth/Cefalù*
▷Graham Greene, *Brighton Rock*
▷Hermann Hesse, *Steppenwolf*
▷Franz Kafka, *The Trial*
▷Malcolm Lowry, *Under the Volcano*

▷Vladimir Nabokov, *Despair*
▷R.K. Narayan, *The English Teacher/Grateful to Life and Death*

Depression and Psychiatry (p 57); Madness (p 59)

ORWELL, George • *(1903–50)*
British writer.

'George Orwell' was the pseudonym of Eric Blair. In his 20s he worked for the Colonial Police in Burma (an experience he later used in the novel *Burmese Days*). He returned to England disgusted with Imperialism and determined never again to work for or support 'the system'. In fact most of his work thereafter was literary: articles, essays and books taking a jaundiced view of British society and attitudes. Commissioned to report on the industrial north of England, he wrote *The Road to Wigan Pier* (1937), an indictment not only of unemployment and poverty but also of the failure of idealists, of all political parties, to find a cure. *Down and Out in London and Paris* (1933) is a description of the life of tramps and other derelicts; *Homage to Catalonia* (1938) is a withering account of the failure of the International Brigade in the Spanish Civil War. During the 1930s Orwell published three ▷Wellsian novels, about people dissatisfied with the constricting middle-class or lower-middle-class lives they led. It was not until 1945, when the second world war seemed to have blown away forever the humbug and complacency which Orwell considered the worst of all British characteristics, that he published his first overtly political book, *Animal Farm*. In this Stalinist 'fairy story', pigs turn their farm into a workers' democracy in which 'all animals are equal, but some are more equal than others', and the rule of all quickly degenerates into the tyranny of the few. The success of *Animal Farm* encouraged Orwell to write an even more savage political fantasy, *1984*.

1984 • *(1949)*
In the totalitarian future, Winston Smith's job is to rewrite history, adding to or subtracting from the record people who are in or out of Party favour. He falls in love – a forbidden thing, because it arises from freewill and not by order of the Party – and is betrayed to the Thought Police. He is tortured until he not only admits, but comes to believe, that the Party is right in everything: if it says that 2 + 2 = 5, then that is so. The book ends, chillingly, with the idea that Winston has won the victory over himself: he is happy because he has chosen, of his own free will, to have no choice.

READ ON ▷

▶ **To the savage politics of *1984*:** Victor Serge, *The Case of Comrade Tulayev*; Arthur Koestler, *Darkness at Noon*; ▷Franz Kafka, *The Trial*; ▷Vladimir Nabokov, *Bend Sinister*.

▶ **Future-fantasies of a similarly bleak kind:** ▷Aldous Huxley, *Brave New World*; ▷Anthony Burgess, *A Clockwork Orange*.

▶ ▷Mario Vargas Llosa. *The City and the Dogs/The Time of the Hero*, set in a Peruvian military academy, is that rare thing, an Orwellian political allegory which is also funny.

George ORWELL

1984 *(repression and oppression in grim totalitarian future)*

Alexander **SOLZHENITSYN, ONE DAY IN THE LIFE OF IVAN DENISOVICH** *(repression of dissidents in Stalinist labour-camp)*

Maxim **GORKY, FOMA GORDEEV**
(underbelly of Tsarist Russia in decline)

Nathaniel **HAWTHORNE, THE SCARLET LETTTER**
(religious bigotry in Pilgrim Fathers America)

Margaret **ATWOOD, THE HANDMAID'S TALE**
(grim future: totalitarian, religious oppression, anti-women)

Fay **WELDON, LIFE AND LOVES OF A SHE-DEVIL**
(betrayed wife takes macabre, comic revenge)

William **GOLDING, LORD OF THE FLIES**
(schoolboys revert to barbarism after being marooned from civilisation)

Joseph **CONRAD, HEART OF DARKNESS**
(wilderness as a satanic, engulfing force, human evil symbolised)

Paul **THEROUX, O-ZONE**
(efforts to make a viable post-nuclear society in US wilderness)

Patrick **WHITE, A FRINGE OF LEAVES**
('civilised' woman in distress, rehabilitated by contact with aboriginal, 'primitive' people)

Willa **CATHER, DEATH COMES FOR THE ARCHBISHOP**
(Catholic missionaries test their faith in 1870s Mexican wilderness)

Anthony **BURGESS, A CLOCKWORK ORANGE**
(crime and class-war in future Britain)

Graham **GREENE, BRIGHTON ROCK**
(crime and redemption in 1930s England)

Georges **SIMENON, THE MURDERER**
(criminal psychologically destroyed by guilt)

Orwell's 1930s novels are A Clergyman's Daughter, Keep the Aspidistra Flying *and* Coming Up for Air. *A collection of his essays, articles and letters was published in 1968.*

OTHER PEOPLES, OTHER TIMES
(historical novels set in remote or unusual times)

Jean M. Auel, *Clan of the Cave Bear* (prehistoric Europe)

James Clavell, *Shôgun* (17th-century Japan)

▷Eleanor Dark, *The Timeless Land* (18th-century Australia)

▷Gustave Flaubert, *Salammbô* (ancient Carthage)

▷Norman Mailer, *Ancient Evenings* (ancient Egypt)

Naomi Mitchison, *Early in Orcadia* (prehistoric Orkneys)

▷Robert Silverberg, *Gilgamesh the King* (ancient Sumeria)

▷Sigrid Undset, *Kristin Lavransdatter* (14th-century Norway)

▷Mario Vargas Llosa, *The War of the End of the World* (19th-century Peru)

Ancient Greece (p 9); Bible: Old Testament (p 23)

P

PARENTS AND CHILDREN

Samuel Butler, *The Way of All Flesh*
Margaret Forster, *Private Papers*
▷Hermann Hesse, *Rosshalde*
▷D.H. Lawrence, *Sons and Lovers*
▷Ivan Turgenev, *Fathers and Sons*
▷John Updike, *The Centaur*

Adolescence (p 3); Families: All-engulfing (p 72); Families: Eccentric (p 72); Families: Many Generations (p 72); Growing Up: Teenagers (p 101)

PASTERNAK, Boris • *(1890-1960)*
Russian poet and novelist.

In the USSR Pasternak is remembered chiefly as a poet and translator (of ▷Goethe and Shakespeare). Western readers know him for his 1957 novel *Doctor Zhivago*, and for the savage reaction of the Soviet authorities of the time, who banned the book and made Pasternak renounce his Nobel prize. *Doctor Zhivago* is about a doctor, Zhivago, and a teacher, Lara, caught up in the civil war which followed the 1917 Revolution. Although each is married to someone else and has a child, they fall in love – and the feverishness of their affair is increased by knowledge that neither it nor they will survive the war, since they come from a doomed class, the bourgeoisie. Horrified and powerless, they witness the brutality, class hatred and fury which precede the establishment of the USSR. Despite the reaction of the late-1950s authorities to all this, Pasternak was not really concerned with politics. He was more interested in the idea of people out of step

READ ON ▷

▶ ▷Lev Tolstoy, *Anna Karenina*. ▷Ernest Hemingway, *A Farewell to Arms*. ▷Elizabeth Bowen, *The Heat of the Day*. ▷Margaret Mitchell, *Gone With the Wind*. ▷Iris Murdoch, *The Red and the Green*.

with their time, star-crossed by destiny, and in the way Zhivago's and Lara's relationship was an emotional counterpart to the chaos and destruction all round them. The book ends with Zhivago's poems about Lara, like faded love-letters plucked from the rubble of the past.

PEAKE, Mervyn • *(1911–68)*
British novelist and artist.

Peake earned his living as an artist, drawing cartoons and grotesque, sombre illustrations to such books as *Treasure Island* and *The Hunting of the Snark*. He also made portraits of the main characters in his own novels: unsmiling freaks with distorted limbs and haunted eyes, violently cross-hatched as if with giant cobwebs. He admired ▷Poe and ▷Kafka, and his own work lopes gleefully – and hilariously – down the same dark passages of the imagination, peering into every corner and detailing the horrors that wait behind every moss-grown, slime-streaked door.

GORMENGHAST • *(1946–59)*
The 'Gormenghast' trilogy *Titus Groan*, *Gormenghast* and *Titus Alone* takes place in a mist-shrouded, monstrous kingdom surrounding the crumbling Gothic castle of Gormenghast. Evil broods, waiting to pounce; it is kept at bay only if everyone, from Lord Sepulchrave himself to the physician Prunesquallor, from Nanny Slagg to the demented, crippled scullion Steerpike, lives every second of each day by a precise, bizarre ritual, as compulsive and pointless as the movements of the insane. *Titus Groan* describes the fearful consequences when Steerpike, to further his own dark ambitions, starts fomenting social revolution. *Gormenghast* is about the growing-up of Titus, 77th Earl of Groan: how he learns about his inheritance, uncovers the castle's secrets and begins to chafe against the rituals which choke its people's lives. In *Titus Alone* Titus breaks free of the castle and explores the country outside, an arrogant knight-errant on a terrifying, pointless quest.

Peake's only other novel, Mr Pye, is a gentler story about a man on Sark in the Channel Islands who shows distressing signs of turning into an angel.

> READ ON >

▶ **To *Gormenghast*;**
▷Mary Shelley, *Frankenstein*; ▷Edgar Allan Poe, *The Fall of the House of Usher*; ▷Tom De Haan, *A Mirror for Princes*; ▷J.R.R. Tolkien, *Lord of the Rings*..
▶ **To *Mr Pye*:** Paul Gallico, *Flowers for Mrs Harris*.

Mervyn **PEAKE**

GORMENGHAST *(Titus Groan uncovers his destiny in sinister castle-kingdom)*

Dennis **WHEATLEY, THE KA OF GIFFORD HILLARY**
(while Hillary sleeps, 'other self' leads malign independent life)

James **HERBERT, THE MAGIC COTTAGE**
(young couple move into macabre haunted house)

Bram **STOKER, DRACULA**
(vampire Count)

Stephen **KING, PET SEMETARY**
(ghosts walk in rural Maine)

Edgar Allan **POE, TALES OF MYSTERY AND IMAGINATION** *(madness, buried alive, and living dead)*

SUPERNATURAL TERROR

DERANGEMENT AND MADNESS

Sylvia **PLATH, THE BELL JAR**
(treatment for suicidal depressive mania)

Patricia **HIGHSMITH, THE GLASS CELL**
(man driven mad by prison, has wife been faithful?)

Ken **KESEY, ONE FLEW OVER THE CUCKOO'S NEST**
(lunatics take over the asylum)

Robert **SILVERBERG, TOM O'BEDLAM**
(are Tom's visions madness or manifestations of genuine alien gods?)

Tom **DE HAAN, A MIRROR FOR PRINCES**
(disturbed family of 'medieval' dictator wait for his death)

Ursula **LE GUIN, MALAFRENA**
(Napoleonic Europe — or its mirror)

Robert **SILVERBERG, LORD VALENTINE'S CASTLE**
(young man — good — gathers followers to battle usurper)

Robert **IRWIN, THE ARABIAN NIGHTMARE**
(man on medieval pilgrimage is trapped in his own dreams)

Jack **VANCE, THE BLUE WORLD**
(floating worlds in water-paradise — but beware sea-monsters)

FANTASY SOCIETIES

OLD, DARK HOUSE AND CASTLES

Daphne **DU MAURIER, REBECCA**
(what is the secret of Manderley?)

Angela **CARTER, THE MAGIC TOYSHOP**
(adolescent orphan goes to live with deranged puppeteer-uncle)

Michael **INNES, LAMENT FOR A MAKER**
(who killed the mad Laird of Erchany? What is the meaning behind the curse?)

Susan **HILL, THE WOMAN IN BLACK**
(ghosts walk in rural England)

Henry **JAMES, THE TURN OF THE SCREW**
(who can exorcise the ghosts which haunt the children?)

PERPLEXED BY LIFE
(people battling to understand and control their destiny)

▷Saul Bellow, *Humboldt's Gift*
▷Albert Camus, *The Fall*
▷Erica Jong, *Fear of Flying*
▷Hermann Hesse, *Rosshalde*
▷Iris Murdoch, *The Sandcastle*
▷V.S. Naipaul, *A House for Mr Biswas*
▷Italo Svevo, *The Confessions of Zeno*
▷Angus Wilson, *Anglo-Saxon Attitudes*

PIRANDELLO, Luigi • *(1867-1936)*
Italian writer of novels, short stories and plays.

Although Pirandello is chiefly known for such experimental plays as *Six Characters in Search of an Author*, he was also a prolific short-story writer and the author of six novels about aristocratic and peasant life in late 19th-century Sicily. His 250 stories take as their starting-point the kind of mundane crimes – adultery, fraud, murder – which figure in the 'news in brief' columns of tabloid newspapers: lip-smacking gossip about total strangers. But Pirandello regards each sensational event as the release of a long build-up of tension or psychological panic – and that build-up is his subject. He shows us people trapped by convention, by their own passions and longings, and by the malevolence of others. If you stripped the music from Puccini's operas and boiled their plots and motivation down to half a dozen pages of lucid, implacable prose, the results might be very similar.

Pirandello's novels include The Late Mattia Pascal, The Old and the Young *and* One, None and a Hundred Thousand. *A good, representative story-collection is* Better Think Twice About It.

READ ON ▷

▶ Alberto Moravia, *Roman Tales.* Cesare Pavese, *Nice Summer.* Ivan Klíma, *My First Loves.* William Saroyan, *The Insurance Salesman and Other Stories.* George Moore, *Celibate Lives.* ▷Vladimir Nabokov, *The Real Life of Sebastian Knight* (novel).

PLACES

  Melvyn Bragg, *The Maid of Buttermere* (English Lake District)
▷Emily Brontë, *Wuthering Heights* (Yorkshire moors)
▷Graham Greene, *The Comedians* (Haiti)
▷Thomas Hardy, *Jude the Obscure* (rural Wessex)

▷John Irving, *The Cider House Rules* (rural Maine)
▷Rudyard Kipling, *Kim* (rural India)
▷R.K. Narayan, *The Painter of Signs* (small-town
  India)

Cities: New World (p 44); Cities: Old World (p 44);
Deep South, USA (p 55); Into the Wilderness (p 127);
US Small Town Life (p 246)

PLAIDY, Jean • *(born 1906)*
British novelist.

'Jean Plaidy' is one of the pseudonyms of Eleanor ▷Hibbert. She is the author of over 80 light historical novels, most of them based on the intrigues surrounding European royal marriages, accessions and other political and dynastic events. Several of her best-known books are grouped in series, including the 'Norman Trilogy' (beginning with *The Bastard King*, 1975, about William the Conqueror), the 'Plantagenet Saga' (based on the Wars of the Roses) and the 'Mary Queen of Scots' series.

Plaidy's other books include The Spanish Bridegroom, A Health Unto his Majesty, Flaunting Extravagant Queen, Perdita's Prince, Sweet Lass of Richmond Hill *and* The Prince and the Quakeress.

> **READ ON** ▷

▶ Margaret Irwin, *Young
Bess.* Tyler Whittle,
The Young Victoria.
Anya Seton, *Katherine.*
Caryl Brahms and S.J.
Simon, *No Bed for
Bacon* (an Elizabethan
spoof).

POE, Edgar Allan • *(1809–49)*
US short-story writer.

Poe's miserable life is almost as well-known as his stories. He was an orphan whose foster-father hated him; he was thrown out of university, military college and half a dozen jobs because of the instability of his character; in order to earn a living he suppressed his real ambition (to be a poet) in favour of hack journalism and sensational fiction; he gambled, fornicated, and finally drank himself to death. He was like a man haunted by his own existence – and this is exactly the feeling in his macabre short stories, which are less about the supernatural than about people driven crazy by their own imagination. 'The Fall of the House of Usher' and 'The Premature Burial' recount the terrifying results when people are accidentally entombed alive. The murderer in 'The Tell-tale Heart' buries his victim under the floorboards, only to be haunted by what he takes to be the thud of the dead man's heartbeat. The hero of 'The Pit and the Pendulum' is psychologically tortured by the Spanish Inquisition, first by fear of a

> **READ ON** ▷

▶ **To Poe's stories of
the macabre:** H.P.
Lovecraft, *Dagon and
Other Macabre Tales*;
M.R. James, *Ghost
Stories of an
Antiquary*; Roald Dahl,
Switch Bitch;
▷Stephen King, *Night
Shift*; ▷James Herbert,
Moon (novel).
▶ **To the detection-
stories:** ▷A. Conan
Doyle, *The Adventures
of Sherlock Holmes*;
Edgar Wallace, *The
Four Just Men*; ▷Isaac
Asimov, *Tales of the
Black Widowers*.

swinging, ever-approaching blade and then by the way the walls of his cell move inwards to crush him. In 'The Black Cat' a murderer is given away by the mewing of a cat which he has accidentally walled up with his victim's body. As well as stories of this kind, Poe occasionally wrote lighter mysteries. The best-known of all ('The Murders in the Rue Morgue'; 'The Mystery of Marie Roget') centre on an eccentric investigator who solves crimes by meticulous reconstruction according to the evidence: they are the first-ever detective-stories.

Poe's stories are normally collected nowadays as Tales of Mystery and Imagination. *His other writings include poetry (*The Bells; The Raven*) and vitriolic literary criticism, savaging such contemporaries as Longfellow.*

POLICE PROCEDURAL

Wilkie Collins, *The Woman in White*
Freeman Wills Crofts, *Death of a Train*
Nicholas Freeling, *Cold Iron*
▷Ed McBain, *Lightning*
▷Ruth Rendell, *A Guilty Thing Surprised*
Maj Sjöwall and Per Wahlöo, *The Laughing Policeman*
Martin Cruz Smith, *Gorky Park*

POLITICS (1)

▷Chinua Achebe, *Anthills of the Savannah*
Jorge Amado, *The Violent Land*
David Caute, *News from Nowhere*
▷Richard Condon, *Mile High*
Benjamin Disraeli, *Coningsby*
Martha Gellhorn, *A Stricken Field*
Arthur Koestler, *Darkness at Noon*
▷Mary McCarthy, *The Groves of Academe*

POLITICS (2)

▷George Orwell, *Animal Farm*
Amos Oz, *A Perfect Peace*
▷Salman Rushdie, *Shame*

Victor Serge, *The Case of Comrade Tulayev*
Howard Spring, *Fame is the Spur*
▷C.P. Snow, *The Corridors of Power*
▷Gore Vidal, *Burr*

PORTER, Katherine Anne • *(1890-1980)*
US novelist and short-story writer.

Many of Porter's short stories, set in Texas, are accounts of ordinary matters – the relationship of old and young, swimming, the conversation of farm-workers, the coming of a circus – seen through the eyes of a child. They are wistful and nostalgic, depicting human existence as both beautiful and transient. Her major work, the 500-page novel *Ship of Fools* (1962), is in a harsher, allegorical vein. The ship of fools is the world, and the passengers are the human race, cruising to disaster. Porter's ship is sailing from Vera Cruz to Bremerhaven in 1931. The crew and most of the passengers are German; the other travellers are Mexican, Swedish, Swiss, American, and above all Spanish: 870 plantation-workers being sent home because of a slump in the sugar trade, and a troupe of sinister dancers. At the start of the voyage, the people are determined to be friendly; but soon divisions of class, race, nation and politics begin to surface, and the outcome is war. The lumpishness of this allegory is offset by the refinement of Porter's writing: the book reads like a collaboration by ▷Chekhov and ▷Conrad, unlikely but persuasive.

Porter's story-collections are Flowering Judas; Pale Horse, Pale Rider *(three short novels);* The Leaning Tower *and* The Old Order. *Her* Collected Stories *appeared in 1967.*

POWELL, Anthony • *(born 1905)*
British novelist.

In the 1930s Powell wrote half a dozen novels in a similar vein to those of Rose Macaulay and Evelyn Waugh, satirising the British intellectual and upper classes of the time. The optimistic, aimless young people of *Afternoon Men* drift from party to party, trying to summon up enough willpower to make something of themselves. *From a View to a Death/Mr Zouch: Superman* sets the arts and foxhunting at each other's throats. The hero of *What's Become of Waring?* has to find someone to write the biog-

> **READ ON**

▶ **To Porter's stories:**
▷Eudora Welty, *The Golden Apples*; ▷Willa Cather, *The Troll Garden*; Seán O'Faoláin, *Foreign Affairs*.
▶ **To *Ship of Fools*:**
▷Joseph Conrad, *Typhoon*; ▷Patrick White, *Voss*.

> **READ ON**

▶ **To Powell's 1930s books:** ▷Evelyn Waugh, *Vile Bodies*; Henry Green, *Party Going*; ▷Rose Macaulay, *Crewe Train*.
▶ The mood of elegiac, upper-class malice

raphy of a best-selling travel-writer who has disappeared in circumstances which grow more mysterious, and more unsavoury, by the minute. After the second world war, during which he produced no fiction, Powell abandoned single books for a 12-novel sequence, *A Dance to the Music of Time*, a satirical portrait of 70 years of English high society and establishment life.

A DANCE TO THE MUSIC OF TIME • *(1951–75)*

The sequence follows its characters from Edwardian schooldays to nostalgic, worldly-wise old age. The narrator, Nick Jenkins, discreet as a civil servant, goes everywhere, knows everyone, and writes of his contemporaries (notably the ambition-racked Widmerpool) in elegant, ironic prose. The books move imperturbably from farce to seriousness, from knockabout to reverie. The first three novels, *A Question of Upbringing*, *A Buyer's Market* and *The Acceptance World*, concern the characters' schooldays, their Oxbridge careers and their entry into the glittering smart set of 1920s London. *At Lady Molly's*, *Casanova's Chinese Restaurant* and *The Kindly Ones* are about first jobs, marriages and the establishment of a network of sexual, social, financial and political alliances which will bind their lives. *The Valley of Bones*, *The Soldier's Art* and *The Military Philosophers* take the characters through two world wars, and *Books Do Furnish a Room*, *Temporary Kings* and *Hearing Secret Harmonies* show them coming to terms with post-war austerity, the white heat of the technological revolution and flower-power, reflecting on the change not only in themselves but in every aspect of British establishment life since their schooldays 50 years before.

Powell's other 1930s novels are Venusberg *and* Agents and Patients. *After finishing* A Dance to the Music of Time *he wrote an autobiography,* To Keep the Ball Rolling, *and two other (unrelated) novels,* O, How the Wheel Becomes It! *and* The Fisher King.

characteristic of *A Dance to the Music of Time* is repeated in three other novel sequences – ▷Marcel Proust, *Remembrance of Things Past (A la recherche du temps perdu)*. Simon Raven, *Alms for Oblivion*; Stuart Evans, *Windmill Hill* – and in the single novels Edward Candy, *Scene Changing*; Emma Tennant, *The House of Hospitalities* and ▷Frederic Raphael, *Orchestra and Beginners*.

POWYS, John Cowper • *(1872–1963)*
British novelist and non-fiction writer.

A university professor, Powys wrote books on ▷Dostoevsky, ▷Homer and ▷Rabelais, dozens of articles, reviews and other non-fiction works, and a lively autiobiography. His early novels (*Ducdame*; *Rodmoor*; *Wolf Solent*, all written before 1930) are sombre, ▷Hardyish stories about the farmers and fishermen of the English West Country. After he retired from teaching Powys wrote a series of

READ ON ▷

▶ **To Powys' early novels:** ▷Victor Hugo, *Toilers of the Sea*; ▷George Eliot, *Silas Marner*; ▷Nathaniel Hawthorne, *The Scarlet Letter*.

completely different novels: long, mystical books influenced by Homer and the Old Testament and drawing on English legend and dark ages history. In *A Glastonbury Romance* modern inhabitants of the Glastonbury area (including worshippers and clergy at the Abbey) find their lives mysteriously affected by local legends of King Arthur and of the Holy Grail. In a similar way, *Maiden Castle* describes how unearthing the distant past – some of the characters are archaeologists working on a prehistoric site – disturbs the present. *Owen Glendower* and *Porius* are historical romances, full of wizards, giants and ancient magic. *The Bronze Head* is about Roger Bacon, the first scientist (or last alchemist). In *Atlantis* the hero of Homer's *Odyssey* embarks on a quest to find the lost continent.

▶ **To *A Glastonbury Romance*:** ▷Lawrence Durrell, *The Dark Labyrinth/Cefalù*; Charles Williams, *War in Heaven*.
▶ **To the late historical novels:** ▷Sigrid Undset, *Kristin Lavransdatter*; Peter Vansittart, *Three Six Seven*; Pär Lagerkvist, *The Sibyl*; ▷Gore Vidal, *Creation*.

PRICHARD, Katharine Susannah •
(1883-1969)
Australian novelist.

Prichard was a political activist, and her best-known novels deal with matters of social concern, mainly in the 1920s and 1930s. *Working Bullocks* is the study of a community of timber workers in Western Australia, fighting the introduction of streamlined methods which will destroy their employment prospects. *Coonardoo* is about the confrontation of white people and aborigines. The 'goldfields trilogy' *The Roaring Nineties*, *Golden Miles* and *Winged Seeds* (1946–50) is a densely-organised multi-generation saga, also set in Western Australia, from the goldrush days of the 19th century, through the industrialisation and political confrontation of the 1920s to post-second-world-war decline.

Prichard's other novels include Black Opal *(about a mining community threatened by big-business takeovers),* Intimate Strangers *(about a bickering couple whose marriage is saved by their shared political enthusiasms) and* Haxby's Circus *(about a husband-and-wife team struggling to run a travelling circus).* The Wild Oats of Han, *a children's book, is based on her idyllic childhood in Tasmania.*

> **READ ON** ▷

▶ ▷Émile Zola, *Germinal*. Mrs Gaskell, *Mary Barton*. Upton Sinclair, *The Jungle*. ▷John Steinbeck, *The Grapes of Wrath*.

PRIESTLEY, J.B. (John Boynton) •
(1894-1984)
British novelist and playwright.

As well as plays and non-fiction books, Priestley wrote

> **READ ON** ▷

▶ *Lost Empires* (a darker

over 60 novels. They range from amiable satire (eg *Low Notes on a High Level*, 1956, sending up egghead BBC musicians) to sombre social realism (eg *Angel Pavement*, 1936, about a sleepy 1930s business firm galvanised into new activity and then destroyed by a confidence trickster). His best-loved novel, *The Good Companions* (1929), tells of three people who escape from humdrum lives to join the Dinky Doos concert party in the 1920s. The novel follows the concert party's career in theatres and seaside resorts all over England, and ends with each of the main characters finding self-fulfilment in an entirely unexpected way. The book bulges with show-biz cliché – brave little troupers; lodging-house keepers with hearts of gold; leading ladies and their tantrums; cynical, hung-over leading men – and with warm-hearted nostalgia for the provincial England of the Good Old Days. It is an armchair of a novel, a book to wallow in – and if life was never really like that, so much the worse for life.

story, about a group of music-hall performers in the year of feverish jingoism and imperialist posturing which led up to the first world war); *The Image Men* (a satire about advertising and television).

▶ **To *The Good Companions*:** Bamber Gascoigne, *The Heyday*; Noel Langley, *There's a Porpoise Close Behind Us*. Budd Schulberg, *What makes Sammy Run?* and ▷Len Deighton, *Close Up* give beadier-eyed views of the entertainment business (perhaps because their subject is not music-hall but films).

▶ **To Priestley's books in general:** ▷H.G. Wells, *Tono-Bungay*; James Hilton, *Goodbye, Mr Chips*; Eric Linklater, *Poet's Pub*.

PRIVATE EYES

Andrew Bergman, *The Big Kiss-off of 1944*
▷Raymond Chandler, *Farewell, My Lovely*
▷Dashiell Hammett, *The Maltese Falcon*
Ross Macdonald, *Sleeping Beauty*
John Milne, *Dead Birds*
Jonathan Valine, *Lime Pit*

Classic Detection (p 46); Great Detectives (p 100); Murder Most Mind-Boggling (p 174)

PROUST, Marcel • *(1871-1922)*
French novelist.

Proust's *Remembrance of Things Past* (A la recherche du temps perdu) (1913–27; magnificently translated by C.K.

READ ON ▷

▶ **Good parallels to the sensuous childhood-**

Scott Moncrieff and Terence Kilmartin) is in seven sections: *Swann's Way, Within a Budding Grove, The Guermantes Way, Cities of the Plain, The Captive, The Fugitive, Time Regained*. Each is as long as a normal novel and each can be read both on its own and as part of the whole huge tapestry. The book is a memoir, told in the first person by a narrator called Marcel, of a group of rich French socialites from the 1860s to the end of the first world war. It shows how they react to outside events – the Dreyfus case, women's emancipation, the first world war – and how, as the world moves on, their power and social position wane. Above all, it shows them reacting to each other, to friends, acquaintances and servants: the book is full of love-affairs, parties, alliances and betrayals. Through it all moves Marcel himself, good-natured, self-effacing, fascinated by beauty (both human and artistic: his accounts of music and literature are as deeply-felt as those of people), and with a sharply ironical eye for social and sexual absurdity. Proust developed for the book a system of 'involuntary memory', in which each sensual stimulus – the smell of lilac, the taste of cake dipped in tea – unlocks from the subconscious a stream of images of the past. Though this technique has structural importance in the novel – Proust believed that our present only makes sense when it is refracted through past experience – its chief effect for the reader is to provide pages of languorous, detailed descriptions, prose poems on everything from the feel of embroidery to garden sounds and scents on a summer evening. Proust likes to take his time: at one point Marcel spends nearly 100 pages wondering whether to get up or stay in bed. But only the length at which he works allows him scope for the sensuous, malicious decadence which is the main feature of his work.

Proust's other writings include translations of Ruskin's The Bible of Amiens *and* Sesame and Lilies, *a collection of short stories and literary parodies,* The Pleasures and the Days *(Les Plaisirs et les jours), and* Jean Santeuil, *a draft of part of* Remembrance of Things Past.

evocations of the first part of *Remembrance of Things Past*: Alain Fournier, *The Lost Domain* (Le grand Meaulnes); ▷James Joyce, *Portrait of the Artist as a Young Man*.
► **Echoing the hedonism and decadence of some of Proust's later sections**: Joris-Karl Huysmans, *Against Nature* (A rebours).
► **Good on 'the texture of experience'**: Dorothy Richardson, *Pilgrimage*; ▷Virginia Woolf, *The Waves*; John Dos Passos, *Manhattan Transfer*.
► **Novel-sequences of comparable grandeur**: ▷Anthony Powell, *A Dance to the Music of Time*; Henry Williamson, *The Flax of Dream*. (Williamson's later sequence *A Chronicle of Ancient Sunlight* starts well, but is hijacked half-way through by the author's fascist sympathies.)

PUBLISH AND BE DAMNED
(writers; publishers; agents; readers; fans)

▷Marjorie Allingham, *Flowers for the Judge*
▷Erica Jong, *How To Save Your Own Life*
▷Wyndham Lewis, *The Apes of God*
▷Rose Macaulay, *Crewe Train*
▷Anthony Powell, *What's Become of Waring?*
▷Philip Roth, *Zuckerman Unbound*
▷Tom Sharpe, *The Great Pursuit*

PUZO, Mario • *(born 1920)*
US novelist and screenwriter.

Puzo began his career as a writer of children's books, but in 1969 turned to adult fiction and had one of the biggest commercial successes in publishing history with *The Godfather*. The story concerns the New York mafia family the Corleones. It centres on Don Vito Corleone's handover of authority to his son Michael – a gift akin to being made successor to Genghis Khan – and on the power-struggle, both with outsiders and between members of the family, to which this leads. Present-day events are intercut with flashbacks to Don Vito's Sicilian childhood and his early days in the USA. The plot of *The Godfather* is in a direct line from those of such multi-generation family and big-business sagas as the novels of Harold Robbins. But Puzo's detail of mafia life is as exhaustive and compelling as a government research report. As ▷Le Carré does with spies, he seems to be spilling 'insider' secrets in every line, and his inventions (if they are inventions) are so plausible that it is hard to imagine how the real mafia could be run in any other way. After the 1970s success of the two Godfather films, Puzo turned to screenwriting (among other things, he co-wrote the first Superman film), and his later novels *Las Vegas*, *Fools Die* and *The Sicilian*, though fast-moving and exciting, are like novelised movies, airport-bookstall fodder lacking the documentary earnestness which makes *The Godfather* so compulsive.

READ ON ▷

▶ **Good mafia follow-ups:** ▷Richard Condon, *Prizzi's Honour*; Donald Westlake, *The Mercenaries*; Elmore Leonard, *Glitz*.
▶ **Blockbusters about big business and/or politics:** John Gregory Dunne, *The Red White and Blue*; ▷Jerome Weidman, *I Can Get it for you Wholesale*; Sally Quinn, *Regrets Only*.

PYM, Barbara • *(1913–80)*
British novelist.

Only ▷Jane Austen and ▷Ivy Compton-Burnett wrote about worlds as restricted as Pym's – and she is regularly compared to both of them. Her books are high-Anglican high comedies; she is tart about the kind of pious middle-class ladies who regard giving sherry-parties for the clergy as doing good works, and she is merciless to priests. Much of the charm of her books lies in their ornate, formal dialogue: her characters all speak with the same prissy, self-conscious elegance, like civil servants taught light conversation by Oscar Wilde.

A GLASS OF BLESSINGS • *(1958)*
Wilmet Forsyth is rich, well-bred, happy and dim. She fills her mind with fantasies about the priests and parishioners at her local church, imagining that their lives are a

READ ON ▷

● *Quartet in Autumn*.
▶ ▷Ivy Compton-Burnett, *Pastors and Masters*. A.N. Wilson, *Kindly Light*. Edward Candy, *Scene Changing*. Alice Thomas Ellis, *The Twenty-seventh Kingdom*. J.F. Powers, *Morte d'Urban*. ▷Anita Brookner, *Look at Me*.

whirl of hidden passions, ambitions and frustrations. She imagines herself in love with a handsome evening-class teacher, and assumes that he adores her too. As the book proceeds, every one of these assumptions is proved spectacularly, ludicrously mistaken.

Pym's other novels are Some Tame Gazelle, Excellent Women, Jane and Prudence, Less than Angels, Quartet in Autumn, The Sweet Dove Died, Crampton Hodnett *and* An Academic Question.

PYNCHON, Thomas • *(born 1937)*
US novelist.

Reading Pynchon's satires is like exploring a maze with an opinionated and eccentric guide. He leads us lovingly up every blind alley, breaks off to tell jokes, falls into reverie, ridicules everything and everyone, and refuses to say where he's going until he gets there. *The Crying of Lot 49* (1967) begins with Oedipa Maas setting out to discover why she has been left a legacy by an ex-lover, and what it is; but it quickly develops into a crazy tour of hippie 1960s California, an exploration of drugs, bizarre sex, psychic sensitivity and absurd politics, centring on a group of oddball characters united in a secret society determined to subvert the US postal system. *Gravity's Rainbow* (1973) is a much darker fable, a savage anti-war satire set in a top-secret British centre for covert operations during the second world war. In a mad world, where actions have long ceased to have any moral point, where nothing – on principle – is ever explained or justified, the characters spend their working hours alternately doing what they're told and trying to find out the reason for their existence, and pass their leisure hours in masochistic, joyless sex. On the basis of his short stories and *The Crying of Lot 49*, Pynchon is sometimes claimed as a comic writer. But although *Gravity's Rainbow* is satirical, its jokes are knives, its farce makes us scream with despair not joy.

Pynchon's first and most experimental novel was V *(1963).* Mortality and Mercy in Vienna *is a novella, and* Low-lands *is a collection of short stories.*

READ ON ⟩

▶ **The satirical fury of** *Gravity's Rainbow* **is most nearly matched in:** ▷Joseph Heller, *Catch-22* and William Gaddis, *J.R.* (about a deranged 10-year-old genius in a reform school who trades in stocks and shares and exploits other people's greed).
▶ **Pynchon's more genial, loonier side is paralleled in:** ▷Mario Vargas Llosa, *Aunt Julia and the Scriptwriter*; Terry Southern, *The Magic Christian* and ▷Kurt Vonnegut, *Breakfast of Champions.*
▶ **Midway between despair and farce, recommended follow-ups are:** ▷John Irving, *The Hotel New Hampshire* and ▷Jerzy Kosinski, *The Devil Tree.*

R

RABELAIS, François • *(c 1494–1553)*

French satirist.

At heart Rabelais' *Gargantua* (1534) and *Pantagruel* (1532–3) are simple fairy-tales: accounts of the birth and education of the giant Gargantua and of his son Pantagruel. But Rabelais was really writing satire, sending up the whole of medieval knowledge and belief. The giants study philosophy, mathematics, theology and alchemy; they build an anti-monastery whose rules are not poverty, chastity and obedience but wealth, fornication and licence. Pantagruel's mentor is no dignified greybeard but the con-man Panurge, and the two of them go on a fantastic journey (through countries as fabulous as any of those visited by Sinbad or Gulliver) to find the answer to the question 'Whom shall Pantagruel marry?'. Because Rabelais' heroes are giants, every human appetite is magnified a thousand-fold. It takes 17,913 cows to provide enough milk to feed the infant Gargantua, and when he is learning to wipe his bottom he experiments with so many different substances that it takes two pages just to list them. Much of *Gargantua*'s first half is taken up with a fierce battle between the giants and their neighbours, and in particular with the exploits of the roistering, apoplectic Friar John of the Funnels and Goblets, who is later rewarded by being made Abbot of the Monastery of Do As You Like. Rabelais described his books as a 'feast of mirth', and their intellectual satire is balanced by celebration of physical pleasure of every kind: not for nothing has the word 'rabelaisian' entered the dictionary. The original French, already engorged with puns, jokes, parodies and over-the-top lists of every kind, was inflated to nearly twice the length by the 17th-century translator Thomas Urquhart. His English is funnier, filthier and even more fantastical

READ ON ▷

▶ ▷Laurence Sterne, *Tristram Shandy*.
▷Jonathan Swift, *Gulliver's Travels*.
Giovanni Boccaccio, *Decameron* (short stories). Anon, *The Thousand and One Nights/The Arabian Nights*. Alexander Theroux, *D'Arconville's Cat*. ▷J.P. Donleavy, *The Ginger Man*.

than Rabelais' French: Rabelais would have loved (and stolen back) every word of it.

RAPHAEL, Frederic • *(born 1931)*
US/British novelist and screenwriter.

Raphael's sourly witty TV plays and series, showing the hollow husks that brilliant Oxbridge graduates become in later life, have diverted attention from his 16 novels. These walk in darker, more sinister paths. His subject is the power of evil, whether political, moral or social. Sometimes (as in *Lindmann*, about guilt for a second-world-war atrocity, or in *Like Men Betrayed*, set in the 1940s Greek civil war), evil is an external force, the result of perverted idealism; in other books (*Richard's Things*, about erotic possession and betrayal; *Heaven and Earth*, about artistic and personal integrity) we are ourselves corrupt, battling our own urges and ambitions. The heart of darkness in Raphael's work is concealed by a firework-display of satirical, witty dialogue which some readers find intrusive, others a symptom of his characters' inability to cope with their own despair.

APRIL, JUNE AND NOVEMBER • *(1972)*
Daniel Meyer, a film-director, has spent his youth in a dazzle of artistic, social and sexual triumph. Now, as middle age looms, he begins to suspect that under the Byronic façade his true self has all but disappeared. Affairs follow, with a younger and an older woman; he lets himself be seduced by different life-styles, in grubby, rainy London and on a sun-bleached Greek island, a rich man's paradise. Like all Raphael's main characters, Meyer is a battle-ground between genuineness and the role he plays in life – and the question of which side of him wins is left a cliffhanger until the book's last, most ironical line of all.

Raphael's other novels include The Limits of Love, Orchestra and Beginners *and* Two for the Road. The Glittering Prizes *and* After the War *are novels linked to TV series.* Sleeps Six *and* Oxbridge Blues *are collections of short stories.*

READ ON ⟩

● *Heaven and Earth.*
▶ ▷F. Scott Fitzgerald, *The Great Gatsby.* Vita Sackville-West, *The Edwardians.* ▷Philip Roth, *Zuckerman Unbound.* Rona Jaffe, *Class Reunion.*

RENAISSANCE EUROPE

Caryl Brahms and S.J. Simon, *No Bed for Bacon*
▷Alexandre Dumas, *The Three Musketeers*
▷Dorothy Dunnett, *Niccolò Rising*
Carlos Fuentes, *Terra Nostra*

Stephen Marlowe, *The Memoirs of Christopher Columbus*
▷Jean Plaidy, *Queen of the Realm*
Irving Stone, *The Agony and the Ecstasy*

The Middle Ages (p 170)

RENAULT, Mary • *(1905–83)*
British novelist.

In her 30s and 40s Renault wrote several novels about hospital and wartime life, culminating in *The Charioteer*, the moving story of a homosexual serviceman. In the 1950s she began writing historical novels about ancient Greece. *The King Must Die* and *The Bull from the Sea* are based on the myth of King Theseus of Athens, who killed the Cretan Minotaur; *Fire From Heaven*, *The Persian Boy* and *Funeral Games* are about Alexander the Great. Like ▷Robert Graves, Renault treats people of the past as if they were psychologically just like us, so that even the most bizarre political or sexual behaviour seems both rational and credible.

THE MASK OF APOLLO • *(1966)*
Niko, a Greek actor of the 4th century BC, is used as a go-between by politicians trying to replace the despotic régime in Sicily with an ideal state ruled by a philosopher-king. Political intrigue is interwoven with Niko's own complicated private life, and with his (brilliantly described) theatrical personality: he is as vulnerable, as self-centred, as dedicated and as nervously extrovert as any Broadway or National Theatre star today.

Renault's other Greek books are The Last of the Wine *and* The Praise Singer. *Her novels with 20th-century settings are* Purposes of Love/Promise of Love, Kind Are Her Answers, The Friendly Young Ladies/The Middle Mist, Return to Night, North Face *and* The Charioteer.

RENDELL, Ruth • *(born 1930)*
British novelist.

Rendell's Chief Inspector Wexford novels are atmospheric murder mysteries in traditional style, set in the small towns and villages of the English Home Counties. Like ▷P.D. James, she spends much time developing the character of her detective, a liberal and cultured man appalled at the psychological pressures which drive people to

READ ON >

● *The Last of the Wine.*
▶ Helen Waddell, *Héloise and Abelard*. John Arden, *Silence Among the Weapons*. Naomi Mitchison, *The Corn King and the Spring Queen*. ▷Gore Vidal, *Creation*. Pär Lagerkvist, *The Sibyl*. Henry Treece, *Oedipus*.

READ ON >

▶ **To the Wexford books:** ▷P.D. James, *Shroud for a Nightingale*; Nicholas Freeling, *Love in Amsterdam*.

crime. Those pressures are the subject of Rendell's other books: grim stories of paranoia, obsession and inadequacy. In *Judgement in Stone* (1978), for example, an illiterate housekeeper is terrified that if her problem is discovered she will be sacked – and her cunning, desperate attempts to conceal it begin a ladder of consequences which leads inexorably to murder.

Rendell's Wexford books include A New Lease of Death, Wolf to the Slaughter, A Guilty Thing Surprised, Some Lie and Some Die *and* An Unkindness of Ravens. *Her psychological novels include* The Face of Trespass, The Killing Doll, The Tree of Hands, Live Flesh *and* Talking to Strange Men. The Fallen Curtain, Means of Evil *and* The Fever Tree *are collections of short stories. Rendell also writes as Barbara Vine (*A Dark-Adapted Eye*).*

▶ **To the psychological thrillers:** Joan Fleming, *Young Man I Think You're Dying*; ▷Patricia Highsmith, *The Glass Cell*; John Katzenbach, *The Traveller*.

REVISITING ONE'S PAST

▷Margaret Atwood, *Surfacing*
▷Anita Brookner, *A Start in Life*
▷Bernice Rubens, *Our Father*
▷Graham Swift, *Waterland*
▷Paul Theroux, *Picture Palace*
▷Virginia Woolf, *Mrs Dalloway*

RHYS, Jean • *(1894–1979)*
British novelist.

All Rhys' novels and stories are about the same kind of person, the 'Jean Rhys woman'. She was once vivacious and attractive (an actress, perhaps, or a dancer) but she fell in love with some unsuitable man or men, was betrayed, and now lives alone, maudlin and mentally unhinged. In Rhys' first four novels (published in the 1920s and 1930s), the heroines are casualties of the Jazz Age, flappers crushed by life itself. In her last, 1960s, book *Wide Sargasso Sea* the central character is a victim of the way men think (or fail to think) of women: she is a young Caribbean heiress in the early 1800s, who marries an English gentleman, Mr Rochester, and ends up as the demented creature hidden in the attics of Thornfield Hall in *Jane Eyre*.

GOOD MORNING, MIDNIGHT • *(1939)*
Deserted by her husband after the death of their baby,

READ ON ▷

● *Wide Sargasso Sea.*
▶ **To *Good Morning Midnight*:** Brian Moore, *The Doctor's Wife*; ▷Doris Lessing, *The Golden Notebook*; ▷Mary McCarthy, *The Company She Keeps*; ▷Anita Brookner, *Hôtel du Lac*; Marguerite Duras, *The Lover*; ▷Christopher Isherwood, *A Single Man*.
▶ **To *Wide Sargasso Sea*:** Lisa St Aubin de Terán, *Slow Train to Milan*.

Sasha would have drunk herself to death if a generous
friend had not rescued her and paid for her to spend a
fortnight in Paris. She 'arranges her little life', as she puts
it: a cycle of solitary meals and drinks, barren conversations with strangers, drugged sleep in seedy hotel-rooms.
She is a damned soul, a husk – and then a gigolo, mistak-
ing her for a rich woman, begins to court her, and she has
to gather the rags of her sanity and try to take hold of her
life once more.

Rhys' other novels are Quartet/Postures, After Leaving Mr
Mackenzie *and* Voyage in the Dark. The Left Bank,
Tigers are Better-looking *and* Sleep it off, Lady *are col-
lections of short stories.*

THE RHYTHM OF NATURE
(people in tune with or in thrall to the land)

Pearl S. Buck, *The Good Earth*
Erskine Caldwell, *God's Little Acre*
Neil M. Gunn, *The Well at the World's End*
▷Thomas Hardy, *Far From the Madding Crowd*
▷Susan Hill, *In the Springtime of the Year*
Mikhail Sholokhov, *Virgin Soil Upturned*

The Countryside (p 51)

RICHARDSON, Henry Handel •
(1870–1946)
Australian novelist.

'Henry Handel Richardson' was the pseudonym of Ethel
Robertson. She was born and educated in Australia, but
went to Europe in her late teens and remained there, with
one three-month break, for the rest of her life. Her best-
known books, however (*The Getting of Wisdom*, 1910,
and the Richard Mahony trilogy: see below) are set in
Australia and reflect her own or her parents' experience.
She was interested in 'psychic outsiders', people who felt
that heightened awareness or sensibilities set them apart
from their fellows. *The Getting of Wisdom* is about a
gifted, unhappy adolescent in a late 19th-century boarding
school, who uses love of the arts as an escape from the
oppressive narrowness of the régime. The battle against
depressive illness is a major theme of the Mahony trilogy.
The Young Cosima is about Liszt's daughter Cosima, her
husband Hans von Bülow and her lover Wagner – all of

READ ON ⟩

● *Maurice Guest*
(another study of
depression, this time
about a man ambitious
to be a professional
musician who finds
that he has talent but
no genius, and who is
then further distracted
by falling unhappily in
love).
▶ **To *The Fortunes of
Richard Mahony*:**
▷Gustave Flaubert,
Madame Bovary;
▷Malcolm Lowry,
Under the Volcano.

them exemplars (at least in their own fevered imaginations) of Nietzschean 'superbeings', who are nevertheless racked by feelings and emotions as uncontrollable as anyone else's.

THE FORTUNES OF RICHARD MAHONY ·
(1915–29)
In this trilogy of novels (*Australia Felix, The Way Home, Ultima Thule*) Mahony, a British doctor, goes to Australia to make his fortune in the 1850s gold rush, marries and settles. His gold-prospecting fails, and he turns first to store-keeping and then back to medicine, before making a sudden fortune from shares he thought were worthless. Unable to cope with wealth, he dissipates his money, impoverishes his family and begins a long, anguished slide into depressive mania. His devoted wife takes a job as postmistress in a remote area, nursing her husband and bringing up her uncomprehending, sorrowing family. Although the trilogy is chiefly concerned with Mahony's complex character and his relationship with his family, it is also a compelling account of 19th-century Australian pioneer and outback life.

Richardson's only other novel is Maurice Guest. Two Studies *contains a pair of long short stories;* The End of a Childhood *and* The Adventures of Cuffy Mahony *are collections of short stories;* Myself When Young *is autobiography.*

RICHARDSON, Samuel · *(1689–1761)*
British novelist.

A successful printer, Richardson was compiling a book of sample letters for all occasions when he had the idea of writing whole novels in letter-form. He produced three, *Pamela, Clarissa* and *Sir Charles Grandison.* They are enormously long (over a million words each), and readers even at the time complained of boredom. But the books were still best-sellers, not, as Richardson imagined, because of their high moral tone, but because his sensational theme (the way some people are drawn irresistibly to debauch the innocent) guaranteed success.

CLARISSA, OR THE HISTORY OF A YOUNG LADY
(1748)
To escape from her parents, who have shut her in her room until she agrees to marry a man she loathes, the hapless Clarissa Harlowe elopes with Mr Lovelace, a rake. He tries every possible way to persuade her to sleep with

▶ **To *Maurice Guest*:** ▷Hermann Hesse, *Steppenwolf.*
▶ **To *The Getting of Wisdom*:** ▷Antonia White, *Frost in May.*

> READ ON

● *Pamela.*
▶ Pierre Choderlos de Laclos, *Dangerous Alliances* (Les liaisons dangereuses) is another letter-novel about moral predation, but shorter, wittier and less sentimental. This book apart, Richardson's work has been more pilloried than paralleled. John Cleland, *Fanny Hill* is the memoirs of a prostitute, combining a dismissive view of men with detailed

him, and when she refuses he puts her into a brothel, drugs and rapes her. She goes into a decline and dies of shame. The story is told by means of letters from the main characters, to one another, to friends, relatives and acquaintances. One of Richardson's triumphs – which some critics claim justifies the book's inordinate length – is to reveal Lovelace's villainy only gradually, as Clarissa herself discovers it.

RICHLER, Mordecai • *(born 1931)*
Canadian novelist.

The heroes of Richler's vitriolic black satires are 'outsiders' (for example Jews in a gentile society), poor (they come from big-city slums) or inept (too guileless for their own good). They face a hostile world of crooks, cheats, extortionists, poseurs (often film makers or tycoons) and bullies. Sometimes, like the hero of *The Apprenticeship of Duddy Kravitz* (1959), Richler's men fight back, using the enemies' weapons and winning the battle at the expense of their own souls; others, like the middle-aged hero of *Joshua Then and Now* (1980), are so humbled by the sense of their own inadequacy that instead of fighting the slings and arrows of outrageous fortune (in Joshua's case, the false accusation that he is a sexual deviant), they welcome them. *Joshua Then and Now* and *Cocksure* (1968) (a violent farce about an honest man bewildered by the permissiveness of the 'swinging sixties') are Richler's most savage books, written to lacerate as well as to amuse.

Richler's other novels include A Choice of Enemies, The Incomparable Atuk/Stick Your Neck Out *and* St Urbain's Horseman. Shovelling Trouble *and* Home Sweet Home *are collections of essays and articles, many of them about Canada and its attitude to 'culture'. The Street* is a memoir of his childhood in the backstreets of Montreal, a fascinating parallel to the opening chapters of *The Apprenticeship of Duddy Kravitz.*

descriptions of life and gossip in an 18th-century, high-society London brothel.
▷Henry Fielding, *Tom Jones* mocks Richardson's moral earnestness: far from shrinking from the pleasures of seduction, Tom lives for them. Aphra Behn, *Love-letters between a Nobleman and his Sister,* pre-dating Richardson by 75 years, is the no-holds-barred account of an incestuous affair.

READ ON >

▶ **To *The Apprenticeship of Duddy Kravitz:***
▷Jerome Weidman, *Can Get It for You Wholesale;* ▷Saul Bellow, *The Adventures of Augie March.*
▶ **To *Cocksure:*** Budd Schulberg, *What Makes Sammy Run?;* ▷Gore Vidal, *Myra Breckinridge.*
▶ **To Richler's work in general:** ▷Nathanael West, *Miss Lonelyhearts;* ▷F. Scott Fitzgerald, *The Great Gatsby.*

ROBERTS, Michèle • *(born 1949)*
British poet and novelist.

Much of Roberts' work has a feminist edge, and her latest novel in particular, *Mrs Noah* (1987), is likely to leave the male half of the human race feeling distinctly uncomfortable. It is a dazzling fantasy, set in the present day. A woman visiting Venice with her preoccupied husband fantasises that she is Mrs Noah. The Ark is a vast library, a repository not only of creatures but of the entire knowledge and experience of the human race. She is its curator (or Arkivist), and her fellow-voyagers are five Sibyls and a token male, the Gaffer, a bearded old party who once wrote a best-selling book (the Bible) and has now retired to a tax-heaven in the sky. Each Sibyl tells a story, and each story is about the way men have oppressed women down the centuries. For all its feminist anger, the book is a witty, imaginative tour de force.

READ ON ▷

● *The Wild Girl* (the Gospel according to Mary Magdalene, a stunning reworking of familiar New Testament themes)
► ▷Margaret Atwood, *The Handmaid's Tale*. ▷Joseph Heller, *Catch-22*. Joe Orton, *Head to Toe*.

ROMAN CATHOLICISM (1)

▷Kingsley Amis, *The Alteration*
 Georges Bernanos, *Diary of a Country Priest*
▷Anthony Burgess, *Earthly Powers*
 Rumer Godden, *A Candle for St Jude*
▷Graham Greene, *Monsignor Quixote*
 Nikos Kazantzakis, *The Greek Passion*
▷Thomas Keneally, *Three Cheers for the Paraclete*

ROMAN CATHOLICISM (2)

 David Lodge, *How Far Can You Go?*
 Brian Moore, *The Colour of Blood*
 J.F. Powers, *Morte d'Urban*
 Frederick Rolfe, *Hadrian the Seventh*
▷Muriel Spark, *The Abbess of Crewe*
▷Morris West, *The Devil's Advocate*
▷Antonia White, *Frost in May*

ROSSNER, Judith • *(born 1935)*
US novelist.

Rossner's novels, whether serious, ironical or farcical, are all fuelled by the same polemical, feminist rage against male-oriented society. They treat human life as a straightforward battle of wits between emotional predators and their quarry – a struggle which always ends in psychological mutilation or destruction. In some books, for example *Nine Months in the Life of an Old Maid* (1969, about a ghastly family who get on each others' nerves) the chase is funny and the mode is farce. In others, for example *Looking for Mr Goodbar* (1975, about a woman cruising singles bars in search of love) the events are grim and the mode is tragedy. The theme of emotional depredation has been popular with recent US writers of all kinds, from 'serious' novelists to the authors of big-business and family sagas. Rossner is one of its wittiest exponents.

ROTH, Philip • *(born 1933)*
US novelist.

One of the wryest and wittiest of all contemporary US novelists, Roth writes of Jewish intellectuals, often authors or university teachers, discomforted by life. Their marriages fail; their parents behave like joke-book stereotypes (forever making chicken soup and simultaneously boasting about and deploring their sons' brains); sexual insatiability leads them from one farcical encounter to another; their career-success attracts embarrassing fans and inhibits further work; their defences of self-mockery and irony wear ever thinner as they approach unwanted middle age. In his best-known book, *Portnoy's Complaint* (1969), Roth treated this theme as farce, heavy with explicit sex and Jewish-mother jokes. The majority of his novels are quieter, the tone is more rueful, and he generalises his theme and makes it symbolise the plight of all decent, conscience-stricken people in a world where barbarians make the running. His major 1980s work was a series of novels about a New York Jewish author, Nathan Zuckerman, who agonises over his trade, writes an immensely successful (dirty) book and is immediately harrassed by the way his fame both forces him to live the life of a celebrity and makes him even more of an enigma to his family and friends.

READ ON >

● *Attachments; August.*
▶ Joyce Carol Oates, *The Poisoned Kiss.*
▷Angela Carter, *The Infernal Desire Machines of Doctor Hoffman.* Robert Bloch, *Psycho.* ▷Susan Hill, *The Bird of Night.*
▶ **Similar novels from an earlier period:**
▷Djuna Barnes, *Nightwood;* ▷Christina Stead, *The Man Who Loved Children.*

READ ON >

● *When She was Good.*
▶ Bernard Malamud, *Dubin's Lives.*
▷Bernice Rubens, *Our Father.* ▷John Fowles, *Daniel Martin.*
▷John Updike, *Marry Me.*

THE PROFESSOR OF DESIRE • *(1977)*

David Kepesh, a brilliant young literature teacher, is trying to sort out his life. His views on art and literature, which once seemed the last word in wit and wisdom, now appear to him to have been engulfed by the subjects he studies: he feels like a dwarf trying to shift a mountain. His emotional life is dominated by an insistent craving for physical pleasure which he finds degrading but irresistible and which he longs to replace by love. His mother and father are elderly, tetchy and horrified by the way their son the genius has betrayed his Jewish roots. Kepesh's circumstances seem to him like a maze, as bewildering and terrifying as anything in ▷Kafka – and the book shows him gradually, painfully, discovering the key.

Roth's other books include Letting Go, The Great American Novel *(which uses baseball as a farcical symbol for every red-blooded US tradition or way of thought),* My Life as a Man *and* Our Gang *(a ▷Swiftian satire about the Nixon presidency).* Goodbye Columbus *collects an early novella and five short stories.* The Zuckerman books *are* The Ghost Writer, Zuckerman Unbound, The Anatomy Lesson, The Prague Orgy *and* The Counterlife.

RUBENS, Bernice • *(born 1927)*
British novelist.

Rubens' heroes and heroines are people at the point of breakdown: her novels chart the escalation of tension which took them there or the progress of their cure. Some of the books are bleak: in *The Elected Member/The Chosen People* (1969), for example, a man is driven mad by feeling that he is a scapegoat for the entire suffering of the Jewish people throughout history, and the story deals with his rehabilitation in a mental hospital. In other books, Rubens turns psychological pain to comedy, as if the only way to cope with the human condition were to treat it as God's black joke against the human race. God is even a character in *Our Father* (1987): he pops up in the Sahara, in the High Street, in the parlour, in bed with the heroine and her husband, constantly nagging her to make up her mind about herself – and his persistence leads her to rummage through childhood memories (where it becomes clear that she completely misunderstood her parents' emotional relationship) and to redefine her life.

Rubens' other novels include Madame Sousatzka, I Sent a Letter to my Love, The Ponsonby Post, Sunday Best, The

READ ON ⟩

● *Birds of Passage.*
▶ ▷Paul Theroux, *Picture Palace.*
▷David Cook, *Missing Persons.* ▷Anita Brookner, *Hôtel du Lac.* Susan Fromberg Shaeffer, *Worldly Goods.* ▷Susan Hill, *A Bit of Singing and Dancing* (short stories).

Brothers, A Five Year Sentence, Birds of Passage, Favours, Spring Sonata *and* Mr Wakefield's Crusade.

RUELL, Patrick • *(born 1936)*
British novelist.

'Patrick Ruell' is one of the pseudonyms of ▷Reginald Hill. His fast-moving, uncomplicated adventure stories include *The Castle of the Demon, Red Christmas, Death Takes the Low Road, Urn Burial* and *The Long Kill* (1986, about a marksman stalking human quarry in the English Lake District).

READ ON ⟩

▶ Nelson De Mille, *The Cathedral*. Derek Lambert, *Touch the Lion's Paw*. Russell Braddon, *The Finalists*.

RUSHDIE, Salman • *(born 1947)*
Indian/British novelist and non-fiction writer.

Rushdie writes magic realism, a mesmeric entwining of actuality and fantasy. *Midnight's Children* (1981) is the story of a rich Indian family over the last 80 years, and especially of Saleem, one of 1001 children born at midnight on 15 August 1947, the moment of India's independence from Britain. Saleem's birthtime gives him extraordinary powers: he is, as Rushdie puts it, 'handcuffed' to India, able to let his mind float freely through its history and to share in the experience of anyone he chooses, from Gandhi or Nehru to the most insignificant beggar in the streets. He represents India's own awareness of itself, and his family story (which he himself tells) is the account of a whole people and a continent. Its filters, his perception and personality, make it mysterious and magical: time coalesces, 'real' politics blur with fantasy, a child's memories and magnifications are just as valid as newspaper accounts. The effect is to change reality to metaphor – and Rushdie uses this to make several sharp political points. In *Shame* (1983) he goes still further. This novel is set in a dream-country, Peccavistan ('Sinned' rather than Sind), whose geography and history are like Pakistan's seen in a distorting mirror. We witness a power-struggle between members of the Harappa dynasty and their friends/rivals/enemies the Hyders. Interwoven with it all is the story of Omar Khayyam Shakil, a bloated, brilliant physician, and his wife Sufiya Zinobia, a mental defective inhabited by a demon which periodically breaks out in homicidal fury. Describing Rushdie's books is like summarising dreams: the telling bleaches them of wit, poetry and compulsion. Like ▷Márquez, he reinvents reality and makes fantasy seem more plausible than truth itself.

READ ON ⟩

▶ ▷Gabriel García Márquez, *One Hundred Years of Solitude*. Augusto Roa Bastos, *I, The Supreme*. ▷Angela Carter, *Nights at the Circus*. Lisa St Aubin de Terán, *The Keepers of the House*. ▷Günter Grass, *The Tin Drum*.

Salman **RUSHDIE**

SHAME *(feud between ruling families in fantasy-state 'Peccavistan')*

Jeanette **WINTERSON, THE PASSION**
(Napoleon)

Augusto **ROA BASTOS, I THE SUPREME**
(Francia, dictator of Paraguay)

Evelyn **WAUGH, BLACK MISCHIEF**
(England-educated 1930s black African ruler)

Miguel **ASTURIAS, THE PRESIDENT**
(corruption and jackboot evil in South America)

Michael **MOORCOCK, GLORIANA**
(state and ruler one gross, monstrous entity)

DICTATORS

Chinua **ACHEBE, ANTHILLS OF THE SAVANNAH**
(emerging African totalitarian state)

Nadine **GORDIMER, A SPORT OF NATURE**
(white girl joins South African freedom fighters)

Gore **VIDAL, BURR**
('traitor' who tried to set up rival republic to Jeffersonian America)

Timothy **MO, AN INSULAR POSSESSION**
(British imperialism and Hong Kong)

Authur **KOESTLER, DARKNESS AT NOON**
(treason-trial of old-guard revolutionary in unnamed but Stalinist dictatorship)

George **ORWELL, ANIMAL FARM**
(animals declare republic which degenerates into dictatorship)

POLITICS

Isabel **ALLENDE, THE HOUSE OF THE SPIRITS**
(political and personal evolution in rich South American family over 100 years.)

Gabriel García **MÁRQUEZ, ONE HUNDRED YEARS OF SOLITUDE** *(sprawling family dominate small town in fantasy South America)*

Peter **CAREY, ILLYWHACKER**
(132-year-old Australian conman tells his story)

Gerald H. **MORRIS, DOVES AND SILK HANDKERCHIEVES** *(magic and realism in 1900s English mining village)*

Günter **GRASS, THE FLOUNDER**
(fisher-couple and talking fish live through all German history)

John **IRVING, THE WORLD ACCORDING TO GARP**
(evolution of writer in fantasy New England town)

MANY GENERATIONS

Rushdie's other works include Grimus *(an early, experimental novel) and* The Jaguar Smile *(non-fiction: a report on Nicaragua and on the effect of US policies in central America).*

S

SALINGER, J.D. (Jerome David) •
(born 1919)
US novelist and short-story writer.

Salinger's only novel, *The Catcher in the Rye* (1951), is a rambling monologue by 17-year-old Holden Caulfield. He has run away from boarding school just before Christmas, and is spending a few days drifting in New York City while he decides whether to go home or not. He feels that his childhood is over and his innocence lost, but he detests the phoney, loveless grown-up world (symbolised by plastic Christmas baubles and seasonal fake goodwill). He thinks that to be adult is a form of surrender, but he can see no way to avoid it. He wanders the city, talking aimlessly to taxi-drivers, lodging-house keepers, bar-tenders, prostitutes and his own kid sister Phoebe, whom he tries to warn against growing up. Finally, inevitably, he capitulates – or perhaps escapes, since we learn that what we have just read is his 'confession' to the psychiatrist in a mental home. Salinger pursued the question of how to recover moral innocence in his only other publications, a series of short stories about the gifted, mentally unstable Glass family. 'Franny and Zooey', the most moving of the stories, shows Zooey Glass, an actor, talking his sister Franny out of a nervous breakdown. It is a performance of dazzling technical brilliance and full of loving-kindness, but – and this is typical of Salinger's grim view of human moral endeavour – although it helps Franny momentarily, it contributes nothing whatever to the good of the world at large.

The Glass family stories are collected in Franny and Zooey; Nine Stories/For Esmé, with Love and Squalor *and* Raise High the Roofbeam, Carpenters.

▷ **READ ON**

▶ **To *The Catcher in the Rye*:** ▷Carson McCullers, *The Member of the Wedding*; ▷Willa Cather, *My Antonia*; ▷John Updike, *The Centaur*; Truman Capote, *Breakfast at Tiffany's*; Alan Sillitoe, *Saturday Night and Sunday Morning*.
▶ **To 'Franny and Zooey':** Sylvia Plath, *The Bell Jar*; ▷Susan Hill, *The Bird of Night*.

SARTRE, Jean-Paul • *(1905–80)*
French novelist, poet and philosopher.

The philosophy of existentialism, which Sartre developed in essays, plays, novels and monographs, says that Nothingness is the natural state of humanity: we exist, like animals, without ethics or morality. But unlike beasts we have the power to make choices, and these give moral status: they are a leap from Nothingness to Being. For some people, the choice is the leap of faith, and belief in God gives them moral status; for others the choice is to make no choice at all, to drift the way the world leads them without taking moral initiatives. For Sartre's characters, the leap into being involved taking responsibility, making moral decisions from which there was no turning back. His vast novel *The Roads to Freedom* (1945–9; in three volumes, *The Age of Reason*, *The Reprieve* and *Iron in the Soul/Troubled Sleep*) tackles this theme exactly: the questions of what moral decisions to make and how to make them. It describes a group of young people trying to sort out their personal lives and at the same time to cope with the moral and intellectual challenges of fascism, communism, colonialism and the second world war. The book is packed with intellectual, political and philosophical discussion and argument: a complex read. But few writings better give the intellectual 'feel' of the 1930s and 1940s, the matrix from which so many of today's ideas were born.

Sartre's main philosophical monograph is Being and Nothingness. *His plays include* The Flies, The Victor/Men Without Shadows, Crime Passionel *and* Huis Clos/No Exit/In Camera. Nausea/The Diary of Antoine Roquentin *is an autobiographical novel about a young intellectual in the 1920s and 1930s.* The Wall/Intimacy *is a collection of short stories.*

SAYERS, Dorothy L. (Dorothy Leigh) •
(1893–1957)
British novelist.

The writer Colin Watson cruelly but accurately described Sayers' kind of crime fiction as 'snobbery with violence'. The fascination of her books is not only in the solving of bizarre crimes in out-of-the-ordinary locations (an advertising agency; an Oxford women's college; an East Anglian belfry), but also in the character of her detective, the super-sleuth Lord Peter Wimsey. He is a languid, monocled aristocrat, whose foppish manner conceals the facts

> **READ ON** >

● *Nausea.*
▶ ▷Albert Camus, *The Plague.* Arthur Koestler, *Darkness at Noon.* ▷Frederic Raphael, *Like Men Betrayed.*
▶ **Novels discussing similar personal dilemmas, but with different backgrounds and cultural conditions:** ▷Lev Tolstoy, *War and Peace;* ▷Ford Madox Ford, *The Good Soldier;* ▷Olivia Manning, *The Levant Trilogy.*

> **READ ON** >

● *Gaudy Night.*
▶ Amanda Cross, *No Word from Winifred.* ▷Michael Innes, *Hamlet, Revenge!* Robert Robinson, *Landscape with Dead Dons.* John Dickson Carr, *Poison in Jest.*

that he has a first-class Oxford degree, was in army intelligence during the first world war, collects rare books, plays the piano like Rubinstein, dances like Astaire and seems to have swallowed a substantial dictionary of quotations. He is aided and abetted by his manservant Bunter, a suave charmer adept at extracting confidences from the cooks, taxi-drivers, waitresses, barbers and vergers who would collapse in forelock-tugging silence if Wimsey himself ever deigned to speak to them. Seldom have detective stories been so preposterous or so unputdownable.

HAVE HIS CARCASE · *(1932)*

In a sleepy seaside resort, someone has cut the throat of a gigolo – and the plot thickens when it is discovered that he was romantically involved with a lonely, rich and foolish widow. But where do the men with the patently-false hair and beards come into it? Why are there no footprints in the sand? What connects the crime with the Russian ex-royal dynasty? All these mysteries are as nothing compared to the greatest cliffhanger of all: will Wimsey's persistent charm ever wear down Harriet Vane, the best-selling crime-novelist, until she agrees to marry him?

The Wimsey/Vane romance is also featured in Strong Poison, Gaudy Night *and* Busman's Honeymoon. *Sayers' other Wimsey books – which some admirers prefer to those involving Harriet Vane – include* Murder Must Advertise, Hangman's Holiday *and* The Nine Tailors.

Rex Stout, *Fer de Lance.* ▷Ruth Rendell, *Some Lie and Some Die.*

SCHOOLS

Nicholas Best, *Tennis and the Masai*
▷Charles Dickens, *Nicholas Nickleby*
James Hilton, *Goodbye, Mr Chips*
▷James Joyce, *Portrait of the Artist as a Young Man*
▷John Le Carré, *Call for the Dead*
▷H.H. Richardson, *The Getting of Wisdom*
▷John Updike, *The Centaur*
▷Evelyn Waugh, *Decline and Fall*

Adolescence (p 3)

SCOTT, Walter · *(1771–1832)*
British novelist and poet.

Scott began his career not with novels but with poems, in a style similar to Scottish folk-ballads and the lyrics of Robert Burns. In 1814, piqued because his verse was out-

READ ON ⟩

● *Ivanhoe; The Heart of Midlothian.*
▶ Harrison Ainsworth,

sold by Byron's, he turned instead to historical novels, and wrote 29 in the next 18 years. They are swaggering tales of love, bravery and intrigue, many of them centred on events from Scottish history and set in the brooding landscapes of the highlands and islands.

ROB ROY · (1817)

In the 1710s, Osbaldistone and Rashleigh are rivals for the hand of Diana Vernon. Rashleigh embezzles money and frames Osbaldistone. Osbaldistone escapes to the highlands of Scotland, where he seeks help from Rob Roy, an outlaw who (like Robin Hood centuries before him) robs the rich to help the poor, rights wrongs and fights a usurping power (in his case, the English) on behalf of an exiled, true royal prince (James Stuart, the Old Pretender). Osbaldistone's quest to clear his name becomes inextricably bound up with the Jacobite Rebellion, and it is not until Rashleigh (who, not unexpectedly, supports the English and betrays Rob Roy to them) is killed that justice prevails and Osbaldistone and Diana at last find happiness.

Scott's other novels include Waverley, Guy Mannering, Old Mortality, The Heart of Midlothian, The Bride of Lammermoor, Ivanhoe, Kenilworth, The Fortunes of Nigel, Quentin Durward, Redgauntlet *and* Castle Dangerous.

SEGAL, Erich · *(born 1937)*
US novelist and non-fiction writer.

Love Story (1970), Segal's first novel, was one of the most affecting romances of the century. A true three-handkerchief weepie, it tells of the idyllic, doomed love-affair between two college students, one of whom falls terminally ill. The book, and the film made from it, moved audiences to tears from Manchester to Melbourne, from Peking to Peoria. In a later romance, *Oliver's Story* (1977), Segal took up the life of one of the young people from the earlier book, eight years later. Oliver falls in love again, only to be haunted by the thought that he is betraying his earlier, 'eternal' love.

The Tower of London. James Fenimore Cooper, *Last of the Mohicans.* ▷Victor Hugo, *Notre-Dame de Paris.* ▷Alexandre Dumas, *The Man in the Iron Mask.* Nigel Tranter, *Montrose: the Captain General.*

> ## READ ON ⟩

▶ *Love Story*'s ecstatic sadness is matched in ▷Boris Pasternak, *Doctor Zhivago* and ▷Margaret Mitchell, *Gone With the Wind* and Philip Roth, *Letting Go. Love Story*'s unselfconscious sentimentality is parallelled in Richard Bach, *Jonathan Livingstone Seagull*, though its plot (an 'outsider' allegory about a bird longing to fly free) could hardly be more different.

SHARPE, Tom • *(born 1928)*
British novelist.

If, as many foreigners maintain, British humour is obsessed with the functions of the lower body, then Sharpe is our comic Laureate. In each of his books he chooses a single target – polytechnic life, publishing, Cambridge University, the landed gentry – and demolishes it magnificently, comprehensively, by piling slapstick on crudity like a demented circus clown. Sharpe's heroes live in a state of unceasing, ungovernable panic, and are usually crippled by lust, forever tripping over their own erections. His old men are gluttonous, lecherous and senile, prone to perversion and prey to strokes and heart attacks; his matrons are whooping whip-wielding Boadiceas, scything down every bedable male in sight. If your humorous fancy is for penises trapped in briar-patches, condoms ballooning above Cambridge spires or maniacs burying sex-dolls in wet cement, Sharpe's books are for you.

RIOTOUS ASSEMBLY • *(1973)*
Kommandant van Heerden, police chief of the sleepy South African town of Piemburg, wants a quiet life and an invitation to join the exclusive British Country Club. His assistant Verkramp wants van Heerden's job. Konstabel Els wants to keep on playing with his electrodes and fucking kaffirs. But Miss Hazelstone phones to say that she has just shot her black cook – and that it was not a 'garbage-disposal operation' but the result of a lovers' tiff. Van Heerden, thinking that she must be covering up for her brother the bishop, sets out on an investigation which spirals into an orgy of transvestism, voyeurism, bestiality and murder. The South African setting gives this book devastating point: given the situation, even Sharpe's most slapstick satirical excess seems a model of self-restraint.

Sharpe's other books include Wilt *and its sequels* The Wilt Alternative *and* Wilt on High; The Throwback; Porterhouse Blue; Ancestral Vices *and* Vintage Stuff.

SHELLEY, Mary • *(1797–1851)*
British novelist.

After the death of her husband (the poet) in 1822, Shelley began a literary career of her own, editing her husband's work, writing essays, journals and travel-books, and publishing short stories and novels, many on what would now be considered SF themes. Her best-known book is *Frankenstein, or the Modern Prometheus* (1818), about a man

> **READ ON**
>
> ● *Indecent Exposure; Blott on the Landscape.*
> ▶ Colin Douglas, *The Houseman's Tale.* Thorne Smith, *The Bishop's Jaegers.* Howard Jacobson, *Peeping Tom.* ▷J.P. Donleavy, *The Ginger Man.*

> **READ ON**
>
> ▶ **To *Frankenstein*:** ▷H.G. Wells, *The Island of Doctor Moreau*; Bram Stoker, *Dracula*; Gerald Du Maurier, *Trilby.*

who tries to prove the superiority of scientific rationality to the supernatural by usurping God's function and creating life. Although, thanks to Hollywood, Frankenstein's monster has nudged his creator from centre-stage, even the worst Frankenstein films keep to one of Shelley's most fascinating ideas: that the monster is an innocent, as pure as Adam before the Fall, and that its ferocity is a response learned by contact with 'civilised' human beings. Shelley developed the theme of the contrast between innocence and the corruption of civilisation in other books, most notably the future-fantasy *The Last Man* (1826), set in a world where all human beings but one have been destroyed by plague, and the survivor wanders among the monuments of the glorious past like a soul in Hell.

▶ To *The Last Man*:
▷Daniel Defoe, *Robinson Crusoe*; Bernard Malamud, *God's Grace*.

SHIPS AND THE SEA

John Dickson Carr, *The Blind Barber*
▷Joseph Conrad, *The Nigger of the Narcissus*
Paul Gallico, *The Poseidon Adventure*
▷Herman Melville, *Moby-Dick*
Nicholas Monsarrat, *The Cruel Sea*
▷Katherine Anne Porter, *Ship of Fools*
Paul Rodgers, *To Kill a God* (Captain Cook's voyages)
▷Jules Verne, *Twenty Thousand Leagues Under the Sea*
▷Herman Wouk, *The Caine Mutiny*

SHIPWRECK

Martin Boyd, *Nuns in Jeopardy*
▷Daniel Defoe, *Robinson Crusoe*
Nicholas Monsarrat, *Running Proud*
▷Muriel Spark, *Robinson*
▷Kurt Vonnegut, *Galápagos*
▷Patrick White, *A Fringe of Leaves*

SHUTE, Neville • *(1899–1960)*
British/Australian novelist.

'Neville Shute' was the pseudonym of Neville Shute Norway. In the 1920s he worked as an aeronautical engineer, and he later served as a second-world-war naval com-

▶ READ ON ▷

● *A Town Like Alice* (about two survivors from the Japanese mander – experiences which inspired two of his finest books, *Pied Piper* (1942), about a mild-mannered man who rescues a group of children from the nazis and *No Highway* (1948), about an aircraft engineer trying desperately to warn sceptical superiors and politicians of the existence of metal fatigue. In 1950 Shute settled in Australia, and made it the setting for most of his later books. He wrote of ordinary people in a self-effacing style; his books have the immediacy of 'in-depth' newspaper reporting. But the characters of each story are in crisis, and the plot shows them working out moral or ethical dilemmas which have implications far beyond the novel's bounds. Several of his books were filmed, and inspired a whole genre of documentary-style drama about 'issues', now also common on television. Some of Shute's themes (for example the horrific effects of bombing on civilians, the theme of his 1939 novel *What Happened to the Corbetts*, or the existence of metal fatigue) have been overtaken by events, and his once-slangy dialogue has dated. But few popular writers have treated serious themes so grippingly. Despite their age, his novels are unputdownable.

ON THE BEACH • *(1957)*

The book is set in the Melbourne suburbs at some unstated time in the near future. We see perfectly ordinary people (a young couple with a baby; a woman and her US sailor-lover) bustling about their mundane lives. But the background is anything but ordinary: the whole human race is facing imminent annihilation from the nuclear fallout of World War III. As the novel proceeds, and Shute explores the implications of this theme, his characters' attempts to preserve everyday decencies are shown to be not so much survival strategy as a pitiable, pointless evasion of reality.

Shute's early books include So Disdained, Lonely Road *and the excellent war-story* Landfall. *His later novels include* The Far Country, In the Wet, Requiem for a Wren *and* Trustee from the Toolroom. Slide Rule *is an autobiography up to 1938.*

SILVERBERG, Robert • *(born 1934)*
US novelist.

Many of Silverberg's single SF novels are set on Earth in the near future, and – like ▷Ballard's – involve escalation towards catastrophe of trends and ideas of the present day. The theme of *Master of Life and Death* is over-popula-

occupation of Malaya who decide to develop one small settlement in the Australian outback).

▶ **To *On the Beach*:** John Christopher, *The Death of Grass*; ▷George Turner, *The Sea and Summer*.

▶ **To Shute's books involving technology and research:** Nigel Balchin, *The Small Back Room*; ▷C.P. Snow, *The New Men*.

▶ **To Shute's work in general:** H.E. Bates, *The Purple Plain*; ▷Morris West, *The Navigator*; Ernest K. Gann, *The High and the Mighty*; ▷Elizabeth Bowen, *The Heat of the Day*.

READ ON ⟩

▶ **To the single novels:** ▷Robert Heinlein, *Job*; Frederick Pohl, *The* tion. *Recalled to Life* imagines a medical advance which allows us to bring the dead back to life. The hero of *Stochastic Man* is a psychic adviser to presidents who finds that he can genuinely predict the future. *A Time of Changes* imagines human society entirely controlled by drugs. Silverberg is also known for fantasy-series set in worlds of the far future. Majipoor, for example, is a giant planet where magic and science, medieval politics and high technology, aliens and humans, co-exist. In *Lord Valentine's Castle* (first volume of the 'Majipoor' Trilogy, 1979–83), a wandering juggler discovers, by chance use of his psychic powers, that he is the rightful Coronal, or ruler, of the planet, and gathers a company of warriors to unseat the usurper and win back his inheritance. In *The Majipoor Chronicles* a boy discovers the planet's computer-archives, and embarks on a psychic exploration of its teeming, magical history. In *Valentine Pontifex* the Coronal of Majipoor has to undertake his most demanding task yet, a battle against the shape-changers (or Metamorphs) who are destroying crops, trying to starve Majipoor's people into submission and take over Valentine's throne.

Silverberg's other books include Lord of Darkness, Capricorn Games *and two inspired by Biblical and other ancient myth,* Shadrach in the Furnace *and* Gilgamesh the King.

SIMENON, Georges • *(born 1903)*
Belgian novelist.

Simenon is best-known for some 150 crime-stories featuring the pipe-smoking, calvados-drinking Commissaire Maigret of the Paris Police. The books are short and spare; they concentrate on Maigret's investigations in bars, lodging-houses and rain-soaked Paris streets, and on his casual-seeming, fatherly conversations with suspects and witnesses. But Simenon is a far more substantial writer than this suggests. His non-Maigret novels – several hundred, since for 50 years he averaged a book every six or seven weeks – are compelling psychological studies of people distracted by fear, obsession, despair or hate. *Act of Passion* (1947) is the confession of a madman who kills his lover to keep her pure, to prevent her being contaminated by the evil which he feels has corroded his own soul. The hero of *The Man Who Watched the Trains Go By* (1938), outwardly placid and controlled, is in fact so gnawed by the sense of his own inadequacy that he chooses murder as the best way to make his mark on the

Reefs of Space; Ray Bradbury, *The Illustrated Man*.
▶ **To the fantasies:**
▷Piers Anthony, *Vicinity Cluster*; Ian M. Banks, *Consider Phlebas*; ▷Anne McCaffrey, *Dragonflight*.

READ ON ▷

▶ **To *Pedigree*:**
▷Jerome Weidman, *Fourth Street East*.
▶ **To Simenon's non-Maigret novels:** Julian Symons, *The 31st of February*.
▶ **To the Maigret books:** Nicholas Freeling, *Love in Amsterdam*; Maj Sjöwall and Per Wahlöö, *The Laughing Policeman*; Friedrich Dürrenmatt, *The Quarry*.

world. In *The President* (1958) a politician, brooding in enforced retirement, is unexpectedly offered the chance to revenge himself both politically and personally on the man who wronged him. *Ticket of Leave* (1942) is about a woman who falls in love with a paroled murderer. All these books are written in a sinewy, unemotional style, as plain as a police report. Only in one novel, *Pedigree* (1948), does Simenon break out of his self-imposed limits. It is a 500-page account of a boy's growing-up in Belgium in the first 15 years of this century, an evocation not only of trams, gaslight, cobble-stones and teeming back-street life, but of an emerging personality. A fictionalised autobiography, it is one of Simenon's most unexpected and rewarding works.

SINGER, I.B. (Isaac Bashevis) •
(born 1904)
Polish/US novelist and short-story writer.

Singer writes in Yiddish, and maintains that even when he translates his work himself, English dilutes its force. His characters are also Yiddish-speakers, either Middle European Jews – merchants, yeshiva-students, gravediggers, rabbis, drunks – from the ghettos and peasant villages of the 17th-19th centuries, or (in several of his finest stories) present-day settlers in Israel or the USA. They struggle to lead decent lives, uplifted or oppressed by the demands of orthodox Jewish belief and ritual. They are haunted by outside forces beyond their control: supernatural beings – several stories are narrated by dybbuks, ghosts and even the Devil himself – or mindless, vicious anti-semitism. Only one of Singer's novels is contemporary: *The Penitent* (1974), about a Polish-American Jew who returns to Israel and tries to come to terms with his own belief and with the tragic history of his people. The rest have historical settings – except that no Singer fiction is really historical, since everything he writes is a fable, with universal resonance. *Satan in Goray*, *The Magician of Lublin* and *The Slave* are about dark forces, demonic evil breaking out in small, closed communities. In *The Manor*, *The Estate* and *Enemies, a Love Story* the destructive forces are internal, as people's orthodox beliefs are challenged by love-affairs, business-deals, friendships and other such worldly claims.

THE FAMILY MOSKAT • *(1950)*
This is a warm, multi-generation story about a large Jewish family in Warsaw, and Singer's finest novel. The focus is on the human relationships within the family, mag-

---

READ ON ▷

► **To the short stories:**
S.Y. Agnon, *The Bridal Canopy*; Isaac Babel, *Odessa Tales*; ▷Nikolai Gogol, *Arabesques*.
► **To *The Family Moskat*:** I.J. Singer (I.B.'s brother), *The Brothers Ashkenazy*.
► **To Singer's other novels:** Bernard Malamud, *The Fixer*; Nikos Kazantzakis, *The Greek Passion*; ▷Mario Vargas Llosa, *The War of the End of the World*; ▷Jerzy Kosinski, *The Painted Bird*.

nificently and movingly described; but the novel's edge comes from the constant intrusion of grim outside reality, the tormented history of Poland between the Congress of Vienna in 1815 and the second-world-war nazi storming of the Warsaw Ghetto. Counterpoint between inner and outer reality, between public and private life, between flesh and spirit, makes this book not just another family saga but a statement about Jewish (and non-Jewish) humanity at large. In that, *The Family Moskat* is characteristic of Singer's work – it is his universality, not his particularity, which makes him one of the most respected writers of the century.

Singer's short-story collections are Gimpel the Fool, The Spinoza of Market Street, Short Friday, The Séance, A Friend of Kafka, A Crown of Feathers, Passions, Love and Exile *and* Old Love. Collected Stories *is a fat anthology.* In My Father's Court *is a memoir of Singer's Warsaw days as the son of a rabbi, a theological student and a budding writer.*

SMITH, E.E. 'Doc' (Edward Elmer Smith, PhD) •
(1890-1965)
US novelist.

Smith's books are the quintessence of space-opera. Good guys in powerful spaceships battle villains, explore new worlds, use entire planets as weapons, arrange the rise and fall of galactic civilisations. Although his scientific invention has been overtaken by events, and his plots and situations have been endlessly pirated in trashy films and TV series, no SF writer has surpassed him as a teller of straightforward, edge-of-the-seat space yarns. *First Lensman*, the first novel of the 'Lensman' series (1950–60; *Triplanetary*, 1948, is a prologue) is a splendid introduction to his work. Faced with the ever-growing power of criminals, from space pirates to intergalactic drug barons, the police are falling further and further behind until Virgil Samms, head of the Triplanetary Service, receives word that he will find help on Arisia, a ghost-planet hitherto shunned by space-travellers.

READ ON ⟩

● *Skylark of Space* (first of the 4-novel 'Skylark' series); *The Imperial Stars* (first of the 10-novel 'Family d'Alembert' series).
▶ David A. Kyle, *The Dragon Lensman* (first of a trilogy of Lensman sequels authorised by the Smith estate). Vonda N. McIntyre, *Enterprize – the First Adventure* (a powerful book using characters from the TV series *Star Trek*). ▷Harry Harrison, *Star Smashers of the Galaxy Rangers* (a merciless spoof).

SMITH, Wilbur • *(born 1933)*
South African novelist.

Smith's novels, set in South Africa, are swaggering adventure yarns in the tradition of ▷H. Rider Haggard. Their backgrounds are war (especially the Boer War), mining and jungle exploration; their heroes are free spirits, revelling in the lawlessness and vigour of frontier life. (John Wayne played their US equivalents in a hundred films.) *Shout at the Devil* (1968) is typical: the story of lion-hunting, crocodile-wrestling, ivory-poaching Flynn O'Flynn, whose Robin Hood humiliations of the sadistic German commissioner Fleischer take a serious turn when war is declared – this is 1914 – and he falls into a German trap.

> **READ ON** ▷

● *The Diamond Hunters* (about a safari to find hidden diamonds); *Gold Mine*; *A Sparrow Falls*.
▶ ▷Desmond Bagley, *Running Blind*. John Gardner, *The Secret Generation*. Hammond Innes, *Campbell's Kingdom*. ▷H. Rider Haggard, *King Solomon's Mines*.

SNOW, C.P. (Charles Percy) • *(1905–80)*
British novelist.

Snow's main work is the novel-sequence 'Strangers and Brothers' (1940–74). Though many characters recur, each book is self-contained. As the series proceeds, Lewis Eliot (the narrator of all 11 novels) rises from humble provincial beginnings to become a barrister, a civil servant and a senior government official. Snow's preoccupation was power: how people influence each other, the working of committees and hierarchies, the morality of office. He coined the phrase 'the corridors of power' – and he offers unrivalled glimpses of the people who tramp those corridors, of real individuals behind the establishment façade. *The Masters*, one of the key books in the sequence, describes the alliances and compromises required to elect a new master for a Cambridge college. *The New Men*, about scientists working on the first atomic bomb, is a study of responsibility: should we use our skills for ends we feel are wrong? In *The Conscience of the Rich*, about family loyalty, a rich young man rejects the future his father plans for him and becomes a doctor. *The Sleep of Reason*, the bleakest of all Snow's books, discusses our moral responsibility for others' evil; it was based on a horrific real 1960s case of multiple child-murder. Snow's themes are large, but his books are blander and less agonised than this suggests. His characters – especially the imperturbable committee-men (never women) who keep things going and the mavericks who let feelings interfere with common sense – are fascinating, and his scenes of discussion and persuasion are brilliantly done: he keeps us on the edge of our seats about such apparently trivial matters as whether

> **READ ON** ▷

▶ ▷Anthony Trollope, *Can You Forgive Her?* (the first novel in the 'Palliser' sequence). ▷Angus Wilson, *The Old Men at the Zoo*. Pamela Hansford Johnson (Lady Snow), *Error of Judgement*. ▷Gore Vidal, *Washington, D.C.* ▷Neville Shute, *No Highway*.

someone will end up saying 'yes' or 'no'.

The books in the sequence are Strangers and Brothers, The Light and the Dark, A Time of Hope, The Masters, The New Men, Homecomings, The Conscience of the Rich, The Affair, The Corridors of Power, The Sleep of Reason *and* Last Things. *Snow's other novels include two thrillers,* Death Under Sail *and* A Coat of Varnish, *and a fascinating study (*The Search*) of the excitement and passion of scientific research.*

SOLZHENITSYN, Alexander • *(born 1918)*
Russian novelist and non-fiction writer.

Denounced for treason in 1945 (he was a Red Army soldier who criticised Stalin), Solzhenitsyn spent eight years in a labour camp where he developed stomach cancer, and after nine months in a cancer hospital was sent into internal exile. He turned this bitter experience into novels – the prison-camp books *One Day in the Life of Ivan Denisovich* (1961) and *The First Circle* (1968); *Cancer Ward* (1968) – and their publication outside the USSR made him one of the most famous of all 1960s Soviet dissidents. He was finally expelled from the USSR in 1974, for writing an exhaustive description of the location, history and methods of the Russian prison-camp system, *The GULAG Archipelago* (1974–8). Few writers have ever surpassed him as a chronicler of human behaviour at its most nightmarish: his personal history authenticates every word he wrote.

Solzhenitsyn's only other novel is August 1914, *about the stirrings of the Russian Revolution.*

READ ON ▷

► ▷Fyodor Dostoevsky, *Notes from the House of the Dead.* Arthur Koestler, *Darkness at Noon.* ▷Vladimir Nabokov, *Bend Sinister.* André Brink, *Looking on Darkness.* ▷Thomas Pynchon, *Gravity's Rainbow.* William Styron, *Sophie's Choice.*

SOMETHING NASTY...

Roald Dahl, *Kiss Kiss* (short stories)
▷James Herbert, *Moon*
▷Stephen King, *Pet Sematary*
▷Ruth Rendell, *Live Flesh*

Good and Evil (p 94)

SOUTH AFRICA

J.M. Coetzee, *In the Heart of the Country*
▷Nadine Gordimer, *Burger's Daughter*
Dan Jacobson, *A Dance in the Sun*
David Karp, *The Day of the Monkey*
Alan Paton, *Cry, The Beloved Country*
▷Tom Sharpe, *Riotous Assembly*
Carolyn Slaughter, *The Innocents*
▷Wilbur Smith, *Rage*

SPARK, Muriel • *(born 1918)*
British novelist.

Spark made her name in the 1960s: her tart black come-dies seemed just the antidote to the fey optimism of the time. Her books' deadpan world is a distorted mirror-im-age of our own, a disconcerting blend of the bland and the bizarre. In *Memento Mori* old people are mysteriously tel-ephoned and reminded that they are about to die. In *Robinson* a plane-load of ill-assorted people (among them the standard Spark heroine, a Catholic with Doubts) crashes on an island where laws and customs are hourly remade at the whim of the sole inhabitant. In *The Prime of Miss Jean Brodie* an Edinburgh schoolmistress tries to brainwash her pupils into being nice, conforming gels. *The Abbess of Crewe* reworks convent politics in terms of Watergate; the hero of *The Only Problem*, a scholar work-ing on the Book of Job, finds its events parallelling those in his own life. Spark develops these ideas not in farce but in brisk, neat prose, as if they were the most matter-of-fact happenings in the world. The results are eccentric, unsettling and hilarious.

THE GIRLS OF SLENDER MEANS • *(1963)*
A group of young ladies lives in a run-down London club for distressed gentlefolk. It is 1945, and there is rumoured to be an unexploded bomb in the garden. The girls are excited by the possibility of imminent destruction: they find it almost as thrilling as the thought of sex. They bus-tle about their busy, vapid lives: pining after film stars, writing (unanswered) letters to famous writers, bargaining for black-market clothing coupons. The book is an alle-gory about seedy-genteel, self-absorbed Britain under the threat of nuclear extinction; for all Spark's breezy hu-mour, the novel is haunted by the questions of where

READ ON ⟩

● *The Ballad of Peckham Rye; The Bachelors.*
▶ Ronald Firbank, *The Eccentricities of Cardinal Pirelli*. ▷Rose Macaulay, *The Towers of Trebizond*. Alice Thomas Ellis, *The 27th Kingdom*. ▷Anita Brookner, *Look at Me*. ▷John Updike, *The Witches of Eastwick*.

we'll be and how we'll behave when the bomb goes up.

Spark's other novels include The Mandelbaum Gate *(her most serious book, about a half-Jewish Catholic convert visiting Jerusalem at the height of Arab-Israeli tension),* The Driver's Seat, Not to Disturb, The Takeover *and* Territorial Rights. The Stories of Muriel Spark *is a generous short-story collection.*

STEAD, Christina • *(1902–83)*
Australian novelist.

Although Stead was born in Australia, she lived most of her life, and set many of her books, in Europe (especially Paris) and the USA. She writes of these places, however, not as a native but as a visitor, in a detached, ironic tone as if she were an anthropologist describing the behaviour of some unlikely, uncongenial tribe. In *The Beauties and Furies*, a savage moral tale about adultery, a young wife runs off to 1930s Paris and has an affair with a handsome but ruthless sexual adventurer; in the end he drops her and goes in search of younger prey. *House of all Nations*, an 800-page blockbuster about the insidious corruption of money, centres on the customers, staff and owners of a private European bank, and especially on its chief Jules Bertillon, a man whose moral sense and conscience have atrophied in the face of 'market forces'. Stead was a socialist, and this book is a devastating, if covert, assault on the pre-second-world-war European capitalist system. *The Man Who Loved Children*, set in the USA but based on Stead's own experience, is a story of stifling family life at the turn of the century, presided over by a monstrous, bullying father; the whole thing is seen through the eyes of his daughter, Louise, as she grows from terrified, adoring childhood to rebellious adolescence and adulthood.

Stead's other novels include For Love Alone, Dark Places of the Heart/Cotter's England, The People With the Dogs, Miss Herbert (The Suburban Wife) *and the long, ironic 'romance'* Letty Fox, Her Luck. The Salzburg Tales *is a collection of macabre, satirical and bawdy short stories modelled on Chaucer's* Canterbury Tales.

STEEL, Danielle
US novelist.

If there can be such a thing as feminist romance, that is what Steel writes. Her young women are briskly in charge

---

READ ON

▶ **To *The Beauties and Furies:*** ▷Jean Rhys, *After Leaving Mr Mackenzie*; Patrick Hamilton, *Hangover Square*; ▷Djuna Barnes, *Nightwood*.
▶ **To *House of All Nations:*** ▷John Galsworthy, *The Forsyte Saga*; ▷Jerome Weidman, *A Family Fortune*.
▶ **To *The Man Who Loved Children:*** ▷Ivy Compton-Burnett, *A Family and a Fortune*; ▷Angela Carter, *The Magic Toyshop*.

READ ON

▶ Helen Van Slyke, *The Rich and the*

of their own destinies, and regard men not as knights in shining armour but as equal partners – an attitude which some of her men find hard to take. Melting femininity is present, in that the books are about love-affairs, but so is melting masculinity: where emotion and sentiment are concerned, all human beings are one. Her books include *Crossings*, *Loving*, *The Promise* and *Full Circle* (1985), whose heroine is involved with the 1970s protest movement in the USA, fighting for civil rights and the end of the Vietnam war.

STEINBECK, John • *(1902–68)*
US novelist.

Until Steinbeck settled to writing in 1935, he moved restlessly from one job to another: he was a journalist, a builder's labourer, a house-painter, a fruit-picker and the caretaker of a lakeside estate. This experience gave him first-hand knowledge of the dispossessed, the unemployed millions who suffered the brunt of the US Depression of the 1930s. Their lives are his subject, and he writes of them with ferocious, documentary intensity and in a style which seems exactly to catch their habits of both mind and speech. The ruggedness of his novels is often enhanced by themes borrowed from myth or the Old Testament. *To A God Unknown* (1933) is about an impoverished farmer who begins worshipping ancient gods and ends up sacrificing himself for rain. *Tortilla Flat* (1935) about 'wetbacks' (illegal Mexican immigrants to California) uses the story of Arthur, Guinevere and Lancelot from British myth. *East of Eden* (1952) is based on the story of Cain and Abel. Though Steinbeck never thrusts such references down his readers' throats, they add to the grandeur and mystery which, together with documentary grittiness, are the overwhelming qualities of his work.

THE GRAPES OF WRATH • *(1938)*
The once-fertile Oklahoma grain-fields have been reduced to a dust-bowl by over-farming, and the Joad family are near starvation. Attracted by leaflets promising work in the fruit-plantations of California, they load their belongings into a battered old car and travel east. In California they find every plantation surrounded by destitute, desperate people: there are a thousand applicants for every job. The plantation-owners pay starvation-wages and sack anyone who objects; the workers try to force justice by strike action – and are beaten up by armed vigilantes. When Tom Joad, already on the run for murder, is caught up in the fight for justice and accidentally kills a man; it is time for Ma to gather the family together again and move on.

Righteous. Mary Wesley, *The Camomile Lawn*. Charlotte Vale Allen, *Promises*. ▷Alice Walker, *Meridian*.

READ ON ⟩

● *Of Mice and Men* (a tragedy about the friendship between two ill-matched farmworkers, Lennie – a simple-minded giant of a man – and the weedier, cleverer George).
▶ Erskine Caldwell, *God's Little Acre*. ▷Edith Wharton, *Ethan Frome*. ▷William Faulkner, *The Hamlet*. Upton Sinclair, *The Jungle*. ▷Victor Hugo, *Toilers of the Sea*. ▷Somerset Maugham, *Liza of Lambeth*.

There must be a place for them somewhere; there must be a Promised Land.

Steinbeck's shorter novels include Cannery Row, The Pearl *and* The Short Reign of Pippin IV. *His short stories, usually about 'wetbacks', share-croppers and other victims of the US system, are in* The Red Pony *and* The Long Valley. The Acts of King Arthur and his Noble Knights *is a straightforward retelling of British myth;* The Portable Steinbeck *is a packed anthology.*

STENDHAL • *(1783-1842)*
French novelist and non-fiction writer.

'Stendhal' was a pseudonym used by the French diplomat Henri-Marie Beyle. As well as fiction (four novels; a dozen short stories) he published essays on art, literature and philosophy and several autobiographical books. Unlike most early 19th-century writers – even ▷Balzac and ▷Dickens – who concentrated on surface likenesses, painting word-pictures of events, people and places without introspection, Stendhal was chiefly interested in his characters' psychology. The main theme of his novels was the way outsiders, without breeding or position, must make their way in snobbish, tradition-stifled society by talent or personality alone. His books give the feeling that we are watching the evolution of that personality, that we are as intimate with his people's psychological development as if they were relatives or friends.

SCARLET AND BLACK (Le rouge et le noir) •
(1830)
The book is a character-study of Julien Sorel, a carpenter's son who rises in the world by brains, sexual charm and ruthlessness. He becomes first tutor to the children of the local Mayor, then the Mayor's wife's lover, and finally secretary to an aristocratic diplomat whose daughter falls in love with him. In ten years he has travelled from humble origins to the verge of a dazzling marriage and a brilliant career. But then the Mayor's wife writes a letter denouncing him as a cold-hearted adventurer, his society acquaintances reject him, and he returns to his native town to take revenge.

Stendhal's other completed novels are Armance, The Abbess of Castro *and* The Charterhouse of Parma. The Life of Henri Brulard *and* Memoirs of an Egoist *are fictionalised autobiography.*

READ ON ⟩

● *The Charterhouse of Parma.*
▶ **To *Scarlet and Black*:** ▷André Gide, *Strait is the Gate*; ▷Nikolai Gogol, *Dead Souls*; ▷George Eliot, *Middlemarch*; ▷Honoré de Balzac, *Lost Illusions*: John Braine, *Room at the Top*; ▷Jerome Weidman, *I Can Get it for You Wholesale.*
▶ **To *The Charterhouse of Parma*:** Umberto Eco, *The Name of the Rose.*

STERNE, Laurence • *(1713–68)*
British novelist.

Sterne's only novel, *The Life and Opinions of Tristram Shandy, Gentleman* (1760–7) is less a story than a gloriously rambling conversation. Tristram sets out to tell his life-story (beginning with the moment of his conception, when his mother's mind is less on what she is doing than on whether his father has remembered to wind the clock). But everything he says reminds him of some anecdote or wise remark, so that he constantly interrupts himself. It takes 300 pages, for example, for him to get from his conception to the age of seven, and in the meantime we have had such digressions as a treatise on what the size and shape of people's noses tells us about their characters, an explanation of how the boy came to be called Tristram by mistake for Trismegistus (and what each name signifies), accounts of the Tristapaedia (the system devised for Tristram's education), the curse of Ernulphus of Rochester and the misfortunes of Lieutenant le Fever; we have also had the novel's preface (placed not at the beginning but as the peroration to Book III), and many musings on life, love and the pursuit of happiness by Tristram's father, Uncle Toby and Corporal Trim. The reader is constantly exhorted, nudged and questioned; there is even a blank page in case you have urgent thoughts of your own to add. We never know how Tristram's life turns out; instead, we are copiously informed about Uncle Toby's love-affair, Tristram's travels in France and the adventures of the King of Bohemia. Sterne himself called *Tristram Shandy* 'a civil, nonsensical, good-humoured book'; it is the most spectacular shaggy-dog story ever told.

Sterne's other writings include sermons – he was a Yorkshire parson – and A Sentimental Journey, *a discursive, half-fictionalised account of the towns and people he saw and the tales he heard during six months' travelling in France.*

STEVENSON, R.L. (Robert Louis) • *(1850–94)*
British writer of novels, short stories and non-fiction.

Apart from the brief psychological thriller *Dr Jekyll and Mr Hyde* (1886, about a man who uses drugs to change himself from kindly family doctor to deformed killer and back again), Stevenson's chief works are historical adventure-stories. They have been hijacked by child readers, but (except perhaps in *Treasure Island*, 1883) there is also

READ ON

▶ ▷François Rabelais, *Gargantua*. Miguel de Cervantes Saavedra, *Don Quixote*. Tobias Smollett, *The Expedition of Humphrey Clinker*. ▷John Kennedy Toole, *A Confederacy of Dunces*. Flann O'Brien, *At Swim-Two-Birds*. ▷Saul Bellow, *Henderson the Rain King*.

READ ON

▶ **To *Dr Jekyll and Mr Hyde*:** ▷H.G. Wells, *The Invisible Man*; Gaston Leroux, *The Phantom of the Opera*; James Hogg, plenty to interest adults: Stevenson's evocation of scenery (especially Scotland), the psychological complexity of his characters, and the feeling (which he shared with ▷Tolstoy) that each human life is part of a vast historical, moral and cultural continuum.

Stevenson's historical novels include The Black Arrow *(a story of the Wars of the Roses),* Weir of Hermiston *(about an Edinburgh 'hanging-judge' in the early 19th century) and the Jacobite trilogy* Kidnapped, Catriona *and* The Master of Ballantrae. *His lighter fiction includes* The Wrong Box, The Wrecker *and* The Ebb-tide. The Merry Men *and* Island Nights' Entertainment *contain short stories. He also wrote poetry, travel books (eg* Travels with a Donkey*) and plays.*

Confessions of a *Justified Sinner.*
▶ **To the adventure stories:** ▷Daniel Defoe, *Robinson Crusoe*; ▷Walter Scott, *The Heart of Midlothian*; John Masefield, *Jim Davis*; ▷John Buchan, *Castle Gay*; ▷A. Conan Doyle, *The Valley of Fear*; ▷Desmond Bagley, *Running Blind.*

STEWART, Mary • *(born 1916)*
British novelist.

Stewart's romantic adventure stories are set in magnificently-evoked, exotic parts of Europe and the Mediterranean. Her books include *Madam Will You Talk?*, *Wildfire at Midnight*, *Thunder on the Right*, *Nine Coaches Waiting*, *The Moon-spinners*, *Airs Above the Ground*, *The Gabriel Hounds*, *Touch Not the Cat* and *This Rough Magic* (1964), in which a girl, holidaying on Corfu, is caught up not only in sorcery – Corfu is the 'magic island' of Shakespeare's *The Tempest* – but in a gun-running conspiracy between Greece and Albania. Stewart also wrote a trilogy based on the legends of Merlin and King Arthur; the first volume is *The Crystal Cave* (1970).

READ ON ⟩

● *The Gabriel Hounds.*
▶ Anne Bridge, *Illyrian Spring.* Helen MacInnes, *The Venetian Affair.* ▷Dorothy Dunnett, *Dolly and the Cookie Bird.*

SVEVO, Italo • *(1861-1928)*
Austrian/Italian novelist.

Svevo was a businessman in Trieste; his firm made underwater paint. Despite encouragement from his friend ▷James Joyce, he never took his writing seriously until the last year of his life, when a French translation of *The Confessions of Zeno* (1922) brought him European fame. His books are ironical comedies. Their ineffective, bewildered heroes blunder about in society, looking for some point to their existence – and the chief irony is that they are genuinely the 'zeros' they think they are, their existence has no point at all. *The Confessions of Zeno* is the autobiography of a man who wants to give up smoking. He explains that his addiction is actually psychological, since every cigarette he smokes reminds him, in ▷Prous-

READ ON ⟩

▶ ▷Franz Kafka, *The Castle.* ▷Saul Bellow, *Herzog.* Alberto Moravia, *The Conformist.* Joaquin Machado de Assis, *The Heritage of Quincas Borba.* William Cooper, *Scenes from Married Life.* William Boyd, *The New Confessions.*

tian fashion, of some past experience, so that to give up smoking would be to surrender his own history; he writes of his Oedipal relationship with his father (whom he accidentally killed), of his prolonged, ludicrous courtship of the wrong woman, and of his treatment by a psychiatrist sicker than himself. The book is as dreamlike and terrifying as ▷Kafka's novels – indeed, Svevo exactly shared Kafka's vision of the world as an absurd, endless and sinister labyrinth.

Svevo's other novels are A Life, As A Man Grows Older *and the shorter* Tale of the Good Old Man and the Pretty Girl.

SWIFT, Graham • *(born 1949)*
British novelist.

Swift's novels centre on apparently ordinary people – shopkeepers, housewives, clerks – under psychological stress. They have reached turning-points in what have seemed boring, routine lives, and the novels show them mentally rerunning the past to find explanations for their feelings, either to themselves or to others. In *Waterland* (1983) the main character is an elderly history teacher, and the event he is remembering is the discovery, forty years before, of a boy's body in a drainage-ditch in the English Fens. In front of a bored, cheeky class, he begins thinking aloud about the reasons for the boy's death – and his monologue ranges through the history of the Fens (one of the remotest and most mysterious English regions), the story of several generations of his own family, and, not least, an account of the rivalry between his mentally subnormal brother Dick and Freddie Parr, the boy found drowned.

Swift's other novels are The Sweet Shop Owner, Shuttlecock *and* Out of This World. Learning To Swim *is a collection of short stories.*

SWIFT, Jonathan • *(1667-1745)*
British/Irish satirist and journalist.

Swift was a savage satirist, pouring out poems, articles

READ ON ⟩

● *Out of This World* (in which, in alternate monologues, the son and grand-daughter of a first-world-war hero, an arms manufacturer, reflect on the way the old man's obsessive love for them has poisoned both their lives).

▶ Peter Benson, *The Levels* (also set in Fen-country). Gerald H. Morris, *Doves and Silk Handkerchieves* and ▷John Irving, *The Cider House Rules* are similarly multi-layered, mysterious stories, set respectively in a Yorkshire mining village at the turn of the 20th century and in rural Maine before, during and after the second world war.

READ ON ⟩

▶ Voltaire, *Candide.*

and essays attacking the follies of his time. *Gulliver's Travels* (1726) differs from his other work only in that the edge of its satire is masked by fairy tale – indeed, the satire is often edited out so that the book can be sold for children. Gulliver is a compulsive explorer, despite the moral humiliation he suffers after every landfall. In Lilliput the people (who are six inches high) regard him as an uncouth, unpredictable monster – particularly when he tells them some of the ideas and customs of his native England. In Brobdignag he becomes the pet of giants, and tries without success to convince them of the value of such civilised essentials as law-courts, money and guns. He visits Laputa and Lagado, cloud-cuckoo-lands where science has ousted common sense; on the Island of Sorcerers he speaks to great thinkers of the past, and finds them in despair at what has become of the human race. Finally he is shipwrecked among the Houynhyms, horses equipped with reason who regard human beings as degenerate barbarians, and who fill him with such distaste for his own species that when he returns to England he can hardly bear the sight, sound or smell of his own family. Throughout the book, Gulliver doggedly preaches the glories of European 'civilisation' (that is, the customs and beliefs of the Age of Enlightenment), and arouses only derision or disgust.

Samuel Butler, *Erewhon*. ▷Nathanael West, *A Cool Million*.

▶ **Equally lacerating satires on aspects of late 20th-century life:** Michael Frayn, *A Very Private Life*; ▷Thomas Pynchon, *The Crying of Lot 49*; ▷Angela Carter, *The Passion of New Eve*.

T

TAYLOR, Elizabeth • *(1912–75)*
British novelist and short-story writer.

A large part of Taylor's art consists in appearing to have no art at all: few authors have ever seemed so self-effacing in their work. As each novel or story begins, it is as if a net curtain has been drawn aside to reveal ordinary people in a normal street. The setting is the outskirts of some large English town; the people are housewives, bus-conductors, labourers, schoolchildren; there seems to be no drama. But as the story proceeds, an apparently unfussy chronicle of ordinary events and conversations builds up enormous psychological pressure, which Taylor then releases in a shocking or hilarious happening which opens speculation wide about whatever will happen when the book is closed. Her artistry – subtle, gentle and unsettling – is at its peak in short stories; her novels, thanks to larger casts, more varied settings and longer time-schemes, tend more to wry social comedy than to the sinister.

THE DEVASTATING BOYS • *(1972)*
The people in this story collection are typical Taylor characters: an elderly couple in the countryside who decide to offer a holiday to two black children from the city slums; a young West Indian, utterly alone in London on the eve of his birthday; an ll-year-old child taking a bus home from a hateful piano lesson; a blue-rinsed widow with an orderly routine of life. Something unexpected happens to each of them, a psychological bombshell. They were as unremarkable as our neighbours – but after these stories, our neighbours will never seem the same again.

Taylor's short stories are collected in Hester Lilly, The Blush *and* A Dedicated Man. *Her novels include* At Mrs Lippincote's, A View of the Harbour, A Game of Hide-

---

> **READ ON**

● *Hester Lilly*; *The Wedding Group* (novel).
▶ **To the stories:** V.S. Pritchett, *The Camberwell Beauty and Other stories*; William Trevor, *Angels at the Ritz*; Mary Gordon, *Temporary Shelter*; Joyce Carol Oates, *Crossing the Border*.
▶ **To the novels:** ▷Susan Hill, *A Change for the Better*; ▷Barbara Pym, *Excellent Women*; ▷Angus Wilson, *Late Call*; Theodore Fontane, *Effi Briest*.

and-seek, The Wedding Group, Blaming, A Wreath of Roses, Mrs Palfrey at the Claremont *and* The Soul of Kindness.

TERRORISTS/FREEDOM FIGHTERS

Jerzy Andrzeyewski, *Ashes and Diamonds*
▷Joseph Conrad, *Under Western Eyes*
Rosalind Laker, *This Shining Land*
▷John Le Carré, *The Little Drummer Girl*
▷Doris Lessing, *The Good Terrorist*
Primo Levi, *If Not Now, When?*
▷Frederic Raphael, *Like Men Betrayed*
Idries Shah, *Kara Kush*

War: Behind the Lines (p 253)

THACKERAY, William Makepeace •
(1811-63)
British novelist and journalist.

Until the success of *Vanity Fair*, when he was 36, Thackeray earned his living as a journalist and cartoonist (especially for Punch magazine) and as a humorous lecturer. His first intention in his novels was to write 'satirical biographies', letting the reader discover the follies of the world at the same time as his naive young heroes and heroines. But the characters took over, and his books now seem more genial and affectionate than barbed. He invented characters as grotesque as ▷Dickens', caricatures of human viciousness or folly, but he wrote of them with a kind of disapproving sympathy, a fellow-feeling for their humanity, which Dickens lacks. Humbug, ambition and the seven deadly sins are Thackeray's subjects – and so are friendship, kindness and warm-heartedness. At a time when many English novels were more like sermons, clamorous for reform, he wrote moral comedies, showing us what fools we are.

VANITY FAIR • *(1847–8)*
The book interweaves the lives of two friends, gentle Amelia and calculating, brilliant Becky Sharp. Becky is an impoverished orphan determined to make her fortune; Amelia believes in love, marriage and family life. Each of them marries; Amelia's husband has an affair with Becky, and dies at Waterloo with her name on his lips; Becky's husband finds her entertaining a rich, elderly admirer and

READ ON ▷

● *Pendennis.*
▶ ▷Jane Austen, *Emma.*
▷Arnold Bennett, *The Card.* ▷H.G. Wells, *Tono-Bungay.*
▷Eudora Welty, *The Ponder Heart.*
▷Barbara Pym, *No Fond Return of Love.*

abandons her. In the end, each girl gets what she longed for, but not in the way she hoped. Amelia, after ten years pining for her dead husband, is cruelly told by Becky of his infidelity, and turns for comfort to a dull, kind man who has worshipped her from afar, and who now offers her marriage, a home and all the comforts of obscurity. Becky's son inherits his father's money and gives her an annuity on condition that she never speaks to him again; we see her at the end of the book, queening it in Bath, an idle, rich member of the society she has always aspired to join and whose values Thackeray sums up in the title of the book.

Thackeray's other books include Pendennis *(the story of a selfish young man, spoilt by his mother, who goes to London to make his fortune as a writer) and its sequel* The Newcomes, Henry Esmond *and its sequel* The Virginians, *and a number of shorter tales and stories including* Barry Lyndon, The Great Hoggarty Diamond *and the spoof fairy-tale* The Rose and the Ring.

THEROUX, Paul • *(born 1941)*
US novelist and non-fiction writer.

Some of Theroux's most enjoyable books are about travelling. *The Great Railway Bazaar* takes him by a succession of weird and wonderful old steam trains from London to Tokyo and back again. In *The Old Patagonian Express* he takes public transport from Boston to the southernmost tip of South America. *The Kingdom by the Sea* is the waspish account of a journey round the coastal resorts of seedy 1980s Britain. In all of them the narrator, the writer himself, feels detached, an observer of events rather than a participant – and the same is true of the people in Theroux's novels. They live abroad, often in the tropics; like the heroes of ▷Graham Greene (the author Theroux most resembles) they feel uneasy both about the society they are in and about themselves; they fail to cope. The hero of *Saint Jack* (1973), a US pimp in Singapore, hopes to make a fortune providing R and R for his servicemen compatriots, but the pliability of his character makes him the prey for every conman and shark in town. In *The Mosquito Coast* (1981) an ordinary US citizen, depressed by life, uproots his family and tries to make a new start in the Honduran jungle, with tragic, farcical results. *Picture Palace* (1978) is the life-story of a famous photographer who has hidden all her life behind her camera, reduced existence to images on film, and now, in withered old age, agonisingly contrasts her memories of youth, warmth and

READ ON ▷

▶ **To O-Zone:** ▷Russell Hoban, *Riddley Walker*; Robie Macauley, *A Secret History of Time to Come*; Keith Roberts, *Kiteworld*.
▶ **To Theroux's novels in general:** ▷Graham Greene, *Our Man in Havana*; Timothy Mo, *Sour Sweet*.
▶ **To the short stories:** ▷Lawrence Durrell, *Antrobus Complete*.
▶ **To the travel-books:** Gordon Meyer, *The River and the People*; Jonathan Raban, *Coasting*.

affection with the dusty prints which are all she has to show for them.

O-ZONE • *(1986)*

The O-Zone or Outer Zone is an American county evacuated after a nuclear accident and left as a no-go area. After 15 years a group of New Yorkers visits it on a sensation-seeking spree – and finds not desert but a self-contained society of mutant, brutalised human beings. Later, two of the New Yorkers return to the O-Zone, seeking to come to terms with the nightmare as their ancestors once tried to tame the wilderness.

Theroux's other novels include Waldo, Fong and the Indians, The Black House, The Family Arsenal *and* Doctor Slaughter. Sinning With Annie, The Consul's File *and* The London Embassy *are collections of short stories.*

TOLKIEN, J.R.R. (John Ronald Reuel) •
(1892–1973)
British novelist.

In 1939 Tolkien, a teacher of Anglo-Saxon literature at Oxford University, published a children's book (*The Hobbit*), about a small furry-footed person who steals a dragon's hoard. Bilbo Baggins was a hobbit, and his quest was the prologue to an enormous adult saga in which elves, dwarves, wizards, ents, human beings and hobbits unite to destroy the power of evil (embodied by the Dark Lord Sauron and his minions the Ring-wraiths and the orcs). The three volumes of *The Lord of the Rings*, published in the mid-1950s, started a vogue for supernatural fantasy-adventure which has spread world-wide and taken in films, quiz-books and role-play games as well as fiction. Tolkien outstrips his imitators not so much because of his plot (which is a simple battle between good and bad, with the moral issues explicit on every page) as thanks to his teeming professorial imagination. He gave his made-up worlds complete systems of language, history, anthropology, geography and literature. Reading him is like exploring a library; his invention seems inexhaustible.

Although The Hobbit *and* The Lord of the Rings *are self-contained, Tolkien published several other volumes filling in chinks of their underlying history, explaining matters only sketched in the main narrative, and adding even more layers of linguistic, historical and anthropological fantasy. The chief books are* The Silmarillion *and* Unfin-

> **READ ON**

▶ ▷Stephen Donaldson, *The Chronicles of Thomas Covenant.*
▷Piers Anthony, *A Spell for Chameleon.*
▷David Eddings, *The Belgariad Quintet.*
Terry Pratchett, *The Colour of Magic* is a spectacular spoof, hardly less fantastical and engrossing than Tolkien's original.

ished Tales. Lost Tales *(three volumes) contain notes and drafts, chiefly of interest to addicts.* Farmer Giles of Ham *and* The Adventures of Tom Bombadil *are short stories for children.*

TOLSTOY, Lev Nikolaevich • *(1828–1910)*
Russian novelist.

In his 60s and beyond Tolstoy became famous as a kind of moral guru or secular saint: he preached the equal 'value' of all human beings, and suited actions to words by giving away his wealth, freeing his serfs and living an austere life in a cottage on the edge of his former estate. A similar view underlies his fiction. His ambition was to enter into the condition of each of his characters, to show the psychological complexity and diversity of the human race. His books are not tidily organised, with every event and emotion shaped to fit a central theme, but reflect the sprawl of life itself. The result was a psychological equivalent of ▷Balzac's 'snapshots' in *The Human Comedy.* Whether Tolstoy is showing us a coachman who comes and goes in half a page, or a major character who appears throughout a book, he invites us to feel full sympathy for that person, makes us flesh out his or her 'reality' in terms of our own.

WAR AND PEACE • *(1869)*
The book begins with people at a St Petersburg party in 1805 discussing the political situation in France, where Napoleon has just been proclaimed emperor. Tolstoy then fills 100 pages with seemingly random accounts of the lives and characters of a large group of relatives, friends, servants and dependants of three aristocrats, Andrey Bolkonsky, Pierre Bezuhov and Natasha Rostov. Gradually all these people become involved both with one another and with the gathering storm as Napoleon's armies sweep through Europe. The story culminates with the 1812 French invasion of Russia, Napoleon's defeat and his retreat from Moscow. The war touches the lives of all Tolstoy's people, and in particular resolves the triangle of affection between his central characters. The effects of war are the real subject of *War and Peace.* It contains 539 separate characters – the range is from Napoleon to the girl who dresses Rostov's hair, from Bolkonsky to an eager young soldier sharpening his sword on the eve of battle – and Tolstoy shows how their individual nature and feelings are both essential to and validated by the vast

READ ON ▷

● *Anna Karenina.*
▶ **To *War and Peace*:**
  ▷Émile Zola, *The Downfall*, (La débâcle).
  ▷I.B. Singer, *The Family Moskat*; André Malraux, *Man's Estate.*
▶ **To *Anna Karenina*:**
  ▷Ivan Turgenev, *On the Eve*; ▷George Eliot, *Romola*; ▷Gustave Flaubert, *Madame Bovary*; ▷Boris Pasternak, *Doctor Zhivago.*

Lev TOLSTOY

Jeanette WINTERSON, THE PASSION

Anthony BURGESS, THE NAPOLEON SYMPHONY

NAPOLEON

'ALL HUMAN LIFE IS HERE'

STENDHAL, SCARLET AND BLACK (*middle- and upper-class life in Napoleonic France*)

Miguel de CERVANTES SAAVEDRA, DON QUIXOTE (*fantasy knight-errantry in Renaissance Spain*)

Johann Wolfgang von GOETHE, THE APPRENTICESHIP OF WILHELM MEISTER (*young man travels 18th-century Europe, learning about life and love*)

Charles DICKENS, DAVID COPPERFIELD (*English city society in the 1830s*)

Mark TWAIN, THE ADVENTURES OF HUCKLEBERRY FINN (*small-town life on Mississippi before American Civil War*)

Ivan TURGENEV, FATHERS AND SONS (*landed class resist fashionable revolutionary ideas, 1860s*)

Nicolai GOGOL, DEAD SOULS (*conman tours rural estates, buying up dead serfs' 'souls'*)

Fyodor DOSTOEVSKI, THE IDIOT (*psychological disintegration of count dismissed by family as simpleton*)

Maxim GORKY, FOMA GORDEEV (*brutal upbringing in barge-owning family on 19th-century Volga*)

TSARIST RUSSIA

WAR AND PEACE *(tapestry of Russian life during Napoleonic Wars)*

NAPOLOENIC WARS

Bernard **CORNWELL, SHARPE'S REGIMENT**

C.S. **FORESTER, THE GUN**

William **THACKERAY, VANITY FAIR**

Boris **PASTERNAK, DOCTOR ZHIVAGO**
(tragic love in chaos of Russian revolution)

Ernest **HEMINGWAY, A FAREWELL TO ARMS**
(love-affair overshadowed by World War I)

Olivia **MANNING, FORTUNES OF WAR**
(World War II: effects on civilians in Balkans and Egypt)

William **STYRON, SOPHIE'S CHOICE**
(US woman haunted by memory of nazi concentration camps)

Kazuo **ISHIGURO, A PALE VIEW OF HILLS**
(Japanese woman coping with memories of Hiroshima)

FALLOUT OF WAR

tapestry of human affairs of which they are part.

Tolstoy's other novels include Anna Karenina *(in which an adulterous and tragic love-affair is used to focus a picture of the stifling, morally incompetent aristocratic Russian society of the 1860s),* The Death of Ivan Illich, The Kreutzer Sonata, Master and Man *and* Resurrection. *His autobiographical books include* Childhood, Boyhood, Youth *and* A Confession.

TOOLE, John Kennedy • *(1937–69)*
US novelist.

A Confederacy of Duncos (1980), Toole's only novel, was published posthumously: it had collected so many rejection-slips that he killed himself. It is a no-holds-barred comic grumble against the 20th-century world in general and the city of New Orleans in particular. Its anti-hero, Ignatius J. Reilly, is a narcissistic, hypochondriacal, towering genius who regards himself as too good for the world. He has successfully avoided working for 30 years, living in a fetid room in his mother's house and alternately masturbating, playing the lute and scribbling brilliant thoughts on a succession of supermarket notepads. At last his mother sends him out to find a job – with catastrophic results. Bored after one hour in a trouser-factory, he sets about destabilising staff-management relations; hired to sell hot-dogs, he eats his stock; in all innocence, he takes up with drug-addicts, whores and corrupt police. If Ignatius were likeable (say, like Voltaire's Candide), the satire might seem more genial and sympathetic; but he is a revolting example of how, in Toole's view, there is no excuse for the clinical brilliance of the brain being shackled to such a bag of guts as the human body. *A Confederacy of Duncos* is witty, slapstick, Rabelaisian, Falstaffian – and offers the human species no reason at all for self-congratulation or for hope.

TRAINS

▷Agatha Christie, *Murder on the Orient Express*
  Freeman Wills Crofts, *Death of a Train*
▷Graham Greene, *Stamboul Train*
▷Jaroslav Hašek, *The Good Soldier Švejk*
▷Patricia Highsmith, *Strangers on a Train*
▷John Masters, *Bhowani Junction*

READ ON ▷

▶ Robert Coover, *The Universal Baseball Association*. Frederick Rolfe, *Hadrian the Seventh*. Peter Carey, *Illywhacker*. B.S. Johnson, *Christie Malry's Own Double-Entry*. Martin Amis, *The Rachel Papers*.

TROLLOPE, Anthony • *(1815–82)*
British novelist.

Until Trollope was 52 he worked for the Post Office, travelling in Europe, the USA, north Africa and all over the British Isles. He turned his foreign experience into travel books, and used his British observations in 47 novels, many of them written, in the fashion of the time, for serial publication in magazines. His style is genial and expansive, and his books deal with such characteristic Victorian themes as class, power, money and family authority. His favourite characters are the upper-middle class of small towns and the surrounding estates. His plots involve the exercise of authority by the older generation and, by the young, all kinds of pranks, kicking over the traces, unsuitable love-affairs and mockery of their elders' stuffiness. Trollope's best-loved novels are in two six-book series, the 'Barsetshire' books (1855–67), about intrigue and preferment in a cathedral city, and the 'Palliser' books (1864–80), about politics on the wider stages of county and country. Each novel is self-contained, but recurring characters and cross-references between the books, added to Trollope's easy-going style, give the reader a marvellously comfortable sensation, as of settling down to hear about the latest scrapes of a group of well-loved friends.

BARCHESTER TOWERS • *(1857)*
The second novel in the Barsetshire sequence is high comedy. Imperious Mrs Proudie, wife of the timid new Bishop of Barchester, brings the Reverend Obadiah Slope into the Palace to help dominate her husband and run the diocese. But Slope is a snake in the grass, determined to make a rich marriage for himself, to win preferment in the church, even to defy Mrs Proudie if that will advance his cause. Their power-struggle is the heart of the book, a stately but furious minuet which soon sweeps up all Trollope's minor characters: rich, pretty Widow Bold, apoplectic Archdeacon Grantly, flirtatious Signora Vesey-Negroni, saintly Mr Harding, bewildered Parson Quiverful and his 14 squalling brats.

The Barsetshire novels are The Warden, Barchester Towers, Doctor Thorne, Framley Parsonage, The Small House at Allington *and* The Last Chronicle of Barset. *The Palliser novels are* Can You Forgive Her?, Phineas Finn, The Eustace Diamonds, Phineas Redux, The Prime Minister *and* The Duke's Children. *Trollope's other novels include* The Bertrams, Orley Farm, The Belton Estate, The Way We Live Now *and* Mr Scarborough's Family.

READ ON ▷

▶ **To the Barsetshire books:** Angela Thirkell, *High Rising* (first of a series set in Barsetshire and borrowing Trollope's characters); Elizabeth Goodge, *Cathedral Close*; Hugh Walpole, *The Cathedral*; ▷Barbara Pym, *Crampton Hodnett*.

▶ **To the Palliser books:** ▷John Galsworthy, *The Forsyte Saga*; Benjamin Disraeli, *Coningsby*; ▷Christina Stead, *House of All Nations*.

▶ **To Trollope's work in general:** Oliver Goldsmith, *The Vicar of Wakefield*; Louis Auchincloss, *The Great World and Timothy Colt*; ▷Barbara Taylor Bradford, *A Woman of Substance*.

TURGENEV, Ivan Sergeevich • *(1818–83)*
Russian novelist and playwright.

A rich man, Turgenev spent much of his life travelling in Europe, and was welcomed abroad as the leading Russian writer of his time. He was less popular in Russia itself. Although his limpid style (influenced by his friend ▷Flaubert) and his descriptions of nature were admired, his wistful satire, treating all human endeavour as equally absurd, won favour with neither conservatives nor radicals. His favourite characters are members of the leisured class, and his stories of disappointed ambition, failed love-affairs and unfocussed dissatisfaction anticipate not so much later revolutionary writings as the plays of ▷Chekhov.

FATHERS AND SONS • *(1861)*
Arkady, a student, takes his friend Bazarov home to meet his father. The old man is impressed by Bazarov's vigorous character and outspoken views – which are that none of the old moral and social conventions have intrinsic validity, and that people must decide for themselves how to live their lives. (This attitude to life, 'nihilism', was widespread among Russian intellectuals in the 1860s and 1870s.) The novel soon leaves politics to explore the effects of Bazarov's character on his own life. He falls in love, and disastrously misinterprets his beloved's wish for friendship as the proposal of a 'free' liaison; he visits his parents, who cannot reconcile their admiration for their son with bewilderment at his ideas; he quarrels with the traditionalist Pavel, Arkady's uncle, and fights an absurd duel with him; he nurses serfs during a typhus epidemic and becomes fatally infected. Although Bazarov always regarded his own existence as futile, after his death it becomes apparent that he has changed the lives and attitudes of every other person in the story.

Turgenev's novels include Rudin, A Nest of Gentlefolk, On the Eve, Smoke *and* Virgin Soil. A Hunter's Notes/A Sportsman's Sketches *contains short stories and poetic descriptions of country scenes.* A Month in the Country, *a Chekhovian comedy, is his best-known play.*

TURNER, George • *(born 1916)*
Australian novelist.

The Sea and Summer (1987), Turner's best-known novel, is set in New Melbourne, Australia, three generations from now. The human race has pillaged the environment

---

READ ON ▷

● *Torrents of Spring* (the story of a man torn by love for two women, a beautiful girl and the wife of an old school friend).
▶ ▷Gustave Flaubert, *Sentimental Education.* George Moore, *The Lake.* ▷L.P. Hartley, *The Go-Between.* ▷Willa Cather, *The Professor's House.* ▷Anton Chekhov, *The Lady With the Little Dog* (and other short stories).

READ ON ▷

● *Beloved Son.*
▶ ▷Anthony Burgess, *A Clockwork Orange.*

to the point where the atmosphere itself is in revolt: the ice-caps are melting and water is lapping at the lower floors of the kilometre-high tower-blocks where the Swill live. The Swill make up ninety per cent of the population; they are unemployed and unemployable, an urban under-class surviving on state handouts, denied education and kept in check by army patrols and razor-wire. The Sweet, by contrast, have privilege, wealth and culture – so long as they keep their jobs. The book is about the relationship between Billy Kovacs, a Swill 'tower boss' (gang-ruler) and a Sweet family fallen on hard times. Although the sit-uation suggests SF, *The Sea and Summer* is, rather, a novel about character and relationships. The quality of Turner's writing, the harshness of his judgements and his depiction of people coping with a horrifying, doomed so-ciety, are ▷Dickensian in both range and rage.

Turner's other novels include The Cupboard Under the Stairs, Vaneglory *and* Yesterday's Men.

TWAIN, Mark • *(1835–1910)*
US novelist and journalist.

'Mark Twain' was the pseudonym of Samuel Clemens. A former steam-boat captain on the Mississippi, soldier, gold-miner and traveller, he wrote breezy, good-humoured accounts of his experiences, with an eye for quirky cus-toms, manners and characters. His favourite form was the short story or comic, factual 'sketch' of half a dozen pages, and several of his books are collections of such pieces. He wrote three historical novels, *Personal Recol-lections of Joan of Arc* (serious: the biography of Joan by a former page and secretary), *The Prince and the Pauper* (about a beggar-boy changing places with King Edward VI of England, his exact double) and *A Connecticut Yan-kee in King Arthur's Court* (in which a man, transported back in time, startles Camelot with such 'magic' items as matches, a pocket watch and gunpowder). In Twain's best-loved books, *The Adventures of Tom Sawyer* (1876) and *The Adventures of Huckleberry Finn* (1886), he wove reminiscences of boyhood and of life on the Mississippi into an easy-going, fictional form. *Tom Sawyer* is about the scrapes, fancies and fears of boyhood. The heroes of *Huckleberry Finn*, a boy and a runaway slave, pole a raft down the Mississippi, beset by conmen, bounty-hunters and outraged citizens, and fall into slapstick adventures each time they land. Twain is regarded in the USA as a founding father of American literature, and dismissed in Europe as a children's author; he offers far slyer, far

Keith Roberts, *Kiteworld*. Ray Bradbury, *Fahrenheit 451*. ▷Paul Theroux, *O-Zone*. ▷David Cook, *Sunrising*.

READ ON ⟩

▶ **To *Huckleberry Finn*:** Alphonse Daudet, *Tartarin of Tarascon*; ▷Henry Fielding, *Tom Jones*; H.E. Bates, *The Darling Buds of May*.
▶ **To Twain's travel-books:** ▷Robert Louis Stevenson, *Travels With a Donkey* (and its sibling, ▷John Steinbeck, *Travels with Charlie*); ▷Laurence Sterne, *A Sentimental Journey*; Laurie Lee, *As I Walked Out One Midsummer Morning*.

gentler, pleasures than either view suggests.

Twain's satires include Pudd'nhead Wilson *and* Extract from Captain Stormfield's Visit to Heaven *(funny) and* The Mysterious Stranger *(serious).* Tom Sawyer Abroad *and* Tom Sawyer Detective *are novels, following Tom's adventures in adult life. Twain's short stories are collected in* The Celebrated Jumping Frog of Calaveras County and Other Sketches *and* The Man That Corrupted Hadleyburg. *His books of travel and reminiscence include* The Innocents Abroad, Roughing It, A Tramp Abroad *and* Life on the Mississippi.

U

UNDSET, Sigrid • *(1882–1949)*
Norwegian novelist.

Outside Norway, Undset is best-known for *Kristin Lavransdatter* (1920–22), a novel-trilogy set in medieval times. It follows the life of Kristin, a landowner's daughter who flies in the face of convention by insisting on marrying the man she loves. He is arrogant and unyielding, even when his political enemies imprison him and strip him of wealth and lands. Only Kristin stands by him: the book's subject is the growth of her soul, the way her Christian devotion transcends humiliation and despair. The book's bleak subject-matter is offset by Undset's warm feeling for her characters, and by her detailed, perceptive picture of 14th-century life and thought.

READ ON ▷

● *The Master of Hestviken.*
▶ Helen Waddell, *Héloise and Abelard.* Umberto Eco, *The Name of the Rose.* Janet Lewis, *The Trial of Sören Kvist.*

UNLOOKED-FOR FRIENDSHIPS

▷David Cook, *Winter Doves*
▷Tove Jansson, *The Summer Book*
▷Alison Lurie, *Foreign Affairs*
▷Joseph Olshan, *A Warmer Season*
▷C.P. Snow, *The Light and the Dark*
▷John Steinbeck, *Of Mice and Men*
▷Morris West, *The World is Made of Glass*

UPDIKE, John • *(born 1932)*
US novelist and short-story writer.

Updike's short stories (most of them written for the *New Yorker*) are witty anecdotes about the snobberies and love-affairs of ambitious Long Island couples, or single, bril-

READ ON ▷

● *Of the Farm.*
▶ ▷Philip Roth, *The*

liant jokes (for example treating bacteria under a microscope as if they were guests at a trendy cocktail party). Some of his novels are in a similarly glittering, heartless style. In *Couples* (1968) a small group of bored Connecticut commuters changes sex-partners as carelessly as if playing a party game. In *The Witches of Eastwick* (1984) three bored young widows set themselves up as a coven of amateur witches, only to become sexually ensnared by a devilishly charming man. The hero of *A Month of Sundays* is a 'progressive' clergyman tortured by lust. Updike's other novels are deeper, concentrating more on the underlying pain than on the ludicrous surface of his characters' lives. The 'Rabbit' trilogy (*Rabbit, Run*; *Rabbit Redux*; *Rabbit is Rich*, 1960–81) tells the life of an ex-school sports champion who finds emotional maturity and happiness almost impossible to grasp. The hero of *Roger's Version*, a middle-aged professor, is thrown into moral turmoil by the possibility of devising a computer-program to prove the existence of God. *Marry Me*, one of Updike's most moving books, is a tragi-comedy about an adulterous affair.

THE CENTAUR · *(1963)*

George Caldwell, an eccentric, ineffective science teacher at Olinger High School in the 1950s, deflects his feelings of inadequacy by fantasising that he is Chiron, the centaur who taught the heroes of Greek myth (which makes his headmaster Zeus and his colleagues Athene, Hephaestus and Hercules), and that he has terminal stomach cancer. The book describes three days in his life, during which he is forced to come to terms with himself and with his adolescent son Peter, who idolises him. Myth-reminiscences start and end the book; its heart is more straightforward, a moving account of small-town life and of the inarticulate love between Peter and his perplexed, exasperating father.

Updike's other novels include The Poorhouse Fair, Of the Farm, The Coup *and two made from stories about a neurotic writer,* Bech, a Book *and* Bech is Back. *His story-collections include* The Same Door, Pigeon Feathers, Museums and Women, The Music School *and* Trust Me.

US SMALL TOWN LIFE

Sherwood Anderson, *Winesburg, Ohio*
▷John Cheever, *Bullet Park*
▷John Irving, *The Cider House Rules*

Ghost Writer. Arthur Laurents, *The Way We Were*. ▷Frederic Raphael, *Heaven and Earth*. ▷Angus Wilson, *Hemlock and After*. Brian Moore, *The Great Victorian Collection*.

Garrison Keillor, *Lake Wobegon Days*
Arthur Laurents, *The Way We Were*

Deep South, USA (p 55)

V

VARGAS LLOSA, Mario • *(born 1936)*
Peruvian novelist.

An admirer of ▷Márquez, Vargas Llosa uses magic realism to give a similarly mordant view of South American life and politics. His books with contemporary settings are his sharpest: *Aunt Julia and the Scriptwriter* (1983) sends up big-city life; *The City and the Dogs/The Time of the Hero* (1962) is a satire on fascism set in a gung-ho, brutal military academy. His finest book, *The War of the End of the World* (1981), is quieter. Ostensibly a historical novel about the setting-up (and savage dismantling by the authorities) of a religious community for drop-outs and derelicts – the kind of people Christ himself might have chosen to wait for the apocalypse at the turn of the 19th/20th centuries – it spreads tendrils of fantasy into every area of social, religious, military and political life.

Vargas Llosa's other novels include The Green House, Conversation in the Cathedral *and* Captain Pantoja and the Special Service. The Cubs *is a collection of short stories.* The Perpetual Orgy *is a book-length musing about* ▷Flaubert's Madame Bovary, *part literary criticism, part reconstruction, part anthology: it is magic realism and non-fiction, hand in hand.*

VERNE, Jules • *(1828–1905)*
French novelist.

Verne began writing in the 1860s, the heyday of both exploration and popular science – and his inspiration was to mix the two. His stories mimic the memoirs of real-life explorers of the time, fabulous adventures narrated in sober, business-like prose – and, by stirring in scientific

---

READ ON ▷

▶ **To Vargas Llosa's fiction:** ▷Isabel Allende, *Of Love and Shadows*; ▷Gabriel García Márquez, *The Autumn of the Patriarch*; Augusto Roa Bastos, *I the Supreme.*
▶ **To *The Perpetual Orgy*:** Julian Barnes, *Flaubert's Parrot.*

READ ON ▷

▶ ▷A. Conan Doyle, *The Lost World.* ▷H.G. Wells, *The First Men in the Moon.* ▷H. Rider Haggard, *She.*

wonders impossible or unlikely at the time, he tips them into fantasy. His heroes are not tethered to the surface of the Earth: they tunnel towards its core (*Journey to the Centre of the Earth*), live underwater (*Twenty Thousand Leagues Under the Sea*) and ride rockets into space (*From the Earth to the Moon*; *Round the Moon*). Alternately with these 'scientific' adventure-stories, Verne produced tales of more orthodox derring-do: *Michel Strogoff*, for example, is a gentleman-adventurer whose bravery saves Civilisation as We Know It; in *Round the World in Eighty Days* Phileas Fogg embarks on a crazy balloon-journey to win a bet. Modern science has outstripped most of Verne's inventions, but few later SF writers have bettered him in straight-down-the-line, thrill-in-every-paragraph adventure.

VIDAL, Gore • *(born 1925)*
US novelist and non-fiction writer.

Vidal made his name as a tart-tongued, witty commentator on 1960s and 1970s life, a favourite chat-show guest. Whatever the topic, from the rotation of crops to the horror of nazi concentration camps, from zen to flower-arranging, he had something interesting to say. The same protean brilliance fills his novels. Whether their subject is homosexuality (*The City and the Pillar*, 1948/65), the excesses of the film industry (*Myra Breckinridge*, 1968) or US politics (the tetralogy *Burr*, *1876*, *Washington DC* and *Empire* 1967–86), they are original, stimulating and engrossing. This is particularly so in his historical novels, where he makes his alternative view of past events seem more attractive than reality itself. *Julian* is a study of the last pagan Roman emperor, who tried to stop the rush of Christianity in the name of (as Vidal sees it) the more humane, more generous Olympian religion. *Creation* is the memoirs of an imaginary Persian nobleman of the 5th century BC, who went as ambassador to India, China and Greece and knew Confucius, Buddha and Socrates. *Lincoln* refocuses our view of the thoughts and achievements of the 16th US president.

KALKI • *(1978)*
Teddy Ottinger, a test pilot, is summoned to the Tibetan ashram of the mysterious Kalki. Born an American, James Kelly, Kalki has settled in the Himalayas after the Vietnam war and announced that he is the tenth avatar of the god Vishnu and that his coming to earth means the end of the present cycle of human existence. The book, a witty intellectual thriller, shows how Kalki's prophecy is ful-

C.S. Lewis, *That Hideous Strength*. Edgar Rice Burroughs, *Pirates of Venus*. ▷E.E. 'Doc' Smith, *The Imperial Stars*. ▷Kurt Vonnegut, *The Sirens of Titan*.

READ ON ⟩

● *Duluth*.
▶ To *Kalki*: ▷Richard Condon, *Winter Kills*; ▷Kurt Vonnegut, *Galápagos*.
▶ To Vidal's historical novels: Peter Green, *The Sword of Pleasure* (set in republican Rome); John Hersey, *The Wall* (about US missionaries in China); John Barth, *The Sotweed Factor* (set in Maryland in the time of the Pilgrim Fathers).
▶ To Vidal's novels in general: ▷Kingsley Amis, *The Alteration*; ▷Patrick White, *The Twyborn Affair*; ▷Muriel Spark, *The Ballad of Peckham Rye*.

filled, and what happens to Teddy and the few other survivors in a world left unchanged except that all human life has ceased.

Vidal's other novels include Williwaw, In a Yellow Wood, The Season of Comfort, Two Sisters, Myron *and* Duluth. *He also wrote detective stories (including* Death in the Fifth Position) *under the name* Edgar Box. A Thirsty Evil *is a collection of short stories.*

VONNEGUT, Kurt • *(born 1922)*
US novelist.

SF ideas shape Vonnegut's novels – and so do autobiography, political and social satire, loonish humour and a furious, nagging rage at the way the human race is pillaging the world. *Galápagos* (1985) begins at the moment of nuclear apocalypse (which is triggered by a bomber-pilot fantasising that firing his missile is like having sex). A group of people, gathered in Ecuador for the 'Nature Cruise of the Century', find that their ship has become a Noah's Ark: they are the sole survivors of humankind. They land in the Galápagos Islands, equipped with no technology except a computer whose memory is stuffed with 1000 dead languages and a million quotations from the world's great literature, and set about survival. At first they are hampered, as (Vonnegut claims) the human race has been handicapped throughout its existence, by the enormous size of their brains, attics of unnecessary thought. But Galápagos is the cradle of the evolutionary theory – and that may be humanity's last hope.

Vonnegut's other novels are Player Piano; The Sirens of Titan; Mother Night; Cat's Cradle; God Bless You, Mrs Rosewater; Slaughterhouse Five; Breakfast of Champions; Slapstick; Jailbird; Palm Sunday *and* Deadeye Dick. Canary in a Cathouse *and* Welcome to the Monkeyhouse *contain short stories.*

> **READ ON**

● *Cat's Cradle; The Sirens of Titan.*
▶ ▷Brian Aldiss, *The Primal Urge.* Frederick Pohl, *The Coming of the Quantum Cats.*
▷Michael Moorcock, *The Final Programme.*
▷Russell Hoban, *Riddley Walker.*
▷Walter M. Miller, *A Canticle for Leibowitz.*
Bamber Gascoigne, *Cod Strewth.*

W

WALKER, Alice • *(born 1944)*
US novelist, poet and non-fiction writer.

The background to Walker's books is the struggle for equal rights in the US over the last 30 years, first by blacks and then by women. Radical politics are not, however, her main concern. She writes wittily, ironically, about the follies of human life, and she is as merciless to her idealistic, college-educated activists as she is to their slobbish, mindless opponents. If ▷Mary McCarthy or ▷Alison Lurie had written about black, feminist politics, these might have been their books. *Meridian* (1976), Walker's second novel, is the splendidly ironical study of a southern black activist, educated to be a 'lady' (in the 1920s white meaning of the term), who becomes a leader in the equal-rights movements of the 1960s. When we see Meridian years later, all battles won, holed up in the small southern town of Chickokema where apart from the coming of equality nothing momentous has ever happened, she is totally confused about where all her energy, her driving-force, has gone. Was this really what her life was for?

Walker's other novels are Third Life of Grange Copeland *and* The Color Purple *(also a film). In* Love and Trouble *and* You Can't Keep a Good Woman Down *are short-story collections. She has also published poetry (*Once; Revolutionary Petunias; Willie Lee, I'll See You in the Morning*) and a book of essays,* In Search of Our Mother's Garden.

> **READ ON** ▷

- ● *The Color Purple.*
- ▶ **To Walker's elegant, tart style:** ▷Mary McCarthy, *The Group;* ▷Muriel Spark, *The Girls of Slender Means.*
- ▶ **To her view of the bizarreness lurking inside perfectly ordinary-seeming human beings:** ▷John Irving, *The World According to Garp;* ▷Tove Jansson, *Sun City.*
- ▶ **To her politics:** ▷Lisa Alther, *Kinflicks;* Ralph Ellison, *Invisible Man.*

Lew **WALLACE**

BEN-HUR *(Christian and pagan antagonism in ancient Rome)*

Jeanette **WINTERSON, BOATING FOR BEGINNERS**
(Noah's flood)

Thomas **MANN, JOSEPH AND HIS BROTHERS**
(- seen as allegory of 1930s fascist Europe)

Joseph **HELLER, GOD KNOWS**
('memoirs' of King David)

BIBLE OLD TESTAMENT

THE FIRST CHRISTIANS

George **MOORE, THE BROOK KERITH**
(Joseph of Arimathea)

Pär **LAGERKVIST, BARABBAS**
(- before, during and after Christ's crucifixion)

Lloyd C. **DOUGLAS, THE ROBE**
(effects on Roman centurion and others who inherit Christ's robe at crucifixion)

Frank **SLAUGHTER, THE SHOES OF THE FISHERMAN**
(Peter)

Henryk **SIENKIEWYCZ, QUO VADIS?**
(first Christian converts, first martyrs)

Anthony **BURGESS, THE KINGDOM OF THE WICKED**
(missionary journeys of Paul, Luke and Barnabas)

Pasquale Festa **CAMPANILE, FOR LOVE, ONLY FOR LOVE** *(Joseph)*

Severia **HURÉ, I, MARY, DAUGHTER OF ISRAEL**
(Mary)

Robert **GRAVES, KING JESUS**
(fulfilment of all Old Testament prophecy)

Michèle **ROBERTS, THE WILD GIRL**
(Gospel according to Mary Magdalene)

JOSEPH, MARY AND JESUS

WALLACE, Lew • *(1827-1905)*
US novelist.

Ben-Hur (1880), the best-known of Wallace's historical romances, is set in Palestine in the reign of the Roman Emperor Nero. The Jewish aristocrat Judah Ben-Hur and the Roman general Messala, once friends, quarrel over politics. Messala falsely accuses Ben-Hur of treason; Ben-Hur's lands are confiscated, his wife and mother are thrown into prison (where they contract leprosy) and he himself is condemned to the galleys. He escapes, leads a resistance-movement against the Romans, wreaks vengeance on Messala during a chariot-race in the Coliseum (the book's action-climax), rescues his mother and wife and takes them to be healed by the preacher Jesus. They are converted to Christianity, and the book ends with a moving scene as they witness Christ's crucifixion. Wallace's Christianity is somewhat preachy, but his depiction of the grandeur and decadence of ancient Rome, of the resistance-movement in Palestine and of the fervour of early Christian converts is unsurpassed.

Wallace's other novels include The Fair God, *a novel of Cortez' invasion of Mexico, and* The Prince of India, *which culminates in a magnificent description of the Turkish siege of Constantinople in 1453. Wallace's* Autobiography *is almost as swaggering as his fiction, particularly about his time as a general during the American Civil War.*

WAR: BEHIND THE LINES

▷Noel Barber, *A Woman of Cairo*
▷Elizabeth Bowen, *The Heat of the Day*
  Elizabeth Darrell, *At the Going Down of the Sun*
▷Jaroslav Hašek, *The Good Soldier Švejk*
▷Ernest Hemingway, *A Farewell to Arms*
▷Thomas Keneally, *Schindler's Ark*
▷Neville Shute, *What Happened to the Corbetts*
▷Lev Tolstoy, *War and Peace*

Terrorists/Freedom Fighters (p 234); War: Front Line (p 254)

READ ON ⟩

▶ **To *Ben-Hur*:** Henryk Sienkiewycz, *Quo Vadis?*; Lord Lytton, *The Last Days of Pompeii*.
▶ **To Wallace's work in general:** ▷Walter Scott, *Ivanhoe*; ▷Victor Hugo, *Notre-Dame de Paris*.

WAR: FRONT LINE

▷Len Deighton, *Bomber*
Emma Drummond, *Forget the Glory*
William Fairchild, *The Poppy Factory*
▷Joseph Heller, *Catch-22*
▷Ernest Hemingway, *For Whom the Bell Tolls*
Alistair Maclean, *The Guns of Navarone*
▷Norman Mailer, *The Naked and the Dead*
Erich Maria Remarque, *All Quiet on the Western Front*

WAUGH, Evelyn • *(1903–66)*
British novelist.

Waugh's main work was a series of tart satires on 1930s attitudes and manners. His vacuous, amiable heroes stumble through life, unsurprised by anything that happens. By chance, they land in the centre of affairs (political, business and sexual) and their presence triggers a sequence of ever more ludicrous events. Innocence is their only saving grace: Waugh's views were that the world is silly but dangerous, and that those who think they understand it are the most vulnerable of all. He was particularly venomous about British high society, depicting the ruling class as a collection of alcohol-swilling Hooray Henries or Henriettas, whose chief pastimes are partying (if young) and interfering in public life (if old). That class apart, the range of his scorn was vast. *Decline and Fall* sends up (among other things) the English prep school system, *Black Mischief* mocks tyranny in an African state emerging from colonialism, *Scoop* satirises gutter journalism and *The Ordeal of Gilbert Pinfold* (1957) mercilessly details the hallucinations of an alcoholic author on a detestable ocean cruise. The second-world-war trilogy *Sword of Honour* (1965) sets Waugh's foolish heroes in the context of truly dangerous, genuinely lunatic real events, and *Brideshead Revisited* (1945) is a more serious book still, the study of an aristocratic Catholic family collapsing under the weight of centuries of unconsidered privilege.

A HANDFUL OF DUST • *(1934)*
The book begins with standard Waugh farce: a pin-headed society wife, Brenda Last, takes a lover to occupy her afternoons. But the effect on her husband Tony and son John is devastating, and the book moves quickly from

> READ ON

● *Scoop.*
▶ William Boyd, *A Good Man in Africa.*
▷Malcolm Bradbury, *Eating People is Wrong.* David Lodge, *How Far Can You Go?*
▷P.H. Newby, *The Picnic at Sakkara.*
▷John Updike, *The Coup.*

farce to tragedy. Waugh never abandons the ridiculous – no one else would have placed his hero in impenetrable tropical jungle, the slave of a megalomaniac who makes him read *Edwin Drood* aloud – but he also writes with compassion for his characters, involving us in their loneliness as his shallower novels never do.

Waugh's other novels are Vile Bodies, Put Out More Flags *and* The Loved One. *His travel-books include* Remote People *and* Waugh in Abyssinia. *His* Diaries *and his autobiography* A Little Learning *are a revealing blend of pity for himself and mercilessness to others.*

WEBSTER, Jan • *(born 1924)*
British novelist.

Webster writes family sagas, spanning many generations. Her best-known books are the sequence *Colliers Row*, *Saturday City* and *Beggarman's Country*, set in the Glasgow slums.

READ ON

▶ ▷Maisie Mosco, *Almonds and Raisins*. Helen Forrester, *Twopence to Cross the Mersey*. Sarah Shears, *Louise*.

WEDDINGS

Elizabeth Colegate, *Statues in a Garden*
▷Carson McCullers, *The Member of the Wedding*
Elizabeth North, *Worldly Goods*
▷Eudora Welty, *Delta Wedding*

WEEPIES

▷Charlotte Brontë, *Jane Eyre*
▷Daphne Du Maurier, *Rebecca*
▷Brenda Jagger, *A Song Twice Over*
▷Norah Lofts, *The Brittle Glass*
▷Margaret Mitchell, *Gone With the Wind*
▷Boris Pasternak, *Doctor Zhivago*
▷Erich Segal, *Love Story*
Mrs Henry Wood, *East Lynne*

WEIDMAN, Jerome • *(born 1913)*
US novelist.

The typical Weidman hero is a successful banker or businessman. Forced by some crisis to look back over the past, he recounts the story of his life and the influences which have made him what he is. Many of the men are Jewish, the sons of poor European immigrants in the early years of the century; the novels are warm-hearted, Dickensian stories of the struggle for existence in the sweatshops and back-streets of 1930s New York, and of young men rising, by brains, luck or adroitness – some of them are crooks – to the positions they hold today. Without exception, Weidman's characters are creations of the American dream – and every one of them feels compromised, as if material success has eroded the moral value-system which helped their parents in their first years in the USA, and which supported their own childhood and growing up.

OTHER PEOPLE'S MONEY • *(1967)*
In 1915, three-year-old Victor is made the foster-son of rich Walter Weld and his wife. Five years later another orphan, Philip Brandwine, joins the household. The novel recounts the boys' childhood, their young manhood, their service in the second world war – and their rivalry for the love of Harriet Weld, their foster-sister. Its subsidiary theme is the character-clash between the two men: Philip is charismatic, dazzling and untrustworthy, Victor is meticulous, earnest and unquestioningly loyal. Their relationship collapses during the second world war, only to be rebuilt afterwards, in the agonising reunion which starts and ends the book. Over everything hovers an enigma, unsolved until the book's last page: what was there about the boys that made the Welds take them as foster-sons in the first place?

Weidman's novels include I Can Get it for You Wholesale, Your Daughter Iris, The Enemy Camp, The Center of the Action, The Temple *and* A Family Fortune. *His short-story collections include* The Horse That Could Whistle Dixie, My Father Sits in the Dark *and* The Death of Dickie Draper. Praying for Rain *is autobiography.*

WELDON, Fay • *(born 1933)*
British novelist and screen-writer.

A TV dramatist, Weldon writes novels in short, screenplay-like scenes full of dialogue: her books are like sinis-

READ ON ▷

● *Fourth Street East* (and its sequels *Last Respects* and *Tiffany Street*).
▶ Budd Schulberg, *What Makes Sammy Run?*.
▷Mordecai Richler, *The Apprenticeship of Duddy Kravitz*. ▷Saul Bellow, *The Adventures of Augie March*. E.L. Doctorow, *World's Fair*. Louis Auchincloss, *Venus in Sparta*.

READ ON ▷

● *The Hearts and Lives of Men*.

ter sit-coms turned into prose. In the 1970s she was regarded as a leading feminist writer, and 'women's experience' is a major theme. Her heroines are ordinary people resisting the need to define themselves as someone else's wife, lover or mother, and missing the traditional cosiness such roles afford. Individuality can only be bought at the cost of psychic discomfort – and this is often intensified by the malice of others and by the hostility of the environment: witchcraft and the venomousness of nature add spice to Weldon's plots. Her books are fast, funny and furious; but their underlying ideas, especially for male chauvinist pigs, are no joke at all.

PUFFBALL • *(1980)*

Liffey, married to boring, ambitious Richard, longs to live in a country cottage; Richard wants a child. They strike a bargain, move to the wolds near Glastonbury and do their best to get Liffey pregnant. Almost at once the idyll turns to nightmare. The cottage has few facilities; there are no commuter-trains to London; their neighbour is a child-beater and an amateur witch. As the baby grows in Liffey's womb and Richard, alone in London for five days a week, consoles himself, Mabs (the neighbour) tries every trick of witchcraft, from potions to pin-stuck wax models, to make Liffey abort her child. *Puffball* is a romantic novel for grown-up people – and the games Weldon plays with our longing for a happy ending give the plot some of its most devastating, satisfying twists.

Weldon's other novels include Down Among the Women, Female Friends, The President's Child, Little Sisters, Praxis, Watching Me Watching You, The Life and Loves of a She-Devil, The Shrapnel Academy *and* The Heart of England. The Rules of Life *is an SF novella.*

WELLS, H.G. (Herbert George) •
(1866–1946)
British writer of novels, short stories and non-fiction.

Wells' early novels were science fantasies, imagining what it would be like if people could travel in time (*The Time Machine*, 1895) or space (*The First Men in the Moon*, 1901), or how the Earth might defend itself against extra-terrestrial attacks (*The War of the Worlds*, 1898). Like ▷Verne, Wells predicted many inventions and discoveries now taken for granted: in *The War in the Air* (1908) for example, he forecast fleets of warplanes and bombers in the days when the Wright brothers were still headline news. For all their scientific wonders, these novels are full of pessimism about society: wherever peo-

▶ ▷Margaret Atwood, *Life Before Man.* Marge Piercy, *The High Cost of Living.* Mary Gordon, *The Company of Women.* Penelope Mortimer, *Long Distance.* Alice Thomas Ellis, *Unexplained Laughter.* Maggie Gee, *Light Years.*

READ ON

▶ **To Wells' SF:** ▷Jules Verne, *Twenty Thousand Leagues Under the Sea*; C.S. Lewis, *Out of the Silent Planet*; H.P. Lovecraft, *The Shadow over Innsmouth.*
▶ **To his social comedies:** ▷Arnold Bennett, *The Card*; Hugh Walpole, *Mr*

ple go, they find barbarism, oppression and misery. *The Island of Doctor Moreau* (1896), about a mad scientist hybridising humans and animals on a lonely island, brings the pessimism nearer home. Side by side with such morbid fantasies, Wells wrote a series of utterly different books. They are genial social comedies, about ordinary people (shop-assistants, clerks) who decide that the way to find happiness is to break out and 'make a go of things'. Sometimes (as in *Ann Veronica*, about a 1910s girl determined on emancipation despite the wishes of her family) Wells' message is polemical; but most of the books – *Love and Mr Lewisham*, *Kipps*, *The History of Mr Polly* – replace propaganda with an indulgent, enthusiastic view of human enterprise.

TONO-BUNGAY • *(1909)*

George Ponderevo goes to live with his uncle Toby. He helps Toby market a marvellous new elixir, Tono-Bungay: it is the answer to the world's problems, the health, wealth and happiness of humankind in a bottle. The Tono-Bungay fortune swells by the minute – and then George discovers that the product is 99% distilled water. The discovery presents George with unresolvable moral dilemmas of all kinds. Does it matter what Tono-Bungay is made of, if it does what it claims to do? Is Toby a crook or does he genuinely believe he is benefiting humankind? How can George bankrupt those he loves – and in the process destroy his own chances of a happy marriage and a prosperous home? He puts off the decision, and in the meantime continues his hobby: pioneer aviation. In the end, technology – the lighter-than-air-machine itself – comes to the rescue: a charming example of Wells' view that all moral and social dilemmas can be solved by science.

Wells' other science-fantasies include When the Sleeper Wakes, The Food of the Gods *and the story-collections* Tales of Space and Time *and* The Country of the Blind and Other Stories. *His other novels include* Mr Blettsworthy on Rampole Island, *a savage anti-totalitarian satire.*

WELTY, Eudora • *(born 1909)*

US novelist and short-story writer.

Unlike such writers as ▷Faulkner or ▷McCullers, who saw the southern United States as a kind of hell tenanted by freaks and degenerates, Welty treated them as paradise. The countryside is lush; birds and animals teem; all nature is in harmony. Human beings are at the heart of the

Perrin and Mr Traill; ▷David Cook, *Missing Persons.*

> READ ON

● *Losing Battles* (more farcical, set not among cotton barons but in a sleepy, dim-witted farming-community, but idyll – and Welty shows them as uncomprehending innocents. The 'Negroes' – she is writing about times long gone – are children of nature, at peace with their environment. The 'White Folks', by contrast, feel edgy. They sense that they are corrupt, that their presence threatens Eden; but they have no idea what the matter is, and all they can do is live as they always have and hope that things will be all right, that nothing will change. The surface events in Welty's books are a mosaic of ordinariness – parties, children's games, chance meetings in town or at the bathing-station – but underlying them all is a sense of fragility, of impending loss. Her characters are living in a dream, comfortable and comforting, but it is only a dream, and already we, and they, sense the first chill of wakefulness.

DELTA WEDDING · *(1946)*

In the 1920s, nine-year-old Laura travels to her uncle's plantation in the Mississippi Delta, to help in preparations for her cousin's wedding. She revels in the eccentric, affectionate rough-and-tumble of cousins, great-aunts, visitors (and dozens of blacks, as friendly and unconsidered as household pets); she climbs trees, bakes cakes, guesses riddles, listens to gossip as the wedding-dress is sewn. Welty also shows the preparations through the eyes of the bride's parents, the bride and groom themselves, and an assortment of servants, friends and neighbours. The wedding brings a whole community into focus – and we are shown, with persistent, gentle irony, that it is not just the bride and groom who must undergo a rite of passage, but the South itself.

Welty's other novels are The Robber Bridegroom, The Ponder Heart, The Optimist's Daughter *and* Losing Battles. *Her short stories are collected in* A Curtain of Green, The Wide Net, The Golden Apples *and* The Bride of Innisfallen.

WEST, Morris · *(born 1916)*
Australian novelist.

West's books are fast-moving moral thrillers, stories not of espionage or crime but of the solution of ethical dilemmas. The hero of *The Shoes of the Fisherman* is a saintly iron-curtain prelate who is elected Pope. *The Clowns of God* is about another Pope forced to abdicate because he has seen a vision predicting the imminent end of the world, and proposes to publicise the fact. In *The Navigator* (1981) a group of people sails to find the Polynesian

with the same undertone of devastating moral condemnation).
▶ ▷Randall Jarrell, *Pictures from an Institution*. ▷L.P. Hartley, *The Go-Between*. ▷Colette, *The Ripening Seed*. ▷Evelyn Waugh, *Brideshead Revisited*. Robert Penn Warren, *All the King's Men*. Lillian Hellman, *Pentimento*.

READ ON >

● *The Devil's Advocate*.
▶ ▷Jerome Weidman, *The Temple*. Frank Slaughter, *Epidemic*. ▷Neville Shute, *Requiem for a Wren*. ▷C.P. Snow, *The Sleep of Reason*. ▷Thomas Keneally,

paradise to which all human souls, the myth says, go after death; they are led by a man who is either a visionary, a charlatan or mad. *The Ambassador* (1965) is about a conscientious US ambassador who resigns over his country's policy in South Vietnam. Moral dilemmas like these are nowadays more common in films than in novels – and anyone who enjoyed *Platoon*, say, or *The Killing Fields* will find the experience of West's novels much the same.

Three Cheers for the Paraclete. Brian Moore, *The Colour of Blood*.

THE WORLD IS MADE OF GLASS · *(1983)*

In Vienna in 1913, the psychiatrist Jung treats a woman who regards him more as a confessor than a healer – and the experience brings him hard up against his sense of his own moral failure, both as a doctor and as a man.

West's other novels include Children of the Sun, The Devil's Advocate, Daughter of Silence, The Tower of Babel, Summer of the Red Wolf, The Salamander *and* Harlequin.

WEST, Nathanael · *(1906–40)*
US novelist and screenwriter.

West wrote rubbishy films for a living: their titles include *Rhythm in the Clouds, Born to be Wild* and *Hallelujah I'm a Bum*. To please himself, he wrote four satirical novels, dark black comedies a million miles from Hollywood. The hero of *Miss Lonelyhearts* (1933) is a cynical newspaperman assigned to the agony column. He begins by despising the wretches who write for advice, but soon begins to pity them and finally leaves his desk to intervene in one case personally, with fatal but farcical results.

West's other novels are The Dream Life of Balso Snell, A Cool Million *and* The Day of the Locust.

> **READ ON**

● *The Day of the Locust* (a bleakly funny send-up of Hollywood).
▶ Joe Orton, *Head to Toe*. Budd Schulberg, *What Makes Sammy Run?*. ▷Aldous Huxley, *After Many a Summer*. ▷Mordecai Richler, *Cocksure*. Thorne Smith, *The Bishop's Jaegers*.

WHARTON, Edith · *(1862–1937)*
US writer of novels, short stories and non-fiction.

A society hostess, Wharton caused outrage by writing with ironical rage about the complacency and shallowness of her own class. (She later described high society as 'frivolous…, able to acquire dramatic significance only through what its frivolity destroys'.) In 1907 she moved to Europe and broadened her scope, writing two Hardyesque rural tragedies (*Ethan Frome, Summer*), several books set in Europe (including *The Reef*, which her friend ▷Henry James admired) and some atmospheric ghost stories. But she regularly returned to her favourite theme, the stifling

> **READ ON**

● *The Custom of the Country*.
▶ Ellen Glasgow, *Barren Ground*. Louis Auchincloss, *A World of Profit*. ▷George Eliot, *Middlemarch*. ▷William Thackeray, *Vanity Fair*. ▷Elizabeth Taylor, *The Wedding*

Edith WHARTON

THE HOUSE OF MIRTH *(woman rebels against 1900s New York high society)*

Thomas **HARDY, FAR FROM THE MADDING CROWD**
(tragic life and love in 19th-century rural England)

William **THACKERAY, VANITY FAIR**
(two girls' ambitions to conquer 1810s English high society)

'PLAYTHINGS OF DESTINY'

Theodore **DREISER, AN AMERICAN TRAGEDY**
(ambition, crime and punishment in lower-class 1920s New York)

Nathaniel **HAWTHORNE, THE HOUSE OF THE SEVEN GABLES** *(New England family cursed for generations because of religious intolerance)*

Gustave **FLAUBERT, MADAME BOVARY**
(mid-19th-century small-town France)

Margaret **ATWOOD, THE HANDMAID'S TALE**
(21st-century fundamentalist Republic of Gilead)

STIFLING COMMUNITIES

Olivia **MANNING, THE RAIN FOREST**
(retreat for psychological misfits on island 'paradise')

Alison **LURIE, THE WAR BETWEEN THE TATES**
('progressive' US university)

Emily **BRONTË, WUTHERING HEIGHTS**
(1800s Yorkshire: a woman loves brutal, 'child-of-nature' foster-brother)

Helen **WADDELL, HÉLOISE AND ABELARD**
(12th-century Paris: a monk falls in love with beautiful pupil)

AGAINST THE ODDS

Victor **HUGO, NOTRE DAME DE PARIS**
(14th-century Paris: hunchback tries to protect beautiful gipsy from men who would debauch her)

Hermann **HESSE, GERTRUD**
(1890s German university: two students, friends, love the same woman)

Anthony **TROLLOPE, DOCTOR THORNE**
(snobbery, illegitimacy and inheritance among 19th-century English landed gentry)

Sinclair **LEWIS, BABBITT**
(wealthy, morally empty merchant tries to break free of sterile small-town conformity)

PRESSURE TO CONFORM

Angus **WILSON, LATE CALL**
(widow lives with uncongenial son in soulless 1960s British 'new town')

John **UPDIKE, RABBIT, RUN**
(ex-high-school sports star tries to adjust to adult mediocrity)

conventions of 1870s-1920s New York high life – and it is
on this that her reputation rests. Her enemies put her down
as a clumsy imitator of James. But whereas he showed his
characters' psychological innerness, she was interested in
manners, in events. She also wrote shorter, wittier sentences, and crisper dialogue. Except that her subject-matter is so sombre, she is more like Oscar Wilde than
James.

THE HOUSE OF MIRTH • *(1905)*

Lily Bart, a beautiful, sharp-witted girl, has been conditioned to luxury from birth. Unfortunately she is an orphan, living on a small allowance. She gambles at cards,
loses, and because of her moral scruples (she refuses to
work off her debts by becoming the mistress of a wealthy
creditor), she ends up poorer and more desperate than
ever. Faced with the choice of marrying either a rich man
she despises (not least because he is a Jew, something her
WASPish upbringing has taught her to abhor) or the penniless man she loves, she chooses neither – and soon afterwards, as the result of scandalous accusation, loses her
position in society. She moves into cheap lodgings and
sinks into despair. She has achieved moral integrity, broken free of her upbringing, but in the process, because of
that upbringing, she has destroyed herself.

Wharton's other New York books include the novels The
Custom of the Country, The Age of Innocence *and* Old
New York, *and the short-story collections* The Descent of
Man, Xingu, Certain People *and* Human Nature. Ghosts
contains ghost-stories, and A Backward Glance *is autobi-
ography, interesting on her friendship with Henry James.*

WHITE, Antonia • *(1899-1979)*
British novelist.

A journalist and translator (notably of ▷Colette), White is
remembered for four deeply-felt autobiographical novels.
Frost in May (1933) is the story of a child at a grim convent boarding school. The nuns' mission is to 'break' each
pupil like a horse – to tame her for Christ – and the book
remorselessly charts the series of small emotional humiliations they inflict on the heroine, which have entirely the
opposite effect to the one they planned. In the later novels
White's heroine works as an actress (*The Lost Traveller*,
1950), tries to combine serious writing with work as a
copy-writer (*The Sugar House*, 1952), and finally (*Beyond
the Glass*, 1954), in the course of a terrifying mental illness, exorcises the ghosts of Catholicism and her relationship with her father, the influences which have both de-

Group. Mary Wesley,
Not That Sort of Girl.

> READ ON

▶ **To *Frost in May*:**
▷James Joyce,
*Portrait of the Artist as
a Young Man*; Jane
Gardam, *Bilgewater*;
▷Thomas Keneally,
*Three Cheers for the
Paraclete.*

▶ **To *Beyond the Glass*:**
Sylvia Plath, *The Bell
Jar.*

▶ **To White's work in
general:** ▷Rosamond
Lehmann, *Dusty
Answer*; ▷Rose

fined and deformed her life.

White's other books include the short-story collection Strangers, *and* The Hound and the Falcon, *an account in letter-form of her return to Catholicism.*

WHITE, Patrick • *(born 1912)*
Australian novelist and playwright.

White was interested in Nietzsche's idea of 'superbeings', people endowed with qualities or abilities which set them apart from the rest of the human race. But White's characters are cursed, not blessed, by difference: their chief attribute is a cantankerous individuality which makes it impossible for them to adjust to society or it to them. In some books (eg *Riders in the Chariot*, about anti-semitism, or *The Vivisector*, about a convention-defying painter) the 'enemy' is the stifling gentility of lower-middle-class Sydney suburbanites. In others (eg *The Tree of Man*, about a young farmer in the 1900s, or *A Fringe of Leaves*, 1976, see below), the battle is more symbolic, against the wilderness itself. But wherever conflict takes place, it is of epic proportions: White's craggy prose puts him in the company of such past writers as ▷Melville or ▷Conrad, and in the 20th century only ▷Golding equals his blend of fast-paced story-telling and brooding philosophical allegory.

VOSS • *(1957)*
In 1857, financed by a group of Sydney businessmen, a group of explorers sets out to cross Australia. The expedition is led by the German visionary Voss: physically awkward, ill-at-ease in towns and houses, speaking a tortured, poetic English which sounds as if he learned it by rote, phrase by painful phrase. The other members include an ex-convict and a dreamy aboriginal boy, Jackie, torn between the white people's culture and his own. White balances reports of the expedition's struggle against the desert and to understand one another with accounts of the life of Laura Trevelyan, a young woman fascinated by Voss (at first as a larger-than-life character, an epic personality, and then as a vulnerable human being) as she waits in Sydney, like a medium hoping for spirit-messages, for news of him.

White's other novels are Happy Valley, The Living and the Dead, The Aunt's Story *(a comedy about an indomitable spinster travelling alone),* The Solid Mandala, The Eye of the Storm *and* The Twyborn Affair. The Burnt Ones *and* The Cockatoos *are collections of short stories.*

Macaulay, *The World My Wilderness.*

> READ ON

● *A Fringe of Leaves* (about a woman shipwrecked in Queensland in the 1840s, who is captured by aborigines and brought to terms not only with an alien culture but with her feelings about the 'civilisation' she knew before).
▶ **To *Voss*:** ▷William Golding, *Darkness Visible*; ▷H.H. Richardson, *The Fortunes of Richard Mahony*; Paul Bowles, *The Sheltering Sky*; ▷Joseph Conrad, *The Nigger of the Narcissus.*
▶ **To *A Fringe of Leaves*:** ▷D.H. Lawrence, *The Plumed Serpent*; ▷Katharine Susannah Prichard, *Coonardoo.*
▶ **To White's work in general:** ▷Christina Stead, *The Man Who Loved Children*; Joyce Cary, *The Horse's Mouth*; ▷Elizabeth Taylor, *Blaming.*

Flaws in the Glass is an autobiography, good on White's own battles against the wilderness (he was an outback farmer) and against convention (he is homosexual).

WILDER, Thornton • *(1897–1975)*
US novelist and playwright.

Wilder is known for plays as well as novels: *The Matchmaker* (source of the musical *Hello, Dolly*), *Our Town*, *The Skin of Our Teeth* and many others. His works explore an idea he called 'simultaneity'. Time is not progressive but circular, our destinies move in cycles, and when people's cycles coincide (like the overlapping Olympic rings), that is the moment of simultaneity, of crisis, in all their lives. In his best-known novel, *The Bridge of San Luis Rey* (1927), the moment of simultaneity is the collapse of a bridge in 18th-century Peru; the book tells the lives of each of the five people killed in the disaster, reaching a climax at the exact instant when the bridge falls in.

THE IDES OF MARCH • *(1948)*
This historical novel charts, in a series of imaginary letters, the converging destinies of a group of people in ancient Rome; it ends on the morning of the Ides of March, 44 BC, as Julius Caesar leaves for the senate-house where (history tells us) he was due to be assassinated. The letter-writers are Caesar himself, Brutus, Cassius, Mark Antony, the poet Catullus, the dissolute aristocrats Clodius and Clodia (symptomatic of the decadent old ruling families Caesar was hoping to replace), and Wilder's purpose is to show how, given those people and circumstances, Caesar's death and the ensuing civil war were inevitable.

Wilder's other novels are The Cabala, The Woman of Andros, Heaven's My Destination, The Eighth Day *and* Theophilus North.

WILSON, Angus • *(born 1913)*
British novelist and short-story writer.

Wilson is a nuclear-age successor to the great Victorian novelists. His plots are expansive, his pages teem with characters and his style is pungently satirical. His middle-class heroes and heroines, often members of the professions, have large, quarrelsome families; adultery, homosexuality, shady dealing and the conflict between public

---

> **READ ON** ▷

● *The Bridge of San Luis Rey.*
▶ **To *The Ides of March*:** Marguerite Yourcenar, *Memoirs of Hadrian*; John Arden, *Silence Among the Weapons*; ▷Mary Renault, *The Last of the Wine*; Hilda Doolittle ('H.D.'), *Hedylus*.
▶ **Other books, of different periods and on different themes, but all concerned with our perception of time:** ▷James Joyce, *Ulysses*; ▷Lawrence Durrell, *Tunc* and *Numquam*; ▷Salman Rushdie, *Midnight's Children*.
▶ **To Wilder's work in general:** ▷Günter Grass, *The Flounder*; Osbert Sitwell, short stories.

> **READ ON** ▷

● *As If By Magic.*
▶ **To Wilson's novels:** ▷Iris Murdoch, *The Sandcastle*; ▷Willa Cather, *The Professor's House*;

and private duty shape their lives. The 'public' plot of *Hemlock and After* (1952) is about a novelist trying to establish a writers' centre in a large, old house; the 'private' plot concerns his anguish about his own homosexuality. *The Old Men at the Zoo* (1961) is a satire set in a future Britain threatened by a united Europe and defeated by its own penchant for replacing action with committee rhetoric. The heroine of *The Middle Age of Mrs Eliot* (1958), unexpectedly widowed, throws off the home-counties mask and embarks on a raffish odyssey across the world, a quest to find herself. In *Late Call* (1964) another lower-middle-class matron, forced to live with her widowed, unloved son, has to come to terms with the soulless New Town he lives in, a reflection both of his own inner desolation and of the emotional wasteland between them where once was love. *Setting the World on Fire* (1980) is a study of the lives and relationships of two brothers, one a finicky lawyer, the other an artist (an experimental theatre director). As well as his novels, Wilson's short stories are much admired. They are sharp anecdotes of emotional ineptness, often involving the clash between middle-aged parents and their children or between ill-matched lovers.

ANGLO-SAXON ATTITUDES • *(1956)*
Gerald Middleton is a rich, successful academic (a historian of Anglo-Saxon England). His personal life is a shambles: he lives apart from his wife, dislikes his children and grandchildren, squabbles with his colleagues and has lost touch with his friends. Faced with the need to accept or reject an important academic task, he begins to think again about the greatest, and oddest, archaeological discovery of his youth 50 years before: an obscene pagan statue in the tomb of a 7th-century Christian missionary. Was it a hoax – and if so, if this is yet another lie on which he has built his life, what can he do now to set things right?

Wilson's other novels are No Laughing Matter *and* As If By Magic. The Wrong Set, Such Darling Dodos *and* A Bit Off the Map *are collections of short stories.*

WODEHOUSE, P.G. (Pelham Grenville) •
(1881–1975)
British novelist.

In the 1920s and 1930s Wodehouse wrote Broadway shows, and he once described his novels as 'musical comedy without the music'. There are over 100 of them, gloriously frivolous romps set in high society 1920s England

Peter Taylor, *A Summons to Memphis.*
▶ **To the short stories:**
V.S. Pritchett, *The Camberwell Beauty*; Mary Gordon, *Temporary Shelter.*

> **READ ON**

● *Summer Lightning.*
▶ Ben Travers, *Rookery Nook* (novel version).
Richard Gordon,

or among dyspeptic US newspaper magnates and film tycoons. Wodehouse's gormless heroes are in love with 'pips' and 'peacherinos'. Before they can marry they must persuade dragon-like relatives (usully aunts) to give reluctant consent or to part with cash – and the persuasion often involves stealing valuable jewels (to earn undying gratitude when they are 'found' again), smuggling the girl into the house disguised (so that the radiance of her personality will charm all opposition) or blackmail (threatening to reveal embarrassing secrets of the relative's misspent youth). There are two main novel-series, the Jeeves books (in which Bertie Wooster consistently makes an ass of himself, usually by being the fall-guy in Jeeves' machiavellian schemes), and the Blandings books (in which Lord Emsworth's prize pig bulks large). Other books tell of the multifarious members of the Mulliner family and the Drones Club, of golfers, cricketers and incompetent crooks; in all of them the season is high summer, every cloud is lined with silver, and happy endings are distributed 'in heaping handfuls' (to quote Wodehouse's own immortal phrase).

LEAVE IT TO PSMITH • *(1923)*
Before Eve Halliday will marry him, Freddie Threepwood needs £1000 to start a bookmaker's business. He goes to Blandings Castle to ask his father Lord Emsworth. But Lord Emsworth has no access to his own fortune: that route is guarded by Lady Constance Keeble and her sidekick the Efficient Baxter. The plot spirals to include poets who are not everything they seem, stolen jewels, a purloined pig – and above all the machinations of the endlessly, irritatingly good-humoured Psmith.

Wodehouse's Blandings books include Galahad at Blandings, Heavy Weather, Pigs Have Wings *and* Uncle Fred in the Springtime. *His Jeeves books include* Joy in the Morning, The Inimitable Jeeves, Jeeves in the Offing *and* The Code of the Woosters. *His other novels include* Money in the Bank, Uncle Dynamite, The Luck of the Bodkins *and* Quick Service. The Man Upstairs, The Clicking of Cuthbert, Eggs and Crumpets *and* Meet Mr Mulliner *are short-story collections, and* Performing Flea *is autobiography.*

WOLFE, Thomas • *(1900–38)*
US novelist.

Wolfe's life's work was an incoherent, multi-million-word torrent of autobiographical prose, an attempt to make epic

Doctor in the House. Patrick Dennis, *Auntie Mame.* The same kind of gormless farce, transplanted to California, updated to the 1980s and set among incompetent crooks and gangsters is in Donald Westlake's Dortmunder books, eg *Bank Shot* or *Who Stole Sassi Manoon?*.

> **READ ON** >

▶ ▷John O'Hara, *From the Terrace.*

fiction of ordinary US life. His models were ▷Homer, Shakespeare and ▷Dickens – and his work is every bit as grand as that suggests. He and his publishers organised some of the material into two long novels, telling the story of Eugene Gant, a young Carolina writer, from boyhood to first success. The first and most accessible book, *Look Homeward, Angel* (1929), tells of Eugene's childhood as the youngest member of a sprawling, bickering slum family, of his awakening to culture and of his heart-breaking realisation that to 'follow art' he must abandon his family and everything it stands for and chop off his own roots. *Of Time and the River* (1935) continues the story, following Eugene through college and to Paris, charting his artistic friendships, his learning about sex and love, and his first attempts at writing. After Wolfe's death two other novels, *The Web and the Rock* and *You Can't Go Home Again*, were assembled from his manuscripts. They follow another writer, George Weber – an adult version of Eugene Gant – through marriage, divorce, disillusion with the USA and hostility to European fascism in the 1930s.

▷Lawrence Durrell, *The Black Book*. ▷H.H. Richardson, *The Fortunes of Richard Mahony*. James Jones, *From Here to Eternity*.

WOOLF, Virginia • *(1882-1941)*
British novelist and non-fiction writer.

As well as novels, Woolf published two dozen non-fiction books: biographies (one of Flush, Elizabeth Barrett Browning's pet dog), diaries, essays on feminism and on literature. She was fascinated by psychology, and her nine novels set out to show, in prose, the workings of the subconscious mind. Instead of narrating strings of events she lets her characters run on in a 'stream-of-consciousness' style which gradually builds a clear picture of their personalities. She developed the technique from Freud's case-histories, but her characters are not psychologically damaged, as Freud's patients were: she tells us the jumble of thoughts and memories in ordinary men and women, and she is particularly good at showing moments of radiant inner happiness. *Mrs Dalloway* (1925), the interior monologue of a middle-class woman preparing to give a dinner-party, reveals her feelings about herself and her past as well as the urgent claims of the coming evening. In *To the Lighthouse* (1927) a group of adults and children is shown on a summer holiday – the trip to the lighthouse is a promised birthday treat for one of the children – and then in the same place ten years later, when the trip is finally made. Despite war and death in the intervening years, the influence of the dead mother is as strong as in her lifetime. *The Waves* (1931), Woolf's most complex book, traces six people's reactions to experience from childhood to maturity, showing how apparently small 'real' past

READ ON ▷

▶ ▷Marcel Proust, *Swann's Way* (the first part of *Remembrance of Things Past)*. ▷Jean Rhys, *Good Morning, Midnight*. D.M. Thomas, *The White Hotel*. Dorothy Richardson, *Pilgrimage*. Anaïs Nin, *Seduction of the Minotaur*. ▷Margaret Atwood, *Surfacing*. Gertrude Stein, *Three Lives*. ▷Iris Murdoch, *The Sea, the Sea*.

events continue to affect the personality as waves shape and reshape the shore.

Woolf's other novels are The Voyage Out, Night and Day, Jacob's Room, Orlando, The Years *and* Between the Acts. Haunted House *and* Mrs Dalloway's Party *are collections of short stories.*

WOUK, Herman • *(born 1915)*
US novelist and playwright.

Wouk's best-known novel, *The Caine Mutiny* (1951), is a tense study of life on a second-world-war US mine-sweeper whose crew judge the captain unfit for command. Its culminating sequence, a court-martial of the mutineers during which the captain is tricked into revealing his paranoia, was made into a hit Broadway play and a Humphrey Bogart film – and the book itself inspired a score of other novels, films and plays about the craziness not only of war but of the hierarchies of command: they range from the James Cagney/Henry Fonda film comedy *Mr Roberts* to ▷Heller's novel *Catch-22*. Wouk himself wrote two other powerful second-world-war books, *The Winds of War* and *War and Remembrance*. His other novels, several made into blockbuster films, include *Marjorie Morningstar* (1955, the story of a young woman who goes to New York to make her way in show-business and who finds romance instead), *Youngblood Hawke* (1962, a tragic-comic satire about a genius-novelist – based on ▷Thomas Wolfe – who is corrupted as soon as he begins meeting agents, publishers and publicists), and *The City Boy* (1948, a wisecracking story about a poor but cheerful New York Jewish family during the Depression).

WYNDHAM, John • *(1903–69)*
British novelist and short-story writer.

Wyndham's novels are less SF than thrillers, set on Earth, with SF overtones: he called them 'logical fantasies'. In

READ ON ▷

▶ **To *The Caine Mutiny*:** Erich Maria Remarque, *All Quiet on the Western Front* (set before, during and after the first world war); Nicholas Monsarrat, *The Cruel Sea* (a powerful thriller about British anti-submarine warfare in the second world war); Pierre Boulle, *The Bridge Over the River Kwai* (set in a Japanese labour camp in Burma during the second world war); ▷Norman Mailer, *The Naked and the Dead* (set in a US training camp during the second world war).
▶ **To *Marjorie Morningstar*:** ▷Willa Cather, *The Song of the Lark.*
▶ **To *The City Boy*:** ▷Jerome Weidman, *Fourth Street East*; ▷Mordecai Richler, *The Apprenticeship of Duddy Kravitz.*

READ ON ▷

▶ Bob Shaw, *Night Walk.*

The Midwich Cuckoos (1957) an alien race seeks to colonise Earth not by force of arms but by fertilising women – and the story begins, in the quiet English countryside (a favourite Wyndham location), as the half-alien children approach puberty. In *Chocky* (1968) a small boy has an invisible confidant – not a figment of his imagination, but a being from outer space. *The Day of the Triffids* (1951) begins with two simultaneous disasters, the sudden blinding of all human beings and the growth of enormous, mobile, predatory plants; the novel concerns the hero's attempts to organise resistance and save the human race.

Wyndham's other novels include The Chrysalids, The Kraken Wakes *and* Trouble With Lichen. *His short stories are collected in* The Seeds of Time, Consider Her Ways *and* Web.

▷James Herbert, *The Magic Cottage*. ▷H.G. Wells, *The Time Machine*.

Y

YERBY, Frank • *(born 1916)*
US novelist.

Yerby's early books, serious novels about racism, were published in the second world war, and found few readers. In 1945 he changed his style, began to write historical romances – and became one of the best-selling authors of the century. Superficially his books are straightforward 'bodice-rippers', passion-and-crinoline melodramas set in the American Deep South. But his persistent underlying theme is the equality of all people, white or black, and this gives his work an edge unusual in romance. In the 1960s he broadened his scope, writing books set in ancient Greece, Biblical Palestine, Victorian England and present-day Washington, D.C.

Yerby's romances include The Foxes of Harrow, The Golden Hawk, Floodtide, A Woman Called Fancy, The Devil's Laughter, Bride of Liberty, Griffin's Way *and* A Darkness at Ingraham's Crest. *His other novels include* The Saracen Blade, The Serpent and the Staff, Goat Song, Judas My Brother *and* Hail the Conquering Hero.

READ ON ▷

► **To the romances:**
▷Margaret Mitchell, *Gone With the Wind*; Kathleen Winsor, *Forever Amber*; Colleen McCullough, *The Thorn Birds*.
► **To Yerby's other books:** Lloyd C. Douglas, *The Big Fisherman*; ▷John Galsworthy, *The Man of Property*; Allen Drury, *A Shade of Difference*.

Z

ZOLA, Émile • *(1840-1902)*
French novelist and non-fiction writer.

Zola won scandalous fame at 27 with his novel *Thérèse Raquin*, about a pair of lovers who murder the woman's husband. The book's financial success let him take up fiction full-time, and he began a 20-novel series designed to show – in a scientific way, he claimed, as species are described – every aspect of late 19th-century French life. Although each novel is self-contained, their main characters are all members of the two families which give the series its name, *The Rougons and the Macquarts*. Zola's scheme echoed ▷Balzac's in *The Human Comedy*, and like Balzac he was interested in exact description, what he called 'naturalism'. But his morbid and pessimistic nature led him to concentrate on the harsher aspects of human existence, so that his characters often seem less like real human beings than the people dragged into sermons to illustrate the effects of drink, lust or poverty. Outside France, Zola's best-known books are *Germinal* (1885, about conditions in the coal-mines, and including a strike and a major accident), *Earth* (La Terre) (1887, about subsistence farming), *The Belly of Paris* (Le ventre de Paris) (1873, about the food-markets of the city), *The Boozer* (L'assommoir) (1871) and *For Women's Delight* (1883, about the staff and customers of a department store).

NANA • *(1880)*
The subject is sex. Nana's mother was a country girl who went to Paris to seek her fortune, became a laundress but was destroyed by drink – this is the story of *The Boozer*. Nana grows up as a street-urchin, and later becomes an actress and singer. She is beautiful but corrupt, morally brutalised by her childhood. She sets out systematically to destroy men: Zola thinks of her first as one of the Sirens

> ### READ ON
>
> ● *Thérèse Raquin.*
> ▶ ▷Somerset Maugham, *Liza of Lambeth.* Theodore Fontane, *Effi Briest.* Frank Norris, *The Pit.* Theodore Dreiser, *An American Tragedy.* ▷John Steinbeck, *The Grapes of Wrath.* George Gissing, *New Grub Street.*

in myth, drawing men irresistibly to her by the beauty of her voice, and then as a spider, preying on them even as she mates with them. He pities neither Nana nor her victims: like his other novels, this panorama of big-city life is painted entirely in shades of black.

Other books in the series include The Human Beast *(La* bête humaine*) (about the gangs of navvies who built railroads),* Money *(set among financiers) and* The Downfall *(La débâcle) (a devastating picture of the 1870 Commune and siege of Paris, which Zola saw as a cleansing operation, ridding the city of the corruption which had led to the misery described in his other books). In his last years he finished the first three books of another series,* The Four Gospels*: their titles are* Fertility, Work *and* Truth.

INDEX

Bold   type   indicates   main   entries.

A

Aaron's Rod   146
Abbess of Castro, The   228
Abbess of Crewe, The   177, 207, 225
Absalom, Absalom!   75
Absence of a Cello, The   119
Absent Without Leave   25
Academic Question, An   199
Academic Year   132, 168
Acceptance World, The   194
According to Mark   27
Achebe, Chinua   **1**, 27, 52, 94, 140–1, 192, 211
Achilles His Armour   9, 98–99
Acker, Kathy   37, 123
Ackroyd, Peter   27
Acquainted with the Night   25
Across the River and Into the Trees   112
Act of Passion   63, 220
Act of Will   30
Acts of King Arthur and his Noble Knights, The 228
Ada   47, 72, 177
Adam Bede   71, 104
Adam, One Afternoon   36
Adams, Alice   130
Adams, Douglas   **2**, 12
Adams, Richard   10, 153
Adamson, Grant   84
Advancement of Learning, An   119
Adventurers, The   87
Adventures of Augie March, The   20, 60–61, 76, 206, 256
Adventures of Cuffy Mahony, The   205
Adventures of Huckleberry Finn, The   55, 60–61, 238–9, 243
Adventures of Sherlock Holmes, The   65, 191
Adventures of Tom Bombadil, The   237
Adventures of Tom Sawyer, The   42, 85, 243
Advertisements for Myself   160
Aeneid   121
Aerodrome, The   138
Affair, The   66, 224
African Queen, The   80

African Stories   151
After Leaving Mr Mackenzie   204, 226
After Many a Summer   125, 260
Afternoon Men   77, 126, 193
After the War   201
Against Nature   89, 197
Agee, James   119
Agents and Patients   194
Age of Innocence, The   43, 48, 106, 262
Age of Reason, The   214
Agnes Grey   32
Agnon, S.Y.   221
Agony and the Ecstasy, The   11, 202
Aiken, Joan   15, 116–7
Ainsworth, Harrison   215
Airport   103
Airs Above the Ground   10, 230
Albatross, The   120
Albert's Bridge   50
Aldington, Richard   80, 152
Aldiss, Brian   **4**, 24, 112, 250
Aleph, The   28
Alexandria Quartet, The   43, **68**, 69, 136–7
Alice In Wonderland   74
Alien Heat, An   171
Allan, Becky   3
Allan Quatermaine   103
Allbeury, Ted   3, **5**, 83, 147
Allen, Charlotte Vale   227
Allen, Woody   28
Allende, Isabel   **5**, 72, 94, 163, 175, 211, 248
Allingham, Margery   **5**, 11, 43, 131, 164, 197
All On a Summer's Day   85
All Quiet on the Western Front   110–111, 254, 268
All That Swagger   85
All the King's Men   259
Almonds and Raisins   73, 173, 255
Alms for Oblivion   194
Along the Arno   52
Alpha List, The   5
Alteration, The   9, 207, 249
Alther, Lisa   **6**, 57, 60–61, 101, 134, 251
Amado, Jorge   192
Ambassador, The   82, 260
Ambassadors, The   82, 130

Ambitions 30
Ambler, Eric **7**, 47, 147
Amelia 76
Amen Corner, The 17
America 91, 138, 139, 156–7
American Baby, The 172
American Dream, An 160, 169
American Notes 59
American Tragedy, An 18, 271
Ames, Delano 44–45, 47
Amis, Kingsley **8**, 26, 27, 58, 82, 132, 156–7,
    183, 207, 249
Amis, Martin 35, 58, 77, 125, 177, 240
Amos Barton 43
An Artist of the Floating World 179
An Astrologer's Day 180
Anatomy Lesson, The 209
Ancestral Vices 166, 217
Ancient Evenings 98–99, 159, **160**, 186
And All the Stars a Stage 24
Anderson, Sherwood 21, 174, 182, 246
And Gazelles Leaping 179
Andrews, Virginia **10**
Andrzeyewski, Jerzy 234
And Where Were You, Adam? 25
Angelou, Maya 17
Angel Pavement 21, 60–61, 196
Angels at the Ritz 233
Anglo-Saxon Attitudes 59, 190, **265**
Animal Family, The 132
Animal Farm 184, 192, 211
Animal-lover's Book of Beastly Murder, The
    119
An Insular Possession 82
Anna Karenina 187, 237, 240
Anna of the Five Towns 21
Anne of Austria 10
Annerton Pit 62
Ann Lee's 29
Ann Veronica 21, 258
Another Country 16
Another Death in Venice 119
Anthills of the Savannah 2, 27, 192, 211
Anthony, Evelyn **10**
Anthony, Piers **10**, 70, 167, 220, 236
Antic Hay 125, 152
Anti-Death League, The 9
Antiphon, The 19
Antrobus Complete 69, 235
An Unofficial Rose 175
Any God Will Do **48**, 159
Anywhen 24
Ape and Essence 124, 125
Apes of God, The 152, 197
Appleby on Ararat 127
Apple Tree, The 67
Appletree Saga, The 122
Appointment with Yesterday 118
Apprenticeship of Duddy Kravitz, The 43,
    60–61, 206, 256, 268
Apprenticeship of Wilhelm Meister, The 60–61,
    90, 101, 160, 238–9

April, June and November 146, **201**
April's Grave 122
Apuleius 76
Arabesques 91, 221
Arabian Nightmare, The 150, 189
Arabian Nights, The 19, 103, 200
Archer, Jeffrey **11**, 84
Arden, John 27, 98–99, 202, 264
Are You Listening, Rabbi Löw? 63
Arigato 49
Aristos, The 84
Armance 228
Armstrong, Thomas 173
Arrow of God 1
Arrowsmith 151
Artamonov Affair, The 95
Artist Among the Missing 162
Artist of the Floating World, An 27, 79, 114,
    129
Art of Living and Other Stories, The 35
As A Man Grows Older 231
Ashes and Diamonds 234
As If By Magic 264, 265
As I Lay Dying 75
Asimov, Isaac 4, **11**, 23, 74, 108, 191
As I Walked Out One Midsummer Morning 243
Aspects of Love 47
Asturias, Miguel 211
At Lady Molly's 194
Atlantis 195
At Mrs Lippincote's 233
Atrocity Exhibition, The 18
At Swim-Two-Birds 63, 135, 229, 261
Attachments 208
At the Going Down of the Sun 253
At the Jerusalem 50, 169
Atwood, Margaret **12**, 20, 27, 34, 37, 65, 86,
    203, 207, 257, 261, 267, 272
Auchincloss, Louis 241, 256, 260
Auel, Jean M. 112, 186
August 208
August Folly 20
August 1914 123, 224
Auntie Mame 2, 156–7, 266
Aunt Julia and the Scriptwriter 199, 248
Aunt's Story, The 263
Austen, Jane **13**, 14, 115, 116–7, 124, 183,
    234
Australia Felix 205
Autobiography of Henry VIII, The 15
Autumn of the Patriarch, The 98–99, 164, 248
Aviator, The 51
Axelrod, George 58
Ayesha: The Return of She 103
Ayrton, Michael 11, 28

B

Babbitt 151, 261

Babel, Isaac   221
Bach, Richard   216
Bachelor of Arts, The   180
Bachelors, The   225
Bachman, Richard   142
Back to Bool Bool   85
Backward Glance, A   133, 262
Bagley, Desmond   **16**, 115, 223, 230
Bailey, Paul   26, 27, 50, 57, 63, 140–1, 169
Bainbridge, Beryl   26
Bait of Lies   3
Balchin, Nigel   219
Baldwin, James   3, **16**, 60–61, 145
Balkan Trilogy, The   68, 161
Ballad and the Source, The   **149**, 183
Ballad of Peckham Rye, The   158, 225, 249
Ballad of the Sad Café, The   18, 55, 75, 169
Ballard, J.G.   **17**, 23, 27, 49, 50, 74, 96, 171
Balloonist, The   62
Balthazar   68
Balzac, Honoré de   **18**, 160, 183, 228
Bamboo Bloodbath   10
Banking on Death   46, 171
Banks, Iain   169
Banks, Ian M.   220
Banks, Lynne Reid   12, 80, 101
Bank Shot   171, 266
Barabbas   23, 252
Barbary Shore   160
Barber, Noel   **19**, 253
Barchester Towers   14, **241**
Bardin, John Franklin   174
Barefoot in the Head   4
Barker, A.L.   25
Barnaby Rudge   59
Barnes, Djuna   **19**, 183, 208, 226
Barnes, Julian   27, 50, 177, 183, 248
Baron in the Trees, The   35
Barren Ground   260
Barry, Jane   122
Barry Lyndon   235
Barth, John   30, 84, 93, 136–7, 177, 249
Barthelme, Richard   177
Basso, Hamilton   151
Bastard King, The   170, 191
Bates, H.E.   72, 85, 219, 243
Bath Tangle   115
Battle Lost and Won, The   162
Battle of Pollocks Crossing, The   27
Bawden, Nina   27
Bay of Silence, The   175
Beano, The   23
Bear Raid, The   79
Beastly Beatitudes of Balthazar B, The   63
Beau Geste   122
Beauties and Furies, The   21, 226
Beautiful and Damned, The   77, 125
Beauvallet   114
Beauvoir, Simone de   36, 150
Bech, a Book   156–7, 246
Bech is Back   246
Beckett, Samuel   28

Beckoning Lady, The   6, 164
Beerbohm, Max   **19**, 66, 133, 156–7
Before Adam   153
Before Lunch   22
Beggar Maid, The   26, 174
Beggarman's Country   255
Behn, Aphra   206
Being There   110–111, 143
Belgariad, The   73, 236
Bell, The   **176**
Bell Jar, The   159, 213, 252, 262
Bellow, Saul   18, **20**, 24, 36, 60–61, 76,
   136–7, 143, 151, 190, 206, 229, 230, 256
Belly of Paris, The   271
Beloved Son   242
Belton Estate, The   241
Bend in the River, A   26, 178
Bend Sinister   177, 184, 224
Bengtsson, Frans   68, 112
Ben Hur   123, 252, 253
Bennett, Arnold   **21**, 65, 78, 88, 234, 257
Bennetts, Pamela   37
Benson, E.F.   **22**, 86
Benson, Peter   231
Benzoni, Juliette   37
Berger, John   26, 84
Berger, Thomas   106
Bergman, Andrew   104, 196
Berlin Game   57, 115
Berlin Stories, The   128
Bernanos, Georges   114, 207
Bertrams, The   241
Best, Nicholas   215
Best Stories of Saroyan   162
bête humaine, La   272
Betrothed, The   123
Better Think Twice About It   190
Between the Acts   140–1, 268
Beyond the Glass   57, 262
Bhowani Junction   165, 240
Big Chapel, The   25
Big Fisherman, The   270
Big Kissoff of 1944, The   104, 196
Big Mama's Funeral   164
Big Sleep, The   39, 40
Bilgewater   3, 262
Billiards at Half-Past Nine   24, 25, 151
Billion Year Spree   4
Bill the Conqueror   116–7
Billy Budd   49, 170
Binchy, Maeve   3, **23**, 130
Bingham, John   44–45
Bingley, Margaret   113
Bird of Night, The   26, 119, 159, 161, 208, 213
Birds of America   14, 76, 101, 128, 168
Birds of Passage   209, 210
Birds of the Air, The   154
Birthstone   68, 174
Bishop's Jaegers, The   217, 260
Bissell, Richard   6
Bit Off the Map, A   265
Bit of Singing and Dancing, A   120, 209

Black Arrow, The   230
Black as He's Painted   164
Black Beech and Honeydew   164
Blackboard Jungle, The   124
Black Book, The   69, 154, 267
Black Easter   24, 92, 170
Black House, The   51, 83, 119, 236
Black Ice   124
Black Lamp, The   120
Black Mischief   211, 254
Black Moon, The   96
Blackmore, R.D.   31, 96
Black Opal   195
Black Robe   92, 127, 140–1
Black Swan   178
Black Tower, The   132
Blackwood, Caroline   26
Blaming   234, 263
Bleak House   59
Blessing, The   41
Blind Barber, The   218
Blind Date   144
Blind Man With a Pistol   167
Blish, James   23, 43, 82, 92, 170
Bliss   40, 142, 163
Blithedale Romance, The   107
Bloch, Robert   183, 208
Blood and Guts in High School   37, 123
Bloodlines   144
Blood of the Lamb, The   58
Blood Red, Sister Rose   139
Blood Sport   85
Bloody Chamber, The   35, 37
Blott on the Landscape   217
Blue Angel, The   123
Bluebeard's Egg   13
Blue Movie   76
Blues for Mr Charlie   17
Blue World, The   150, 189
Blush, The   233
Boat, The   106
Boating for Beginners   23, 252
Boccaccio, Giovanni   19, 200
Bodily Harm   13
Bogarde, Dirk   76
Böll, Heinrich   24, 114, 151, 181
Bomber   57, 110–111, 254
Bonecrack   85
Bone People, The   27, 123, 124
Bonjour Tristesse   46
Book, A   19
Book and the Brotherhood, The   27, 174, 176
Book of Common Prayer, A   65, 154
Book of Daniel, The   139, 140–1
Book of Imaginary Beings, The   28
Book of Laughter and Forgetting, The   143
Book of Mrs Noah, The   96
Book of Repulsive Women, The   19
Book of Sand, The   28
Books Do Furnish a Room   194
Bookshop, The   26
Books of Corum, The   172

Boozer, The   165, 271
Borges, Jorge Luis   28, 35
Boston Adventure   182
Bostonians, The   131
Bottle Factory Outing, The   26
Boule de Suif   166
Boulle, Pierre   268
Bouvard and Pécuchet   78
Bowen, Elizabeth   25, 28, 101, 106, 131, 158, 161, 162, 187, 219, 253
Bowen, Marjorie   122
Bowles, Paul   36, 263
Box, Edgar   250
Boyd, Martin   29, 218
Boyd, William   2, 8, 27, 156–7, 230, 254
Boyhood   240
Boy Who Followed Ripley, The   118
Bradbury, Malcolm   8, 27, 30, 156–7, 254
Bradbury, Ray   4, 220, 243
Braddon, Russell   210
Bradford, Barbara Taylor   30, 88, 241
Bragg, Melvyn   104, 145, 190
Brahms, Caryl   6, 181, 191, 201
Braine, John   182, 228
Branch, Pamela   44–45, 47
Brautigan, Richard   127, 172
Brave New World   34, 86, 125, 184
Breakfast at Tiffany's   213
Breakfast in the Ruins   172
Breakfast of Champions   199, 250
Break In   84
Breaking of Bumbo, The   77
Breaking Point, The   67
Breaking Strain, The   165
Brent of Bin Bin   53, 85
Brickfield, The   106
Bridal Canopy, The   221
Bride of Innisfallen, The   259
Bride of Lammermoor, The   216
Bride of Liberty   270
Bride of Lowther Fell, The   159
Bride of Pendorric, The   121
Brideshead Revisited   51, 254, 259
Bridge, Anne   116–7, 230
Bridge of San Luis Rey, The   84, 264
Bridge Over the River Kwai, The   268
Brief Candles   125
Briefing for a Descent into Hell   25, 150
Brien, Alan   15
Brigadier and the Golf Widow, The   41
Brightfount Diaries, The   4
Brighton Rock   100, 166, 183, 272
Bring Larks and Heroes   139
Bring the Monkey   85
Brink, André   26, 94, 107, 224
British Museum is Falling Down, The   124
Brittle Glass, The   116–7, 152, 255
Broad Highway, The   66
Broch, Hermann   161
Brontë, Charlotte   31, 67, 88, 183, 255
Brontë, Emily   31, 96, 190, 261
Bronze Head, The   195

Brookes, Terry   10
Brook Kerith, The   23, 38, 252
Brookner, Anita   27, **32**, 53, 72, 106, 154, 175, 183, 198, 203, 209, 225
Brothers, The   173, 209
Brothers and Sisters   48, 166
Brothers Ashkenazy, The   221
Brothers Karamazov, The   63
Brown, George Douglas   31
Brown, Roy   57
Brown on Resolution   **80**
Bruno's Dream   25
Bryers, Paul   156–7
Buchan, John   **33**, 44–45, 103, 122, 230
Buck, Pearl S.   204
Buddenbrooks   29, 73, 75, 87, 160
Buddwing   124
Bulgakov, Mikhail   93
Bullet in the Ballet, A   6
Bullet Park   40, 246
Bullets for the Bridegroom   7
Bullfighters, The   159
Bull from the Sea, The   202
Bulwer-Lytton, Edward   9
Burford, Eleanor   115
Burger's Daughter   94, 225
Burgess, Anthony   22, 26, **33**, 54, 93, 98–99, 120, 132, 136–7, 176, 184, 207, 238–9, 242, 252
Burmese Days   184
Burning World, The   17, 24
Burnt Ones, The   263
Burnt-out Case, A   36, 101
Burr   193, 211, 249
Burroughs, Edgar Rice   103, 249
Busman's Honeymoon   215
Busy Body, The   7
Butler, Richard   5
Butler, Samuel   48, 187, 232
Butterfield 8   182
Buyer's Market, A   194
Byatt, A.S.   32, 158
Bystander   95

C

Cabala, The   264
Cage Me a Peacock   20
Cain, James M.   104
Caine Mutiny, The   110–111, 218, 268
Cakes and Ale   165, 166
Cal   74
Caldwell, Erskine   204, 227
California Time   76, 177
Call for the Dead   148, 215
Call It Sleep   145
Call of the Wild   152, **153**
Calvino, Italo   11, 28, **35**, 163, 170
Calypso   167

Camberwell Beauty, The   233, 265
Cambridge Murders, The   66
Camera Obscura/Laughter in the Dark   178
Camomile Lawn, The   227
Campanile, Pasquale Festa   252
Campbell's Kingdom   112, 115, 223
Camus, Albert   20, **36**, 63, 190, 214
Canary in a Cathouse   250
Cancer Ward   224
Candide   231
Candle for St Jude, A   207
Candy   110–111
Candy, Edward   32, 194, 198
Cannery Row   228
Cannibals and Missionaries   168
Canticle for Leibowitz, A   86, 170, 250
Can You Forgive Her?   87, 223, 241
Capote, Truman   213
Capricorn Games   220
Captain Blood   66, 115, 122
Captain Fantom   119
Captain Horatio Hornblower   80
Captain Pantoja and the Special Service   5, 248
Captains and the Kings, The   161
Captains Courageous   143
Captain Singleton   55
Captive, The   197
Card, The   21, 22, 234, 257
Cardboard Crown, The   29
Cardinal and the Queen, The   10
Carey, Peter   27, 140–1, 145, 211
Caroline Type   47
Carr, J.L.   27
Carr, John Dickson   64, 100, 214, 218
Carr, Philippa   **37**, 115
Carre, John Le   82
Carrie   92, 93, 142
Carter, Angela   19, 35, **37**, 72, 86, 142, 189, 208, 210, 226, 232
Carter, Peter   120
Carter, P. Youngman   6
Cary, Joyce   11, 136–7, 152, 165, 263
Casanova's Chinese Restaurant   194
Case Book of Sherlock Holmes, The   64, 65
Case of Comrade Tulayev, The   184, 193
Case of Confidence, A   82
Case of Conscience, A   23
Case of the Gilded Fly, The   6
Case of the Howling Dog, The   42
Cashelmara   123
Cast a Cold Eye   168
Castang's City   44–45
Castle, The   **138**, 139, 230
Castle Dangerous   216
Castle Gay   230
Castle of Crossed Destinies, The   35, 36
Castle of Otranto, The   183
Castle of the Demon, The   210
Castle of Wizardry   70
Casualties   80
Casuarina Tree, The   166
Catalina   166

Cat and Mouse 97
Catcher in the Rye, The 29, 101, 136–7, 213
Catch-22 74, 108, **109**, 110–111, 138, 199, 207, 254, 268
Cathedral, The 210, 241
Cathedral Close 241
Cather, Willa 29, **38**, 82, 101, 127, 129, 158, 176, 193, 213, 242, 264, 268, 272
Cat Jumps, The 29
Catriona 230
Cat's Cradle 105, 250
Cat Who Walks Through Walls, The 108
Cause for Alarm 8
Caute, David 94, 192
Caves of Alienation, The 152
Caves of Steel, The 11
Cefalù 69, 84, 175, 183, 195
Celebrated Jumping Frog of Calaveras County and Other Sketches, The, 244
Celestial Omnibus 83
Celibate Lives 190
Centaur, The 40, 119, 187, 213, 215, **246**
Centre of the Action, The 151, 256
Centres of Ritual 68
Certain Blindness, A 85
Certain People 262
Cervantes Saavedra, Miguel de 76, 90, 91, 121, 229, 238–9
César Birotteau 18
Chandler, Raymond **39**, 104, 196
Change for the Better, A 119, 233
Change of Skin, A 5
Changes, The 62
Changing Places 30
Chant of Jimmie Blacksmith, The 26, 139
Chapterhouse of Dune 113
Charioteer, The 202
Charmed Life, A 168, 174
Charterhouse of Parma, The 228
Charteris, Leslie 79
Charter to Danger 8
Chase, James Hadley 39
Chatterton 27
Chatwin, Bruce 123, 140–1
Checkmate 68
Cheever, John **40**, 124, 140–1, 159, 162, 246
Chekhov, Anton 15, **41**, 91, 162, 242
Chéri 47
Chesterton, G.K. 46, 64
Chevalier, Gabriel 22
Chike and the River 2
Childermass 109
Childers, Erskine 33
Childhood 240
Childhood at Brindabella 85
Childhood's End 46
Children are Civilians Too 25
Children at the Gate 12
Children of Dune 113
Children of Dynmouth, The 26
Children of Tender Years 5
Children of the Frost 153

Children of the Game, The 48
Children of the Sun 260
Children's Children 173
Child's History of England, A 59
China Syndrome, The 103
Chinese Agenda, The 79
Chocky 119, 269
Choice of Enemies, A 5, 206
Choirboys, The 167
Chosen People, The 209
Christie, Agatha **42**, 44–45, 100, 240
Christie Malry's Own Double-Entry 240
Christine 142
Christmas Carol, A 59
Christopher, John 219
Chronicle of a Death Foretold 164
Chronicles of Castle Brass, The 172
Chronicles of the Black Sword, The 172
Chronicles of Thomas Covenant, The 236
Chrysalids, The 86, 269
Churchill Commando, The 5
Cider House Rules, The **128**, 191, 231, 246
Cider With Rosie 23, 132
Circles of Deceit 27
Cities of the Plain 89, 197
City and the Dogs, The 110–111, 184, 248
City and the Pillar, The 249
City Boy , The 268
City Life 177
City of Illusions 149
City of Night, The 17
City of Spades 21
Clan of the Cave Bear 186
Clap Hands, Here Comes Charlie 85
Clarissa, or the History of a Young Lady **205**
Clarke, Arthur C. **43**
Clash of Cymbals, A 24
Class Reunion 7, 168, 201
Claudius the God 97
Clavell, James 82, 159, 165, 186
Clayhanger 21, 22, 88
Clea 68
Clear Light of Day, The 26, 179
Cleary, Jon 11
Cleland, John 205
Clemens, Samuel 243
Clergyman's Daughter, A 186
Clicking of Cuthbert, The 266
Clochemerle 22
Clock Without Hands 169
Clockwork Orange, A **34**, 120, 184, 242, 272
Closed Circuit 122
Close Quarters 93, 140–1
Close to Home 65
Close-Up 57, 76, 196
Clouded Hills 130
Cloven Viscount, The 35
Clown, The 24, 114
Clowns of God, The 259
Clubbable Woman, A 119
Clutch of Constables 164
Coasting 235

Coat of Varnish, A   224
Cobbold, Richard   181
Cockatoos, The   85, 263
Cockpit   144
Cocksure   206, 260
Cocteau, Jean   48
Code of the Woosters, The   14, 266
Cod Strewth   170, 181, 250
Coetzee, J.M.   27, 56, 94, 225
Coffin, Peter   104
Coffin for Dimitrios   7
Cold Comfort Farm   51
Cold Iron   192
Colegate, Elizabeth   255
Colegate, Isabel   79, 161
Coleman, Bob   76, 115
Colette   3, **46**, 89, 259
Collector, The   83, 169
Colliers Row   73, 255
Collins, Hunt   124
Collins, Jackie   144
Collins, Wilkie   192
Color Purple, The   55, 251
Colour of Blood, The   27, 207, 260
Colour of Magic, The   2, 73, 236
Come Away, Death   42
Comedians, The   49, 101, 190
Comfort Me with Apples   58
Comfort of Strangers, The   27, 89, 93, 169
Coming First   156–7
Coming from Behind   118, 156–7, 168
Coming of the Quantum Cats, The   250
Coming Up for Air   186
Company of Women, The   257
Company She Keeps, The   154, 168, 183, 203
Complete Robot, The   11
Compton-Burnett, Ivy   **47**, 72, 75, 166, 198, 226
Concrete Island   17
Condition of Muzak   172
Condon, Richard   2, 5, 8, 47, **48**, 110–111, 124, 159, 192, 198, 249
Confederacy of Dunces, A   63, 134, 136–7, 181, 229, 240
Confederates   26, 139
Conference-ville   172
Confession, A   240
Confessional   147
Confessions of a Justified Sinner   230
Confessions of Felix Krull, Confidence Man, The   48, 54, 60–61, 76, 107, 160, 161
Confessions of Zeno, The   136–7, 190, 230
Confidence Man, The   170
Confidential Agent, The   100
Conformist, The   230
Coningsby   192, 241
Conjunction, The   25
Connecticut Yankee in King Arthur's Court, A   243
Conrad, Joseph   3, **49**, 63, 92, 101, 127, 153, 169, 178, 193, 218, 234, 263, 272
Conran, Shirley   144

Conscience of the King, The   122
Conscience of the Rich, The   87, 223, 224
Conservationist, The   53, 94
Consider Her Ways   269
Consider Phlebas   220
Constance   27, 69
Consul's File, The   236
Continental Op, The   104
Conversation in the Cathedral   248
Cook, David   41, **50**, 60–61, 181, 183, 209, 243, 245, 258
Cookson, Catherine   14, **50**
Cool Million, A   232, 260
Coonardoo   195, 263
Cooper, James Fenimore   127, 216
Cooper, William   8, 230
Coover, Robert   28, 63, 108, 172, 240
Cop Hater   167
Corn King and the Spring Queen, The   9, 97, 202
Cornwell, Bernard   80, 120, 238–9
Coroner's Pidgin   6
Corpse Diplomatique   44–45
Corridors of Power, The   193, 224
Corydon   89
Cosmic Inferno   4
Cosmicomics   12, 35, 36
Cotillion   115
Cotter's England   226
Cotton Comes to Harlem   17
Couens, Frederick   120
Count Belisarius   9, 97
Counterfeiters, The   60–61, 89, 101
Counterlife, The   209
Countess of Charny, The   67
Count of Monte Cristo, The   67
Country Girls, The   23, 46
Country of the Blind and Other Stories, The   258
Coup, The   246, 254
Couples   86, 246
Courtesy of Death, The   122
Courtney, Caroline   116–7, 121
Cousin Bette   18, 160
Cousin Phyllis   88
Cover Her Face   132
Coward, Noël   142
Cox, Richard   51
Crampton Hodnett   66, 199, 241
Crane, Stephen   110–111
Cranford   14, 86, 88
Creation   98–99, 195, 202, 249
Creatures of Circumstance   101
Crewe Train   158, 165, 193, 197
Crime and Punishment   **63**
Crime at Christmas   44–45
Crispin, Edmund   6, 44–45, 126, 174
Crofts, Freeman Wills   44–45, 192, 240
Crome Yellow   125
Crooked House, The   42
Cross, Amanda   214
Crossing, The   5, 83

Crossings 227
Crossing the Border 233
Crown of Feathers, A 222
Crowther Chronicles, The 173
Cruel Sea, The 218, 268
Crusoe's Daughter 55, 67, 149, 175
Cry Guilty 85
Crying of Lot 49, The 199, 232
Cry of the Halidon, The 154
Crystal Cave, The 230
Crystal Singer, The 167
Cry, the Beloved Country 94, 225
Cubs, The 248
Cujo 142
Cupboard Under the Stairs, The 243
Curé of Tours, The 18
Currents of Space, The 12
Curse Not the King/Rebel Princess 10
Curtain of Green, A 259
Curtis, Peter 152
Cussler, Clive 2
Custom House, The 128
Custom of the Century, The 14, 260, 262
Cut Me In 124
Cut-Rate Kingdom, The 142
Cuts 30
Cyberiad, The 150
Cyclops 2

D

Daffodil Affair, The 6, 62, 126
Dagon and Other Macabre Tales 191
Dahl, Roald 91, 142, 191, 224
Dain Curse, The 104
Daisy Miller 131
Damiano 62
Dance in the Sun, A 225
Dance to the Music of Time, A **194**, 197
Dancing Girls 13
Dangerous Ages 159
Dangerous Alliances 205
Danger Tree, The 162
Dangling Man 21
Daniel, Glyn 66
Daniel Deronda 71, 90
Daniel Martin 4, 83, 146, 208
Darby, Catherine 67
D'Arconville's Cat 136–7, 200
Darcy, Clare 115, 116–7
Darfsteller, The 170
Dark, Eleanor 53, 127, 136–7, 140–1, 175, 186
Dark, The 113
Dark-Adapted Eye, A 203
Dark as the Grave Wherein My Friend is Laid 153
Dark Design, The 74
Dark Labyrinth, The 69, 84, 175, 183, 195

Dark Light Years, The 4
Darkness and Day 48
Darkness at Ingraham's Crest, A 270
Darkness at Noon 184, 192, 211, 214, 224
Darkness Visible 53, 93, 263
Dark Places of the Heart 226
Dark Shore, The 122
Dark Side of the Street, The 115
Darling Buds of May, The 72, 85, 243
Darrell, Elizabeth 253
Date With Death 167
Daudet, Alphonse 243
Daughter of Silence 260
Daughter of the Sea 152
Daughter of Time 44–45
Daughters and Sons 48
'*Daughters of England*' series 37
David Copperfield **59**, 60–61, 101, 238–9
Davidson, Lionel 16, 49, 139
Davidson, Max 181
Davies, Andrew 54
Davies, Robert 14
Davies, Robertson 27, **54**, 118, 132, 136–7, 140–1, 145, 156–7
Day After Judgement, The 24
Day After Tomorrow, The 108
Day of Creation, The 17, 171
Day of My Delights 29
Day of the Butterfly 152
Day of the Jackal, The 2, 83, 140–1
Day of the Locust, The 76, 260
Day of the Monkey, The 225
Day of the Triffids, The 269
Dayworld 73
Dead Birds 196
Dead Cert 85
Deadeye Dick 250
Dead March in Three Keys 152
Dead Souls **91**, 228, 238–9
Dead Zone, The 142
Dean's December, The 21
Death and the Visiting Firemen 62
Death at the President's Lodgings 127
Death Comes for the Archbishop **38**, 127, 272
Death in Ecstasy 164
Death in Leningrad 43, 146, 147
Death in the Afternoon 112
Death in the Family, A 119
Death in the Fifth Position 250
Death in Venice 161
Death of a Fat God 6
Death of a Ghost 5, 11
Death of an Expert Witness 131
Death of a Train 44–45, 192, 240
Death of Dickie Draper, The 256
Death of Grass, The 219
Death of Ivan Illich, The 240
Death of the Heart, The **28**, 101, 106, 158
Death of Virgil, The 161
Death on the Nile 42, 100
Death Takes the Low Road 210
Death to the French 80

Death Under Sail   224
Death Watch   100
Deathworld I   105
Deathworld II   105
Deathworld III   105
De Beauvoir, Simone   71
Debits and Credits   142, 143
Decameron   19, 200
Decline and Fall   2, 215, 254
Dedicated Man, A   28, 233
Deer Park, The   160
Defence, The   177
Defoe, Daniel   **55**, 76, 92, 218, 230
De Haan, Tom   12, **56**, 67, 73, 114, 148, 188, 189
Deighton, Len   7, **56**, 66, 76, 85, 110–111, 115, 147, 196, 254
Delta Wedding   23, 51, 55, 75, 169, 255, **259**
De Maupassant, Guy   41, 166
Demelza   96
De Mille, Nelson   210
Demon Lover, The   29
Dennis, Patrick   2, 156–7, 266
Derek Lambert   210
Desai, Anita   26, 133, 179
Descent of Man, The   262
Desert of Love, The   167
Desire and Pursuit of the Whole, The   89
Despair   63, 177, 184
Destinies of Darcy Dancer, Gentleman, The   63
Details of a Sunset   178
Detection Unlimited   114
Devastating Boys, The   **233**
Devil on Lammas Night, The   122
Devil's Advocate, The   207, 259, 260
Devil's Alternative, The   83
Devil's Child   113
Devil's Cub   115
Devil's Laughter, The   270
Devils of Loudon, The   107
Devil's Own, The   152
Devil Take the Blue-Tail Fly   174
Devil Tree, The   143, 199
De Vries, Peter   34, 40, **58**, 76, 86, 124, 156–7
Diamond Hunters, The   223
Diamonds are Forever   79
Diary of a Country Priest   114, 207
Diary of a Nobody, The   133, 181
Diary of Antoine Roquentin, The   214
Diary of Samuel Marchbanks, The   54
Dickens, Charles   3, 6, 18, 50, **58**, 60–61, 88, 101, 123, 140–1, 181, 215, 238–9
Dickenson, Carter   44–45
Dickinson, Gordon   12
Dickinson, Peter   **59**, 122, 164, 174
Dickson, Carter   126
Didion, Joan   65, 154
Died in the Wool   164
Different Face, A   162
Difficult Young Man, A   29
Dinosaur Planet   168
Dirk Gently's Holistic Detective Agency   2

Dirty Story   7
Diski, Jenny   32, 175
Disorderly Knights, The   68
Dispossessed, The   149
Disraeli, Benjamin   70, 192, 241
Distant Likeness, A   63
Diversity of Creatures, A   143
Doctor Brodie's Report   28
Doctor Faustus   160, 169, 176
Doctor Fischer of Geneva   101
Doctor in the House   118, 266
Doctor Mirabilis   24
Doctor No   79, 147
Doctorow, E.L.   139, 140–1, 256
Doctor Slaughter   236
Doctor's Wife, The   26, 203
Doctor Thorne   241, 261
Doctor Zhivago   170, 187, 216, 237, 238–9, 255
Documents Relating to the Sentimental Agents in the Volyen Empire   151
Dodge, David   7, 44–45
Dodo   10, 140–1
Dodsworth   151
Dogs of War, The   51, 83
Dog Years   97
Dolly and the Cookie Bird   68, 230
Dolly and the Doctor Bird   68
Dolly and the Nanny Bird   68
Dolly and the Singing Bird   68
Dolly and the Starry Bird   68
Dolores   47
Domain, The   113
Dombey and Son   18, 59
Donaldson, Stephen   62, 73, 148, 236
Donleavy, J.P.   **63**, 118, 200, 217
Don Quixote   28, 75, 76, 90, 91, 121, 229, 238–9
Don't Go to Sleep in the Dark   118
Don't, Mr Disraeli   181
Don't Tell Alfred   19
Doolittle, Hilda   98–99, 161, 264
Doon   113
Dosadi Experiment, The   74, 113
Dos Passos, John   197
Dostoevski, Fyodor   **63**, 95, 153, 224, 238–9
Double Hook, The   123
Douglas, Colin   30, 217
Douglas, Lloyd C.   252, 270
Doves and Silk Handkerchieves   163, 211, 231
Dove's Nest and Other Stories, The   163, 174
Doves of Venus, The   162
Do With Me What You Will   182
Down Among the Women   257
Down and Out in London and Paris   184
Downfall, The   237, 272
Doyle, Arthur Conan   44–45, **64**, 73, 100, 103, 122, 191, 230, 248
Drabble, Margaret   **65**, 71, 150
Dracula   217, 252
Dragondrums   167
Dragonflight   73, 167, 220

Dragon for Edward, A 37
Dragon in the Sea, The 113
Dragon Lensman, The 222
Dragonquest 167
Dragonsinger 167
Dragonsong 167
Dream Life of Balso Snell, The 68, 138, 260
Dream Lover, The 162
Dream of John Ball, A 173
Dreamtigers 28
Dreiser, Theodore 18, 21, 166, 271
Dresden Green, The 84
Dressmaker, The 26
Dr Frigo 8
Driver's Seat, The 226
Dr Jekyll and Mr Hyde 229
Droll Tales 18
Drowned World, The 17, 49
Drowning Pool, The 39, 104
Drummond, Emma 254
Drury, Allen 154, 270
Dubin's Lives 208
Dubliners 134, 135
Dublin Four 23
Ducdame 194
Duchess in Disguise 116–7
Duke's Children, The 241
Duluth 249, 250
Dumas, Alexandre **66**, 115, 123, 201, 216
Du Maurier, Daphne 31, **67**, 96, 114, 152, 170, 183, 189, 255
Du Maurier, Gerald 217
Dune 12, 23, 113
Dune Messiah 113
Dunmore, Spencer S. 51
Dunne, Colin 124
Dunne, John Gregory 198
Dunnett, Dorothy 10, **67**, 201, 230
Duras, Marguerite 203
Durrell, Gerald 132
Durrell, Lawrence 27, 43, **68**, 84, 136–7, 153, 175, 183, 195, 235, 264, 267
Dürrenmatt, Friedrich 44–45, 220
Dusty Answer 150, 262
Dutiful Daughter, A 139
Dvořák in Love 176
Dwarf, The 56, 170

E

Eagle Has Landed, The 44–45, 115
Early Asimov, The 12
Early in Orcadia 186
Early Stories 67
Earth 271
Earth Children 112
Earthly Powers 27, 33, 93, 136–7, 207
Earthman Come Home 24, 46

Earthworks 4
East and West 81
Easterman, Daniel 83
East Lynne 255
East of Eden 227
Eating People is Wrong 8, 30, 254
Ebb-tide, The 230
Ebony Tower, The 29, 84
Eccentricities of Cardinal Pirelli, The 225
Echoes 3, 23
Echoing Grove, The 150
Eco, Umberto 93, 170, 174, 228, 245
Eddings, David 62, **70**, 73, 236
Edible Woman, The 13, 65
Edith's Diary 118
Edwardians, The 79, 201
Edwin Drood 59, 255
Effi Briest 233, 271
Egan, Lesley 44–45, 167
Egg and I, The 85
Eggs and Crumpets 266
Egleton, Clive 79
1876 249
Eighth Day, The 96, 264
Eighty Million Eyes 167
Einstein's Monsters 35
Elders and Betters 48
Elected Member, The 25, 209
Elective Affinities 90
Electra 9, 121
Eleven 119
Eliot, George 50, 65, **70**, 90, 104, 145, 183, 194, 228, 237, 260
Ellis, Alice Thomas 27, 154, 168, 174, 198, 225, 257
Ellison, Ralph 16, 134, 251
Elmer Gantry 151
Elyza 116–7
Emma 13, 15, 234
Emperor's Snuff Box, The 64
Empire 249
Empire of the Sun 18, 27, 50, 74
Enchanter's Endgame 70
Encounters 29
Enderby's Dark Lady 34, 54, 132
Ending Up 9, 26, 183
End of a Childhood, The 205
End of All Songs, The 172
End of Solomon Grundy, The 44–45
End of the Affair, The 101
End of the Chapter 88
End of the Road, The 30
Enemies, a Love Story 221
Enemies of the System 4
Enemy Camp, The 256
England, Barry 25
England, Their England 133, 146
English Assassin, The 143, 171
English Teacher, The 78, 128, 179, 180, 184
Enigma of Arrival, The 178
Enormous Radio, The 41
Enright, D.J. 132, 168

Enter a Murderer   164
Enterprize – the First Adventure   222
Envious Casca   114
Epidemic   259
Epitaph for a Spy   8
Erewhon   232
Erik Brighteyes   103
Error of Judgement   223
Esmond in India   133
Estate, The   221
Eternal Fire   75
Eternal Moment, The   83
Ethan Frome   51, 104, 227, 260
Et nunc manet in te   89
Eugenia   115
Eugénie Grandet   18
Europeans, The   52, 133
Eustace and Hilda   41, 106
Eustace Diamonds, The   241
Evans, Stuart   68, 152, 194
Eva Trout   25, 28, 29, 131
Evenings on a Farm   91
Everlasting Secret Family and Other Secrets, The   172
Every Little Crook and Nanny   124
Evidence of Things Not Seen   17
Excellent Women   199, 233
Executioner's Song, The   159
Exile and the Kingdom   37
Exit of a Dragonfly   93
Expedition of Humphrey Clinker, The   229
Experience of India, An   133
Extract from Captain Stormfield's Visit to Heaven   244
Eyeless in Gaza   89, 125
Eye of the Storm, The   263

F

Fabrications   28
Fabulous Riverboat, The   74
Face Me When You Walk Away   85
Face of Trespass, The   203
Face on the Cutting-room Floor, The   174
Facial Justice   106, 125
Fahrenheit 451   243
Fairchild, William   254
Fair God, The   253
Fairly Dangerous Thing, A   119
Falconer   40, 140–1, 159
Fall, The   20, 36, 63, 190
Fallen Curtain, The   203
Fall of Moondust, A   46
Fall of the House of Usher, The   188
False Colours   130
Falstaff   15, 145, 181
Fame is the Spur   193
Family and a Fortune, A   48, 226
Family and Friends   32, 72

Family Arsenal, The   236
Family Fortune, A   171, 226, 256
Family Madness, A   142
Family Moskat, The   73, 160, **221**, 222, 237
Fanny Hill   205
Far, Far the Mountain Peak   165
Far Away and Long Ago   132
Far Country, The   219
Farewell, My Lovely   **39**, 40, 196
Farewell to Arms, A   **112**, 187, 238–9, 253
Farewell to France   19
Far From the Madding Crowd   **105**, 204
Farmer, Philip José   **73**, 108
Farmer Giles of Ham   237
Farnol, Jeffery   66
Far Pavilions, The   81, 116–7, 171
Farre, Rowena   10
Farrell, J.G.   19, 26, **74**, 126, 142, 165
Farther Adventures of Robinson Crusoe, The   55
Farthest Shore, The   149
Father and his Fate, A   48
Father Brown Stories, The   64
Fathers and Sons   187, 238–9, **242**
Faulkner, William   53, 72, **74**, 227
Favours   210
Fear of Flying   134, 190
Felix Holt   71
Female Friends   257
Female Man, The   37
Fer de Lance   215
Fertility   272
Fever Tree, The   203
Fiasco   150
Fictions   28, 35
Fielding, Henry   55, 59, **75**, 116–7, 243
Field of Blood   82
Fiesta   10, 112
Fifth Business   54
Fifth Queen, The   79
Figures in a Landscape   25
Files on Parade   182
Filmi, Filmi, Inspector Ghote   44–45, 76
Final Curtain   **164**
Finalists, The   210
Final Programme, The   171, 250
Financial Expert, The   179, 180
Financiers, The   171
Finnegans Wake   135
Firbank, Ronald   77, 225
Firefly Summer   23
Firefox   33
Fire From Heaven   202
Fire Next Time, The   16
Fireside, Caroline   116–7
Firestarter   142
Fireworks   38, 142
First Circle, The   224
First Lensman   222
First Men in the Moon, The   43, 248, 257
Fisher King, The   194
Fitzgerald, F. Scott   **77**, 125, 153, 201, 206
Fitzgerald, Penelope   26

Fitzgerald, Valerie 19, 126
Five-Year Sentence, A 26, 210
Fixer, The 91, 221
Flag on the Island, A 179
Flanagan, Mary 11, 65, 174
Flashman 81, 120
Flaubert, Gustave 70, **78**, 160, 183, 186, 204, 237, 242, 261
Flaubert's Parrot 27, 177, 248
Flaunting Extravagant Queen 191
Flaws in the Glass 264
Flax of Dream, The 197
Fleming, Ian **78**, 147
Fleming, Joan 203
Fletch 39, 47
Flight from the Enchanter, The 89, 101, 176
Flint and Roses 130
Floodtide 270
Flounder, The **96**, 211, 264
Flowering Judas 193
Flowers for Adonis 9
Flowers for Mrs Harris 188
Flowers for the Judge **6**, 197
Flowers in the Attic 10
Flyaway 16
Flying Colours 80
Flying to Nowhere 27
Foe 56
Fog, The 113
Follett, Ken 2, 33, 44–45, **79**
Foma Gordeev 3, **95**, 153, 238–9, 272
Fong and the Indians 82, 236
Fontane, Theodore 233, 271
Food of the Gods, The 258
Fools Die 198
Forbes, Colin 115
Ford, Elbur 115
Ford, Ford Madox 29, **79**, 101, 214
Foreign Affairs 7, 14, 41, **154**, 180, 193, 245
For Esmé, with Love and Squalor 172, 213
Forester, C.S. 16, **80**, 120, 165, 238–9
Forever Amber 116–7, 270
Forfeit 85
Forget the Glory 254
For Love Alone 226
For Love, Only for Love 252
Forrester, Helen 255
Forster, E.M. 15, 51, 52, **81**, 82, 126, 130, 133, 183
Forster, Margaret 159, 187
Forsyte Saga, The 72, **87**, 171, 226, 241
Forsyth, Frederick 2, 3, 11, 51, **83**, 140–1
Fortunes of Nigel, The 216
Fortunes of Richard Mahony, The 150, 204, **205**, 263, 267
Fortunes of War 19, 161, 238–9
For Whom the Bell Tolls 112, 159, 254
For Women's Delight 271
Foster, Alan Dean 10, 70
Foundation Saga, The 4, **12**, 23, 74, 108
Found in the Street 118

Foundling, The 115
Four-Dimensional Nightmare, The 18
Four Forsyte Stories 88
Four-gated City, The 150
Four Gospels, The 272
Four Just Men, The 191
Fournier, Alain 197
Fourth Protocol, The 3, 11, 83
Fourth Street East 43, 165, 220, 256, 268
Fowles, John 4, 29, **83**, 93, 104, 136–7, 140–1, 146, 169, 181, 208
Foxes of Harrow, The 270
Framley Parsonage 241
Franchise Affair, The 10
Francis, Dick 11, **84**
Frankenstein 188, 217
Frankenstein Unbound 4
Franklin, Miles 3, 14, 29, 53, **85**
Franny and Zooey 57, 213
Fraser, George Macdonald 81, 120
Fraternity 88
Frayn, Michael 30, 73, 125, 128, 173, 180, 181, 232
Freedom Trap, The 16
Free Fall 93
Freeling, Nicholas 44–45, 84, 192, 202, 220
Freemantle, Brian **85**
Fremlin, Celia 10, 118
French, Marilyn 134, 150
French Bride, The 10
French Lieutenant's Woman, The **84**, 104, 181
Frenchman's Creek 67
Friday's Child 115
Friend from England, A 32
Friendly Young Ladies, The 202
Friend of Kafka, A 222
Friends and Heroes 162
Fringe of Leaves, A 38, 140–1, 218, 263, 272
Frisch, Max 20, 138
From a View to a Death 193
From Here to Eternity 267
From London Far 126
From Russia With Love 78, 79
From Scenes Like These 25
From the Diary of a Snail 97
From the Earth to the Moon 249
From the Terrace 266
Frost in May 3, 205, 207, 262
Fuentes, Carlos 5, 98–99, 163, 201
Fuentes, R. 10
Fugitive, The 197
Full Circle 227
Fuller, John 27
Fullerton, Alexander 115
Full Term 127
Funeral Games 202
Funeral in Berlin 57
Funny Side, The 140–1
Further Adventures of Tom Jones, The 115
Futility and Other Animals 172
Futurological Congress, The 150

G

G   26, 84
Gabriel Hounds, The   230
Gabriel's Lament   27, 50
Gaddis, William   199
Gad's Hall   152
Galahad at Blandings   266
Galápagos   96, 108, 218, 249, 250
Gallico, Paul   10, 43, 103, 188, 218
Galsworthy, John   72, **87**, 171, 226, 241, 270
Gambler, The   64, 95
Game for Heroes, A   122
Game of Hide-and-seek, A   233
Game of Kings, The   68
Games at Twilight   133
Gangway!   43, 66
Gann, Ernest K.   51, 219
Gardam, Jane   3, 26, 55, 67, 106, 149, 175, 262
Garden Party, The   163
Gardens of Delight, The   148
Gardner, Erle Stanley   42
Gardner, John   35, 79, 223
Gargantua   106, 145, 181, 200, 229
Garnett, David   47
Garrick Year, The   65
Gary, Romain   153
Gascoigne, Bamber   6, 62, 170, 181, 196, 250
Gaskell, Mrs   14, 15, 31, 43, 50, 59, 70, 86, **88**, 104, 173, 195
Gaskin, Catherine   50
Gaudy, The   127
Gaudy Night   66, 214, 215
Gébler, Carlo   36
Gee, Maggie   257
Gellhorn, Martha   192
Gemini Contenders, The   33, 154
Gemini Girls   50
Genet, Jean   17, 95
Genetrix   167
Genius and the Goddess, The   125
Gentleman and Ladies   119
Gentleman of France   66
Gentlemen at Gyang Gyang   85
Gentlemen Prefer Blondes   77
George, Margaret   15
George, Peter   57, 110–111
Germinal   88, 195, 271
Gertrud   90, 113, 114, 176, 261
Get off the Unicorn   168
Get Ready for Battle   133
Getting of Wisdom, The   176, 204, 205, 215
Ghose, S.N.   179
Ghosts   262
Ghost Stories of an Antiquary   191
Ghost Writer, The   209, 245
Gibbon, Lewis Grassic   88
Gibbons, Stella   51
Gide, André   47, 60–61, **89**, 101, 114, 228
Gideon Planish   151

Gift, The   178
Gildenfire   63
Giles Goat-boy   93, 136–7, 177
Gilgamesh the King   186, 220
Gimpel the Fool   222
Ginger Griffin, The   116–7
Ginger Man, The   63, 118, 200, 217
Giovanni's Room   17
Gipsy's Baby, The   150
Girls in Their Married Bliss   46
Girls of Slender Means, The   251, **225**
Gissing, George   18, 181, 271
Give the Boys a Great Big Hand   167
Glance Away, A   17
Glanville, Brian   52, 171
Glasgow, Ellen   113, 182, 260
Glass Bead Game, The   56, 113, 114, 173
Glassblowers, The   67
Glass Cell, The   118, 203, 252
Glass Key, The   104
Glass of Blessings, A   14, 86, 124, **198**
Glastonbury Romance, A   195
Glittering Prizes, The   201
Glitz   198
Gloriana   171, 211
Glory   178
Glory Road   167
Gnur Bodi   120
Go, Lovely Rose   47, 164
Go, Tell it on the Mountain,   3, 16, 60–61, 145
Goat Song   270
Go-Between, The   81, 82, 106, 242, 259
God and his Gifts, A   48
God Bless You, Mrs Rosewater   250
Godden, Rumer   3, 207
God Emperor of Dune   113
Godfather, The   198
God Knows   15, 23, 98–99, 109, 252
God on the Rocks   26
God's Grace   218
God's Little Acre   204, 227
Gods of Riverworld   74
Goethe, Johann Wolfgang von   60–61, **89**, 101, 160, 238–9
Gog   110–111
Gogol, Nicolai Vasilevich   **91**, 221, 228, 238–9
Going to Meet the Man   17
Golden Apples, The   174, 193, 259
Golden Apples of the Sun, The   4
Golden Ass, The   76
Golden Bowl, The   130
Golden Fleece, The   9, 97, 121
Golden Hawk, The   270
Golden Keel, The   16, 115
Golden Miles   195
Golden Notebook, The   57, 150, 203
Goldfinger   **79**
Golding, William   20, 26, 36, 41, 52, 53, 55, 84, **91**, 92, 119, 120, 140–1, 170, 263, 272
Gold Mine   223
Goldsmith, Oliver   241
Goncharov, Ivan   91

Gone with the Wind 31, 55, 170, 187, 216, 255, 270
Good Apprentice, The 27
Good as Gold 108
Good Behaviour 27, 48, 261
Goodbye Again 116–7
Goodbye Columbus 102, 209
Goodbye Mickey Mouse 56
Goodbye, Mr Chips 196, 215
Goodbye to an Old Friend 85
Goodbye to Berlin 43, 128
Good Companions, The 6, 196
Good Earth, The 204
Goodge, Elizabeth 241
Gooding Girl, The 30
Good Man in Africa, A 8, 254
Good Morning, Midnight 19, 20, 134, 159, **203**, 267
Good Soldier, The 79, 214
Good Soldier Švejk, The 91, 106, 107, 109, 110–111, 138, 240, 253
Good Terrorist, The 27, 146, 151, 234
Gordimer, Nadine 13, 26, 53, **94**, 102, 211, 225
Gordon, Mary 233, 257, 265
Gordon, Richard 118, 265
Gorky, Maxim 3, **95**, 153, 171, 238–9, 272
Gorky Park 167, 192
Gormenghast 183, **188**, 189
Goshawk Squadron 25
Gossip from the Forest 26, 139
Graduate, The 2, 47, 102
Graduate Wife, The 168
Graham, James 16, 122
Graham, Winston 73, **96**
Grand Babylon Hotel, The 21
Grand Man, A 50
grand Meaulnes, Le 197
Grand Sophy, The 115
Grant, Joan 97, 98–99
Grapes of Wrath, The 3, 59, 195, **227**, 271
Grass, Günter 5, **96**, 110–111, 210, 211, 264
Grass is Singing, The 150
Grateful to Life and Death 128, 179, 184
Graves, Robert 9, 15, 76, 86, **97**, 98–99, 121, 158, 165, 173, 202, 252
Gravity's Rainbow 110–111, 199, 224
Gray, Alasdair 138
Great American Novel, The 209
Great Balls of Fire 105
Great Expectations 59
Great Fortune, The 162
Great Gatsby, The **77**, 201, 206
Great Granny Webster 26
Great Hoggarty Diamond, The 235
Great Pursuit, The 197
Great Short Stories of O'Hara, The 182
Great Victorian Collection, The 246
Great World and Timothy Colt, The 241
Greek Fire 96
Greek Passion, The 207, 221
Green, Henry 193

Green, Peter 9, 98–99, 249
Green Brain, The 113
Greene, Graham 7, 36, 44–45, 49, 80, **100**, 112, 122, 129, 146, 166, 183, 190, 207, 235, 240, 272
Green Equinox, The 26
Greengage Summer, The 3
Green Hills of Africa, The 112
Green House, The 248
Greenmantle 33
Griffin's Way 270
Grimmelshausen, Von 106
Grimus 212
Grossmith, George and Weedon 133, 181
Group, The 7, 168, 251
Group Portrait with Lady **24**
Groves of Academe, The 30, 118, 156–7, **168**, 192
Growing Up 162
Guardian of the Heart 121
Guareschi, Giovanni 133, 179
Guermantes Way, The 136–7, 197
Guerrillas 178
Guest and his Going, A 180
Guest of Honour, A 94
Guide, The 180
Guilty Thing Surprised, A 192, 203
Gulag Archipelago, The 224
Gulliver's Travels 73, 92, 200, 232
Gun, The 16, 80, 165, 238–9
Gun for Sale, A 80, 100, 122
Gunn, Neil M. 38, 204
Guns of Navarone, The 112, 254
Guy Mannering 216

H

Habit of Loving, The 151
Hadrian the Seventh 97, 207, 240
Haggard, H. Rider 33, **103**, 115, 223, 248
Haggard, William 122
Hailey, Arthur **103**
Hail the Conquering Hero 270
Hail to the Chief 124
Hall, Adam 57
Halliday, Dorothy 68
Hamilton, Patrick 226
Hamlet, Revenge! 214
Hamlet, The 75, 227
Hammett, Dashiel 39, **104**, 196
Handful of Dust, A **254**
Hand in Glove 164
Handl, Irene 72, 176
Handmaid's Tale, The 12, **13**, 27, 34, 37, 86, 207, 261, 272
Hand-reared Boy, A 4
Hangman's Holiday 215
Hangover Square 226
Happy Endings 50

Happy Families Are All Alike   40
Happy Return, The   80
Happy Valley   263
Harcourt, Palma   79
Hard Times   59, 88, 123, 181
Hardy, Thomas   31, 51, 70, **104**, 145, 190, 204
Hare, Cyril   42, 44–45
Harlequin   260
Harris, Macdonald   62
Harrison, Harry   2, **105**, 222
Harris' Requiem   150
Harrod-Eagles, Cynthia   121
Hart-Davis, Duff   5
Hartley, L.P.   40, 41, 81, 82, **106**, 242, 259
Harvest Comedy   80
Hašek, Jaroslav   91, **106**, 109, 110–111, 138, 240, 253
Hatter's Ghosts, The   118
Haunted House   152, 268
Have his Carcase   **215**
Have Space-suit, Will Travel   43
Hawthorne, Nathaniel   3, 63, **107**, 140–1, 169, 194, 272
Haxby's Circus   195
'H.D.'   161, 264
Headbirths   97
Head to Toe   138, 207, 260
Health Unto his Majesty, A   191
Hearing Secret Harmonies   194
Heart Clock   119
Heart is a Lonely Hunter, The   169
Heart of Darkness   **49**, 92, 127, 153, 272
Heart of England, The   51, 92, 257
Heart of Midlothian, The   215, 216, 230
Heart of the Matter, The   **101**
Hearts and Lives of Men, The   256
Heat And Dust   26, 81, 82, 126, 128, 133
Heat of the Day, The   28, 161, 187, 219, 253
Heaven and Earth   201, 246
Heaven's My Destination   151, 264
Heavy Weather   266
Hedylus   98–99, 161, 264
Heights of Rimring, The   5
Heinlein, Robert   43, **108**, 167, 171, 219
Heiress, The   10
Heller, Joseph   15, 23, 36, 74, 78, 98–99, **108**, 110–111, 136–7, 138, 199, 207, 252, 254
Helliconia Spring   4, 112
Helliconia Summer   4
Helliconia Trilogy, The   **4**, 24
Helliconia Winter   4
Hell is Always Today   115
Hellman, Lillian   259
Héloïse and Abelard   56, 202, 245, 261
Hemingway, Ernest   10, 39, 101, **109**, 153, 159, 187, 238–9, 253, 254
Hemlock and After   246, 265
Henderson the Rain King   20, 229
Henry Esmond   235
Herbert, Frank   12, 23, 74, **112**
Herbert, James   **113**, 142, 191, 224, 252, 269
Hercules My Shipmate   9, 97, 121

Here Comes Everybody   33
Here Lies   162
Here's O'Hara   182
Heretics of Dune   113
Hergesheimer, John   166
Heritage, The   24
Heritage and its History, A   48
Heritage of Quincas Borba, The   230
Hero, The   80
Herodotus   97
Heroes and Villains   37, 38
Hersey, John   34, 249
Herzog   20, 21, 43, 230
Hesse, Hermann   36, 38, 51, 56, 89, 90, 93, **113**, 161, 173, 175, 176, 183, 187, 190, 205, 261
Hester Lilly   233
Heyday, The   6, 62, 196
Heyer, Georgette   14, 15, **114**, 116–7, 130
Hibbert, Eleanor   37, **115**, 120, 191
Hide My Eyes   5, 6
Higgins, Jack   44–45, **115**, 147, 176
High and the Mighty, The   219
High Citadel   16
High Cost of Living, The   7, 257
High History of the Runestaff, The   172
High Hunt   70
High Place, The   122
High Rise   17
High Rising   124, 241
Highsmith, Patricia   10, 44–45, **118**, 131, 142, 166, 203, 240, 252
High Wind in Jamaica, A   41, 50
High Window, The   40
Hilda Lessways   22, 65, 78
Hill, Reginald   **119**, 210
Hill, Susan   26, 50, 92, **119**, 159, 161, 175, 189, 204, 208, 209, 213, 233
Hilton, James   103, 196, 215
Himalayan Concerto, The   165
Himes, Chester   17, 167
Him With the Foot in his Mouth   21
Hindsight   62
Hired Man, The   104
Hireling, The   106
His Last Bow   65
His Master's Voice   150
Histories   97
History Man, The   **30**
History of Mr Polly, The   60–61, 258
History of the Eternal Champion, The   172
Hitchhiker's Guide to the Galaxy, The   2, 12
Hitchman, Janet   24
Hoban, Russell   34, **120**, 127, 170, 235, 250
Hobbit, The   236
Hodge, Jane Aiken   37, 115, 116–7
Hogan, Desmond   19
Hogg, James   229
Hold the Dream   30
Holiday   26
Hollow Lands, The   172
Holt, Tom   22

Holt, Victoria   115, **120**
Holtby, Winifred   71
Holy Sinner, The   35, 56, 161, 170
Homage to Catalonia   112, 184
Homage to Qwert Yuiop   34
Home and the World, The   133, 179
Homecomings   224
Homer   9, 120, **121**
Homer's Daughter   97, 121
Honorary Consul, The   101
Honourable Schoolboy, The   146
Hooker, Richard   110–111
Hope, Anthony   115, **122**
Hope, Christopher   178
Hornblower and the Atropos   81
Hornblower in the West Indies   81
Horse and Two Goats, A   180
Horse's Mouth, The   11, 136–7, 152, 165, 263
Horse That Could Whistle Dixie, The   256
Horse Under Water   8, 57, 85, 147
Hotel   103
Hôtel du Lac   27, 32, 106, 203, 209
Hotel New Hampshire, The   48, 54, 72, 127, 199
Hot-house   4
Hot Wind from Hell, A   122
Hound and the Falcon, The   263
Hound of the Baskervilles, The   44–45, 65, 100
Hour of the Lily, The   3, 49
House and its Head, A   48, 72
House at Old Vine, The   152
House at Sunset, The   152
Housebreaker of Shady Hill, The   41
House for Mr Biswas, A   82, **178**, 190
Household, Geoffrey   33, 44–45, 51, 80, **122**
Householder, The   133
House in Paris, The   29
Houseman's Tale, The   30, 217
House of All Nations   87, 171, 226, 241
House of Hospitalities, The   194
House of Mirth, The   60–61, 261, **262**
House of the Seven Gables, The   107
House of the Spirits, The   72, 163, 175, 211
House of the Wolfings, The   173
House on the Strand, The   67
House that Nino Built, The   133
House With the Green Shutters, The   31
Howard, Audrey   30
Howard, Elizabeth Jane   32
Howards End   51, 81, 183
Howatch, Susan   67, **122**
How Far Can You Go?   207, 254
How I Became a Holy Mother   133
How I Grew   168
How To Save Your Own Life   134, 197
Huckleberry Finn   59, 243
Hudson, W.H.   132
Hughes, Richard   41, 50
Hugo, Victor   43, 60–61, 63, **123**, 140–1, 169, 170, 194, 216, 227, 253, 261
Hulme, Keri   27, **123**, 172
Human Age, The   152

Human Beast, The   272
Human Comedy, The   18, 237, 271
Human Factor, The   100, 146
Human Nature   262
Humboldt's Gift   **20**, 136–7, 190
Hunter, Evan   **124**, 167
Hunters and the Hunted, The   167
Hunter's Notes, A   242
Hunting of the Snark, The   188
Huntingtower   33
Huré, Severia   22, 252
Hutchinson, R.C.   26
Huxley, Aldous   34, 86, 89, 107, **124**, 152, 184, 260
Huysmans, Joris-Karl   89

I

I Can Get It For You Wholesale   95, 198, 206, 228, 256
I, Claudius   9, 15, **97**, 98–99
I, Mary, Daughter of Israel   22, 252
I, The Supreme   15, 97, 98–99, 210, 211, 248
Ice Age, The   66
Ice-cream War, An   27
Ice is Coming, The   73
Ice Schooner, The   172
Ides of March, The   9, **264**
Idiot, The   63, 153, 238–9
If Beale Street Could Talk   17
If it Die   89
If Not Now, When?   234
If There be Thorns   10
I Hear America Swinging   58
I Know Why the Caged Bird Sings   17
Iliad   121
Illearth War, The   63
I'll Take Manhattan   144
Illusionist, The   27
Illustrated Man, The   220
Illyrian Spring   230
Illywhacker   27, 140–1, 145, 211, 240
Image Men, The   166, 196
Imaginary Friends   12, 149, 154
Immaterial Murder Case, The   152
Immoralist, The   47, **89**
I'm Not Stiller   20, 138
Imperial Earth   46
Imperial Highness   10
Imperial Stars, The   222, 249
Impossible Object, The   25
I'm the King of the Castle   50, 92, **119**
In a Free State   25, 26, 178
In a German Pension   41, 163
In a Yellow Wood   250
Incomparable Atuk, The   206
In Custody   27
Indecent Exposure   217
Indian Widow, The   121

In Evil Hour 164
Infamous Army, The 114
Infernal Desire Machines of Doctor Hoffman, The 19, 38, 208
Informer, The 74
Inheritors, The 52, 91
In High Places 103
Inimitable Jeeves, The 266
Injured Party, The 32, 154
In My Father's Court 222
Innes, Hammond 112, 115, 223
Innes, Michael 6, 46, 51, 62, **126**, 189, 214
Innocence of Father Brown, The 46
Innocent Blood 132
Innocent Erendira and other Stories 28, 164
Innocents, The 225
In Our Time 112
Inquest on Bouvet 100
In Search of Love and Beauty 133
Inside Mr Enderby 34
Instant in the Wind, An 26
Insular Possession, An 27, 74, 165, 211
Insurance Salesman and Other Stories, The 190
In the Heart of the Country 94, 225
In Their Wisdom 26
In the Name of the Father 147
In the Springtime of the Year 119, 175, 204
In the Wet 219
Intimacy 214
Intimate Strangers 195
Into Your Tent I'll Creep 58
Intruder in the Dust 74, 75
Invincible, The 150
Invisible Cities 28, 35, 36
Invisible Man 16, 134, 229, 251
Invitation to a Beheading 177
Invitation to the Waltz 150
Ipcress File, The 56
Irish Journal 25
Iron Heel, The 153
Iron in the Soul 214
Irving, John 6, 48, 54, 62, 72, **127**, 191, 199, 211, 231, 246, 251
Irwin, Margaret 114, 191
Irwin, Robert 150, 189
Isabelle 89
I Sent a Letter to my Love 209
Isherwood, Christopher 43, **128**, 175, 203
Ishiguro, Kazuo 27, 79, 114, **128**, 179, 238–9
Island 125
Island Nights' Entertainment 166, 230
Island of Doctor Moreau, The 113, 142, 153, 217, 258
Island Pharisee, The 88
Islands in the Stream 112
Island Tales 153
It 113, 142
Italian Assets 5
Italian Folk-Tales 36
It Can't Happen Here 151
Ivanhoe 215, 216, 253
I Will Fear No Evil 108

I Would be Private 159

J

Jack of Eagles 24
Jacob, Naomi 120
Jacobson, Dan 225
Jacobson, Howard 8, 54, 118, 140–1, 145, 156–7, 168, 217
Jacob's Room 268
Jaffé, Rona 7, 168, 201
Jagger, Brenda **130**, 255
Jaguar Smile, The 212
Jailbird 250
Jake's Thing 8, 26
Jalna 51
Jamaica Inn 67, 115, 152
James, Henry 28, 52, 71, 81, 82, 87, 92, 106, 119, **130**, 133, 154, 189
James, M.R. 191
James, P.D. 6, 46, 118, **131**, 202
Jane and Prudence 199
Jane Eyre **31**, 32, 67, 183, 203, 255
Jansson, Tove **132**, 179, 183, 245, 251
Jarrell, Randall 30, 54, 118, **132**, 156–7, 259
Jassy 152
Jean Santeuil 197
Jeeves in the Offing 266
Jeremy Poldark 96
Jerome, Jerome K. 20, 85, **133**
Jerusalem the Golden 65, 150
Jest of God, A 150
Jesus on Mars 73
Jewel in the Skull, The 171
Jhabvala, Ruth Prawer 26, 81, 82, 126, 128, **133**
Jill 106
Jim Davis 230
Job 108, 219
John Barleycorn 153
John Brown's Body 25
John MacNab 33, 122
Johnson, B.S. 240
Johnson, Pamela Hansford 223
Johnston, Jennifer 26, 161
Joining Charles 29
Jolley, Elizabeth 140–1
Jonathan Livingstone Seagull 216
Jones, James 267
Jong, Erica **134**, 190, 197
Joris-Karl Huysmans 197
Joseph 26
Joseph, Marie 50
Joseph and his Brothers 23, 159, 160, 252
Joseph Andrews 75, 76
Joshua Then and Now 206
Journal of the Plague Year, A 56
Journals of Susannah Moodie, The 13
Journey from This World to the Next, A 76

Journeying Boy, The 127
Journey to the Centre of the Earth 73, 249
Journey to the Interior, A 33, 180
Joyce, James 19, 59, 75, 121, **134**, 136–7, 197, 215, 262, 264
Joy in the Morning 266
J.R. 199
Judas Flowering 37
Judas My Brother 270
Judd, Alan 66
Jude the Obscure 70, 105, 145, 190
Judgement in Stone 203
Juggernaut 16
Julian 9, 249
July's People 94
Jungle, The 88, 195, 227
Jungle Book 143
Jungle Lovers 34
Justine 68
Just-so Stories 143

K

Kafka, Franz 35, 91, **138**, 156–7, 177, 183, 184, 230
Kalki 17, 100, **249**
Kama Sutra 74
Kane and Abel 11
Kangaroo 146
Ka of Gifford Hillary, The 252
Kara Kush 74, 234
Karp, David 225
Katherine 191
Katzenbach, John 203
Kaye, M.M. 19, 81, 116–7
Kazantzakis, Nikos 207, 221
Keane, Molly 27, 48, 261
Keating, H.R.F. 6, 44–45, 62, 76, 164, 174
Keepers of the House, The 210
Keeping Up Appearances 159
Keep the Aspidistra Flying 186
Keillor, Garrison 247
Kellerman, Jonathan 57
Kellow, Kathleen 115
Kemelman, Harry 44–45, 46
Keneally, Thomas 6, 26, 27, 53, **139**, 140–1, 207, 253, 259, 262
Kenilworth 216·
Kent, Alexander 80
Kesey, Ken 159, 252
Key To Rebecca, The 33, 44–45, 79
Khufra Run, The 16
Kid from Riga, The 147
Kidnapped 68, 120, 230
Killer in the Rain 40
Killing Bottle, The 40, 106
Killing Doll, The 203
Kilroy, Thomas 25
Kim 82, 126, **143**, 191

Kind Are Her Answers 202
Kindly Light 198
Kindly Ones, The 194
Kinflicks 6, 60–61, 101, 134, 251
King, Francis 128
King, Stephen 92, 93, 113, **142**, 191, 224, 252
King and Joker 62
Kingdom of the Wicked, The 22, 34, 98–99, 252
Kingfisher 115
King Fisher Lives 26
King Hereafter 68
King Jesus 97, 252
King Must Die, The 9, 97, 121, 202
King, Queen, Knave 178
King's General, The 67
King Solomon's Mines 103, 115, 223
Kipling, Rudyard 82, 126, **142**, 166, 191
Kipps 14, 52, 59, 76, 258
Kiss Kiss 142, 224
Kiss Me Again Stranger 67
Kiteworld 235, 243
Kits Hill 122
Klíma, Ivan 190
Klingsor's Last Summer 114
Knulp 114
Koestler, Arthur 184, 192, 211, 214, 224
Koontz, Dean R. 113
Kornbluth, C.M. 125
Kosinski, Jerzy 110–111, **143**, 177, 199, 221
Kraken Wakes, The 269
Krantz, Judith 30, 87, **144**, 171
Kreutzer Sonata, The 240
Kristin Lavransdatter 104, 186, 195, 245
Kruse, John 3, 49
Kundera, Milan 35, 143
Kyle, David A. 222

L

Labyrinths **28**
Lace 144
Laclos, Pierre Choderlos de 205
Lady Chatterley's Lover 146
Lady in the Lake, The 39, 40, 104
Lady Living Alone 152
Lady With the Little Dog and Other Stories, The **41**, 162, 242
Lagerkvist, Pär 23, 56, 170, 195, 202, 252
Lake, The 242
Laker, Rosalind 116–7, 234
Lake Wobegon Days 247
Lament for a Lost Lover 37
Lament for a Maker 127, 189
Lampedusa, Giuseppi Tomaso di 75
Lampitt, Dinah 183
Lanark 138
Landfall 110–111, 219
Landlocked 150

Land of Mist, The   65
Landscape with Dead Dons   214
Landslide   16
Langley, Noel   20, 196
Langrigg, Roger   140–1
Lantana Lane   53
Lantern Network, The   5
Lardner, Ring   153, 182
Larkin, Philip   106
Lark Rise to Candleford   132
L'assommoir   165, 271
Last and the First, The   48
Last Chronicle of Barset, The   60–61, 241
Last Days of Pompeii, The   9, 253
Last Gamble, The   96
Last House-Party, The   62
Last Letters from Hav   27
Last Man, The   218
Last of Chéri, The   47
Last of Mr Norris, The   128
Last of the Mohicans, The   127, 216
Last of the Wine, The   202, 264
Last Place God Made, The   115
Last Respects   256
Last Summer   124
Last Things   224
Last Tycoon, The   77
Las Vegas   198
Late Bourgeois World, The   94
Late Call   233, 261, 265
Late George Apley, The   24
Late Mattia Pascal, The   190
Later Adventures of Tom Jones, The   76
Lathen, Emma   46, 164, 171
Lathe of Heaven, The   149
Laughing Policeman, The   192, 220
Laurels Are Poison   46, 126
Laurence, Margaret   150
Laurents, Arthur   246, 247
Lawley Road   180
Lawrence, D.H.   21, 88, **145**, 187, 263
Leacock, Stephen   133
Leaf-storm and other Stories   164
Leaning in the Wind   83, 180
Leaning Tower, The   41, 169, 193
Lear, John   43, 146, 147
Learning To Swim   231
Leave it to Psmith   **266**
Leaven of Malice   54
Le Carré, John   3, 5, 57, 94, **146**, 147, 154, 215, 234
L'Éducation sentimentale   78
Lee, Harper   3, 55, 75
Lee, Laurie   23, 132, 243
Left Bank, The   204
Left Hand of Darkness, The   4, 112, 148
Le Guin, Ursula   4, 73, 112, **148**, 167, 189
Lehmann, Rosamond   **149**, 175, 183, 262
Lem, Stanislaw   43, **150**
Lenin: the Novel   15
Lenz, Siegfried   24
Leonard, Elmore   198

Leopard, The   75
Le rouge et le noir   228
Leroux, Gaston   229
Lessing, Doris   12, 25, 27, 57, 146, **150**, 203, 234
Lesson in Love, A   46, 89
Lesson of the Master, The   131
Less than Angels   199
Let Me Count the Ways   58
Letting Go   6, 209, 216
Letty Fox, Her Luck   226
Levanter, The   7
Levant Trilogy, The   69, 161, 214
Levels, The   231
Levi, Primo   234
Lewis, C.S.   56, 73, 92, 148, 249, 257
Lewis, Janet   1, 38, 71, 245
Lewis, Roy   85
Lewis, Sinclair   86, **151**, 261
Lewis, Wyndham   11, 109, **152**, 197
liaisons dangereuses, Les   197, 205
Lie Down in Darkness   75
Lie Down With Lions   2
Life, A   78, 231
Life and Adventures of Mr Duncan Campbell, The   55
Life and Death of Jonathan Wild the Great, The   76
Life and Loves of a She-Devil, The   94, 257, 272
Life & Times of Michael K   27
Life Before Man   12, 257
Life for the Stars, A   24
Life in the West   4
Life of Henri Brulard, The   228
Life of Klim Samgin, The   95
Life, the Universe and Everything   2
Life to Come, The   83
Light and the Dark, The   224, 245
Light a Penny Candle   23, 130
Light in August   75
Lightning   7, 192
Light of Day, The   **7**, 47
Lights of Skaro, The   44–45
Light That Failed, The   143
Light Years   257
Like Birds Like Fishes   133
Like Men Betrayed   201, 214, 234
Lilac Bus, The   23
Limbo   125
Lime Pit   196
Limits of Love, The   201
Lincoln   249
Lindmann   201
Linklater, Eric   106, 196
Lion of Boaz-Jachin and Jachin-Boaz, The   120
List of Adrian Messenger, The   147
Literary Lapses   133
Little Company, The   53
Little Dorrit   59, 140–1.
Little Drummer Girl, The   94, 146, 148, 234
Little House on the Prairie, The   23, 85

Little Learning, A 255
Little Mexican, The 125
Little Sister, The 40
Little Sisters 257
Little Wilson and Big God 34
Little World of Don Camillo, The 179
Live Flesh 118, 142, 203, 224
Lively, Penelope 26, 27, 119
Lively Dead, The 59, 62, 174
Lives of Girls and Women 174
Livia 69
Living and the Dead, The 263
Livingstone's Companions 94
Liza of Lambeth 3, 18, 165, 227, 271
Lizard in the Cup, The 62
Local Anaesthetic 97
Lockwood Concern, The 60–61, 182
Lodge, David 4, 27, 30, 34, 124, 154, 156–7, 207, 254
Lofts, Norah 116–7, 120, **152**, 255
Lois the Witch 88
Loitering with Intent 27
Lolita 177
London, Jack 10, 88, 112, **152**
London Embassy, The 236
London Match 57
Lonely Girl, The 46
Lonely Road 219
Long Distance 257
Longest Journey, The 81
Long Goodbye, The 40
Long Kill, The 44–45, 210
Long March, The 159
Long Ships, The 68, 112
Long Valley, The 228
Long Way from Verona, A 106
Look at All Those Roses 29
Look at Me **32**, 154, 183, 198, 225
Look at the Harlequins! 177
Look Homeward, Angel 55, 134, 145, 267
Looking for Mr Goodbar 208
Looking Glass War, The 148
Looking on Darkness 224
Look to the Lady 6
Loos, Anita 77
Lord Foul's Bane 63, 148
Lord Hornblower 81
Lord Jim 49
Lord of Darkness 220
Lord of the Far Islands 121
Lord of the Flies 41, 91, 92, 93, 119, 272
Lord of the Rings, The 62, 70, 73, 188, 236
Lord Valentine's Castle 73, 189, 220
Lorna Doone 31, 96
Losing Battles 258, 259
Lost Domain, The 197
Lost Empires 195
Lost Honour of Katherina Blum, The 24, 181
Lost Horizon 103
Lost Illusions 228
Lost Lady, A 38
Lost Tales 237

Lost Traveller, The 262
Lost World, The 64, 73, 103, 248
Lotte in Weimar 161
Lot to Ask, A 180
Louise 255
Love 38
Love and Exile 222
Love and Friendship 154
Love and Mr Lewisham 258
Love and Napalm: Export USA 18
Love and Trouble, In 251
Lovecraft, H.P. 191, 257
Loved One, The 52, 156–7, 255
Love in a Cold Climate 22, 158
Love in Amsterdam 202, 220
Love-letters between a Nobleman and his Sister 206
Lover, The 203
Love Story 116–7, 216, 255
Love Talker, The 10
Love Unknown 8
Loving 227
Low-flying Aircraft 18
Low-lands 199
Low Notes on a High Level 156–7, 196
Lowry, Malcolm 101, 134, **153**, 183, 204
Lucia in Wartime 22
Lucia Triumphant 22
Lucinda Brayford 29
Luck of the Bodkins, The 266
Lucky 144
Lucky Jim 8, 132, 156–7
Lucy Gayheart 39
Ludlum, Robert 33, 79, 122, 147, **154**
Lunar Caustic 153
Lung, The 74
Lurie, Alison 7, 12, 14, 15, 118, 124, 149, **154**, 156–7, 168, 180, 245, 251, 261
Lyall, Gavin 57
Lying Days, The 94
Lyonesse 62
Lytton, Lord 253

M

Macaulay, Rose 101, 149, **158**, 165, 181, 193, 197, 225, 262
Macauley, Robie 120, 235
MacAvoy, R.A. 62
MacDonald, Betty 85
MacDonald, Greg 39, 47, 118
MacDonald, Philip 147
MacDonald, Ross 39, 104, 196
Macdonell, A.G. 133
Machado de Assis, Joaquin 230
MacInnes, Colin 21
MacInnes, Helen 10, 33, 116–7, 230
Mackenzie, Compton 158
Mackerel Plaza, The 58, 86

MacLaverty, Bernard   74
Maclean, Alastair   112, 254
Madame Bovary   70, **78**, 183, 204, 237, 248, 261
Madame Sousatzka   209
Madam Will You Talk?   230
Madder Music   58
Madeleine   89
Madonna of the Astrolabe, The   127
Maggot, A   84, 93, 140–1
Magic Christian, The   199
Magic Cottage, The   252, 269
Magician of Lublin, The   221
Magician's Gambit   70
Magic Labyrinth, The   74
Magic Mountain, The   90, 160, **161**
Magic Toyshop , The   37, 72, 189, 226
Magister Ludi   113
Magnet, The   95
Magus, The   83, 84, 136–7
Mahjong Spies, The   103, 147
Maiden Castle   195
Maid of Buttermere, The   145, 190
Maigret's Pipe   42
Mailer, Norman   98–99, 104, 110–111, 112, **159**, 169, 186, 254, 268
Main Street   86, 151
Majipoor Chronicles, The   220
Make Room! Make Room!   105
Making Good Again   49, 139
Making of the Representatives for Planet 8, The   151
Malacia Tapestry, The   4
Malafrena   73, 148, 189
Malamud, Bernard   20, 91, 208, 218, 221
Malaysian Trilogy, The   34
Male Response, The   4
Malgudi Days   180
Mallen Girl, The   50
Mallen Litter, The   51
Mallen Streak, The   51
Malraux, André   237
Maltese Falcon, The   39, 104, 196
Man and Two Women, A   151
Man Called Spade, A   104
Man Called Thin, A   104
Manchurian Candidate, The   2, 5, 8, 49
Mandarins, The   36, 71
Mandelbaum Gate, The   130, 226
Maneater of Malgudi, The   179
Man from St Petersburg, The   79
Manhattan Transfer   197
Man in the Iron Mask, The   66, 123, 216
Mann, Heinrich   123
Mann, Thomas   23, 29, 35, 48, 54, 56, 60–61, 73, 75, 76, 87, 90, 106, 159, **160**, 169, 170, 176, 252
Manning, Olivia   19, 68, **161**, 175, 214, 238–9, 261
Man of Property, The   87, 270
Man of the People, A   2
Manor, The   221

Manservant and Maidservant   48
Man's Estate   237
Mansfield, Katherine   15, 40, 41, 142, **162**, 174
Mansfield Park   13, 15, 115
Mansfield Revisited   15, 116–7
Mansion, The   75
Mantel, Hilary   156–7
Man That Corrupted Hadleyburg, The   244
Manticore, The   54
Mantissa   83
Man Upstairs, The   266
Man Who Killed Himself, The   118
Man Who Loved Children, The   72, 90, 208, 226, 263
Man Who Watched the Trains Go By, The   220
Man Without Qualities, The   160
Man With the Golden Gun, The   79
Man With the President's Mind, The   5
Many Inventions   143
Manzoni, Alessandro   123
Mapp and Lucia   **22**, 86
Maras Affair, The   8
Marchbanks' Almanac   54
Margaret Catchpole   181
Mario the Magician   161
Marjorie Morningstar   268
Markstein, George   79
Marlowe, Stephen   15, 98–99, 181, 202
Marquand, J.P.   24
Márquez, Gabriel García   28, 73, 98–99, **163**, 210, 211, 248
Marriage Between Zones Three, Four and Five, The   151
Marry Me   183, 208, 246
Marsh, Ngaio   46, 131, **164**
Marshall, James Vance   92
Marsten, Richard   124
Martha Quest   13, 150
Martin Chuzzlewit   59
Mary Anne   67
Mary Barton   **88**, 173, 195
Masculine Ending   6
Masefield, John   230
M*A*S*H   110–111
Mask of Apollo, The   6, 98–99, **202**
Mask of Dimitrios, The   7, 147
Mason, Anita   27
Masqueraders, The   115
Master and Man   240
Master and Margharita, The   93
Master of Ballantrae, The   230
Master of Hestviken, The   245
Master of Life and Death   17, 219
Masters, John   74, 142, **165**, 240
Masters, The   126, 223, 224
Matarese Circle, The   154
Match for a Murderer   68
Matheson, Richard   142
Matter of Conscience, A   79
Matter of Honour, A   11, 84
Maugham, Somerset   3, 11, 18, 21, 59, 60–61, 81, 101, 142, **165**, 227, 271

Mauriac, François   18, 63, 72, **166**
Maurice   83
Maurice Guest   57, 204, 205
Mavor, Elizabeth   26
Mayor of Casterbridge, The   104, 105
May We Borrow Your Husband?   101
Mazemaker, The   11
Mazes and Monsters   168
McBain, Ed   124, **167**, 192
McCabe, Cameron   174
McCaffrey, Anne   73, **167**, 220
McCarthy, Mary   7, 14, 30, 76, 101, 118, 128,
   154, 156–7, **168**, 174, 183, 192, 203, 251
McCullers, Carson   18, 47, 55, 75, 119, 166,
   169, 213, 255
McCullough, Colleen   14, 170, 270
McCutcheon, Hugh   122
McEwan, Ian   27, 89, 93, 169
McGinley, Patrick   143
McIntyre, Vonda N.   222
Means of Evil   203
Mechanismo   105
Medea   98–99
Medusa Frequency, The   120
Meeting at Telgte, The   97
Meeting by the River, A   128, 175
Meeting for Burial   24
Meet Mr Mulliner   266
Melville, Herman   49, **169**, 218
Member of the Wedding, The   47, 169, 213,
   255
Memento Mori   183, 225
Memoirs of a Catholic Girlhood   168
Memoirs of a Cavalier   55
Memoirs of an Egoist   228
Memoirs of a Survivor   151
Memoirs of Captain George Carleton   55
Memoirs of Christopher Columbus, The   15,
   98–99, 181, 202
Memoirs of Hadrian   9, 97, 98–99, 264
Memoirs of Sherlock Holmes, The   **64**
Memorial Service, A   127
Memory-Hold-the-Door/The Three Hostages   33
Men and Wives   48
Mensonge   30
Men Without Women   101, 112
Mercenaries, The   124, 198
Meridian   227, 251
Merlin   181
Mermaid   131
Mermaids on the Golf Course   119, 142
Merry Men, The   230
Methuselah's Children   108
Meyer, Gordon   235
Meyer, Nicholas   64
Micah Clarke   65
Michel Strogoff   249
Middle Age of Mrs Eliot, The   28, 60–61, 175,
   265
Middlemarch   65, **71**, 145, 183, 228, 260
Middle Mist, The   202
Middleton, Stanley   26, 150

Midnight Plus One   57
Midnight's Children   27, 126, 127, 136–7, 210,
   264
Midsummer Century   24
Midwich Cuckoos, The   92, 269
Mighty and their Fall, The   48
Miguel Street   179
Milan, Victor   171
Mile High   49, 110–111, 192
Military Philosophers, The   194
Millar, Margaret   131
Millenium Hall   173
Miller, Walter M.   86, **170**, 250
Mill on the Floss, The   50, 70, 71
Millstone, The   65, 71
Milne, John   39, 196
Mimic Men, The   179
Mind to Murder, A   132
Ministry of Fear, The   44–45
Mirgorod   91
Mirror for Princes, A   12, 56, 67, 73, 114,
   148, 188, 189
Misalliance, A   32, 53, 175
misérables, Les   60–61, 63, 123, 140–1
Misery   142
Miss Harriet   41
Miss Herbert (The Suburban Wife)   226
Missing Persons   50, 183, 209, 258
Miss Lonelyhearts   206, 260
Miss Silver Investigates   42
Mistral's Daughter   144
Mistress of Mellyn   121
Mitchell, Gladys   42, 44–45, 46, 62, 64, 126
Mitchell, Margaret   31, 55, **170**, 187, 216, 255,
   270
Mitchison, Naomi   9, 97, 186, 202
Mitford, Nancy   19, 22, 41, 72, 158
Mixture of Frailties, A   14, 54
Mo, Timothy   27, 74, 82, 165, 178, 211, 235
Moby-Dick   **169**, 218
Modern Comedy, A   87, 88
Moggach, Deborah   65, 169
Moll Flanders   55, 76
Molloy, Michael   147
Money   125, 272
Moneychangers, The   103
Money in the Bank   266
Monsarrat, Nicholas   98–99, 112, 218, 268
Monsieur   69
Monsignor Quixote   100, 207
Montezuma's Daughter   103
Montfords, The   29
Montherlant, Henri de   159
Month in the Country, A   27
Month of Sundays, A   246
Montrose: the Captain General   216
Moon   113, 191, 224
Moon and Sixpence, The   11, 165, 166
Moonraker   79
Moons of Jupiter, The   174
Moon-spinners, The   230
Moon Tiger   27

Moorcock, Michael 73, 143, **171**, 211, 250
Moore, Brian 26, 27, 92, 127, 140–1, 203, 207, 246, 260
Moore, George 23, 38, 190, 242, 252
Moorhouse, Frank **172**
Morag's Flying Fortress 105, 128
Moravia, Alberto 182, 190, 230
Moreau's Other Island 4
More Die of Heartbreak 21
More Pricks than Kicks 28
More Spook Stories 22
Moreta 167
More Women than Men 48
More Work for the Undertaker 6
Morris, Gerald H. 127, 163, 211, 231
Morris, Jan 27
Morris, William 86, **173**
Mortal Coils 125
Mortality and Mercy in Vienna 199
Morte d'Urban 198, 207
Mortimer, Penelope 65, 257
Mosby's Memoirs 21
Mosco, Maisie 73, **173**, 255
Moscow Quadrille 5
Moscow Set 57
Mosley, N. 25
Mosquito Coast, The 49, 127, 175, 235
Mother 95
Mother and Son 48
Mother Night 250
Mothers and Sons 75
Mountolive 68
Mousetrap 42
Moving Toyshop, The 44–45, 126, 174
Mr Blettsworthy on Rampole Island 258
Mr Campion and Others 6
Mr Campion's Farthing 6
Mr Midshipman Hornblower 81, 120
Mr Norris Changes Trains 128
Mr Palomar 36
Mr Perrin and Mr Traill 257
Mr Prohack 22
Mr Pye 188
Mrs Ames 22
Mr Sammler's Planet 18, 21, 24, 143, 151
Mr Sampath 178, 180
Mr Scarborough's Family 241
Mrs Dalloway 65, 134, 136–7, 149, 203, 267, 268
Mrs Eckdorff in O'Neill's Hotel 25
Mrs Harris in New York 43
Mrs Noah 207
Mrs Palfrey at the Claremont 26, 234
Mr Standfast 33
Mr Stone and the Knights Companion 179
Mrs Wallop 58
Mr Wakefield's Crusade 210
Mr Zouch: Superman 193
Much Else in Italy 29
Munro, Alice 26, **174**
Murari, T.N. 116–7, 126
Murder at the Vicarage **42**

Murderer, The 272
Murder in Focus 68
Murder in Mesopotamia **42**
Murder in Style 100
Murder in the Round 68
Murder is Announced, A 42
Murder, Maestro, Please 47
Murder Must Advertise 215
Murder of Quality, A 148
Murder of Roger Ackroyd, The 42
Murder on the Orient Express 42, 240
Murder's Little Sister 44–45
Murdoch, Iris 25, 26, 27, 28, 31, 58, 78, 89, 101, 116–7, 136–7, 149, **174**, 175, 187, 190, 264, 267
Museums and Women 246
Music School, The 246
Musil, Robert 24, 160
My Antonia 29, 38, 39, 82, 213
My Apprenticeship 47, 95
My Brilliant Career 3, 14, 29, 85
My Career Goes Bung 85
My Childhood 95
My Cousin Rachel 67, 96
My Enemy the Queen 121
Myers, L.P. 159
My Family and Other Animals 132
My Father Sits in the Dark 256
My First Loves 190
My Heart and My Flesh 80
My Life and Times 133
My Life as a Man 209
My Life in the Bush of Ghosts 1
My Mortal Enemy 39
Myra Breckinridge 37, 206, 249
Myron 250
Myself and Michael Innes 127
Myself When Young 67
Mysterious Stranger, The 244
Mystic Masseur, The 178
My Universities 95

N

Nabokov, Vladimir 30, 47, 63, 72, 132, 156–7, **177**, 184, 190, 224
Nabokov's Dozen 178
Nabokov's Quartet 178
Naipaul, V.S. 25, 26, 82, **178**, 190
Naive and Sentimental Lover, The 146, 148
Naked and the Dead, The 110–111, 112, 159, 254, 268
Naked Sun, The 11
Name of the Rose, The 93, 170, 174, 228, 245
Nana 3, 18, 169, **271**
Napoleon Symphony, The 34, 238–9
Narayan, R.K. 78, 82, 126, 128, 178, **179**, 184, 191
Narziss and Goldmund 93, 113, 114

National Lampoon   113
Nature of Passion, The   133
Nausea   214
Navigator, The   219, 259
Near and the Far, The   159
Nest of Gentlefolk, A   242
Nest of Vipers, The   63, 72, **166**
Net of Circumstance, The   85
Never Leave Me   116–7
New Arrivals, Old Encounters   4
Newby, P.H.   25, 82, 83, **180**, 254
Newcomes, The   235
New Confessions, The   230
New Dominion, A   133
New Grub Street   18, 181, 271
New Lease of Death, A   203
New Life, A   20
New Maps of Hell   9
New Men, The   219, 223, 224
News From Nowhere   86, 94, 173, 192
New Shirt, A   19
New York Dance, A   47
Niccolò Rising   68, 201
Nice and the Good, The   25
Nice Summer   190
Nicholas Nickleby   58, 59, 215
Nigger of the Narcissus, The   49, 169, 218, 263
Night Among the Horses, A   19
Night and Day   268
Nightmare Abbey   90
Night of Error   16
Night of Errors, A   127
Nightrunners of Bengal   74, 142, 165
Nights at the Circus   38, 210
Night's Black Agent   44–45
Night She Died, The   42
Night Shift   142, 191
Night Walk   268
Nightwood   19, 183, 208, 226
Nin, Anaïs   172, 267
Nine Billion Names of God, The   46
Nine Coaches Waiting   116–7, 230
Nine Months in the Life of an Old Maid   208
Nine Stories   172, 213
Nine Tailors, The   44–45, 215
1985   34
1984   12, 86, 138, **184**, 272
Ninety-three   123
Ninja's Revenge   10
No Barrier   53
No Bed for Bacon   191, 201
Nobody Knew They Were There   124
Nobody Knows My Name   17
No Comebacks   83
No Country for Young Men   26
Nocturne   80
No Fond Return of Love   234
No Highway   219, 223
No Laughing Matter   109, 265
No Longer at Ease   1
No Man's Wit   159
No Name in the Street   16

Non-Existent Knight, The   35
No, Not Bloomsbury   30
Non-stop   4
Noonday Devil, The   66
No One Writes to the Colonel   164
No Orchids for Miss Blandish   39, 104
Norris, Frank   271
North, Elizabeth   23, 255
North and South   50, 59, 70, 88, 173
Northanger Abbey   15, 183
North Face   202
Nostromo   49, 101, 178
Not a Penny More Not a Penny Less   11
Notes From the House of the Dead   64, 224
Notes from Underground   64
Notes of a Native Son   16
Not For Publication   94
Nothing Like the Sun   34
Nothing Personal   17
Nothing Sacred   38
Notre Dame de Paris   43, 123, 170, 216, 253, 261
Not That Sort of Girl   262
Not to Disturb   226
Nowhere City, A   155
No Word from Winifred   214
Nœud de Vipères, Le   63, 166
Number of the Beast   108, 171
Numquam   68, 264
Nuns in Jeopardy   218
Nye, Robert   15, 145, **181**

O

O, How the Wheel Becomes It   194
Oasis, The   168
Oates, Joyce Carol   182, 208, 233
Oblomov   91
O'Brien, Edna   23, 46, 174
O'Brien, Flann   63, 135, 229, 261
Obscure Destinies   39
Occasion for Loving   94
Occupying Power, The   10
Octopussy   79
Odessa File, The   83
Odessa Tales   221
Odyssey   9, 97, 120, 121, 195
Oedipus   202
O'Faolain, Julia   26
O'Faoláin, Seán   41, 193
Offshore   26
Of Human Bondage   21, 59, 60–61, 165
O'Flaherty, Liam   74
Of Love and Shadows   5, 94, 248
Of Mice and Men   227, 245
Of the Farm   245, 246
Of Time and the River   267
Ogniblat L'Artsau, Mrs   182
O'Hara, John   60–61, **182**, 266

O'Hara Generation, The   182
Oh What A Paradise it Seems   40
Old and the Young, The   190
Old Blastus of Bandicoot   85
Old Curiosity Shop, The   59
Old Devils, The   **8**, 27
Oldest Confession, The   49
Oldfield, Pamela   30
Old Forest, The   182
Old Goriot   **18**, 183
Old Gringo, The   163
Old Hall, New Hall   51
Old Ladies, The   18
Old Love   222
Old Man and the Sea, The   109, 112, 153
Old Men at the Zoo, The   223, 265
Old Mortality   216
Old New York   262
Old Order, The   193
Old Wives' Tale, The   **21**, 22
Oliver's Story   216
Oliver Twist   3, 50, 58, 59
Olshan, Joseph   245
Omoo   169
On a Pale Horse   10
Once and Future King, The   70, 73
One Day in the Life of Ivan Denisovich   140–1, 224, 272
One Fat Englishman   9
One Flew Over the Cuckoo's Nest   159, 252
One Foot in the Grave   62
One Human Minute   150
158-Pound Marriage, The   128
One Hundred Years of Solitude   5, 73, **163**, 210, 211
One Man's Meat   119
One, None and a Hundred Thousand   190
One of Ours   39
One Step from Earth   105
One Tree, The   63
On Forsyte Change   88
On Her Majesty's Secret Service   79
Onions, Oliver   104, 152
Only Children   15, 154
Only Problem, The   225
Only When I Larf   57, 66
On the Beach   **219**
On the Eve   237, 242
Operation Pax   **127**
O Pioneers!   39
Optimist's Daughter, The   259
Opus   12
Orchestra and Beginners   194, 201
Orczy, Baroness   14, 66
Ordeal of Gilbert Pinfold, The   159, 254
Orientations   142
Original Sins   7
Origin of the Brunists, The   107
Orlando   163, 268
Orley Farm   241
Orphan Island   159
Orsinian Tales   149

Orton, Joe   138, 207, 260
Orwell, George   12, 86, 112, 138, **184**, 192, 211, 272
Osterman Weekend, The   154
Other Fires   95
Other Friday, The   55
Other People's Money   48, **256**
Other Side of Paradise, The   19
Other Side of the Fire, The   168
Other Women   7, 57
Our Ancestors   **35**, 36, 163, 170
Our Father   175, 203, 208, 209
Our Gang   209
Our Man in Havana   7, 100, 235
Our Mutual Friend   59
Outbreak of Love   29
Out of India   133
Out of the Silent Planet   56, 73, 257
Out of This World   231
Outsider, The   36
Overload   103
Overture to Death   164
Owen Glendower   195
Oxbridge Blues   201
Oz, Amos   192
O-Zone   125, 235, **236**, 243, 272

P

Pain   156–7
Painted Bird, The   143, 177, 221
Painter of Signs, The   179, 191
Pair of Blue Eyes, A   105
Pale Fire   **178**
Pale Horse, Pale Rider   71, 193
Pale View of Hills, A   129, 238–9
Pal Joey   182
Palm Sunday   250
Palm-wine Drinkard, The   178
Pamela   205
Pantagruel   200
Paper Dragon, The   124
Paper Men, The   20, 93
Paper Thunderbolt   **127**
Parade's End   29, 79, 101
Parasites, The   67
Parents and Children   48
Parker, Dorothy   162
Parsifal Mosaic, The   122, 147, 154
Parson's Daughter, The   14
Party Going   193
Pascali's Island   26
Pasley, Malcolm   139
Passage of Arms   8
Passage to India, A   52, 81, 82, **83**, 126, 133
Passenger   142
Passion, The   211, 238–9
Passion of New Eve, The   **37**, 86, 232
Passions   222

Passmore 26
Pasternak, Boris 170, **187**, 216, 237, 238–9, 255
Pastoral Symphony, The 89, 114
Pastors and Masters 48, 198
Past Through Tomorrow, The 108
Path to the Nest of Spiders, The 36
Paton, Alan 94, 225
Pauper, Brawler and Slanderer 123
Pavese, Cesare 190
Pawn in Frankincense 68
Pawn of Prophecy 62, 70
Paying Guests 22
Payment Deferred 80
Peacock, Thomas Love 90
Peake, Mervyn 48, 183, **188**, 189
Pearce, Mary 122
Pearl, The 228
Pebble in the Sky 12
Peck, Richard 73
Pedigree 220, 221
Peeping Tom 8, 54, 217
Pemberton, Margaret 116–7
Pendennis 60–61, 181, 234, 235
Penitent, The 221
Penmarric 67, 123
Pentimento 259
People of the Abyss, The 88
People Who Knock on the Door, The 10, 118, 166
People With the Dogs, The 226
Perdita's Prince 10, 191
Perelandra 92, 148
Perfect Happiness 119
Perfect Spy, A 3, 82, 146, 147, 148
Perfect Woman, A 106
Performing Flea 266
Perpetual Orgy, The 248
Persian Boy, The 202
Persian Prince, The 10
Persian Ransom, The 10
Personal Recollections of Joan of Arc 243
Persuasion 15
Petal on the Wind 10
Peter Abelard 170
Peter Camenzind 89, 114, 161
Peters, Elizabeth 10
Peter Smart's Confessions 26, 57, 140–1
Petronius 97, 121, 145, 181
Pet Sematary 142, 224, 252
Phantom of the Opera, The 229
Philosopher's Pupil, The 149
Phineas Finn 241
Phineas Redux 241
Photogenic Soprano, The 68
Piano-players, The 34, 176
Pickwick Papers 59
Picnic at Sakkara 82, 180, 254
Picture Palace 203, 209, 235
Pictures from an Institution 30, 54, 118, 132, 156–7, 259
Pied Piper 219

Piercy, Marge 7, 257
Pigeon Feathers 246
Pigs Have Wings 266
Pilgrimage 197, 267
Pincher Martin 55, 93, 120
Pirandello, Luigi **190**
Pirates of Venus 249
Pistols for Two 115
Pit, The 271
Place in the Sun, A 73
Plague, The **36**, 214
Plague Dogs, The 36, 153
Plaidy, Jean 10, 67, 114, 115, 170, **191**, 202
Plain Murder 80
Plain Tales from the Hills 142
Planet of Exile 149
Planet of the Damned 105
Plantagenet Prelude, The 68
Plath, Sylvia 159, 213, 252, 262
Playback 40
Player Piano 250
Playmaker, The 6, 53, 139, 140–1
Play Room, The 162
Pleasure of Ruins, The 159
Pleasures and the Days, The 197
Pledge, The 44–45
Plot it Yourself 100
Plumed Serpent, The 146, 263
Plunkett, James 20, 261
Pnin 30, 177
Poe, Edgar Allan 142, **191**, 252
Poet's Pub 196
Pohl, Frederick 125, 219, 250
Point Counter Point 125
Poison Belt, The 65
Poisoned Kiss, The 208
Poison in Jest 214
Poison Oracle, The 62, 164
Poldark 73
Police at the Funeral 6
Polonaise 116–7
Ponder Heart, The 234, 259
Ponsonby Post, The 209
Poorhouse Fair, The 246
Poppy Factory, The 254
Porius 195
Porky 169
Portable Steinbeck, The 228
porte étroite, La 89
Porter, Joyce 119
Porter, Katharine Anne 41, 71, 169, **193**, 218
Porterhouse Blue 8, 66, 217
Portnoy's Complaint 6, 109, 208
Portrait of a Lady 71, 130, 131
Portrait of an Unknown Man 24
Portrait of Dorian Gray, The 20
Portrait of the Artist as a Young Man 59, 134, 135, 197, 215, 262
Poseidon Adventure, The 103, 218
Possessed, The 64
Postures 204
Potterism 158, 181

Potts, Jean   47, 164
Powell, Anthony   77, 125, 126, 152, **193**, 197
Power and the Glory, The   100, 112
Powers, J.F.   198, 207
Power That Preserves, The   63
Powys, John Cowper   **194**
Poyer, Joe   79
Prague Orgy, The   209
Praise Singer, The   202
Pratchett, Terry   2, 73, 236
Prater Violet   128
Praxis   26, 257
Prayer for the Dying, A   115
Praying for Rain   256
Precious Bane   51
Prelude to Christopher   53
Prelude to Waking   85
Present and the Past, The   48
President, The   211, 221
President's Child, The   257
Prester John   33, 103
Presumed Innocent   2
Prichard, Katharine Susannah   **195**, 263
Prick of Noon, The   58, 76
Pricksongs and Descants   28, 63, 172
Pride and Prejudice   **13**, 14, 15, 124
Pride of Heroes, A   62
Priestley, J.B.   6, 21, 60–61, 156–7, 165, **195**
Primal Urge, The   4, 250
Prime Minister, The   241
Prime Number   105
Prime of Miss Jean Brodie, The   225
Prince and the Pauper, The   243
Prince and the Quakeress, The   191
Prince of India, The   253
Princess Daisy   30, 87, 144
Princess of Mars, A   103
Printer of Malgudi, The   178, 180
Prisoner of Zenda, The   115, 122
Pritchett, V.S.   182, 233, 265
Private Angelo   106
Private Papers   187
Prizzi's Family   48
Prizzi's Honour   47, 48, 124, 198
Proceed, Sergeant Lamb   97
Prodigal Daughter, The   11
Prodigy, The   114
Professor, The   32
Professor of Desire, The   154, **209**
Professor's House, The   39, 129, 242, 264
Promise, The   227
Promise of Love   202
Promises   227
Promises, The   50
Proof   19, 85
Proust, Marcel   41, 81, 89, 102, 130, 136–7, 194, **196**, 267
Providence   32
Psycho   183, 208
Public Image, The   25
Puck of Pook's Hill   143
Pudd'nhead Wilson   244

Puffball   **257**
Pumpkin Eater, The   65
Purple Plain, The   219
Purposes of Love   202
Pursuit of Love, The   72
Put Out More Flags   255
Puzo, Mario   **198**
Pym, Barbara   14, 26, 54, 66, 86, 124, **198**, 233, 234, 241
Pynchon, Thomas   110–111, **199**, 224, 232
Pyramid, The   93

Q

Quarry, The   220
Quartet   204
Quartet in Autumn   26, 54, 198, 199
Queen Lucia   22
Queen of Sorcery   70
Queen of the Realm   202
Queen's Necklace, The   67
Queen's Play   10, 68
Quentin Durward   216
Querelle of Brest   17, 95
Quest for Karla, The   **146**
Question of Upbringing, A   194
Quick Service   266
Quiet American, The   101, 129
Quiller-Couch, Arthur   96
Quiller Memorandum, The   57
Quinn, Sally   144, 198
Quinx   69
Quo Vadis?   23, 252, 253

R

Raban, Jonathan   235
Rabbit is Rich   246
Rabbit Redux   246
Rabbit, Run   151, 246, 261
Rabelais, François   106, 145, 181, **200**, 229
Rachel Papers, The   58, 240
Radcliffe   88, 145
Radiant Way, The   **65**, 66
Rage   225
Rainbow, The   21, 145, 146
Rain Forest, The   162, 175, 261
Rainforest   32, 175
Raise High the Roofbeam, Carpenters   213
Raj Quartet, The   81, 165
Raphael, Frederic   76, 146, 168, 177, 194, **201**, 214, 234, 246
Rap on Race, A   17
Rat, The   97
Rates of Exchange   27, 30
Rathbone, Julian   26
Rats, The   113

Raven, Simon 194
Rayner, Claire 173
Razor's Edge, The 166
Real Life of Sebastian Knight, The 177, 190
Realms of Gold, The 65
Real People 124, 155
Real Thing, The 131
Rebecca 31, 67, 170, 183, 189, 255
Rebel Angels, The **54**, 118, 132, 156–7
Rebel Heiress 115
Rebel Princess 10
Recalled to Life 220
Rechy, John 17
Red Alert 57, 110–111
Red and the Green, The 176, 187
Redback 140–1, 145
Red Badge of Courage, The 110–111
Redburn: his First Voyage 169
Red Christmas 210
Redgauntlet 216
Red Harvest 104
Red Pony, The 228
Red White and Blue, The 198
Red Widow Murders, The 44–45
Reed, Eliot 8
Reef, The 130, 260
Reefs of Space, The 219
Reeman 81
Reflections in a Golden Eye 119, 166, 169
Regency Buck 14, 115, 116–7
Regenesis 115
Regrets Only 144, 198
Reinhart in Love 106
Re Joyce 33
Remarque, Erich Maria 110–111, 254, 268
Remembrance of Things Past 41, 81, 89, 102, 130, 135, 194, 196, 197, 267
Renault, Mary 6, 9, 97, 98–99, 121, **202**, 264
Rendell, Ruth 3, 118, 131, 142, 146, 192, **202**, 215, 224
Rendezvous with Rama 43
Renegade 96
Reprieve, The 214
Requiem for a Nun 75
Requiem for a Wren 219, 259
Restaurant at the End of the Universe, The 2
Restoree 167
Resurrection 240
Return of Sherlock Holmes, The 65
Return of the Native, The 105
Return to Coolami 53, 175
Return to Night 202
Reuben, Reuben 34, 58, 156–7
Revenge for Love, The 152
Revolution and Roses 180
Rhine Journey 27
Rhineman Exchange, The 154
Rhys, Jean 19, 20, 31, 134, 159, **203**, 226, 267
Riceyman Steps 21, 22
Rich and the Righteous, The 226
Richard Bolitho, Midshipman 80

Richardson, Dorothy 197, 267
Richardson, Henry Handel 29, 57, 150, 176, **204**, 215, 263, 267
Richardson, Samuel 75, **205**
Richard's Things 201
Rich Are Different, The 123
Richler, Mordecai 25, 43, 60–61, **206**, 256, 260, 268
Riddle of the Sands, The 33
Riddley Walker 34, 120, 170, 235, 250
Ride a Pale Horse 116–7
Riders in the Chariot 59, 263
Rievers, The 75
Ringed Castle, The 68
Riotous Assembly **217**, 225
Ripening Seed, The 3, **47**, 259
Ripley's Game **118**
Ripley Under Ground 118, 131
Ripple from the Storm, A 150
Rising 26
Risk 11, 85
Rites of Passage 26, 55, 84, 93
River and the People, The 235
Riverworld 108
Roa Bastos, Augusto 15, 97, 98–99, 210, 211, 248
Road, The 153
Road Past Mandalay, The 165
Roads of Earth, The 154
Roads to Freedom, The 214
Road to Lichfield, The 26
Road to Wigan Pier, The 184
Roaring Nineties, The 195
Robber Bridegroom, The 259
Robbins, Harold 87, 198
Robe, The 252
Roberts, Elizabeth M. 80
Roberts, Keith 235, 242
Roberts, Michèle 23, 34, 96, **207**, 252
Robinson 218, 225
Robinson, Derek 25
Robinson, Robert 214
Robinson, Rony 23
Robinson Crusoe **55**, 56, 92, 218, 230
Rob Roy **216**
Rocannon's World 149
Roche, Mazo de la 51
Rocket to Luna 124
Rodda, Charles 8
Rodgers, Paul 218
Rodmoor 194
Roger's Version 246
Rogue Justice 122
Rogue Male 33, 51, 122
Rolfe, Frederick 89, 97, 207, 240
Roll Call, The 22
Roman Tales 190
Romantic Hero, A 162
Romola 71, 237
Rookery Nook 265
Room at the Top 182, 228
Room With a View, A 15, 81

Room with a View, A 130
Rose and the Ring, The 235
Rose Domino, The 115
Rose of Tibet, The 16
Rosshalde 36, 38, 51, **113**, 187, 190
Rossner, Judith **208**
Ross Poldark 96
Roth, Henry 145
Roth, Philip 6, 102, 109, 154, 197, 201, **208**, 216, 245
Rough Shoot, A 122
Rougons and the Macquarts, The 271
Round the Moon 249
Round the World in Eighty Days 249
Round Up 153
Rowan Garth 67
Royal Intrigue 10
Rubens, Bernice 25, 26, 173, 175, 203, 208, **209**
Rude Awakening, A 4
Rudin 242
Ruell, Patrick 44–45, 119, **210**
Rules of Life, The 257
Rumours of Rain 26, 94, 107
Run for Cover 122
Running Blind 16, 223, 230
Running Proud 98–99, 112, 218
Running Scared 118
Rupert of Hentzau 122
Rushdie, Salman · 27, 126, 127, 136–7, 163, 192, **210**, 264, 272
Rush on the Ultimate, A 6, 174
Russ, Joanna 37
Russian Beauty, A 178
Russian Interpreter, The 128, 180
Ruth 88, 104
Ryder 19
Ryder, Jonathan 154

S

Sabatini, Rafael 66, 115, 122
Sackville-West, Vita 79, 201
Safety Net, The 24
Sagan, Françoise 46
Saint Goes On, The 79
Saint Jack 235
Saki 91
Salamander, The 260
Salammbô 78, 160, 186
Salem's Lot 142
Salinger, J.D. 29, 57, 101, 136–7, 172, **213**
Saliva Tree, The 4
Salzburg Tales, The 226
Same Door, The 246
Sandcastle, The 28, 136–7, 176, 190, 264
Sanditon 15
Sands of Mars, The **46**
Sara Band of Two Sisters 37

Saracen Blade, The 270
Sarah Dane 50
Saratoga Barrier, The 113
Saroyan, William 162, 190
Sarraute, Nathalie 24
Sartoris 53, 74, 75
Sartre, Jean-Paul 19, **214**
Satan in Goray 1, 93, 107, 221
Saturday City 255
Saturday Night and Sunday Morning 213
Satyricon 97, 121, 145, 181
Sauce for the Goose 58
Saville 26
Say, Darling 6
Sayers, Dorothy L. 44–45, 66, 100, **214**
Scandalous Woman and Other Stories, A 174
Scarlatti Inheritance, The 154
Scarlet and Black 131, **228**, 238–9
Scarlet Letter, The 3, 63, 107, 140–1, 169, 194, 272
Scarlet Pimpernel, The 14, 66
Scattered Seed 173
Scene Changing 32, 194, 198
Scenes from Clerical Life 71
Scenes from Married Life 230
Scenes from Provincial Life 8
Schindler's Ark 27, **139**, 253
Schirmer Inheritance, The 8
Schlee, Anne 27
School for Love 162
Schulberg, Budd 110–111, 196, 206, 256, 260
Scoop 180, 181, 254
Scorpion God, The 93
Scots Quair, A 88
Scott, Hardiman 3
Scott, Paul 26, 81, 82, 133, 165
Scott, Sarah 173
Scott, Walter 13, **215**, 230, 253
Scruples 144, 171
Sea and Summer, The 17, 43, 86, 219, 242, 243
Sea-Grape Tree, A 149, 150, 175
Seal Morning 10
Seals, The 62, 122
Séance, The 222
Search, The 151, 224
Search for My Great Uncle's Head, The 104
Season in England, A 180
Season in Purgatory 139
Season of Comfort, The 250
Sea, The Sea, The 26, 176, 267
Sea-wolf, The 112, 153
Sebastian 69
Secret Agent, The 3, 49
Secret Diary of Adrian Mole, aged 13¾, The 3
Secret for a Nightingale 120
Secret Generation, The 223
Secret History of Time to Come, A 120, 235
Secret Lives 22
Secret Whispers, The 3, 5, 147
Seduction of the Minotaur 267
Seeds of Time, The 269

Seeds of Yesterday 10
Segal, Erich 116–7, **216**, 255
Seize the Day 21
Self-condemned 152
Semyonov, Julian 146
Sense and Sensibility 15, 116–7
Sentimental Education 78, 242
Sentimental Journey, A 229, 243
Sentinel, The 46
Sepulchre 113, 142
Serenissima 134
Serge, Victor 184, 193
Sergeant Lamb of the Ninth 97, 165
Serpent and the Staff, The 270
Set of Six, A 50
Seton, Anya 191
Setting Free the Bears 127
Setting the World on Fire 128, 265
Seven Against Reeves 152
Seven Days in New Crete 86, 97, 173
Seven-per-cent Solution, The 64
1776 165
Seventh Sanctuary, The 83
Several Perceptions 38
Severed Head, A 58, 116–7, 176
Seymour, Gerald 82, 115
Shade of Difference, A 270
Shadow Dance 38
Shadow Moon 19
Shadow over Innsmouth, The 257
Shadow Play 39
Shadows on our Skin 26
Shadows on the Rock 38
Shadrach in the Furnace 220
Shaeffer, Susan Fromberg 32, 154, 209
Shah, Idries 74, 234
Shall We Tell the President? 11
Shame 27, 163, 192, 210, 272
Shannon, Dell 167
Shaping of a Writer, The 67
Sharpe, Tom 8, 30, 66, 118, 166, 197, **217**, 225
Sharpe's Honour 80
Sharpe's Regiment 120, 238–9
Shaw, Bob 268
Shaw, Irwin 11
She 33, 103, 248
Shears, Sarah 255
She Came to Stay 150
Sheckley, Robert 105
Sheldon, Sidney 144
Shelley, Mary 188, **217**
Sheltered Life, The 182
Sheltering Sky, The 36, 263
Shepherd, The 83
Shikasta 151
Shining, The 142
Ship of Fools 193, 218
Ship of the Line 80
Ship Who Sang, The 167
Shirley 88
Shivering Sands, The 121

Shoes of the Fisherman, The 23, 252, 259
Shôgun 82, 159, 165, 186
Sholokhov, Mikhail 204
Shooting Party, The 79, 161
Short Friday 222
Short Reign of Pippin IV, The 228
Shout at the Devil 103, 115, 223
Shrapnel Academy, The 257
Shrimp and the Anemone, The 106
Shrine 113
Shrinking Man, The 142
Shroud for a Nightingale 132, 202
Shrunken Heads 57
Shulman, Neville 93
Shute, Neville 110–111, **218**, 223, 253, 259
Shuttlecock 231
Siblings, The 57
Sibyl, The 195, 202
Sicilian, The 198
Siddhartha 114
Sido 47
Siege of Krishnapur, The 26, 74, 126, 142, 165
Sienkiewycz, Henryk 23, 252, 253
Sign of Four, The 65
Silas Marner 71, 194
Silence Among the Weapons 27, 98–99, 202, 264
Sillitoe, Alan 213
Silmarillion, The 236
Silverberg, Robert 17, 73, 150, 171, 186, 189, **219**, 252
Simenon, Georges 42, 63, 100, 101, 118, **220**, 272
Simon, S.J. 6, 181, 191, 201
Simplex Simplicissimus 106
Simpson, Dorothy 42
Sinclair, Andrew 77, 110–111
Sinclair, Upton 88, 195, 227
Singapore Grip, The 19, 74
Singer, I.B. 1, 73, 93, 107, 143, 160, **221**, 237
Singer, I.J. 221
Singing Citadel, The 172
Singing Sands, The 174
Single Flame, A 29
Single Man, A 128, 203
Singular Man, A 63
Sinning With Annie 236
Sinuhe the Egyptian 123
Sioux, The 72, 176
Sir Charles Grandison 205
Sirens of Titan, The 2, 249, 250
Sirian Experiments, The 27, 151
Sister Carrie 21, 166
Sitwell, Osbert 264
Sixth Heaven, The 106
Sjöwall, Maj 192, 220
Skeleton Crew 142
Sketches by Boz 59
Skin Deep **62**
Skull Beneath the Skin, The 46, 118, 132

Skvorecky, Joseph   176
Skyfall   105
Skylark of Space   222
Slapstick   250
Slaughter, Carolyn   225
Slaughter, Frank   23, 252, 259
Slaughterhouse Five   250
Slave, The   221
Slay-Ride   85
Sleep and His Brother   62
Sleeping Beauty   196
Sleeping Life, A   131
Sleeping Sword   130
Sleep it off, Lady   204
Sleep of Reason, The   223, 224, 259
Sleeps Six   201
Slide Rule   219
Slow Dawning   53
Slow Train to Milan   203
Small Back Room, The   219
Small House at Allington, The   241
Small Town in Germany, A   146, 148
Small Town Tyrant   123
Small World   4, 27, 34, 154, 156–7
Smiley's People   148
Smith, E.E. 'Doc'   **222**, 249
Smith, Joan   6
Smith, Martin Cruz   2, 140–1, 147, 167, 192
Smith, Thorne   217, 260
Smith, Wilbur   103, 115, **223**, 225
Smoke   242
Smollett, Tobias   229
Snailwatcher, The   119
Snare of the Hunted, The   10, 33
Snow, C.P.   26, 66, 79, 87, 126, 151, 165, 193, 219, **223**, 245, 259
Snow Goose, The   10
So Disdained   219
Solaris   43, 150
Soldier Erect, A   4
Soldier's Art, The   194
Soldier's Embrace, A   94
Soldiers Three   143
Solid Gold Mandala, The   150
Solid Mandala, The   263
Solo   115, 176
So Long, and Thanks for All the Fish   2
Solzhenitsyn, Alexander   123, 140–1, **224**, 272
Some Everyday Folk and Dawn   85
Some Lie and Some Die   203, 215
Some People, Places and Things that will not Appear in my Next Novel,   41
Some Tame Gazelle   199
Something Childish   163
Something Happened   36, 78, 108, 109, 136–7
Something in Disguise   32
Something I've Been Meaning to Tell You   174
Something of Myself   143
Something to Answer For   25, 123, 140–1, 180
Song of the Lark, The   39, 101, 158, 176, 268
Song Twice Over, A   130, 255
Sons and Lovers   88, **146**, 187

Sophie's Choice   139, 224, 238–9
Sophy of Kravonia   122
Sorrows of Young Werther, The   90
Sot-weed Factor, The   84, 249
Soul Hunters   79
Soul of Kindness, The   234
Sound and the Fury, The   72, **75**
Sound of Wings, The   51
Source of Embarrassment, A   168
Sour Sweet   27, 178, 235
Southern, Terry   76, 110–111, 199
South Riding   71
Space Merchants, The   125
Spanish Bridegroom, The   114, 191
Spark, Muriel   25, 27, 130, 158, 177, 183, 207, 218, **225**, 249, 251
Sparrow Falls, A   223
Speak, Memory   132, 178
Spear, The   113
Spearfield's Daughter   11
Spectre, The   95
Spell for Chameleon, A   11, 70, 236
Spellsinger   10, 70
Spillway   19
Spinoza of Market Street, The   222
Spinsters in Jeopardy   164
Spire, The   36, **93**, 170
Spoiled Earth, The   123
Spoilers, The   16
Spoils of Poynton, The   87, 131
Spoilt City, The   162
Spook Stories   22
Sport of Nature, A   13, **94**, 102, 211
Sport of Queens, The   85
Sportsman's Sketches   41, 242
Sprig Muslin   115
Spring, Howard   193
Spring of the Ram, The   68
Spring Sonata   210
Spy Story   57
Spy Who Came in from the Cold, The   5, 57, 148
SS-GB   57
Stafford, Jean   162, 182
Stainless Steel Rat, The   2, 105
Stainless Steel Rat for President, The   105
Stainless Steel Rat Saves the World, The   105
Stainless Steel Rat's Revenge, The   105
Stainless Steel Rat Wants You!, The   105
Stain on the Snow, The   101
Stalky and Co.   143
Stallion Gate   2, 140–1, 147
Stamboul Train   100, 240
Stand, The   142
Stanley and the Women   8
Staring at the Sun   50, 183
Stars and Bars   2, 156–7
Stars Like Dust, The   12
Star Smashers of the Galaxy Rangers   105, 222
Starswarm   4
Start in Life, A   32, 203
Statues in a Garden   255

Status Civilization, The 105
Staying On 26, 82, 133
Staying with Relations 159
Stead, Christina 21, 72, 87, 90, 171, 208, **226**, 241, 263
Steel, Danielle 50, **226**
Stein, Gertrude 267
Steinbeck, John 3, 59, 195, **227**, 243, 245, 271
Stendhal 131, **228**, 238–9
Stephen Hero 135
Steppenwolf 113, 114, 175, 183, 205
Stepping Westward 30, 156–7
Steps 143
Sterne, Laurence 54, 76, 136–7, 145, 200, **229**, 243
Stevenson, R.L. 68, 120, 166, **229**, 243
Stewart, J.I.M. 126, 127
Stewart, Mary 10, 115, 116–7, **230**
Stick Your Neck Out 206
Stirling, Jessica 123
Stochastic Man 220
Stoker, Bram 217, 252
Stone, Irving 202
Stop Press 46
Storey, David 26, 88, 145
Stories, The **40**
Stories of a Lifetime 161
Stories of Muriel Spark, The 226
Storm Island 33, 79
Storm of Time 53
Story, Jack Trevor 105, 128
Story of Ragged Robyn, The 104, 152
Story Teller, The 118
Stout, Rex 44–45, 100, 126, 215
Strait is the Gate 89, 228
Strange Meeting 119
Stranger at the Gates 10
Stranger in a Strange Land 108
Strangers 263
Strangers and Brothers 79, 165, 224
Strangers on a Train 44–45, 118, 240
Strength of the Strong, The 153
Stricken Field, A 192
Stronger Climate, A 133
Strong Poison 215
Strumpet City 21, 261
Stubbs, Jean 122
Study in Scarlet, A 64
St Urbain's Horseman 25, 206
Styron, William 75, 139, 159, 224, 238–9
Success 77, 177
Such Darling Dodos 265
Such Pleasure 29
Suffrage of Elvira, The 179
Sugar House, The 262
Summer 260
Summer Book, The 132, 179, 245
Summer in the Twenties, A 62
Summer Lightning 51, 265
Summer of the Red Wolf 260
Summing Up, The 166
Summons before the Dark, The 151

Summons to Memphis, A 28, 265
Sum of Things, The 162
Sun Across the Sky 53
Sun Also Rises, The 10, 112
Sun City 132, 183, 251
Sunday Best 209
Sundering Flood, The 173
Sunrising 41, **50**, 60–61, 181, 243
Superior Women 130
Surfacing 12, 20, 203, 267
Surfeit of Lampreys 46, 131, 164
Survivor, The 113
Suspension of Mercy, A 118
Sutcliffe, Rosemary 9
Sutton Place 183
Svevo, Italo 78, 136–7, 190, **230**
Swami and Friends 180
Swan in the Evening, The 150
Swann's Way 41, 130, 197, 267
Sweet Danger 6
Sweet Dove Died, The 199
Sweet Dreams 73, 125, 173
Sweet Lass of Richmond Hill 191
Sweet Shop Owner, The 231
Sweets of Pimlico, The 168
Swift, Graham 27, 203, **231**
Swift, Jonathan 73, 92, 200, **231**
Swinnerton, Frank 80
Switch Bitch 191
Sword in the Stone, The 35
Sword of Honour 161, 254
Sword of Pleasure, The 249
Sword of Shannara, The 10
Sybil 71
Sylvia's Lovers 88
Symme's Hole 123
Symons, Julian 44–45, 118, 152, 220
Symphonie pastorale, La 89, 114

T

Table Talk of Samuel Marchbanks, The 54
Tactics of Mistake 12
Tagore, Rabinadrath 133, 179
Taj 116–7, 126
Take a Girl Like You 8
Takeover, The 226
Take Two at Bedtime 6
Talented Mr Ripley, The 118
Tale of the Good Old Man and the Pretty Girl 231
Tale of Two Cities, A 59
Tales of Hearsay 50
Tales of Mystery and Imagination 142, 192, 252
Tales of Mystery and Romance 172
Tales of Natural and Unnatural Catastrophes 119
Tales of Space and Time 258

Tales of the Black Widowers   191
Tales of the Jazz Age   77
Tales of Unrest   49
Talkative Man, The   180
Talking to Strange Men   3, 146, 203
Tamarind Seed, The   10
Tanamera   19
Tanglewood Tales   107
Tannahill, Reay   67
Taps at Reveille   77
Tarka the Otter   10
Tarr   11, 55, 152
Tartarin of Tarascon   243
Tass is Authorized to Announce   146
Taste for Death, A   **131**
Tate, Ellalice   115
Taylor, Elizabeth   233
Taylor, Andrew   47
Taylor, Elizabeth   26, 28, 78, **233**, 260, 263
Taylor, Fred   154
Taylor, Peter   28, 40, 182, 265
Technicolor Time Machine, The   105
Telefon   2, 83, 147
Tell Me How Long the Train's Been Gone   17
Tempest-tost   54, 140–1
Temple, The   256, 259
Temporary Kings   194
Temporary Shelter   233, 265
Temptation of St Anthony, The   78
Tenant of Wildfell Hall, The   32
Ten Creeks Run   85
Tender is the Night   77, 153
Tendrils of the Vine, The   47
Ten Little Indians   42
Ten Little Niggers   42, 44–45
Ten Miles from Anywhere   180
Tennant, Emma   194
Tennis and the Masai   215
Ten North Frederick   182
Ten Teacups, The   126
Terán, Lisa St Aubin de   175, 203, 210
Terminal   115
Terra Nostra   98–99, 201
Terre, La   271
Territorial Rights   226
Tess of the d'Urbervilles   31, 104, 105
Tey, Josephine   10, 44–45, 174
Thackeray, William   14, 15, 60–61, 77, 124, 181, **234**, 238–9, 260
That Hideous Strength   249
That Uncertain Feeling   8, 58
Then There Were None   42
Theophilus North   264
There's a Porpoise Close Behind Us   140–1, 196
Thérèse Desqueyroux   166
Thérèse Raquin   271
Theroux, Alexander   136–7, 200
Theroux, Paul   34, 49, 51, 82, 83, 125, 127, 166, 175, 203, 209, **235**, 243, 272
These Old Shades   115
These Twain   22

They Shall Have Stars   24
They Were Defeated   101, **158**
Things Fall Apart   1, 52, 94, 140–1
Thinking Reed, The   149
Thin Man, The   104
Thinner   142
Third Life of Grange Copeland   251
Third Man, The   100
Thirkell, Angela   19, 22, 124, 241
Thirsty Evil, A   250
31st of February, The   220
Thirty-Nine Steps, The   **33**, 44–45
This Company of Women   73
This Gun for Hire   80, 122
This Rough Magic   115, 230
This Shining Land   234
This Side of Paradise   77
Thomas, Craig   33
Thomas, D.M.   27, 37, 68, 84, 114, 174, 175, 267
Thomas Covenant   73
Thompson, Flora   132
Thorn Birds, The   14, 170, 270
Thorne, Nicola   30, 73
Those Barren Leaves   125
Thousand Nights and One Night, The   200
Three Black Pennies, The   166
Three Cheers for the Paraclete   139, 207, 260, 262
Three Continents   133
Three Hostages, The   33
Three Lives   267
Three Men in a Boat   20, 85, 133
Three Men on a Bummel   133
Three Musketeers, The   **66**, 115, 201
Three Six Seven   9, 82, 98–99, 195
Three Stories   78
Threshold   **149**
Through the Fields of Clover   58
Throwback, The   217
Thunder at Sunset   165
Thunderball   79
Thunder on the Right   230
Thursday the Rabbi Walked Out   44–45
Ticket of Leave   221
Tiffany Street   256
Tiger for Malgudi, A   179
Tiger in the Smoke, The   6, 43, 131
Tigers are Better-looking   204
Tilly Trotter   51
Tilly Trotter Wed   51
Tilly Trotter Widowed   51
Time Dweller, The   172
Time Enough for Love   108
Time It Takes, The   51
Timeless Land, The   53, 127, 140–1, 186
Time Machine, The   73, 257, 269
Time Must Have a Stop   125
Time of Changes, A   220
Time of Hope, A   224
Time of Man, The   80

Time of the Angels, The 176
Time of the Hero, The 110–111, 184, 248
Time Regained 197
Time to Kill, A 122
Tin Drum, The 5, 96, 97, 110–111, 210
Tinker Tailor Soldier Spy 146
Tinniswood, Peter 72
Titus Alone 188
Titus Groan 48, 188
To A God Unknown 227
To Catch a Spy 8
To Have and Have Not 112, 153
Toilers of the Sea, The 123, 169, 194, 227
To Jerusalem and Back 21
To Kill a God 218
To Kill a Mocking Bird 3, 55, 75
Told by an Idiot 158
To Let 87
Tolkien, J.R.R. 70, 73, 188, **236**
Tollgate, The 114
Tolstoy, Lev 121, 187, 214, **237**, 238–9, 253
Tom Brown's Schooldays 81
Tombs of Atuan, The 149
Tom Jones 55, 59, **76**, 116–7, 206, 243
Tom O'Bedlam 150, 171, 252
Tom Sawyer Abroad 244
Tom Sawyer Detective 244
Tono-Bungay 124, 196, 234, **258**
Toole, John Kennedy 63, 134, 136–7, 181, 229, **240**
Too Many Cooks 126
Torrents of Spring, The 112, 242
Tortilla Flat 227
To the Lighthouse 72, 75, 175, 267
Touch Not the Cat 230
Touch of Daniel, A 72
Touch the Lion's Paw 210
Tough Guys Don't Dance 104, 160
Tournier, Michel 55
Towards the End of the Morning 30, 181
Tower of Babel, The 260
Tower of London, The 216
Towers of Trebizond, The 158, 225
To Whom She Will 133
Town, The 75
Town House, The 152
Town Like Alice, A 218
Townsend, Sue 3
To Your Scattered Bodies Go 74
Traffics and Discoveries 143
Tragic Muse, The 131
Traitor's Purse 6
Tranter, Nigel 216
Traveller, if you Come to Spa 25
Traveller, The 203
Travelling Grave, The 106
Travels of Wilhelm Meister, The 89
Travels with a Donkey 230, 243
Travels with Charlie 243
Travels With My Aunt 100
Traven, B. 49, 101, 115
Travers, Ben 265

Treasure Island 188, 229
Treasure of the Sierra Madre, The 49, 101, 115
Treece, Henry 9, 98–99, 121, 202
Tree of Hands, The 203
Tree of Man, The 263
Trembling of a Leaf, The 166
Tremor of Forgery, The 118
Trenhaile, John 103, 147
Trevor, Elleston 57
Trevor, William 25, 26, 233
Trial, The 138, 139, 177, 183, 184
Trial of Sören Kvist, The 1, 38, 71, 245
Trick of the Ga Bolga, The 143
Trilby 217
Trillion Year Spree 4
Triplanetary 222
Tristram Shandy 54, 76, 136–7, 145, 200, 229
Troika 79
Troll Garden, The 193
Trollope, Anthony 14, 60–61, 87, 181, 223, **241**, 261
Troubled Sleep 214
Trouble Makers, The 10
Troubles 74
Trouble With Lichen 269
Trout Fishing in America 127
Troy Town 96
True Stories 13
Trumpet-Major, The 105
Trust 11, 65, 174
Trustee from the Toolroom 219
Trust Me 246
Truth 272
Tuesday the Rabbi saw Red 46
Tulku 62
Tunc 68, 264
Tunnel of Love, The 40, **58**, 124
Turgenev, Ivan 41, 187, 237, 238–9, **242**
Turner, George 17, 43, 86, 120, 219, **242**
Turn of the Screw, The 92, 119, 131, 189
Turow, Scott 2
Turtle Diary 120, 127
Tutuola, Amos 1, 123, 178
Twain, Mark 42, 55, 59, 60–61, 85, 238–9, **243**
Twelve Horses and the Hangman's Noose 44–45, 64
Twenty-seventh Kingdom, The 198
'*Twenty-six Men and a Girl*' 95
Twenty-third Man, The 62
Twenty Thousand Leagues Under the Sea 218, 249, 257
Twenty Years After 66
'*Twixt Land and Sea* 50
Two Faces of January, The 118
Two for the Road 201
Two or Three Graces 125
Twopence to Cross the Mersey 255
Two Sisters 250
Two Studies 205
Two Tales and Eight Tomorrows 105

Two Worlds and their Ways   48
Twyborn Affair, The   152, 249, 263
Typee   169
Typhoon   49, 153, 193
Tyrants Destroyed   178
T Zero   36

U

Ultima Thule   205
Ulysses   19, 75, 121, 134, **135**, 136–7, 153, 264
Unbearable Lightness of Being, The   35
Uncle Dynamite   266
Uncle Fred in the Springtime   266
Uncommercial Traveller, The   59
Under a Glass Bell   172
Under the Greenwood Tree   105
Under the Net   78
Under the Volcano   101, 134, 153, 183, 204
Under the Wheel   114
Under Western Eyes   49, 63, 234
Undset, Sigrid   104, 186, 195, **245**
Unexplained Laughter   257
Unfinished Tales   236
Unguarded House, The   24
Unicorn, The   31
Universal Baseball Association, The   240
Universal History of Infamy, A   28
Unkindness of Ravens, An   203
Unknown Ajax, The   114
Unlimited Dream Company, The   17, 96
Unnatural Causes   132
Unsuitable Job for a Woman, An   6, 132
Unsworth, Barry   26
Unvanquished, The   75
Updike, John   40, 58, 86, 92, 93, 119, 151, 156–7, 183, 187, 208, 213, 215, 225, **245**, 254, 261
Up the Country   53, 85
Urgent Copy   34
Urn Burial   210

V

V   199
Vacant Possession   156–7
Vacillations of Poppy Carewe, The   116–7
Vagaries Malicieux   19
Valentine Pontifex   220
Valine, Jonathan   196
Valley of Bones, The   194
Valley of Fear, The   65, 230
Valmouth   77
Vance, Jack   62, 150, 189

Vaneglory   120, 243
Vanishing Ladies   124
Vanity Fair   14, 15, 77, 124, **234**, 238–9, 260
Vansittart, Peter   9, 82, 98–99, 195
Van Slyke, Helen   226
Vardeman, Robert E.   171
Vargas Llosa, Mario   5, 98–99, 110–111, 184, 186, 199, 221, **248**
Vatican Cellars, The   89
Vendor of Sweets, The   82, 126, **180**
Venetian Affair, The   230
Venusberg   125, 194
Venus in Sparta   256
Vermilion Sands, The   18
Verne, Jules   43, 73, 218, **248**, 257
Vertical Smile, The   49
Very Good Hater, A   119
Very Peculiar Practice, A   54
Very Private Life, A   232
Vestal Fire   158
Vicar of Wakefield, The   241
Vicinity Cluster   167, 220
Vicomte of Bragelonne, The   66
Victim, The   21, 36
Victim of the Aurora, A   142
Vidal, Gore   9, 17, 37, 98–99, 100, 165, 193, 195, 202, 206, 211, 223, **249**
View from Pompey's Head, The   151
View of the Harbour, A   233
Vile Bodies   77, 193, 255
Villette   32
Vine, Barbara   203
Vintage Murder   164
Vintage Stuff   217
Violent Land, The   192
Viper of Milan, The   122
Virgil   121
Virginians, The   235
Virgin in the Garden, The   32, 158
Virgin Soil   242
Virgin Soil Upturned   204
Virgin Soldiers, The   4, 110–111
Vivisector, The   263
Vlemk the Box-painter   35
Voices of Time, The   18
Voices on the Wind   10
Voltaire   231
Vonnegut, Kurt   2, 96, 105, 108, 199, 218, 249, **250**
Voss   53, 92, 127, 175, 193, **263**
Voyage in the Dark   204
Voyage of the Destiny, The   181
Voyage on a Dark Ship   172
Voyage Out, The   268

W

Waddell, Helen   56, 170, 202, 245, 261
Wager, Walter   2, 83, 147

Wahlöo, Per 192, 220
Wainwright, John 85
Waiting Sands, The 122
Waldo 236
Walkabout 92
Walker, Alice 55, 227, **251**
Walking Shadows 154
Wall, The 34, 214, 249
Wallace, Edgar 191
Wallace, Lew 123, 252, **253**
Wallach, Ira 119
Walpole, Horace 183
Walpole, Hugh 18, 241, 257
Waltari, Mika 123
Walter 50
Wambaugh, Joseph 167
Wapshot Chronicle, The 40, 124
Wapshot Scandal, The 40
War and Peace 121, 214, **237**, 238–9, 253
War and Remembrance 268
War Between the Tates, The 118, 154, 156–7, 168, 261
Warden, The 181, 241
War in Heaven 195
War in the Air, The 257
Warleggan 96
Warlord of the Air 73, 171
Warmer Season, A 52, 245
Warner, Rex 138
War of Powers, The 171
War of the End of the World, The 98–99, 186, 221, 248
War of the Worlds, The 43, 257
Warren, Robert Penn 259
Washington DC 223, 249
Washington Square 131
Wasp Factory, The 169
Watcher and Other Stories, The 36
Watcher in the Shadows 44–45, 80, 122
Watching Me Watching You 257
Waterfall, The 65
Waterland 27, 203, 231
Water-Method Man, The 128
Watership Down 10
Waterway 53, 136–7
Watson, Colin 119
Watson, Ian 148
Watson, Sheila 123
Watsons, The 15
Waugh, Evelyn 2, 51, 52, 77, 156–7, 159, 161, 180, 181, 193, 211, 215, **254**, 259
Waverley 216
Waves, The 53, 197, 267
Way Home, The 205
Way of All Flesh, The 48, 187
Wayside Tavern, The 120
Way Some People Live, The 41
Way We Live Now, The 241
Way We Were, The 246, 247
Weather in the Streets, The 150
Web 269
Web and the Rock, The 267

Webb, Charles 2, 47, 102
Webb, Mary 51
Webster, Jan 73, **255**
Wedde, Ian 123
Wedding Group, The 233, 234, 260
Weeks-Pearson, Tony 10, 140–1
Wee Willie Winkie 166
Weidman, Jerome 43, 48, 95, 151, 165, 171, 198, 206, 220, 226, 228, **256**, 259, 268
Weight of the Evidence, The 127
Weir of Hermiston 230
Welcome, John 122
Welcome to the Monkeyhouse 250
Weldon, Fay 26, 51, 92, 94, **256**, 272
Well at the World's End, The 38, 204
Wellington Blue 181
Wells, H.G. 14, 21, 43, 52, 59, 60–61, 73, 76, 113, 124, 142, 153, 196, 217, 229, 234, 248, **257**, 269
Welty, Eudora 23, 51, 55, 75, 169, 174, 193, 234, 255, **258**
Wentworth, Patricia 42
Wesley, Mary 116–7, 227, 262
West, Morris 82, 207, 219, 245, **259**
West, Nathanael 68, 76, 138, 206, 232, **260**
West, Rebecca 149
Westlake, Donald 7, 43, 47, 66, 76, 124, 171, 198, 266
West of Sunset 76
Weyman, Stanley J. 66
Wharton, Edith 14, 43, 48, 51, 60–61, 104, 106, 130, 227, **260**, 261
What Happened to the Corbetts 219, 253
What Maisie Knew 106, 154
What makes Sammy Run? 110–111, 196, 206, 256, 260
What's Become of Waring? 152, 193, 197
What's Bred in the Bone 27, 54, 136–7, 145
What's To Become of the Boy? 25
What the Heart Keeps 116–7
Wheatley, Dennis 252
Wheeler, T. 25
When Blackbirds Sing 29
When God Laughs 153
When in Greece 164
When My Girl Comes Home 182
When She was Good 208
When the Sleeper Wakes 258
When the Wind Blows 44–45
Where All the Girls Are Sweeter 5
Where Am I Now – and Do I Need Me? 58
Where Angels Fear to Tread 81
Where There's a Will 44–45
Where There's Smoke 124
Where the Rivers Meet 30
Whip Hand 85
Whipping Star, The 113
Whisper of the Axe, The 49
Whispers 113
White, Antonia 3, 57, 205, 207, **262**
White, Patrick 38, 53, 55, 59, 92, 127, 140–1, 150, 152, 175, 193, 218, 249, **263**, 272

White, T.H.   35, 70, 73
White Company, The   64, 122
White Dog   153
White Dragon, The   167
White Fang   10, 152
White Goddess, The   97
White Gold Wielder   63
White Hotel, The   27, 37, 84, 114, 175, 267
White-jacket, or The World in a Man-o'-War   169
Whittle, Tyler   191
Who Do You Think You Are?   174
Who Stole Sassi Manoon?   76, 266
Who the Hell Was Sylvia?   119
Why Are We in Vietnam?   159
Wideman, John Edgar   17
Wide Net, The   259
Wide Sargasso Sea   31, 203
Wife to Mr Milton   97, 158
Wilde, Oscar   20
Wilder, Laura Ingalls   23, 85
Wilder, Thornton   9, 84, 96, 151, **264**
Wildfire at Midnight   230
Wild Girl, The   23, 34, 207, 252
Wild Justice   84
Willard and His Bowling Trophy   172
Williams, Charles   195
Williams, G.M.   25
Williams, Tenessee   75
Williamson, Henry   10, 197
Willingham, Calder   75
Willis, Ted   5
Williwaw   250
Wilson, A.N.   8, 168, 198
Wilson, Angus   28, 59, 60–61, 128, 175, 190, 223, 233, 246, 261, **264**
Wilt   30, 118, 217
Wilt Alternative, The   217
Wilt on High   217
Windeater (Te Kaihau), The   123, 172
Windfall   16
Windmill Hill   194
Winds of War, The   268
Wind's Twelve Quarters, The   149
Winesburg, Ohio   21, 174, 182, 246
Winged Pharaoh   97, 98–99
Winged Seeds   195
Wings of the Dove, The   28, 81, **130**
Winner Take Nothing   112
Winsor, Kathleen   116–7, 270
Winter Doves   50, 245
Winter Kills   5, 249
Winter Notes on Summer Experiences   64
Winterson, Jeanette   23, 211, 238–9, 252
Witches of Eastwick, The   58, 92, 93, 225, 246
Witch from the Sea, The   37
Witchwood   33
Within a Budding Grove   81, 102, 197
Within the Tides   50
Without Feathers   28
Wives and Daughters   15, 88

Wodehouse, P.G.   14, 51, 116–7, **265**
Wohl, Burton   103
Wolfe, Thomas   55, 134, 145, **266**
Wolf Solent   194
Wolf to the Slaughter   203
Woman Called Fancy, A   67, 270
Woman in Black, The   119, 189
Woman in White, The   192
Woman of Andros, The   264
Woman of Cairo, A   19, 253
Woman of Rome, The   182
Woman of Substance, A   30, 88, 241
Woman of the Pharisees, The   18, 167
Woman Who Rode Away, The   146
Women in Love   145, 146
Women's Room, The   134, 150
Wonder Book, A   107
Wood, Mrs Henry   255
Wood Beyond the World, The   173
Wooden Overcoat, The   47
Woodhouse, Sarah   121, 152
Woodlanders, The   51, 105
Woods, Sara   85
Woolf, Virginia   53, 65, 72, 75, 134, 136–7, 140–1, 149, 163, 175, 197, 203, **267**
Word for World is Forest, The   148, 167
Work   272
Work and Play   36
Working Bullocks   195
World According to Garp, The   6, 62, 127, 211, 251
World is Made of Glass, The   245, **260**
Worldly Goods   23, 209, 255
World My Wilderness, The   149, 158, 263
World of Apples, The   41
World of Love, A   29
World of Profit, A   260
World of Strangers, A   94
World of Wonders   54
World's End   166
World's Fair   256
World, the Flesh and the Devil, The   67
Wouk, Herman   110–111, 218, **268**
Wounded Land, The   63
Wreath of Roses, A   78, 234
Wrecker, The   230
Wren, P.C.   122
Wrightson, Patricia   73
Writer's Notebook, A   166
Writing on the Wall, The   101
Wrong Box, The   230
Wrong Set, The   265
Wuthering Heights   **31**, 32, 96, 190, 261
Wyndham, John   86, 92, 119, **268**

X

Xingu   262

Y

Years, The   268
Yegor Bulitchev and Others   95, 171
Yerby, Frank   67, **270**
Yesterday's Men   243
You Can't Go Home Again   267
You Can't Keep a Good Woman Down   251
You Know Me, Al   182
Young Bess   114, 191
Youngblood Hawke   268
Young Cosima, The   204
Young Felix   80
Young Man I Think You're Dying   203
Young Patullo   127
Young Törless   24
Young Victoria, The   191

You Only Live Twice   79
Yourcenar, Marguerite   9, 97, 98–99, 264
Your Daughter Iris   256
Youth   49, 240

Z

Zauberberg, Der   161
Zemindar   19, 126
Zen There Was Murder   59, 164
Zola, Émile   3, 18, 88, 165, 169, 195, 237,
   271
Zuckerman Unbound   197, 201, 209
Zuleika Dobson   19, 66, 133, 156–7